ANNUAL EDITIONS

Criminal Justice 10/11

Thirty-Fourth Edition

EDITOR

Joanne Naughton
Mercy College, Dobbs Ferry

Joanne Naughton is an assistant professor of Criminal Justice at Mercy College. Professor Naughton is a former member of the New York City Police Department, where she encountered most aspects of police work as a police officer, detective, sergeant, and lieutenant. She is also a former staff attorney with The Legal Aid Society where she represented indigent criminal defendants, and has taught at John Jay College of Criminal Justice. She received her BA and JD at Fordham University.

ANNUAL EDITIONS: CRIMINAL JUSTICE, THIRTY-FOURTH EDITION

Published by McGraw-Hill, a business unit of The McGraw-Hill Companies, Inc., 1221 Avenue of the Americas, New York, NY 10020. Copyright © 2011 by The McGraw-Hill Companies, Inc. All rights reserved. Previous edition(s) 2008, 2009, 2010. No part of this publication may be reproduced or distributed in any form or by any means, or stored in a database or retrieval system, without the prior written consent of The McGraw-Hill Companies, Inc., including, but not limited to, in any network or other electronic storage or transmission, or broadcast for distance learning.

Some ancillaries, including electronic and print components, may not be available to customers outside the United States.

Annual Editions® is a registered trademark of The McGraw-Hill Companies, Inc.

Annual Editions is published by the **Contemporary Learning Series** group within the McGraw-Hill Higher Education division.

1 2 3 4 5 6 7 8 9 0 WDQ/WDQ 1 0 9 8 7 6 5 4 3 2 1 0

ISBN 978–0–07–805065–7
MHID 0–07–805065–0
ISSN 0272–3816

Managing Editor: *Larry Loeppke*
Developmental Editor: *Dave Welsh*
Editorial Coordinator: *Mary Foust*
Editorial Assistant: *Cindy Hedley*
Production Service Assistant: *Rita Hingtgen*
Permissions Coordinator: *DeAnna Dausener*
Senior Marketing Manager: *Julie Keck*
Marketing Communications Specialist: *Mary Klein*
Marketing Coordinator: *Alice Link*
Director Specialized Production: *Faye Schilling*
Senior Project Manager: *Joyce Watters*
Production Supervisor: *Sue Culbertson*
Cover Graphics: *Kristine Jubeck*

Compositor: Laserwords Private Limited
Cover Images: © Mikael Karlsson (inset); Brand X Pictures (background)

Library in Congress Cataloging-in-Publication Data
Main entry under title: Annual Editions: Criminal Justice. 2010/2011.
   1. Criminal Justice—Periodicals. I. Victor, Joseph L., *comp.* II. Naughton, Joanne. Title: Criminal Justice.
658'.05

Editors/Academic Advisory Board

Members of the Academic Advisory Board are instrumental in the final selection of articles for each edition of ANNUAL EDITIONS. Their review of articles for content, level, and appropriateness provides critical direction to the editors and staff. We think that you will find their careful consideration well reflected in this volume.

ANNUAL EDITIONS: Criminal Justice 10/11
34th Edition

EDITOR

Joanne Naughton
Mercy College, Dobbs Ferry

ACADEMIC ADVISORY BOARD MEMBERS

Preface

In publishing ANNUAL EDITIONS we recognize the enormous role played by the magazines, newspapers, and journals of the public press in providing current, first-rate educational information in a broad spectrum of interest areas. Many of these articles are appropriate for students, researchers, and professionals seeking accurate, current material to help bridge the gap between principles and theories and the real world. These articles, however, become more useful for study when those of lasting value are carefully collected, organized, indexed, and reproduced in a low-cost format, which provides easy and permanent access when the material is needed. That is the role played by ANNUAL EDITIONS.

During the 1970s, Criminal Justice emerged as an appealing, vital, and unique academic discipline. It emphasizes the professional development of students who plan careers in the field, and attracts those who want to know more about a complex social problem and how this country deals with it. Criminal Justice incorporates a vast range of knowledge from a number of specialties, including law, history, and the behavioral and social sciences. Each specialty contributes to our fuller understanding of criminal behavior and of society's attitudes toward deviance.

In view of the fact that the criminal justice system is in a constant state of flux, and because the study of criminal justice covers such a broad spectrum, today's students must be aware of a variety of subjects and topics. Standard textbooks and traditional anthologies cannot keep pace with the changes as quickly as they occur. In fact, many such sources are already out-of-date the day they are published. *Annual Editions: Criminal Justice 10/11* strives to maintain currency in matters of concern by providing up-to-date commentaries, articles, reports, and statistics from the most recent literature in the criminal justice field.

This volume contains units concerning crime and justice in America, victimology, the police, the judicial system, juvenile justice, and punishment and corrections. The articles in these units were selected because they are informative as well as provocative. The selections are timely and useful in their treatment of ethics, punishment, juveniles, courts, and other related topics.

Included in this volume are a number of features designed to be useful to students, researchers, and professionals in the criminal justice field. These include the table of contents, which summarizes each article, and features key concepts in bold italics; *a topic guide* for locating articles on specific subjects; a list of relevant *Internet References*; a comprehensive section on crime statistics; and a glossary. In addition, each unit is preceded by an overview that provides a background for informed reading of the articles, emphasizes critical issues, and presents key points to consider.

We would like to know what you think of the selections contained in this edition of *Annual Editions: Criminal Justice.* Please fill out the postage-paid article rating form on the last page and let us know your opinions. We change or retain many of the articles based on the comments we receive from you, the reader. Help us to improve this anthology—annually.

Joanne Naughton

Joanne Naughton
Editor

Contents

UNIT 1
Crime and Justice in America

The concepts in bold italics are developed in the article. For further expansion, please refer to the Topic Guide.

UNIT 2
Victimology

The concepts in bold italics are developed in the article. For further expansion, please refer to the Topic Guide.

UNIT 3
The Police

The concepts in bold italics are developed in the article. For further expansion, please refer to the Topic Guide.

UNIT 4
The Judicial System

The concepts in bold italics are developed in the article. For further expansion, please refer to the Topic Guide.

UNIT 5
Juvenile Justice

The concepts in bold italics are developed in the article. For further expansion, please refer to the Topic Guide.

UNIT 6
Punishment and Corrections

The concepts in bold italics are developed in the article. For further expansion, please refer to the Topic Guide.

The concepts in bold italics are developed in the article. For further expansion, please refer to the Topic Guide.

Correlation Guide

The *Annual Editions* series provides students with convenient, inexpensive access to current, carefully selected articles from the public press. **Annual Editions: Criminal Justice 10/11** is an easy-to-use reader that presents articles on important topics such as *the justice system, victims, punishment, policing,* and many more. For more information on *Annual Editions* and other *McGraw-Hill Contemporary Learning Series* titles, visit www.mhhe.com/cls.

This convenient guide matches the units in **Annual Editions: Criminal Justice 10/11** with the corresponding chapters in two of our best-selling McGraw-Hill Introductory Criminal Justice textbooks by Inciardi and Bohm/Haley.

Annual Editions: Criminal Justice 10/11	Criminal Justice, 9/e by Inciardi	Introduction to Criminal Justice, 6/e by Bohm/Haley
Unit 1: Crime and Justice in America	**Chapter 1:** "Criminal Justice" in America	**Chapter 1:** Crime and Justice in the United States
Unit 2: Victimology	**Chapter 9:** Police Misconduct and Police Integrity	**Chapter 2:** Crime and Its Consequences
Unit 3: The Police	**Chapter 6:** Police Systems in the United Stated: History and Structure **Chapter 7:** Enforcing the Law and Keeping the Peace: The Nature and Scope of Police Work **Chapter 8:** The Law of Arrest, Search, and Seizure: Police and the Constitution **Chapter 9:** Police Misconduct and Police Integrity	**Chapter 5:** History and Structure of American Law Enforcement **Chapter 6:** Policing: Roles, Styles, and Functions **Chapter 7:** Policing America: Issues and Ethics
Unit 4: The Judicial System	**Chapter 10:** The Structure of American Courts **Chapter 11:** The Courtroom Work Group and the Right to Counsel **Chapter 12:** The Business of the Court: From First Appearance Through Trial **Chapter 13:** Sentencing, Appeal, and the Judgment of Death	**Chapter 8:** The Administration of Justice **Chapter 9:** Sentencing, Appeals, and the Death Penalty
Unit 5: Juvenile Justice	**Chapter 18:** Juvenile Justice: An Overview	**Chapter 13:** Juvenile Justice
Unit 6: Punishment and Corrections	**Chapter 14:** From Walnut Street to Alcatraz: The American Prison Experience **Chapter 15:** Penitentiaries, Prisons, and Other Correctional Institutions: A Look Inside the Inmate World **Chapter 16:** Prison Conditions and Inmate Rights **Chapter 17:** Probation, Parole, and Community-Based Correction	**Chapter 10:** Institutional Corrections **Chapter 11:** Prison Life, Inmate Rights, Release, and Recidivism **Chapter 12:** Community Corrections

Topic Guide

This topic guide suggests how the selections in this book relate to the subjects covered in your course. You may want to use the topics listed on these pages to search the Web more easily.

On the following pages a number of websites have been gathered specifically for this book. They are arranged to reflect the units of this Annual Editions reader. You can link to these sites by going to *http://www.mhhe.com/cls*.

All the articles that relate to each topic are listed below the bold-faced term.

Internet References

The following Internet sites have been selected to support the articles found in this reader. These sites were available at the time of publication. However, because websites often change their structure and content, the information listed may no longer be available. We invite you to visit http://www.mhhe.com/cls for easy access to these sites.

Annual Editions: Criminal Justice 10/11

General Sources

American Society of Criminology
http://www.bsos.umd.edu/asc/four.html

This is an excellent starting place for study of all aspects of criminology and criminal justice, with links to international criminal justice, juvenile justice, court information, police, governments, and so on.

Federal Bureau of Investigation
http://www.fbi.gov

The main page of the FBI website leads to lists of the most wanted criminals, uniform crime reports, FBI case reports, major investigations, and more.

National Archive of Criminal Justice Data
http://www.icpsr.umich.edu/NACJD/index.html

NACJD holds more than 500 data collections relating to criminal justice; this site provides browsing and downloading access to most of the data and documentation. NACJD's central mission is to facilitate and encourage research in the field of criminal justice.

Social Science Information Gateway
http://sosig.esrc.bris.ac.uk

This is an online catalog of thousands of Internet resources relevant to social science education and research. Every resource is selected and described by a librarian or subject specialist. Enter "criminal justice" under Search for an excellent annotated list of sources.

UNIT 1: Crime and Justice in America

Sourcebook of Criminal Justice Statistics Online
http://www.albany.edu/sourcebook/

Data about all aspects of criminal justice in the United States are available at this site, which includes more than 600 tables from dozens of sources. A search mechanism is available.

UNIT 2: Victimology

National Crime Victim's Research and Treatment Center (NCVC)
http://www.musc.edu/cvc/

At this site, find out about the work of the NCVC at the Medical University of South Carolina, and click on Related Resources for an excellent listing of additional web sources.

Office for Victims of Crime (OVC)
http://www.ojp.usdoj.gov/ovc

Established by the 1984 Victims of Crime Act, the OVC oversees diverse programs that benefit the victims of crime. From this site you can download a great deal of pertinent information.

UNIT 3: The Police

ACLU Criminal Justice Home Page
http://www.aclu.org/CriminalJustice/CriminalJusticeMain.cfm

This "Criminal Justice" page of the American Civil Liberties Union website highlights recent events in criminal justice, addresses police issues, lists important resources, and contains a search mechanism.

Law Enforcement Guide to the World Wide Web
http://leolinks.com/

This page is dedicated to excellence in law enforcement. It contains links to every possible related category: community policing, computer crime, forensics, gangs, and wanted persons are just a few.

Violent Criminal Apprehension Program (VICAP)
http://www.state.ma.us/msp/unitpage/vicap.htm

VICAP's mission is to facilitate cooperation, communication, and coordination among law enforcement agencies and provide support in their efforts to investigate, identify, track, apprehend, and prosecute violent serial offenders. Access VICAP's data information center resources here.

UNIT 4: The Judicial System

Center for Rational Correctional Policy
http://www.correctionalpolicy.com

This is an excellent site on courts and sentencing, with many additional links to a variety of criminal justice sources.

Justice Information Center (JIC)
http://www.ncjrs.org

Provided by the National Criminal Justice Reference Service, this JIC site connects to information about corrections, courts, crime prevention, criminal justice, statistics, drugs and crime, law enforcement, and victims.

National Center for Policy Analysis (NCPA)
http://www.public-policy.org/~ncpa/pd/law/index3.html

Through the NCPA's "Idea House," you can click onto links to an array of topics that are of major interest in the study of the American judicial system.

U.S. Department of Justice (DOJ)
http://www.usdoj.gov

The DOJ represents the American people in enforcing the law in the public interest. Open its main page to find information about the U.S. judicial system. This site provides links to federal government web servers, topics of interest related to the justice system, documents and resources, and a topical index.

UNIT 5: Juvenile Justice

Gang Land: The Jerry Capeci Page
http://www.ganglandnews.com

Although this site particularly addresses organized-crime gangs, its insights into gang lifestyle—including gang families and their influence—are useful for those interested in exploring issues related to juvenile justice.

Internet References

Institute for Intergovernmental Research (IIR)
http://www.iir.com

The IIR is a research organization that specializes in law enforcement, juvenile justice, and criminal justice issues. Explore the projects, links, and search engines from this home page. Topics addressed include youth gangs and white collar crime.

National Criminal Justice Reference Service (NCJRS)
http://virlib.ncjrs.org/JuvenileJustice.asp

NCJRS, a federally sponsored information clearinghouse for people involved with research, policy, and practice related to criminal and juvenile justice and drug control, provides this site of links to full-text juvenile justice publications.

Partnership Against Violence Network
http://www.pavnet.org

The Partnership Against Violence Network is a virtual library of information about violence and youths at risk, representing data from seven different federal agencies—a one-stop searchable information resource.

UNIT 6: Punishment and Corrections

American Probation and Parole Association (APPA)
http://www.appa-net.org

Open this APPA site to find information and resources related to probation and parole issues, position papers, the APPA code of ethics, and research and training programs and opportunities.

The Corrections Connection
http://www.corrections.com

This site is an online network for corrections professionals.

Critical Criminology Division of the ASC
http://www.critcrim.org/

Here you will find basic criminology resources and related government resources, provided by the American Society of Criminology, as well as other useful links. The death penalty is also discussed.

David Willshire's Forensic Psychology & Psychiatry Links
http://members.optushome.com.au/dwillsh/index.html

This site offers an enormous number of links to professional journals and associations. It is a valuable resource for study into possible connections between violence and mental disorders. Topics include serial killers, sex offenders, and trauma.

Oregon Department of Corrections
http://egov.oregon.gov/DOC/TRANS/CC/cc_welcome.shtml

Open this site for resources in such areas as crime and law enforcement and for links to U.S. state corrections departments.

UNIT 1

Crime and Justice in America

Unit Selections

1. **What Is the Sequence of Events in the Criminal Justice System?,** *Report to the Nation on Crime and Justice,* Bureau of Justice Statistics
2. **Plugging Holes in the Science of Forensics,** Henry Fountain
3. **Does Proximity to Schools Tempt Former Sex Offenders?,** Cynthia Calkins Mercado, PhD and Brian H. Bornstein, PhD
4. **Stereotype, Then and Now,** Michael Nelson
5. **The Death of the War on Drugs,** Lawrence T. Jablecki, PhD
6. **Of Crime and Punishment: Experts Explore Issues in the Legal Limelight,** Robert Vodde et al.
7. **Serving Life for Providing Car to Killers,** Adam Liptak

Key Points to Consider

- Do you worry when paying bills and making purchases online that someone may be stealing your identity?

- Does the death penalty succeed in deterring others from committing heinous offenses?

- What steps do you think criminal justice should take to modernize and take advantage of the available technology?

Student Website
www.mhhe.com/cls

Internet Reference
Sourcebook of Criminal Justice Statistics Online
http://www.albany.edu/sourcebook/

Crime continues to be a major problem in the United States. Court dockets are full, our prisons are overcrowded, probation and parole caseloads are overwhelming, and our police are being urged to do more. The bulging prison population places a heavy strain on the economy of the country. Clearly, crime is a complex problem that defies simple explanations or solutions. While the more familiar crimes of murder, rape, assault, and drug law violations are still with us, international terrorism has become a pressing worry. The debate also continues about how best to handle juvenile offenders, sex offenders, and those who commit acts of domestic violence. Crime committed using computers and the Internet also demands attention from the criminal justice system.

Annual Editions: Criminal Justice 10/11 focuses directly upon crime in America and the three traditional components of the criminal justice system: police, the courts, and corrections. It also gives special attention to crime victims in the victimology unit and to juveniles in the juvenile justice unit. The articles presented in this section are intended to serve as a foundation for the materials presented in subsequent sections.

The unit begins with "What Is the Sequence of Events in the Criminal Justice System?" an article that reveals that the response to crime is a complex process, involving citizens as well as many agencies, levels, and branches of government. Then, Henry Fountain reports on a study by a panel of experts that said it was time to put more science in forensic science in "Plugging Holes in the Science of Forensics." In "Does Proximity to Schools Tempt Former Sex Offenders?" Mercado and Bornstein look at laws that restrict where sex offenders may reside and their effect on recidivism. In "Stereotype, Then and Now," Michael Nelson writes that in three new books he is distressed to be reminded about the 2006 Duke lacrosse case and

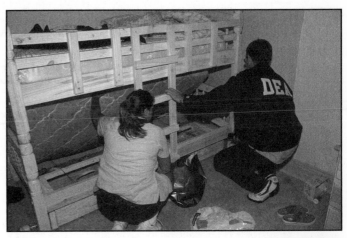

© Mikael Karlsson

just how quick everyone was to make prejudicial assumptions about the athletes.

Next, Lawrence Jablecki is critical of this country's drug policies in "The Death of the War on Drugs." In "Of Crime and Punishment: Experts Explore Issues in the Legal Limelight," Robert Vodde, et al. tell us what a panel of faculty and alumni at a New Jersey university think about many of today's important criminal justice issues.

This unit ends with an article by Adam Liptak, "Serving Life for Providing Car to Killers," which is about another unique aspect of the American justice system—the felony murder rule, whereby an unintended killing during a felony is considered murder.

What Is the Sequence of Events in the Criminal Justice System?

The Private Sector Initiates the Response to Crime

This first response may come from individuals, families, neighborhood associations, business, industry, agriculture, educational institutions, the news media, or any other private service to the public.

It involves crime prevention as well as participation in the criminal justice process once a crime has been committed. Private crime prevention is more than providing private security or burglar alarms or participating in neighborhood watch. It also includes a commitment to stop criminal behavior by not engaging in it or condoning it when it is committed by others.

Citizens take part directly in the criminal justice process by reporting crime to the police, by being a reliable participant (for example, a witness or a juror) in a criminal proceeding and by accepting the disposition of the system as just or reasonable. As voters and taxpayers, citizens also participate in criminal justice through the policymaking process that affects how the criminal justice process operates, the resources available to it, and its goals and objectives. At every stage of the process from the original formulation of objectives to the decision about where to locate jails and prisons to the reintegration of inmates into society, the private sector has a role to play. Without such involvement, the criminal justice process cannot serve the citizens it is intended to protect.

The Response to Crime and Public Safety Involves Many Agencies and Services

Many of the services needed to prevent crime and make neighborhoods safe are supplied by noncriminal justice agencies, including agencies with primary concern for public health, education, welfare, public works, and housing. Individual citizens as well as public and private sector organizations have joined with criminal justice agencies to prevent crime and make neighborhoods safe.

Criminal Cases Are Brought by the Government Through the Criminal Justice System

We apprehend, try, and punish offenders by means of a loose confederation of agencies at all levels of government. Our American system of justice has evolved from the English common law into a complex series of procedures and decisions. Founded on the concept that crimes against an individual are crimes against the State, our justice system prosecutes individuals as though they victimized all of society. However, crime victims are involved throughout the process and many justice agencies have programs which focus on helping victims.

There is no single criminal justice system in this country. We have many similar systems that are individually unique. Criminal cases may be handled differently in different jurisdictions, but court decisions based on the due process guarantees of the U.S. Constitution require that specific steps be taken in the administration of criminal justice so that the individual will be protected from undue intervention from the State.

The description of the criminal and juvenile justice systems that follows portrays the most common sequence of events in response to serious criminal behavior.

Entry into the System

The justice system does not respond to most crime because so much crime is not discovered or reported to the police. Law enforcement agencies learn about crime from the reports of victims or other citizens, from discovery by a police officer in the field, from informants, or from investigative and intelligence work.

Once a law enforcement agency has established that a crime has been committed, a suspect must be identified and apprehended for the case to proceed through the system. Sometimes, a suspect is apprehended at the scene; however, identification of a suspect sometimes requires an extensive investigation. Often, no one is identified or apprehended. In some instances, a suspect is arrested and later the police determine that no crime was committed and the suspect is released.

Prosecution and Pretrial Services

After an arrest, law enforcement agencies present information about the case and about the accused to the prosecutor, who will decide if formal charges will be filed with the court. If no charges are filed, the accused must be released. The prosecutor can also drop charges after making efforts to prosecute (*nolle prosequi*).

A suspect charged with a crime must be taken before a judge or magistrate without unnecessary delay. At the initial appearance, the judge or magistrate informs the accused of the charges and decides whether there is probable cause to detain the accused person. If the offense is not very serious, the determination of guilt and assessment of a penalty may also occur at this stage.

Often, the defense counsel is also assigned at the initial appearance. All suspects prosecuted for serious crimes have a right to be represented by an attorney. If the court determines the suspect is indigent and cannot afford such representation, the court will assign counsel at the public's expense.

A pretrial-release decision may be made at the initial appearance, but may occur at other hearings or may be changed at another time during the process. Pretrial release and bail were traditionally intended to ensure appearance at trial. However, many jurisdictions permit pretrial detention of defendants accused of serious offenses and deemed to be dangerous to prevent them from committing crimes prior to trial.

The court often bases its pretrial decision on information about the defendant's drug use, as well as residence, employment, and family ties. The court may decide to release the accused on his/her own recognizance or into the custody of a third party after the posting of a financial bond or on the promise of satisfying certain conditions such as taking periodic drug tests to ensure drug abstinence.

In many jurisdictions, the initial appearance may be followed by a preliminary hearing. The main function of this hearing is to discover if there is probable cause to believe that the accused committed a known crime within the jurisdiction of the court. If the judge does not find probable cause, the case is dismissed; however, if the judge or magistrate finds probable cause for such a belief, or the accused waives his or her right to a preliminary hearing, the case may be bound over to a grand jury.

A grand jury hears evidence against the accused presented by the prosecutor and decides if there is sufficient evidence to cause the accused to be brought to trial. If the grand jury finds sufficient evidence, it submits to the court an indictment, a written statement of the essential facts of the offense charged against the accused.

Where the grand jury system is used, the grand jury may also investigate criminal activity generally and issue indictments called grand jury originals that initiate criminal cases. These investigations and indictments are often used in drug and conspiracy cases that involve complex organizations. After such an indictment, law enforcement tries to apprehend and arrest the suspects named in the indictment.

Misdemeanor cases and some felony cases proceed by the issuance of an information, a formal, written accusation submitted to the court by a prosecutor. In some jurisdictions, indictments may be required in felony cases. However, the accused may choose to waive a grand jury indictment and, instead, accept service of an information for the crime.

In some jurisdictions, defendants, often those without prior criminal records, may be eligible for diversion from prosecution subject to the completion of specific conditions such as drug treatment. Successful completion of the conditions may result in the dropping of charges or the expunging of the criminal record where the defendant is required to plead guilty prior to the diversion.

Adjudication

Once an indictment or information has been filed with the trial court, the accused is scheduled for arraignment. At the arraignment, the accused is informed of the charges, advised of the rights of criminal defendants, and asked to enter a plea to the charges. Sometimes, a plea of guilty is the result of negotiations between the prosecutor and the defendant.

If the accused pleads guilty or pleads *nolo contendere* (accepts penalty without admitting guilt), the judge may accept or reject the plea. If the plea is accepted, no trial is held and the offender is sentenced at this proceeding or at a later date. The plea may be rejected and proceed to trial if, for example, the judge believes that the accused may have been coerced.

If the accused pleads not guilty or not guilty by reason of insanity, a date is set for the trial. A person accused of a serious crime is guaranteed a trial by jury. However, the accused may ask for a bench trial where the judge, rather than a jury, serves as the finder of fact. In both instances the prosecution and defense present evidence by questioning witnesses while the judge decides on issues of law. The trial results in acquittal or conviction on the original charges or on lesser included offenses.

After the trial a defendant may request appellate review of the conviction or sentence. In some cases, appeals of convictions are a matter of right; all States with the death penalty provide for automatic appeal of cases involving a death sentence. Appeals may be subject to the discretion of the appellate court and may be granted only on acceptance of a defendant's petition for a *writ of certiorari*. Prisoners may also appeal their sentences through civil rights petitions and *writs of habeas corpus* where they claim unlawful detention.

Sentencing and Sanctions

After a conviction, sentence is imposed. In most cases the judge decides on the sentence, but in some jurisdictions the sentence is decided by the jury, particularly for capital offenses.

In arriving at an appropriate sentence, a sentencing hearing may be held at which evidence of aggravating or mitigating circumstances is considered. In assessing the circumstances surrounding a convicted person's criminal behavior, courts often rely on presentence investigations by probation agencies or other designated authorities. Courts may also consider victim impact statements.

The sentencing choices that may be available to judges and juries include one or more of the following:

- the death penalty
- incarceration in a prison, jail, or other confinement facility
- probation—allowing the convicted person to remain at liberty but subject to certain conditions and restrictions such as drug testing or drug restrictions such as drug testing or drug treatment

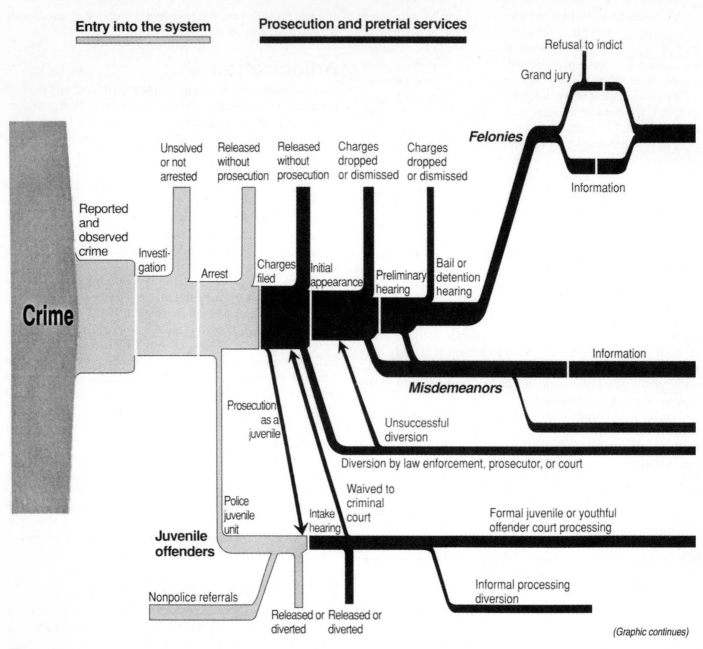

Figure 1
Note: This chart gives a simplified view of caseflow through the criminal justice system. Procedures vary among jurisdictions. The weights of the lines are not intended to show the actual size of caseloads.

- fines—primarily applied as penalties in minor offenses
- restitution—requiring the offender to pay compensation to the victim. In some jurisdictions, offenders may be sentenced to alternatives to incarceration that are considered more severe than straight probation but less severe than a prison term. Examples of such sanctions include boot camps, intense supervision often with drug treatment and testing, house arrest and electronic monitoring, denial of Federal benefits, and community service.

In many jurisdictions, the law mandates that persons convicted of certain types of offenses serve a prison term. Most jurisdictions permit the judge to set the sentence length within certain limits, but some have determinate sentencing laws that stipulate a specific sentence length that must be served and cannot be altered by a parole board.

Corrections

Offenders sentenced to incarceration usually serve time in a local jail or a State prison. Offenders sentenced to less than 1 year generally go to jail; those sentenced to more than 1 year go to prison. Persons admitted to the Federal system or a State prison system may be held in prison with varying levels of custody or in a community correctional facility.

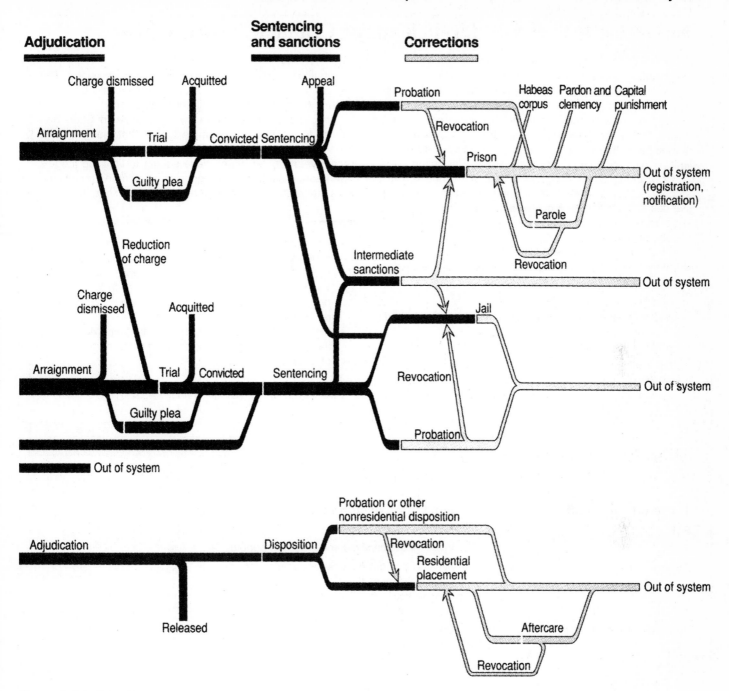

Adjudication

Sentencing and sanctions

Corrections

Figure 1 *(continued)*

Source: Adapted from *The challenge of crime in a free society*. President's Commission on Law Enforcement and Administration of Justice, 1967. This revision, a result of the Symposium on the 30th Anniversary of the President's Commission, was prepared by the Bureau of Justice Statistics in 1997.

A prisoner may become eligible for parole after serving a specific part of his or her sentence. Parole is the conditional release of a prisoner before the prisoner's full sentence has been served. The decision to grant parole is made by an authority such as a parole board, which has power to grant or revoke parole or to discharge a parolee altogether. The way parole decisions are made varies widely among jurisdictions.

Offenders may also be required to serve out their full sentences prior to release (expiration of term). Those sentenced under determinate sentencing laws can be released only after

they have served their full sentence (mandatory release) less any "goodtime" received while in prison. Inmates get goodtime credits against their sentences automatically or by earning them through participation in programs.

If released by a parole board decision or by mandatory release, the releasee will be under the supervision of a parole officer in the community for the balance of his or her unexpired sentence. This supervision is governed by specific conditions of release, and the releasee may be returned to prison for violations of such conditions.

Discretion Is Exercised throughout the Criminal Justice System

Discretion is "an authority conferred by law to act in certain conditions or situations in accordance with an official's or an official agency's own considered judgment and conscience."[1] Discretion is exercised throughout the government. It is a part of decision making in all government systems from mental health to education, as well as criminal justice. The limits of discretion vary from jurisdiction to jurisdiction.

Concerning crime and justice, legislative bodies have recognized that they cannot anticipate the range of circumstances surrounding each crime, anticipate local mores, and enact laws that clearly encompass all conduct that is criminal and all that is not.[2]

Therefore, persons charged with the day-to-day response to crime are expected to exercise their own judgment within limits set by law. Basically, they must decide—

- whether to take action
- where the situation fits in the scheme of law, rules, and precedent
- which official response is appropriate.[3]

To ensure that discretion is exercised responsibly, government authority is often delegated to professionals. Professionalism requires a minimum level of training and orientation, which guide officials in making decisions. The professionalism of policing is due largely to the desire to ensure the proper exercise of police discretion.

The limits of discretion vary from State to State and locality to locality. For example, some State judges have wide discretion in the type of sentence they may impose. In recent years, other states have sought to limit the judge's discretion in sentencing by passing mandatory sentencing laws that require prison sentences for certain offenses.

Notes

1. Roscoe Pound, "Discretion, dispensation and mitigation: The problem of the individual special case," *New York University Law Review* (1960) 35:925, 926.
2. Wayne R. LaFave, *Arrest: The decision to take a suspect into custody* (Boston: Little, Brown & Co., 1964), p. 63–184.
3. Memorandum of June 21, 1977, from Mark Moore to James Vorenberg, "Some abstract notes on the issue of discretion."

Bureau of Justice Statistics (www.ojp.usdoj.gov/bjs/). January 1998. NCJ 167894. To order: 1-800-732-3277.

Who Exercises Discretion?

These criminal justice officials . . .	must often decide whether or not or how to—
Police	Enforce specific laws
	Investigate specific crimes; Search people
Prosecutors	File charges or petitions for adjudication
	Seek indictments
	Drop cases
	Reduce charges
Judges or magistrates	Set bail or conditions for release
	Accept pleas
	Determine delinquency
	Dismiss charges
	Impose sentence
	Revoke probation
Correctional officials	Assign to type of correctional facility
	Award privileges
	Punish for disciplinary infractions
Paroling authorities	Determine date and conditions of parole
	Revoke parole

Recidivism

Once the suspects, defendants, or offenders are released from the jurisdiction of a criminal justice agency, they may be processed through the criminal justice system again for a new crime. Long term studies show that many suspects who are arrested have prior criminal histories and those with a greater number of prior arrests were more likely to be arrested again. As the courts take prior criminal history into account at sentencing, most prison inmates have a prior criminal history and many have been incarcerated before. Nationally, about half the inmates released from State prison will return to prison.

The Juvenile Justice System

Juvenile courts usually have jurisdiction over matters concerning children, including delinquency, neglect, and adoption. They also handle "status offenses" such as truancy and running away, which are not applicable to adults. State statutes define which persons are under the original jurisdiction of the juvenile court. The upper age of juvenile court jurisdiction in delinquency matters is 17 in most States.

The processing of juvenile offenders is not entirely dissimilar to adult criminal processing, but there are crucial differences. Many juveniles are referred to juvenile courts by law enforcement officers, but many others are referred by school officials, social services agencies, neighbors, and even parents, for behavior or conditions that are determined to require intervention by the formal system for social control.

At arrest, a decision is made either to send the matter further into the justice system or to divert the case out of the system, often to alternative programs. Examples of alternative programs include drug treatment, individual or group counseling, or referral to educational and recreational programs.

When juveniles are referred to the juvenile courts, the court's intake department or the prosecuting attorney determines whether sufficient grounds exist to warrant filing a petition that requests an adjudicatory hearing or a request to transfer jurisdiction to criminal court. At this point, many juveniles are released or diverted to alternative programs.

All States allow juveniles to be tried as adults in criminal court under certain circumstances. In many States, the legislature *statutorily excludes* certain (usually serious) offenses from the jurisdiction of the juvenile court regardless of the age of the accused. In some States and at the Federal level under certain circumstances, prosecutors have the *discretion* to either file criminal charges against juveniles directly in criminal courts or proceed through the juvenile justice process. The juvenile court's intake department or the prosecutor may petition the juvenile court to *waive* jurisdiction to criminal court. The juvenile court also may order *referral* to criminal court for trial as adults. In some jurisdictions, juveniles processed as adults may upon conviction be sentenced to either an adult or a juvenile facility.

In those cases where the juvenile court retains jurisdiction, the case may be handled formally by filing a delinquency petition or informally by diverting the juvenile to other agencies or programs in lieu of further court processing.

If a petition for an adjudicatory hearing is accepted, the juvenile may be brought before a court quite unlike the court with jurisdiction over adult offenders. Despite the considerable discretion associated with juvenile court proceedings, juveniles are afforded many of the due-process safeguards associated with adult criminal trials. Several States permit the use of juries in juvenile courts; however, in light of the U.S. Supreme Court holding that juries are not essential to juvenile hearings, most States do not make provisions for juries in juvenile courts.

In disposing of cases, juvenile courts usually have far more discretion than adult courts. In addition to such options as probation, commitment to a residential facility, restitution, or fines, State laws grant juvenile courts the power to order removal of children from their homes to foster homes or treatment facilities. Juvenile courts also may order participation in special programs aimed at shoplifting prevention, drug counseling, or driver education.

Once a juvenile is under juvenile court disposition, the court may retain jurisdiction until the juvenile legally becomes an adult (at age 21 in most States). In some jurisdictions, juvenile offenders may be classified as youthful offenders which can lead to extended sentences.

Following release from an institution, juveniles are often ordered to a period of aftercare which is similar to parole supervision for adult offenders. Juvenile offenders who violate the conditions of aftercare may have their aftercare revoked, resulting in being recommitted to a facility. Juveniles who are classified as youthful offenders and violate the conditions of aftercare may be subject to adult sanctions.

The Governmental Response to Crime Is Founded in the Intergovernmental Structure of the United States

Under our form of government, each State and the Federal Government has its own criminal justice system. All systems must respect the rights of individuals set forth in court interpretation of the U.S. Constitution and defined in case law.

State constitutions and laws define the criminal justice system within each State and delegate the authority and responsibility for criminal justice to various jurisdictions, officials, and institutions. State laws also define criminal behavior and groups of children or acts under jurisdiction of the juvenile courts.

Municipalities and counties further define their criminal justice systems through local ordinances that proscribe the local agencies responsible for criminal justice processing that were not established by the State.

Congress has also established a criminal justice system at the Federal level to respond to Federal crimes such as bank robbery, kidnaping, and transporting stolen goods across State lines.

The Response to Crime Is Mainly a State and Local Function

Very few crimes are under exclusive Federal jurisdiction. The responsibility to respond to most crime rests with State and local governments. Police protection is primarily a function of cities and towns. Corrections is primarily a function of State governments. Most justice personnel are employed at the local level.

From *Report to the Nation on Crime and Justice,* January 1998. Published by Office of Justice/U.S. Department of Justice.

Plugging Holes in the Science of Forensics

HENRY FOUNTAIN

It was time, the panel of experts said, to put more science in forensic science.

A report in February by a committee of the National Academy of Sciences found "serious problems" with much of the work performed by crime laboratories in the United States. Recent incidents of faulty evidence analysis—including the case of an Oregon lawyer who was arrested by the F.B.I. after the 2004 Madrid terrorist bombings based on fingerprint identification that turned out to be wrong—were just high-profile examples of wider deficiencies, the committee said. Crime labs were overworked, there were few certification programs for investigators and technicians, and the entire field suffered from a lack of oversight.

But perhaps the most damning conclusion was that many forensic disciplines—including analysis of fingerprints, bite marks and the striations and indentations left by a pry bar or a gun's firing mechanism—were not grounded in the kind of rigorous, peer-reviewed research that is the hallmark of classic science. DNA analysis was an exception, the report noted, in that it had been studied extensively. But many other investigative tests, the report said, "have never been exposed to stringent scientific scrutiny."

While some forensic experts took issue with that conclusion, many welcomed it. And some scientists are working on just the kind of research necessary to improve the field. They are refining software and studying human decision-making to improve an important aspect of much forensic science—the ability to recognize and compare patterns.

The report was "basically saying what many of us have been saying for a long time," said Lawrence Kobilinsky, chairman of the department of sciences at John Jay College of Criminal Justice in New York. "There are a lot of areas in forensics that need improvement."

Barry Fisher, a past president of the American Academy of Forensic Sciences and a former director of the crime laboratory at the Los Angeles County Sheriff's Department, said he and others had been pushing for this kind of independent assessment for years. "There needs to be a demonstration that this stuff is reliable," he said.

It's not that there hasn't been any research in forensic science. But over the years much of it has been done in crime labs themselves. "It hasn't gotten to the level where they can state findings in a rigorous scientific way," said Constantine Gatsonis, director of the Center for Statistical Sciences at Brown University and co-chairman of the National Academy of Sciences committee. And rather than being teased out in academic papers and debated at scientific conferences, "a lot of this forensic stuff is being argued in the courtroom," Mr. Fisher said. "That's not the place to validate any kind of scientific information."

Much forensic research has been geared to improving technologies and techniques. These studies can result in the kinds of gee-whiz advances that may show up in the next episode of the "C.S.I." series—a technique to obtain fingerprints from a grocery bag or other unlikely source, for example, or equipment that enables analyses of the tiniest bits of evidence.

This kind of work is useful, Dr. Kobilinsky said, "but it doesn't solve the basic problem."

DNA analysis came out of the biological sciences, and much money and time has been spent developing the field, resulting in a large body of peer-reviewed research. So when a DNA expert testifies in court that there is a certain probability that a sample comes from a suspect, that claim is grounded in science.

As evidence to be analyzed, DNA has certain advantages. "DNA has a particular structure, and can be digitized," Dr. Gatsonis said. So scientists can agree, for example, on how many loci on a DNA strand to use in their analyses, and computers can do the necessary computations of probability.

"Fingerprints are a lot more complicated," Dr. Gatsonis said. "There are a lot of different ways you can select features and make comparisons." A smudged print may have only a few ridge endings or other points for comparison, while a clear print may have many more. And other factors can affect prints, including the material they were found on and the pressure of the fingers in making them.

Sargur N. Srihari, an expert in pattern recognition at the University at Buffalo, part of the New York state university system, is trying to quantify the uncertainty. His group did much of the research that led to postal systems that can recognize handwritten addresses on envelopes, and he works with databases of fingerprints to derive probabilities of random correspondence between two prints.

Most features on a print are usually represented by X and Y coordinates and by an angle that represents the orientation of the particular ridge where the feature is located. A single print can have 40 or more comparable features.

Dr. Srihari uses relatively small databases, including an extreme one that contains fingerprints from dozens of identical twins (so the probability of matches is high), and employs the results to further refine mathematical tools for comparison that would work with larger populations.

"These numbers are not easy to come by at this point," he said. The goal is not individualization—matching two prints with absolute certainty—but coming up with firm probabilities that would be very useful in legal proceedings.

Other researchers are compiling databases of their own. Nicholas D. K. Petraco, an assistant professor at John Jay College, is studying microscopic tool marks of the kind made by a screwdriver when a burglar jimmies a window. It has been hypothesized that no two screwdrivers leave exactly the same pattern of marks, although that has never been proved. So Dr. Petraco is systematically making marks in jeweler's wax and other materials, creating images of them under a stereo microscope and quantifying the details, assembling a database that can eventually be mined to determine probabilities that a mark matches a certain tool.

Dr. Petraco, a chemist with a strong background in computer science, looks to industry for ideas about pattern recognition—the tools that a company like Netflix uses, for example, to classify people by the kinds of movies they like. "A lot of computational machinery goes into making those kinds of decisions," he said.

He figures that if something works for industry, it will work for forensic science. "You don't want to invent anything new," he said, because that raises legal issues of admissibility of evidence.

The work takes time, but the good news is that the data stays around forever. So as software improves, the probabilities should get more accurate. "Algorithms and data comparison evolve over time," Dr. Petraco said.

But it may not be possible to develop useful databases in some disciplines—bite mark analysis, for example. "Using a screwdriver, that's very straightforward and simple," said Ira Titunik, a forensic odontologist and adjunct professor at John Jay College. But bites involve numerous teeth, and there are other factors, including condition of the skin, that may make it difficult to quantify them for purposes of determining probabilities.

A few researchers are looking at how errors creep into forensic analysis. The National Institute of Standards and Technology recently established a working group on fingerprints, with statisticians, psychologists and others, "to try to understand the circumstances that lead to human error," said Mark Stolorow, director of the Office of Law Enforcement Standards at the institute.

In Britain, Itiel Dror, a psychologist who studies decision-making processes, is already looking at human factors. "I like to say the mind is not a camera, objectively and passively recording information," said Dr. Dror, who has a consulting firm and is affiliated with University College London. "The brain is an active and dynamic device."

He has conducted studies that show that when working on an identification, fingerprint examiners can be influenced by what else they know about a case. In one experiment, he found that the same examiner can come to different conclusions about the same fingerprint, if the context is changed over time.

The same kinds of contextual biases arise with other decision-makers, said Dr. Dror, who works with the military and with financial and medical professionals. He thinks one reason forensic examiners often do not acknowledge that they make errors is that in these other fields, the mistakes are obvious. "In forensics, they don't really see it," he said. "People go to jail."

Forensics experts say the need for research like Dr. Dror's and Dr. Srihari's does not mean that disciplines like fingerprint analysis will turn out to be invalid. "I have no doubt that fingerprint evidence and firearms evidence, once looked into by the appropriate research entities, are going to be shown to be very reliable and good," said Mr. Fisher, the former American Academy of Forensic Sciences president.

Dr. Kobilinsky said people should not jump to the conclusion that forensic science is bad science. "There's a lot of experience and knowledge that goes into somebody's expertise," he said.

"It's not junk science. But that doesn't mean it shouldn't be improved."

Does Proximity to Schools Tempt Former Sex Offenders?

CYNTHIA CALKINS MERCADO, PhD AND BRAIN H. BORNSTEIN, PhD

Last November, the Supreme Court of Georgia considered the constitutionality of sex offender residency restrictions, one of the more recent policies to gain popularity in the criminal justice arena. Residency restrictions prohibit sex offenders from living or working within a certain distance (typically between 500 and 2,500 feet) of places such as schools, day-care facilities or parks. At least 30 states and many local jurisdictions have residency restrictions in place. Some states, such as Alabama, have exceptions that allow offenders with already established residences to remain when a school or other youth-serving institution later establishes itself in the area. Georgia, however, had no such statutory exception, leaving Anthony Mann in violation of his probation when a child-care facility moved within 1,000 feet of the home that he owned with his wife and a barbeque restaurant he co-owned.

Applying a Fifth Amendment takings analysis, the Georgia Supreme Court noted that "there is no place in Georgia where a registered sex offender can live without being at continual risk of being ejected," (*Mann v. Department of Georgia Corrections et al,* 282 Ga. 754, 755, 2007). The court found the statute to be unconstitutional with regard to Mann's home, but not his work, given that much of the work in running the restaurant could be done off-site.

Other Court Rulings

In another case, Keith Seering and his family left their home and moved into a fold-down camper on rural farmland to comply with Iowa's 2,000-foot residency restriction. However, after the farm owner demanded that they leave the property, Seering challenged the statute's constitutionality. In upholding the residency restriction, the Iowa Supreme Court found no deprivation of Seering's substantive or due process rights (*State v. Seering,* 701 N.W.2d 655, 2005).

Other courts have similarly upheld residency restriction legislation. In 2005, the Eighth Circuit Court of Appeals upheld the same statute at issue in *Seering,* with the court finding that no fundamental right exists to choose where one lives (*Doe v. Miller,* 418 F.3d 950, 2005). The Association for the Treatment of Sexual Abusers (ATSA) petitioned for writ of *certiorari,* noting the national significance of *Doe v. Miller* and arguing that residency restrictions "actually harm the innocent children they are intended to protect" by increasing offender transience (ATSA, 2005). The U.S. Supreme Court, however, declined to hear the case.

What the Research Shows

Although many challenges to residency restriction legislation have survived constitutional scrutiny, some argue that residency restrictions lead to housing instability and housing shortages. Research can inform several issues that may be relevant to these cases. For instance, in Orange County, Fla., research shows that more than 95 percent of residential properties are within 1,000 feet of designated child-dense areas, while 2,500-foot restrictions encompass nearly 100 percent of residential space.

To date, there is still little research on the utility of residency restriction statutes. However, a recent study failed to show that sex offenders who re-offend live closer to schools and parks than those who do not re-offend. Further, research has found that "social or relationship proximity" to children, rather than residential proximity, affects sexual recidivism. Notably, after considering studies on the impact of residency restrictions, both the Colorado and Minnesota legislatures opted not to enact such legislation.

Some evidence suggests that offenders (regardless of the crime they have committed) who become more integrated in the community and lead more stable lives are less likely to re-offend than those who experience change and turmoil. Indeed, it is possible that being able to remain in the same house would provide a source of stability that would reduce re-offending, in much the same way that job stability reduces likelihood of recidivism. Though existing research indicates that residency restrictions limit housing options and that geographical proximity to child-dense community structures may have little effect on recidivism generally, further research might address whether residential instability impacts sexual re-offense patterns. Psychologists and other social scientists can contribute valuable data to this policy debate by studying such questions. It is possible that the benefit produced by residency-restriction statutes is offset by the risks they create.

Acknowledgements—"Judicial Notebook" is a project of APA's Div. 9 (Society for the Psychological Study of Social Issues).

Stereotype, Then and Now

Michael Nelson

Old-style college football bore strong resemblances to contemporary lacrosse. Both games were initially successful on elite Northeastern campuses, then spread south and west. Both were (and still are) bruising "helmet sports." In the era before spring football practice, lacrosse teams were largely manned by football players trying to stay in shape. The storied athlete Jim Thorpe got started in sports by playing football and lacrosse for the Carlisle Indian School.

As recounted in two recently published books, *The Real All Americans: The Team That Changed a Game, a People, a Nation,* by Sally Jenkins (Doubleday, 2007), and *Carlisle vs. Army: Jim Thorpe, Dwight Eisenhower, Pop Warner, and the Forgotten Story of Football's Greatest Battle,* by Lars Anderson (Random House, 2007), the school was founded in Pennsylvania in 1879 by Richard Henry Pratt. He was a cavalry officer who wanted to see the children of defeated American Indian tribes educated to succeed in mainstream America. Utterly unconcerned about preserving tribal culture (Jenkins, in particular, is justly critical of him for that), Pratt was nonetheless wildly progressive for his day: He actually believed that Indians were by nature fully equal to whites.

One way for Carlisle to make a splash in educational circles, Pratt decided, was to start a football team that could compete with the collegiate powers of the day: Harvard, Yale, Penn, Princeton, and, later, Army. Pratt hired Glenn (Pop) Warner, a young Cornell alumnus who was brimming with ideas about how to transform football from a game based on brutal massed attacks to a wide-open contest of speed and agility.

Carlisle played a good brand of football under Warner. It got even better when Thorpe, an athlete of astonishing quickness and grace, came along. Yet Carlisle's story is less interesting for its team's success than for how that success was perceived. As Anderson notes, "every game was framed as an epic battle between wild Indians and refined white players." A pregame article about the 1899 Yale-Carlisle contest in the *New York World* was all too typical: "On one side were the undergraduates of an old and great university. They represent, physically, the perfection of modern athletics, and intellectually, the culture and refinement of the best modern American life. On the other side was the aborigine . . . the redskin . . . developed or veneered, as the case may be, by education."

Any modern reader will be properly outraged by this and the many additional examples offered by Jenkins and Anderson of writers shoehorning Thorpe and other Indian students into stereotyped categories based on prevailing prejudices. The assumption that the Carlisle players, by the mere fact of their birth as Indians, were "wily," "cunning" "savages" (as various contemporary accounts had it) is one that, happily, most Americans have risen above.

It is all the more distressing, then, to be reminded in three new books about the 2006 Duke lacrosse case just how quick professors, administrators, journalists, and prosecutors were to make equally prejudicial assumptions about members of the Duke lacrosse team on the basis of their having been born as white males in mostly upper-middle-class families. *It's Not About the Truth: The Untold Story of the Duke Lacrosse Case and the Lives It Shattered,* by Don Yaeger with the former Duke lacrosse coach Mike Pressler (Threshold Editions, 2007); *A Rush to Injustice: How Power, Prejudice, Racism, and Political Correctness Overshadowed Truth and Justice in the Duke Lacrosse Rape Case,* by Nader Baydoun and R. Stephanie Good (Thomas Nelson, 2007); and the one that has gotten all the attention, *Until Proven Innocent: Political Correctness and the Shameful Injustices of the Duke Lacrosse Rape Case,* by Stuart Taylor Jr. and K.C. Johnson (St. Martin's Press, 2007), make clear that the proclivity of people who should know better to stereotype and stigmatize has not changed, even if the targets have.

The villains in the Duke lacrosse case are legion. They include, most obviously, the runaway Durham district attorney, Mike Nifong, who indicted three Duke students on alarmingly flimsy grounds, then concealed evidence of their innocence. Selena Roberts, the *New York Times* sports columnist who rushed to label the team "a group of privileged players of fine pedigree entangled in a night that threatens to belie their social standing as human beings," was among the most egregious journalistic offenders.

The authors' special condemnation, however, appropriately goes to the grown-ups at Duke, because only they have a specific responsibility, under the terms of the university's handbook, to treat students as "fellow members of the university community, deserving of respect and consideration in their dealings with faculty." Even as evidence accumulated regarding the innocence of the accused and the perfidy of Nifong, the university's president, Richard H. Brodhead, for more than eight months refused to stand by his students, on the ground that they faced felony charges. The moral emptiness of Brodhead's stance was laid bare when, in the face of public pressure and an altered media climate, he used Nifong's decision to drop the bogus rape charge as an occasion to reinstate the students whom he had suspended. The fact that, at the time, those students still faced felony charges for sexual assault and kidnapping undermines Brodhead's claim that his behavior was governed by principled deference to the criminal-justice process.

As for Duke's faculty members, they either rushed to condemn the students (speaking as the so-called Group of 88) or stood by silently for months while their colleagues did. On April 6, 2006, shortly after some protesters banged pots and hoisted banners (the largest read "CASTRATE!!") outside the lacrosse captains' house and others hung "Wanted!" posters around the campus with photos of team members, the Group of 88 ran a full-page ad in the student newspaper. The ad thanked "the protesters making collective noise . . . for not waiting and making yourselves heard." So much for critical thinking based on weighing evidence.

A week after the Group of 88's ad appeared, one of its authors, the literature professor Wahneema Lubiano, wrote an essay describing the students on the lacrosse team as "almost perfect offenders" because they are "the exemplars of the upper end of the class hierarchy, the politically dominant race and ethnicity, the dominant gender, the dominant sexuality, and the dominant social group on campus." Her colleague Houston Baker had already weighed in on March 29 with an open letter to Duke's provost, Peter Lange. Baker demanded that Duke order the "immediate dismissal" of the students and coaches of the lacrosse team because they embodied "abhorrent sexual assault, verbal racial violence, and drunken, white male privilege loosed amongst us."

Rich with villains, the lacrosse case also has a hero: the Duke law professor James Coleman.

As the case unfolded, Coleman played two vital roles in advancing the cause of reason. Officially, he led the university's inquiry into the team's conduct during the previous five years. The result of the inquiry, as detailed in the committee's May 1, 2006, report: Lacrosse players drank too much but were in most other ways exemplary students—strong scholars with a 100-percent graduation rate and many more academic all-Americans than any other lacrosse team in the Atlantic Coast Conference; respectful of the bus drivers, groundskeeper, equipment manager, and others who served the team; and blamelessly free of bullying behavior, racist talk, sexism, and cheating.

Unofficially, Coleman repeatedly made the point that most deserves to be remembered. When it becomes acceptable to treat people badly on the basis of prejudiced stereotypes about their race, gender, and class, it is African-Americans, women, and the poor who have the most to lose. Speaking of Nifong, on the October 15, 2006, edition of *60 Minutes,* Coleman asked, "What are you to conclude about a prosecutor who says to you, 'I'll do whatever it takes to get this set of defendants?' What does it say about what he's willing to do to get poor black defendants?"

The book we really need is a sober, even empathetic account of why people who care about justice can behave so unjustly.

It's too bad that all three of the new Duke lacrosse books are polemics (Taylor-Johnson and Baydoun-Good even hoist the red flag of "political correctness" in their subtitles). For one thing, the persecution of the students was itself so unjust that it doesn't need any rhetorical pumping up. For another, the books' harshly anti-left tone will make them easy to dismiss by the very people who most need to reflect on why prestigious intellectuals erred so heinously. The book we really need is a sober, even empathetic account of why people who care about justice can behave so unjustly, and why scholars who know how harmful prejudice is sometimes succumb to stereotyping of a kind that would have put the sportswriters of the Carlisle era to shame.

MICHAEL NELSON is a professor of political science at Rhodes College and a nonresident senior fellow at the University of Virginia's Miller Center for Public Affairs. His book with John Mason, *How the South Joined the Gambling Nation: The Politics of State Policy Innovation,* has just been published by Louisiana State University Press.

The Death of the War on Drugs

Lawrence T. Jablecki

In his first interview as the nation's new drug czar, Gil Kerlikowske told the *Wall Street Journal* that the phrase "war on drugs" should be retired because it implies that citizens who use illegal substances are enemies of the state to be conquered and destroyed. Instead of viewing the vast majority of these citizens as criminals deserving of punishment, a new paradigm should embrace them as members of our communities deserving of opportunities to establish or renew healthy and productive lives.

There are certainly no new arguments available to employ in support of or in opposition to current U.S. drug policies. Instead, we are locked in an ideological contest between two conflicting and not mutually exclusive philosophical perspectives, both of which have existed for many centuries. More specifically, the contest is between the perspective that a genuinely free society maximizes the rights and freedoms of its citizens, in turn allowing them to think, say, and act as they please as long as they don't harm or injure their fellow citizens. The other perspective emphasizes the claim that a stable social order can't be maintained in the absence of the legal enforcement of a rather long list of the shared moral values of its citizens. In short, this contest is what the eighteenth century Scottish philosopher David Hume called the perpetual struggle between the liberty of the individual and the authority of the state. And what can't be emphasized enough is that this isn't a struggle between the armies of good and evil. Much too often, defenders on both sides are persuaded that truth and justice are on theirs, and they have allowed their zeal to sink to the level of inflammatory attacks on the motivation and personal characteristics of their opponents. Regardless of our moral stance on a cluster of very divisive issues, all of us should heed the sage comments of the philosopher Isaiah Berlin in his 1958 "Two Concepts of Liberty" lecture: "If, as I believe, the ends of men are many, and not all of them are in principle compatible with each other, then the possibility of conflict—and of tragedy—can never be wholly eliminated from human life, either personal or social. The necessity of choosing between absolute claims is then an inescapable characteristic of the human condition."

I am enormously proud to be an American citizen and wouldn't choose to live in another country. I am, however, unequivocally ashamed that during the last thirty years, our criminal justice policies (federal and state) have sealed our identity as the nation that incarcerates a higher percentage of its population than any other country in the world. The dominant crime control policies are driven by a harsh retributive view of punishment committed to the belief that the only criteria are the seriousness of the offense and the criminal history of the defendant. Making no claim to originality, we have been beguiled by an addiction more powerful than all the drugs combined, namely, vengeance. This is a bitter pill that honesty obliges us to swallow.

There is a wealth of scholarly bickering about the feasibility of determining the actual number of non-violent drug offenders in U.S. federal, state, and private prisons. In his 2004 book, *Thinking about Crime: Sense and Sensibility in American Penal Culture* (Oxford University Press), Michael Tonry makes the worthy claim that

Many thousands of people are serving decades long sentences in federal prisons for non-violent drug crimes. Their misfortune is to have been sentenced in federal courts before avoidance of sentencing guidelines by federal judges and prosecutors became common practice. Hundreds of thousands of people, mostly but not only of minority and disadvantaged backgrounds, have spent much of their young adulthood in prison for drug crimes. Their misfortune is that unwisely, but for young people not uncommonly, and typically as a result of peer influences and teenagers' sense of invincibility, they experimented with drug use, got hooked, and got caught—in a time when antidrug policies were unprecedentedly harsh.

It would be a major error in judgment to claim that the tough law-and-order campaigns of those seeking to retain or attain public office and well-financed lobbyists urging the construction of more prisons, particularly private prisons, were solely responsible for the realities presented by Tonry. Members of Congress and state legislators would not have been able to craft and pass harsh penalties without the strong support of their constituents. Fortunately, the opinions and sensibilities of a fast growing number of our citizens are moving in the direction of believing that the war of prohibition, eradication, and harsh penalties are costing far too much in terms of human fatalities and consuming far too much of our federal and state resources. Many groups of vocal dissenters using electronic mass communication are focusing on these items for an agenda for change: the medical use of marijuana; the de-criminalization of the possession of small amounts of marijuana; the still unresolved issue of the wide disparity in the disposition of cases involving crack and powder cocaine; access to clean syringes to reduce the spread of HIV and hepatitis C; and new medical research involving prescription heroin or heroin replacements with the goals of improving health and reducing crime.

The Uniform Crime Report of 2007 compiled by the FBI contains the following data: of the over fourteen million reported arrests, 1.8 million or 13 percent were for drug abuse violations. Of those, 47.5 percent were for marijuana and of that number 89 percent were for possession, the others involving the sale and manufacture or growing. Three of every four persons in the group of drug violators were under the age of thirty. It is a given that many thousands in this group had a significant criminal history and it is equally true that many thousands did not. This means that many thousands of young offenders with no criminal history are caught in the very wide net of criminal justice and the majority of them must endure a grueling process of adjudication which brands them with a conviction and the status of being a criminal.

A radical proposal, which I believe is realistically feasible, would retrain the same professionals who administer our criminal justice systems to create so-called pre-prosecution agreements which still send a message of societal disapproval, but leave no permanent scars. The specific guts of the proposal are as follows: all persons arrested for possessing small amounts of any illegal substance, excluding it's sale or manufacture, who have no criminal history shall be granted a one-time only pre-prosecution agreement not to exceed one year. Within thirty days of accepting this agreement, they shall complete a substance abuse evaluation by a state-certified substance abuse counselor approved by the local jurisdiction and follow any recommendations of said counselor. Within thirty days of successful completion of this agreement the local jurisdiction and the state's criminal records division shall destroy and expunge all records of the case, excepting a list of the participants. Any participant who is arrested and convicted of any new criminal offense before completion of the program is subject to prosecution of the original offense.

The prosecutors in every local jurisdiction of this country have the explicit or inherent authority to create these programs and they certainly have the discretionary authority to dispose of numerous felony arrests by using this option. I am not embracing the claim that people who violate the criminal laws have any kind of a right that obliges the state to provide a comprehensive menu of services to fix the causes of their illegal conduct. I am claiming that there is a compelling public interest to do so.

The demise of the war on drugs can be accomplished if President Obama musters the political courage to use the presidential bully pulpit to win public and congressional support for the National Criminal Justice Commission Act of 2009 coauthored by Senators Jim Webb (D-VA) and Arlen Specter (D-PA). The purpose of this commission is to, in the words of the legislation, "undertake a comprehensive review of the criminal justice system, make findings related to current federal and state criminal justice policies and practices, and make reform recommendations for the president, Congress, and state governments to improve public safety, cost-effectiveness, overall prison administration, and fairness in the implementation of the nation's criminal justice system."

The commission will have eleven members, the chair to be appointed by President Obama and the other ten members to be appointed by various elected officials. Hopefully, the majority of these ten members will be private citizens who are nationally recognized experts and whose collective experience embraces the specified areas of law enforcement, criminal justice, national security, prison administration, prisoner reentry, public health (including drug addiction and mental health), victims' rights and social services.

If this commission is enacted and its final product receives strong public support and congressional approval, it can deal a death blow to the present international perception that the United States is a rogue nation whose criminal justice system is at war with its own citizens.

LAWRENCE T. JABLECKI, PhD, is a lecturer in the Master of Liberal Studies Program at Rice University and an adjunct professor of philosophy in the prison program of the University of Houston at Clear Lake. For eighteen years he was the director of the adult probation department in Brazoria County, Texas.

From *The Humanist,* September/October 2009, pp. 6–8. Copyright © 2009 by Lawrence T. Jablecki, PhD. Reprinted by permission of the author.

Of Crime and Punishment
Experts Explore Issues in the Legal Limelight

Criminal Justice is one of the top fields of interest for today's college students. Perhaps this popularity is based on our intense interest in criminals and law and order. In the United States we grapple every day with the concept of justice, on the streets, in the courtrooms and even in the statehouse. *FDU Magazine* asked facility and alumni to tell us what they think of some of the most high-profile issues in criminal justice today. Their answers reveal the enormously complex considerations that can tip the scales of justice.

ROBERT VODDE ET AL.

The Death Penalty

The sentencing trial of admitted al Qaeda conspirator Zacarias Moussaoui raised many issues relating to the death penalty in the United States—from mitigating circumstances and mental condition to zero tolerance for terrorism. Robert Vodde, director of the University's School of Criminal Justice and former chief of police for Leonia, N.J., explores the most critical issues relating to the death penalty.

Debates surrounding the death penalty center on religious, ethical, political, legal and utilitarian issues. But perhaps the most argued in America is whether invoking the death penalty violates the U.S. Constitution, specifically the Eighth and 14th Amendments; i.e., is it cruel and unusual punishment? In 1972, the U.S. Supreme Court, in *Georgia v. Furman*, ruled that capital punishment was unconstitutional. Four years later, however, the court reversed itself in *Gregg v. Georgia* (1976). Since that decision, close to 7,000 criminals have been sent to death row, of which more than 1,000 have been executed.

The second issue of controversy addresses whether or not putting another human to death is morally and ethically right. As Cardinal Theodore McCarrick posited, can the death penalty "offer the tragic illusion that we can teach that killing is wrong by killing?"

The third issue calls into question the utility of the death penalty; i.e., is it pragmatic? Does it succeed in deterring others from committing heinous offenses such as murder? According to Katherine Beckett and Theodore Sasson in *The Politics of Injustice: Crime and Punishment in America*, there is a conspicuous absence of empirical data to suggest that there is any relationship between capital punishment and a reduction in crime. The authors point to states such as Texas and Florida, which have high execution rates and yet also have the highest homicide rates.

And lastly, does capital punishment discriminate against society's minorities and the disenfranchised, who lack the education, financial resources and influence to provide for a defense comparable to those more fortunate? Beckett and Sasson wrote that in 13 states with death penalty laws, "significant race-of-offender bias" had been documented. Furthermore, advances in DNA technology and forensic science have revealed that many defendants have been convicted based on wrong or tainted evidence or procedural anomalies.

Despite bans on capital punishment by the European Union and Latin America, it appears that most Americans favor the death penalty, although that number seems to be changing. While 75 to 80 percent of Americans polled by Gullup in 1989 favored the death penalty, a similar poll in October 2005 showed that number had dropped to 64 percent.

Putting aside whether the killing of another person is legally, constitutionally, religiously, morally, ethically or politically "right" or "wrong," the question remains: "What is society looking to achieve by taking the life of a fellow human and why?"

Domestic Spying

Americans were forced to weigh their right to privacy with the need to combat terrorism when U.S. President George Bush acknowledged that the government had sanctioned warrantless domestic eavesdropping on Americans. Paulette Laubsch, assistant professor of administrative sciences, and Ronald Calissi, director of FDU's School of Administrative Science, address whether it is sometimes necessary to carry out domestic eavesdropping, or domestic spying, inside the United States without judicial oversight.

September 11, 2001, changed how citizens of the United States view their freedom. As security measures were either imposed or strengthened, individuals were willing to give up some of the freedoms that they have held dear for centuries, if it was good for our security and safety. But as time passes, we start questioning why we cannot do certain things, or more appropriately, why government can restrict our freedoms.

In January 2006, the president acknowledged that he had authorized the National Security Agency (NSA) to intercept international communications from known terrorist agencies. The president has used as justification the Authorization for the Use of Military Force, the Foreign Intelligence Surveillance Act and the Fourth Amendment of the Constitution. Shortly after September 11, he also signed a secret order that allowed the NSA to eavesdrop on international communications that involved both U.S. citizens and residents.

U.S. Attorney General Alberto Gonzalez has determined that existing statutes and our Constitution give legal authority to the president to conduct domestic eavesdropping for the purpose of detecting and preventing another catastrophic attack on America. In the ongoing conflict with al Qaeda and its allies, the president has a primary duty under the Constitution to protect the American people, as well as the full authority necessary to carry out that solemn duty.

Citizens may generally agree that activities involving eavesdropping on terrorists abroad are necessary to ensure our safety and security; but, some of these individuals protest domestic eavesdropping, citing the limitation of our freedoms.

There have been times when so-called spying activities were acceptable. In World War II, the government had segments of the population under investigation, monitoring correspondence and activities. This example, of course, relates to a wartime situation of a different era.

As everyone knows, technology has sped up communication. Cellular phones have become mainstream, and individuals do not need a landline to discuss their concerns or plans. Computers have become a universal method of correspondence. These modalities, including personal digital assistants (PDAs), have made it possible to communicate from anywhere to anywhere at any time. This changes how crimes are planned and carried out. Crime fighting must also change.

Americans need to trust government to do what is necessary to keep the citizenry safe, and that can include warrantless domestic eavesdropping.

Police Profiling

But how does one know from whom we need to be protected? African-Americans in New Jersey have alleged that they have been unfairly targeted for police checks. More recently, Americans of Middle Eastern descent have felt the eye of the law has unfairly profiled them. Are there some cases where institutional or systematic profiles can be legally justifiable? James Kenny, associate professor of criminal justice and a retired supervisory treasury officer, offers his view.

When used properly, profiles are legitimate and effective law-enforcement tools. Most list various personality traits and behaviors associated with a group of persons who have committed crimes in the past. However, as human conduct is affected by many complex and ever-changing variables, these traits and behaviors cannot consistently predict the future behavior of specific individuals. Criminal conduct is more dependent on at-risk individuals possessing the means, motive and ability to commit the offenses.

Profiles used to identify future criminal behaviors can cause great harm. Attempts to single out potentially violent individuals can stigmatize, traumatize and encourage already-troubled persons to act out, making profiling a self-fulfilling prophecy. And, profiling individuals is not very accurate at predicting extreme violence. At-risk individuals are unlikely to commit violence without various environmental, social and interpersonal factors interacting with each other and becoming more serious over time.

Despite the limitations of profiles, their use can alert authorities that an individual may need help and monitoring. The frequency, intensity and immediacy of the at-risk behaviors should dictate the type of intervention. In the less serious cases, the subject should not be viewed as potentially violent, but rather as an individual in need of assistance. At-risk individuals that are identified and helped promptly are unlikely to resort to violence.

Patriot Act

Soon after September 11, the House of Representatives and the Senate passed legislation granting new law-enforcement privileges through the USA Patriot Act. Are all of the privileges granted to the government by the act constitutional? FDU Magazine *sought out Kimberly Scrio, BA'04 (T), a paralegal with Casey & Barnett, LLC, in New York City, to answer this question, which was the topic of her FDU honors thesis.*

During times of national crisis the government is entrusted with the authority to implement any and all means necessary to secure the safety of the people. But at what point do the people begin to question the actions of government?

On October 26, 2001, both the U.S. House of Representatives and the Senate overwhelmingly passed the USA Patriot Act—343 pages of amendments and additions to previous laws designed to eliminate potential barriers in fighting terrorism.

According to the Department of Justice website, the Patriot Act "improves our counterterrorism efforts in several significant ways." It allows authorities to use tools already in use against organized crime and drug trafficking to investigate terrorist activities, facilitates information sharing among government agencies and updates existing law to reflect new technology and technological threats. In addition, the act imposes harsher penalties for those convicted of committing terrorist crimes.

The American Civil Liberties Union (ACLU) asserts that the Patriot Act tramples on the civil liberties of American citizens in several ways. The organization says the act violates the Fourth Amendment, which requires government to show probable cause before obtaining a search warrant. Second, the act violates the First Amendment by imposing a gag order on public employees required to provide government with their clients' personal information. The act also violates the First Amendment by effectively authorizing the FBI to investigate American citizens for, in part, exercising their freedom of speech. And, it eliminates the requirement for government to provide notice to individuals whose privacy has been compromised by a government investigation.

The act does intrude on an individual's right to privacy, but only in cases where the government suspects the individual is involved in terrorist-related activity. If the government is suspicious of an individual's activities, should it not have the ability to investigate that individual? Theoretically, law-abiding citizens will never have to worry about their right to privacy being violated because their activities will never be suspicious.

On the other hand, the Patriot Act does have the potential to trample on citizens' constitutional rights. The act relies on trusting investigators not to intrude upon these rights. Therefore, a strong argument can be made against the act, because, although government officials may not be currently abusing the act, the potential for abuse exists.

Thus the proverbial question once again arises. Should the people entrust the government with the authority granted by the USA Patriot Act in the name of national security, or should the people revolt against the Patriot Act for fear of potential government abuse? The fate of our national security may very well rest upon the answer.

Excessive Force

The use of force by the police has long been a contentious issue. Since the widely publicized Rodney King beating in Los Angeles, major efforts have been made to ensure such incidents do not take place. Patrick Reynolds, assistant director of the School of Criminal Justice, explains the measures taken to combat the use of excessive force.

Without a doubt, the most controversial issue in American policing is the use of force by police officers. On too many occasions, we have seen newspaper headlines reporting that an individual has been brutalized or, worse yet, killed by the police. The consequences of excessive and deadly force have been severe, affecting both police organizations and the communities they serve.

To reduce the occurrence of such incidents, better training and accountability mechanisms have been put in place. Police recruits are being taught that the level of force that they employ should only rise to the level of resistance being offered by a suspect.

Officers are trained to employ a continuum of force that ranges from the least amount, which would be the officer's mere presence, to the other extreme, the use of deadly force. Often the mere presence of a police officer will get most citizens to conform to the law. When an officer meets resistance from a suspect, that officer is legally authorized to escalate the level of force employed, depending on the resistance received from the suspect. The continuum of force ranges from an officer's presence to verbalization, command voice, firm grips, pain compliance, impact techniques and, finally, deadly force.

In addition, officers are taught to control their emotions in volatile confrontations and to utilize force only as needed. The most important issue regarding use of force is whether it was justified and consistent with the resistance being offered. The decision of whether or not to use force is an instantaneous one—and one of the most challenging situations a police officer may encounter. An incorrect decision by a police officer cannot be recalled.

In the vast majority of confrontations requiring the use of force, officers respond in a professional nature and utilize force that is justified. It is the few exceptions where officers overreact and use inappropriate force that seem to capture the media's attention.

Police organizations have gone to great lengths to minimize the number of instances where officers employ excessive force. The stringent hiring processes employed by police agencies exemplify this. Competitive testing, psychological screening and extensive background checks are being employed. Both recruit training and in-service training for seasoned officers focus on making good choices, maintaining professional standards and bridging the gap that has existed for many years between the community and the police.

Law enforcement and police behavior have come a long way in the past decade and will continue to improve, so long as there is full disclosure and analysis of police conduct—both positive and negative.

The War on Drugs

Has the War on Drugs been won or merely forgotten in favor of more dramatic issues? FDU Magazine *asked Richard Gray, assistant professor of criminal justice and a retired substance abuse treatment coordinator for the U.S. Probation Department in Brooklyn, "Are U.S. drug laws effectively reducing the impact of drug use and abuse on our society?"*

The best measurement of the effectiveness of the "War on Drugs" comes from the White House Office of National Drug Control Policy (ONDCP), which states, "The goals of the program are to reduce illicit drug use, manufacturing and trafficking, drug-related crime and violence, and drug-related health consequences."

If we focus on the most basic questions—"Is drug use down?" "Is crime down?" and "Are drugs less available?"—the answer to our larger question becomes apparent.

Drug use. According to National Household Survey on Drug Abuse (NHSDA) drug use by persons over age 12 has remained relatively stable since 1988 (the year the "Drug War" began). During this period, the number of persons who reported drug use in the previous month or the previous year has remained unchanged and the number of persons reporting any drug use has increased by about 7 million.

The organization Monitoring the Future examines access to drugs, drug use and attitudes toward drugs of the nation's junior and senior high school students. According to its 2005 study, there were minor declines in substance abuse by older teens, but previous declines in use among eighth graders had stopped. More importantly, the changes themselves were not statistically significant—they could be explained by chance alone. For all intents and purposes, there was no reduction in substance abuse among school children.

Drug-related crime. In general, crime is down in the United States. According to the Bureau of Justice Statistics, it has decreased significantly since 1993. However, since 1995, drug-related arrests have stayed relatively stable at approximately 1.5 million per year. Although reporting slightly lower arrest rates, the Bureau also reported that arrests for drug abuse violations increased steadily between 1991 and 1996 and remained stable from 1997 to 2005.

Drug availability. If supply is down, you cannot tell by the responses of high school students. The 2005 Monitoring the Future study found that marijuana was judged to be easy or very easy to get by 85 percent of 12th graders. LSD was perceived as less available; however, other hallucinogens have increased steadily in availability. On the brighter side, almost 8 percent fewer 12th graders than in the previous year perceived MDMA (ecstasy) to be fairly easy or easy to get. Despite this, cocaine, crack, hallucinogens, MDMA and amphetamines were rated as easily accessible by between 40 and 50 percent of students.

The government spends about $13 billion per year in its war against drugs. Have they been successful in stopping or significantly impacting substance abuse? Has the drug war decreased drug-related crime? Is the availability of illegal substances down? Insofar as the "War on Drugs" metaphor has failed us, we had best begin to think of a new strategy.

From *FDU Magazine*, Summer/Fall 2006, pp. 16–20. Copyright © 2006 by Fairleigh Dickinson University. Reprinted by permission.

Serving Life for Providing Car to Killers

Adam Liptak

Early in the morning of March 10, 2003, after a raucous party that lasted into the small hours, a groggy and hungover 20-year-old named Ryan Holle lent his Chevrolet Metro to a friend. That decision, prosecutors later said, was tantamount to murder.

The friend used the car to drive three men to the Pensacola home of a marijuana dealer, aiming to steal a safe. The burglary turned violent, and one of the men killed the dealer's 18-year-old daughter by beating her head in with a shotgun he found in the home.

Mr. Holle was a mile and a half away, but that did not matter.

He was convicted of murder under a distinctively American legal doctrine that makes accomplices as liable as the actual killer for murders committed during felonies like burglaries, rapes and robberies.

Mr. Holle, who had given the police a series of statements in which he seemed to admit knowing about the burglary, was convicted of first-degree murder. He is serving a sentence of life without the possibility of parole at the Wakulla Correctional Institution here, 20 miles southwest of Tallahassee.

A prosecutor explained the theory to the jury at Mr. Holle's trial in Pensacola in 2004. "No car, no crime," said the prosecutor, David Rimmer. "No car, no consequences. No car, no murder."

Most scholars trace the doctrine, which is an aspect of the felony murder rule, to English common law, but Parliament abolished it in 1957. The felony murder rule, which has many variations, generally broadens murder liability for participants in violent felonies in two ways. An unintended killing during a felony is considered murder under the rule. So is, as Mr. Holle learned, a killing by an accomplice.

India and other common law countries have followed England in abolishing the doctrine. In 1990, the Canadian Supreme Court did away with felony murder liability for accomplices, saying it violated "the principle that punishment must be proportionate to the moral blameworthiness of the offender."

Countries outside the common law tradition agree. "The view in Europe," said James Q. Whitman, a professor of comparative law at Yale, "is that we hold people responsible for their own acts and not the acts of others."

But prosecutors and victims' rights groups in the United States say that punishing accomplices as though they had been the actual killers is perfectly appropriate.

"The felony murder rule serves important interests," said Mr. Rimmer, the prosecutor in the Holle case, "because it holds all persons responsible for the actions of each other if they are all participating in the same crime."

Kent Scheidegger, the legal director of the Criminal Justice Legal Foundation, a victims' rights group, said "all perpetrators of the underlying felony, not just the one who pulls the trigger" should be held accountable for murder.

"A person who has chosen to commit armed robbery, rape or kidnapping has chosen to do something with a strong possibility of causing the death of an innocent person," Mr. Scheidegger said. "That choice makes it morally justified to convict the person of murder when that possibility happens."

About 16 percent of homicides in 2006 occurred during felonies, according to the Federal Bureau of Investigation. Statistics concerning how many of those killings led to the murder prosecutions of accomplices are not available, but legal experts say such prosecutions are relatively common in the more than 30 states that allow them. About 80 people have been sentenced to death in the last three decades for participating in a felony that led to a murder though they did not kill anyone.

Terry Snyder, whose daughter Jessica was the victim in Mr. Holle's case, said Mr. Holle's conduct was as blameworthy as that of the man who shattered her skull.

"It never would have happened unless Ryan Holle had lent the car," Mr. Snyder said. "It was as good as if he was there."

Prosecutors sometimes also justify the doctrine on the ground that it deters murders. Criminals who know they will face harsh punishment if someone dies in the course of a felony, supporters of the felony murder rule say, may plan their crimes with more care, may leave deadly weapons at home and may decide not to commit the underlying felony at all.

But the evidence of a deterrent effect is thin. An unpublished analysis of F.B.I. crime data from 1970 to 1998 by Anup Malani, a law professor at the University of Chicago, found that the presence of the felony murder rule had a relatively small effect on criminal behavior, reducing the number of deaths during burglaries and car thefts slightly, not affecting deaths during rapes and, perversely, increasing the number of deaths during robberies. That last finding, the study said, "is hard to explain" and "warrants further exploration."

The felony murder rule's defenders acknowledge that it can be counterintuitive.

"It may not make any sense to you," Mr. Rimmer, the prosecutor in Mr. Holle's case, told the jury. "He has to be treated just as if he had done all the things the other four people did."

Prosecutors sought the death penalty for Charles Miller Jr., the man who actually killed Jessica Snyder, but he was sentenced to life without parole. So were the men who entered the Snyders' home with him, Donnie Williams and Jermond Thomas. So was William Allen Jr., who drove the car. So was Mr. Holle.

Mr. Holle had no criminal record. He had lent his car to Mr. Allen, a housemate, countless times before.

"All he did was to say, 'Use the car,'" Mr. Allen said of Mr. Holle in a pretrial deposition. "I mean, nobody really knew that girl was going to get killed. It was not in the plans to go kill somebody, you know."

But Mr. Holle did testify that he had been told it might be necessary to "knock out" Jessica Snyder. Mr. Holle is 25 now, a tall, lean and lively man with a rueful sense of humor, alert brown eyes and an unusually deep voice. In a spare office at the prison here, he said that he had not taken the talk of a burglary seriously.

"I honestly thought they were going to get food," he said of the men who used his car, all of whom had attended the night-long party at Mr. Holle's house, as had Jessica Snyder.

"When they actually mentioned what was going on, I thought it was a joke," Mr. Holle added, referring to the plan to steal the Snyders' safe. "I thought they were just playing around. I was just very naïve. Plus from being drinking that night, I just didn't understand what was going on."

Mr. Holle's trial lawyer, Sharon K. Wilson, said the statements he had given to the police were the key to the case, given the felony murder rule.

"It's just draconian," Ms. Wilson said. "The worst thing he was guilty of was partying too much and not being discriminating enough in who he was partying with."

Mr. Holle's trial took one day. "It was done, probably, by 5 o'clock," Mr. Holle said. "That's with the deliberations and the verdict and the sentence."

Witnesses described the horror of the crime. Christine Snyder, for instance, recalled finding her daughter, her head bashed in and her teeth knocked out.

"Then what did you do?" the prosecutor asked her.

"I went screaming out of the home saying they blew my baby's face off," Ms. Snyder said.

The safe had belonged to Christine Snyder. The police found a pound of marijuana in it, and, after her daughter's funeral, she was sentenced to three years in prison for possessing it.

Not every state's version of the felony murder rule is as strict as Florida's, and a few states, including Hawaii, Kentucky and Michigan, have abolished it entirely.

"The felony-murder rule completely ignores the concept of determination of guilt on the basis of individual misconduct," the Michigan Supreme Court wrote in 1980.

The vast majority of states retain it in various forms, but courts and officials have taken occasional steps to limit its harshest applications.

In August, for instance, Gov. Rick Perry of Texas commuted the death sentence of Kenneth Foster, the driver of a getaway car in a robbery spree that ended in a murder.

Mr. Holle was the only one of the five men charged with murdering Jessica Snyder who was offered a plea bargain, one that might have led to 10 years in prison.

"I did so because he was not as culpable as the others," said Mr. Rimmer, the prosecutor.

Mr. Holle, who rejected the deal, has spent some time thinking about the felony murder rule.

"The laws that they use to convict people are just—they have to revise them," he said. "Just because I lent these guys my car, why should I be convicted the same as these people that actually went to the scene of the crime and actually committed the crime?"

Mr. Rimmer sounded ambivalent on this point.

"Whether or not the felony murder rule can result in disproportionate justice is a matter of opinion," Mr. Rimmer said. "The father of Jessica Snyder does not think so."

UNIT 2
Victimology

Unit Selections

Key Points to Consider

- What is needed in order to switch from calling oneself a "victim" of crime to a "survivor" of crime?

- Why do we need good statistics to talk sensibly about social problems?

- Do you think a violent adult can change after participating in a program?

Student Website

www.mhhe.com/cls

Internet References

National Crime Victim's Research and Treatment Center (NCVC)
http://www.musc.edu/cvc/

Office for Victims of Crime (OVC)
http://www.ojp.usdoj.gov/ovc

For many years, crime victims were not considered an important topic for criminological study. Now, however, criminologists consider that focusing on victims and victimization is essential to understanding the phenomenon of crime. The popularity of this area of study can be attributed to the early work of Hans Von Hentig and the later work of Stephen Schafer. These writers were the first to assert that crime victims play an integral role in the criminal event, that their actions may actually precipitate crime, and that unless the victim's role is considered, the study of crime is not complete.

In recent years, a growing number of criminologists have devoted increasing attention to the victim's role in the criminal justice process. Generally, areas of particular interest include establishing probabilities of victimization risks, studying victim precipitation of crime and culpability, and designing services expressly for victims of crime. As more criminologists focus their attention on the victim's role in the criminal process, victimology will take on even greater importance.

This unit provides a sharp focus on several key issues. The lead article, "Do Batterer Intervention Programs Work?," from the National Institute of Justice, looks at studies that have been conducted on the most common types of programs in New York and Florida. The need for good statistics in order to talk sensibly about social problems is the subject of the next article, "Telling the Truth about Damned Lies and Statistics."

The use of social security numbers by schools, business, and governments for purposes not intended by law can lead to unintended consequences, as discussed by McGill, et al. in "Identity Theft Trends: Abuse of Social Security Numbers." A rape victim's account of her traumatic experience follows

© Jonathan Kitchen/Getty Images

next in "Violence and the Remaking of a Self." The perplexing response of some crime victims is explained by DeFabrique, et al. in "Understanding Stockholm Syndrome."

Next, Susan L. Clayton writes about a Florida judge who spoke about mentally ill offenders in "Judge Steven Leifman Advocates for the Mentally Ill." Finally, "Victim Satisfaction with the Criminal Justice System" presents the results of research on whether the victims of domestic violence who call the police are satisfied with the outcome.

Do Batterer Intervention Programs Work?

Two Studies

For more than a decade, courts have been sending convicted batterers to intervention programs rather than to prison. But do these programs work? Two studies in Florida and New York tested the most common type of batterer intervention. Their findings raise serious questions about the effectiveness of these programs. However, problems conducting the research raise questions about the studies' findings.

JOHN ASHCROFT, DEBORAH J. DANIELS, AND SARAH V. HART

What DID the Researchers Find?

Batterer intervention programs do not change batterers' attitudes and may have only minor effects on behavior, according to these studies. The Florida study found no significant differences between those who had treatment and those who did not as to whether they battered again or their attitudes toward domestic violence. The study did find an apparent relationship between whether an offender was employed or owned a house and whether he reoffended: Those with the most to lose were the least likely to reoffend. In New York, batterers in a 26-week program were less likely to reoffend than those in an 8-week program, but neither group showed any change in attitudes toward women or domestic violence.

What Were the Studies' Limitations?

Researchers face serious problems in studying batterer intervention programs:

- Batterers drop out at high rates.
- Victims often relocate or become difficult to find.
- No measures have been designed to specifically assess batterers' attitudes.
- To protect victims, judges often override random assignment of batterers to a control group.

These research limitations can affect the quality of the collected data, which can, in turn, affect researchers' ability to draw verifiable conclusions. Although both studies tried to address these limitations, they could not avoid them entirely.

Batterer intervention programs have been proliferating in the United States for the past two decades. These programs give batterers an alternative to jail. They usually involve several months of attendance at group therapy sessions that attempt to stop the violence and change the batterers' attitudes toward women and battering.

Mounting evidence indicates that the programs might be ineffective.

Two recent evaluations, one in Broward County, Florida, and the other in Brooklyn, New York,[1] evaluated interventions based on the Duluth model, which is the most commonly used program in the Nation—many States mandate its use (see "Types of Batterer Interventions"). The Broward County study found that the batterer intervention program had little or no effect, and the Brooklyn study found only minor improvement in some subjects. Neither program changed subjects' attitudes toward domestic abuse.

However, limitations in the studies raise additional issues. Are the evaluations correct that these programs don't change batterers' behavior and attitudes, or do shortcomings in the evaluations cover up program effects? There is no adequate answer

Types of Batterer Interventions

The Broward County and Brooklyn batterer intervention programs were based on the Duluth model. The Duluth model's underlying theory is that batterers want to control their partners and that changing this dynamic is key to changing their behavior. Its curriculum uses a "power and control wheel" depicting tactics abusers use to control their partners. Themes counteracting these tactics are discussed in classes and group sessions that attempt to induce batterers to confront their attitudes and behavior.

There are several alternatives to the Duluth model. Cognitive-behavioral intervention views battering as a result of errors in thinking and focuses on skills training and anger management. Another model, group practice, works from the premise that battering has multiple causes and is best addressed through a combined approach that includes an individual needs assessment. Proponents of these programs believe that a more long-term approach than the Duluth model is necessary.*

Programs based on batterer typologies or profiles are gaining popularity. These interventions profile the batterer through a psychological assessment, then classify him by level of risk, substance abuse, and other factors that may influence which intervention is most likely to work for him. Programs based on this approach are still relatively new and not fully evaluated.

A controversial intervention is couples therapy, which views men and women as equally responsible for creating disturbances in the relationship. It is widely criticized for assigning the victim a share of the blame for the continuation of violence.

Note

*Examples of these programs include Emerge and AMEND (Abusive Men Exploring New Directions). See Healey, K., C. Smith, and C. O'Sullivan, *Batterer Intervention: Program Approaches and Criminal Justice Strategies,* Issues and Practices, Washington, DC: U.S. Department of Justice, National Institute of Justice, 1998, NCJ 168638.

to this question. Both issues may need to be addressed in future programs and studies.

Broward County: Does Stake-In-Conformity Matter Most?

The Broward County study found no significant difference between the treatment and control groups in attitudes toward the role of women, whether wife beating should be a crime, or whether the State has the right to intervene in cases of domestic violence. It also found no significant difference between these groups in whether victims expected their partners to beat them again. Moreover, no significant difference was found in violations of probation or rearrests, except that men who were assigned to the program but did not attend all sessions were more likely to be rearrested than members of the control group.

Evaluators tried to determine what could account for differences in men's self-reports of physical violence. They considered whether the offender was assigned to treatment; the number of classes he attended; and such stake-in-conformity variables as marital status, residential stability, and employment. These last factors proved crucial.

Attending the program had no effect on the incidence of physical violence. Rather, offenders who were employed, married, and/or owned a home were less likely to batter again. Younger men and men with no stable residence (regardless of age) were more likely to abuse their partners. Older men who owned a home were less likely to do so.

Twenty-four percent of men in both the experimental and control groups were rearrested at least once during their year on probation. Again, attending the program had no effect. Rather, whether an offender was employed (a stake-in-conformity variable) seemed to have more influence on whether he was rearrested.

Brooklyn: Is Longer Treatment More Effective?

The Brooklyn study unintentionally had two experimental groups of offenders. After the study was underway, defense attorneys objected to the 26-week program's duration and cost and advised their clients not to participate. To preserve the study, offenders were offered an accelerated 8-week program, which created a second experimental sample.

Batterers assigned to 26 weeks of treatment were less likely than the control group and those assigned to 8-week classes to be arrested again for a crime against the same victim. Neither program changed batterers' attitudes toward domestic violence. There were significant differences in reoffending, however. Even though more offenders completed the shorter program, the 26-week group had fewer criminal complaints than either the control group or the 8-week group.

Men who attended the longer treatment committed fewer new violent acts than those who attended the shorter treatment or those who had no treatment. This may suggest that providing treatment for a longer period of time helped reduce battering during the term of treatment and for some time thereafter.

Program and Research Issues

Concerns about research methodology cloud most batterer intervention program evaluations, and these two studies were no exception. The major issues are—

- *Maintaining sample integrity.* Keeping assignments to batterer programs truly random is consistently a challenge.[2]
- *Low attendance, high attrition, difficulty following up.* High dropout and low response rates can lead to overly positive estimates of program effects.

- *Inadequate data sources.* Official records used to validate batterer and victim reports may be collected inconsistently across jurisdictions; also, they capture only those violations that reach the authorities. Evidence suggests that batterers often avoid rearrest by switching to psychological and verbal abuse.[3]
- *Difficulty measuring outcomes.* Evaluators lack good survey instruments to measure batterer behavior and attitudes. The revised Conflict Tactics Scale (CTS2) used in these studies was not designed for before and after measurements.[4] The Brooklyn study raised another issue common to batterer intervention program studies: Do evaluations examine the effects of the intervention or the effects of assignment to a treatment group?[5]
- *Who is defining success?* A final concern is broader in scope: Is a mere reduction in violence enough? These studies considered a reduction in violence to be a success based on the premise that it is unrealistic to expect batterers to abandon violent behavior after one intervention. But a "statistically significant reduction in violence" may mean little to a battered woman.[6]

A "statistically significant reduction in violence" may mean little to a battered woman.

New Directions for Protecting Victims

The bottom line is: What are the best ways to protect victims? Batterer intervention programs are one approach, although much remains to be learned about them—specifically, which program works best for which batterer under which circumstances.[7] But perhaps what is needed is a whole new approach.

Rethinking Intervention

The models that underlie batterer intervention programs may need improvement. New approaches based on research into the causes of battering and batterer profiles[8] may be more productive than a one-size-fits-all approach.[9] Researchers may also draw lessons from other disciplines, such as substance abuse interventions—for example, that length of treatment may influence the outcome.[10]

Improvements in how programs are put into practice may also be necessary, since variations in how programs are carried out may reduce their effectiveness. Researchers have noted greater effects in demonstration programs implemented by researchers than in practical programs implemented by juvenile or criminal justice agencies. Thus, the degree to which a program is faithful to the intervention model may determine how well it works. For example, some programs have few sanctions for dropping out, whereas others closely monitor attendance. This suggests the need to test the effectiveness of close monitoring and required attendance.

Although these studies focus on male batterers, women batter as well. The dynamics of battering appear to differ for men and women, which suggests a need for intervention programs designed specifically for female batterers. Currently, it appears that most women batterers are being placed in male-dominated batterer intervention programs.

Linking Batterer Programs to Other Programs and Responses

Batterer intervention programs may be effective only in the context of a broader criminal justice and community response to domestic violence that includes arrest, restraining orders, intensive monitoring of batterers,[11] and changes to social norms that inadvertently tolerate partner violence.

If monitoring is partly responsible for lower reoffense rates, as the Brooklyn experiment suggests, judicial monitoring may be a useful approach. The Judicial Oversight Demonstration initiative—a collaboration among the National Institute of Justice, the Office on Violence Against Women, and three local jurisdictions—is testing this idea.[12] Other innovations might include mandatory intervention (indeterminate probation) until the batterer no longer endangers his partner, an approach that has been used with sex offenders.[13]

Improving Evaluations

Although the quality of batterer intervention program evaluations has improved,[14] barriers remain. By collaborating, researchers, practitioners, and policymakers may be able to develop better strategies and improve the rigor of experimental evaluations.

For example, researchers need to find better ways to maintain contact with batterers and victims and better instruments than the revised CTS2.[15] They need to develop more reliable ways of validating batterer and victim reports than relying strictly on official records of rearrests and probation violations. Statistical tools can be applied to correct for nonrandom assignment and other problems.[16]

Since batterer intervention programs are a relatively new response to a critical social problem, it is too early to abandon the concept. More work needs to be done to determine the causes of battering and test new responses.

Notes

1. Davis, R.C., B.G. Taylor, and C.D. Maxwell, *Does Batterer Treatment Reduce Violence? A Randomized Experiment in Brooklyn,* final report to the National Institute of Justice, Washington, DC: National Institute of Justice, 2000, NCJ 180772; Feder, L., and D.R. Forde, *A Test of the Efficacy of Court-Mandated Counseling for Domestic Violence Offenders: The Broward Experiment,* final report to the National Institute of Justice, Washington, DC: National Institute of Justice, 2000, NCJ 184752.

2. Compromises in random assignment may have diluted the Brooklyn program's impact.

3. See Gondolf, E.W., "Patterns of Reassault in Batterer Programs," *Violence and Victims* 12(4)(1997): 373–87; and

Harrell, A.V., *Evaluation of Court-Ordered Treatment for Domestic Violence Offenders,* final report to the State Justice Institute, Washington, DC: The Urban Institute, 1991.

4. The revised CTS2 assesses offender reports of abuse. See Straus, M.A., S.L. Hamby, S. Boney-McCoy, and D.B. Sugarman, "The Revised Conflict Tactics Scale (CTS2): Development and Preliminary Psychometric Data," *Journal of Family Issues* 17(3)(1996): 283–316. Concerns about the types of batterers studied and the effects of mandating treatment are discussed in Davis, et al., *Does Batterer Treatment Reduce Violence?* 15–17.

5. The Broward study statistically tested for this possibility and found no treatment effect.

6. See Edleson, J.L., "Controversy and Change in Batterer's Programs," in *Future Interventions with Battered Women and Their Families,* ed. J.L. Edleson and Z.C. Eisikovitz, Thousand Oaks, CA: Sage Publications, 1996.

7. Gondolf, E.W., "Batterer Programs: What We Know and Need to Know," *Journal of Interpersonal Violence* 12(1)(1997): 83–98.

8. Holtzworth-Munroe, A., and G.L. Stuart, "Typologies of Male Batterers: Three Subtypes and the Differences Among Them," *Psychological Bulletin* 116(3)(1994): 476–97. Also see Wexler, D.B., "The Broken Mirror: A Self Psychological Treatment Perspective for Relationship Violence," *Journal of Psychotherapy, Practice, and Research* 8(2)(1999): 129–41.

9. Healey, K., C. Smith, and C. O'Sullivan, *Batterer Intervention: Program Approaches and Criminal Justice Strategies,* Issues and Practices, Washington, DC: U.S. Department of Justice, National Institute of Justice, 1998, NCJ 168638.

10. Taxman, F.S., "12 Steps to Improved Offender Outcomes: Developing Responsive Systems of Care for Substance-Abusing Offenders," *Corrections Today* 60(6)(1998): 114–117, 166. Also see Howard, K.I., K. Moras, and W. Lutz, "Evaluation of Psychotherapy: Efficacy, Effectiveness, and Patient Progress," *American Psychologist* 51(10)(1996): 1059–1064.

11. A. Klein, cited in Healey, et al., *Batterer Intervention: Program Approaches and Criminal Justice Strategies,* 10.

12. "Experiment Demonstrates How to Hold Batterers Accountable," *National Institute of Justice Journal* 244 (July 2000): 29.

13. Hafemeister, T.L., "Legal Aspects of the Treatment of Offenders With Mental Disorders," in R.M. Wettstein, ed., *Treatment of Offenders With Mental Disorders,* New York: Guilford Press, 1998: 44–125.

14. Davis, R.C., and B.G. Taylor, "Does Batterer Treatment Reduce Violence? A Synthesis of the Literature," *Women and Criminal Justice* 10(2)(1999): 69–93.

15. See Gondolf, E.W., "Batterer Programs: What We Know and Need to Know;" and Sullivan, C.M., M.H. Rumptz, R. Campbell, K.K. Eby, and W.S. Davidson, "Retaining Participants in Longitudinal Community Research: A Comprehensive Protocol," *Journal of Applied Behavioral Science* 32(3)(1996): 262–76.

16. See Jackson, S., et al., *Batterer Intervention Programs: Where Do We Go From Here?* NIJ Special Report, Washington, DC: U.S. Department of Justice, National Institute of Justice, June 2003, NCJ 195079: 26.

From *National Institute of Justice Report,* September 2003, pp. ii, 1–8.

Telling the Truth about Damned Lies and Statistics

JOEL BEST

The dissertation prospectus began by quoting a statistic— a "grabber" meant to capture the reader's attention. The graduate student who wrote this prospectus undoubtedly wanted to seem scholarly to the professors who would read it; they would be supervising the proposed research. And what could be more scholarly than a nice, authoritative statistic, quoted from a professional journal in the student's field?

So the prospectus began with this (carefully footnoted) quotation: "Every year since 1950, the number of American children gunned down has doubled." I had been invited to serve on the student's dissertation committee. When I read the quotation, I assumed the student had made an error in copying it. I went to the library and looked up the article the student had cited. There, in the journal's 1995 volume, was exactly the same sentence: "Every year since 1950, the number of American children gunned down has doubled."

This quotation is my nomination for a dubious distinction: I think it may be the worst—that is, the most inaccurate—social statistic ever.

What makes this statistic so bad? Just for the sake of argument, let's assume that "the number of American children gunned down" in 1950 was one. If the number doubled each year, there must have been two children gunned down in 1951, four in 1952, eight in 1953, and so on. By 1960, the number would have been 1,024. By 1965, it would have been 32,768 (in 1965, the F.B.I. identified only 9,960 criminal homicides in the entire country, including adult as well as child victims). By 1970, the number would have passed one million; by 1980, one billion (more than four times the total U.S. population in that year). Only three years later, in 1983, the number of American children gunned down would have been 8.6 billion (nearly twice the earth's population at the time). Another milestone would have been passed in 1987, when the number of gunned-down American children (137 billion) would have surpassed the best estimates for the total human population throughout history (110 billion). By 1995, when the article was published, the annual number of victims would have been over 35 trillion—a really big number, of a magnitude you rarely encounter outside economics or astronomy.

Thus my nomination: estimating the number of American child gunshot victims in 1995 at 35 trillion must be as far off—as hilariously, wildly wrong—as a social statistic can be. (If anyone spots a more inaccurate social statistic, I'd love to hear about it.)

Where did the article's author get this statistic? I wrote the author, who responded that the statistic came from the Children's Defense Fund, a well-known advocacy group for children. The C.D.F.'s *The State of America's Children Yearbook 1994* does state: "The number of American children killed each year by guns has doubled since 1950." Note the difference in the wording—the C.D.F. claimed there were twice as many deaths in 1994 as in 1950; the article's author reworded that claim and created a very different meaning.

It is worth examining the history of this statistic. It began with the C.D.F. noting that child gunshot deaths had doubled from 1950 to 1994. This is not quite as dramatic an increase as it might seem. Remember that the U.S. population also rose throughout this period; in fact, it grew about 73 percent—or nearly double. Therefore, we might expect all sorts of things— including the number of child gunshot deaths—to increase, to nearly double, just because the population grew. Before we can decide whether twice as many deaths indicate that things are getting worse, we'd have to know more. The C.D.F. statistic raises other issues as well: Where did the statistic come from? Who counts child gunshot deaths, and how? What is meant by a "child" (some C.D.F. statistics about violence include everyone under age 25)? What is meant by "killed by guns" (gunshot-death statistics often include suicides and accidents, as well as homicides)? But people rarely ask questions of this sort when they encounter statistics. Most of the time, most people simply accept statistics without question.

Certainly, the article's author didn't ask many probing, critical questions about the C.D.F.'s claim. Impressed by the statistic, the author repeated it—well, meant to repeat it. Instead, by rewording the C.D.F.'s claim, the author created a mutant statistic, one garbled almost beyond recognition.

But people treat mutant statistics just as they do other statistics—that is, they usually accept even the most implausible claims without question. For example, the journal editor who accepted the author's article for publication did not bother to consider the implications of child victims doubling each year. And people repeat bad statistics: The graduate student copied the garbled statistic and inserted it into the dissertation prospectus. Who knows whether still other readers were impressed by the author's statistic and remembered it or repeated it? The article remains on the shelf in hundreds of libraries, available to anyone who needs a dramatic quote. The lesson should be clear: Bad statistics live on; they take on lives of their own.

Some statistics are born bad—they aren't much good from the start, because they are based on nothing more than guesses or dubious data. Other statistics mutate; they become bad after being mangled (as in the case of the author's creative rewording). Either way, bad statistics are potentially important: They can be used to stir up public outrage or fear; they can distort our understanding of our world; and they can lead us to make poor policy choices.

T he notion that we need to watch out for bad statistics isn't new. We've all heard people say, "You can prove anything with statistics." The title of my book, *Damned Lies and Statistics*, comes from a famous aphorism (usually attributed to Mark Twain or Benjamin Disraeli): "There are three kinds of lies: lies, damned lies, and statistics." There is even a useful little book, still in print after more than 40 years, called *How to Lie With Statistics*.

We shouldn't ignore all statistics, or assume that every number is false. Some statistics are bad, but others are pretty good. And we need good statistics to talk sensibly about social problems.

Statistics, then, have a bad reputation. We suspect that statistics may be wrong, that people who use statistics may be "lying"—trying to manipulate us by using numbers to somehow distort the truth. Yet, at the same time, we need statistics; we depend upon them to summarize and clarify the nature of our complex society. This is particularly true when we talk about social problems. Debates about social problems routinely raise questions that demand statistical answers: Is the problem widespread? How many people—and which people—does it affect? Is it getting worse? What does it cost society? What will it cost to deal with it? Convincing answers to such questions demand evidence, and that usually means numbers, measurements, statistics.

But can't you prove anything with statistics? It depends on what "prove" means. If we want to know, say, how many children are "gunned down" each year, we can't simply guess—pluck a number from thin air: 100, 1,000, 10,000, 35 trillion, whatever. Obviously, there's no reason to consider an arbitrary guess "proof" of anything. However, it might be possible for someone—using records kept by police departments or hospital emergency rooms or coroners—to keep track of children who have been shot; compiling careful, complete records might give us a fairly accurate idea of the number of gunned-down children. If that number seems accurate enough, we might consider it very strong evidence—or proof.

The solution to the problem of bad statistics is not to ignore all statistics, or to assume that every number is false. Some statistics are bad, but others are pretty good, and we need statistics—good statistics—to talk sensibly about social problems. The solution, then, is not to give up on statistics, but to become better judges of the numbers we encounter. We need to think critically about statistics—at least critically enough to suspect that the number of children gunned down hasn't been doubling each year since 1950.

A few years ago, the mathematician John Allen Paulos wrote *Innumeracy*, a short, readable book about "mathematical illiteracy." Too few people, he argued, are comfortable with basic mathematical principles, and this makes them poor judges of the numbers they encounter. No doubt this is one reason we have so many bad statistics. But there are other reasons, as well.

Social statistics describe society, but they are also products of our social arrangements. The people who bring social statistics to our attention have reasons for doing so; they inevitably want something, just as reporters and the other media figures who repeat and publicize statistics have their own goals. Statistics are tools, used for particular purposes. Thinking critically about statistics requires understanding their place in society.

While we may be more suspicious of statistics presented by people with whom we disagree—people who favor different political parties or have different beliefs—bad statistics are used to promote all sorts of causes. Bad statistics come from conservatives on the political right and liberals on the left, from wealthy corporations and powerful government agencies, and from advocates of the poor and the powerless.

In order to interpret statistics, we need more than a checklist of common errors. We need a general approach, an orientation, a mind-set that we can use to think about new statistics that we encounter. We ought to approach statistics thoughtfully. This can be hard to do, precisely because so many people in our society treat statistics as fetishes. We might call this the mind-set of the Awestruck—the people who don't think critically, who act as though statistics have magical powers. The awestruck know they don't always understand the statistics they hear, but this doesn't bother them. After all, who can expect to understand magical numbers? The reverential fatalism of the awestruck is not thoughtful—it is a way of avoiding thought. We need a different approach.

One choice is to approach statistics critically. Being critical does not mean being negative or hostile—it is not cynicism. The critical approach statistics thoughtfully; they avoid the extremes of both naive acceptance and cynical rejection of the numbers they encounter. Instead, the critical attempt to evaluate numbers, to distinguish between good statistics and bad statistics.

The critical understand that, while some social statistics may be pretty good, they are never perfect. Every statistic is a way of summarizing complex information into relatively simple numbers. Inevitably, some information, some of the complexity, is lost whenever we use statistics. The critical recognize that this is an inevitable limitation of statistics. Moreover, they realize that every statistic is the product of choices—the choice between defining a category broadly or narrowly, the choice of one measurement over another, the choice of a sample.

People choose definitions, measurements, and samples for all sorts of reasons: Perhaps they want to emphasize some aspect of a problem; perhaps it is easier or cheaper to gather data in a particular way—many considerations can come into play. Every statistic is a compromise among choices. This means that every definition—and every measurement and every sample—probably has limitations and can be criticized.

Being critical means more than simply pointing to the flaws in a statistic. Again, every statistic has flaws. The issue is whether a particular statistic's flaws are severe enough to damage its usefulness. Is the definition so broad that it encompasses too many false positives (or so narrow that it excludes too many false negatives)? How would changing the definition alter the statistic? Similarly, how do the choices of measurements and samples affect the statistic? What would happen if different measures or samples were chosen? And how is the statistic used? Is it being interpreted appropriately, or has its meaning been mangled to create a mutant statistic? Are the comparisons that are being made appropriate, or are apples being confused with oranges? How do different choices produce the conflicting numbers found in stat wars? These are the sorts of questions the critical ask.

As a practical matter, it is virtually impossible for citizens in contemporary society to avoid statistics about social problems. Statistics arise in all sorts of ways, and in almost every case the people promoting statistics want to persuade us. Activists use statistics to convince us that social problems are serious and deserve our attention and concern. Charities use statistics to encourage donations. Politicians use statistics to persuade us that they understand society's problems and that they deserve our support. The media use statistics to make their reporting more dramatic, more convincing, more compelling. Corporations use statistics to promote and improve their products. Researchers use statistics to document their findings and support their conclusions. Those with whom we agree use statistics to reassure us that we're on the right side, while our opponents use statistics to try and convince us that we are wrong. Statistics are one of the standard types of evidence used by people in our society.

It is not possible simply to ignore statistics, to pretend they don't exist. That sort of head-in-the-sand approach would be too costly. Without statistics, we limit our ability to think thoughtfully about our society; without statistics, we have no accurate ways of judging how big a problem may be, whether it is getting worse, or how well the policies designed to address that problem actually work. And awestruck or naive attitudes toward statistics are no better than ignoring statistics; statistics have no magical properties, and it is foolish to assume that all statistics are equally valid. Nor is a cynical approach the answer; statistics are too widespread and too useful to be automatically discounted.

It would be nice to have a checklist, a set of items we could consider in evaluating any statistic. The list might detail potential problems with definitions, measurements, sampling, mutation, and so on. These are, in fact, common sorts of flaws found in many statistics, but they should not be considered a formal, complete checklist. It is probably impossible to produce a complete list of statistical flaws—no matter how long the list, there will be other possible problems that could affect statistics.

The goal is not to memorize a list, but to develop a thoughtful approach. Becoming critical about statistics requires being prepared to ask questions about numbers. When encountering a new statistic in, say, a news report, the critical try to assess it. What might be the sources for this number? How could one go about producing the figure? Who produced the number, and what interests might they have? What are the different ways key terms might have been defined, and which definitions have been chosen? How might the phenomena be measured, and which measurement choices have been made? What sort of sample was gathered, and how might that sample affect the result? Is the statistic being properly interpreted? Are comparisons being made, and if so, are the comparisons appropriate? Are there competing statistics? If so, what stakes do the opponents have in the issue, and how are those stakes likely to affect their use of statistics? And is it possible to figure out why the statistics seem to disagree, what the differences are in the ways the competing sides are using figures?

At first, this list of questions may seem overwhelming. How can an ordinary person—someone who reads a statistic in a magazine article or hears it on a news broadcast—determine the answers to such questions? Certainly news reports rarely give detailed information on the processes by which statistics are created. And few of us have time to drop everything and investigate the background of some new number we encounter. Being critical, it seems, involves an impossible amount of work.

In practice, however, the critical need not investigate the origin of every statistic. Rather, being critical means appreciating the inevitable limitations that affect all statistics, rather than being awestruck in the presence of numbers. It means not being too credulous, not accepting every statistic at face value. But it also means appreciating that statistics, while always imperfect, can be useful. Instead of automatically discounting every statistic, the critical reserve judgment. When confronted with an interesting number, they may try to learn more, to evaluate, to weigh the figure's strengths and weaknesses.

Of course, this critical approach need not—and should not—be limited to statistics. It ought to apply to all the evidence we encounter when we scan a news report, or listen to a speech—whenever we learn about social problems. Claims about social problems often feature dramatic, compelling examples; the critical might ask whether an example is likely to be a typical case or an extreme, exceptional instance. Claims about social problems often include quotations from different sources, and the critical might wonder why those sources have spoken and why they have been quoted: Do they have particular expertise? Do they stand to benefit if they influence others? Claims about social problems usually involve arguments about the problem's causes and potential solutions. The critical might ask whether these arguments are convincing. Are they logical? Does the proposed solution seem feasible and appropriate? And so on.

Being critical—adopting a skeptical, analytical stance when confronted with claims—is an approach that goes far beyond simply dealing with statistics.

Statistics are not magical. Nor are they always true—or always false. Nor need they be incomprehensible. Adopting a critical approach offers an effective way of responding to the numbers we are sure to encounter. Being critical requires more thought, but failing to adopt a critical mind-set makes us powerless to evaluate what others tell us. When we fail to think critically, the statistics we hear might just as well be magical.

JOEL BEST is a professor of sociology and criminal justice at the University of Delaware. This essay is excerpted from *Damned Lies and Statistics: Untangling Numbers From the Media, Politicians, and Activists*, published by the University of California Press and reprinted by permission. Copyright © 2001 by the Regents of the University of California.

Identity Theft Trends: Abuse of Social Security Numbers

MICHAEL MCGILL

The U.S. Social Security Administration (SSA) Office of the Inspector General (OIG) was created in 1995 as a result of the Social Security Independence and Program Improvements Act of 1994. Since its inception, the OIG's statutory mission has been to prevent and detect fraud, waste, abuse, and mismanagement of the SSA's programs and operations. To accomplish this mission, the OIG directs, conducts, and supervises a comprehensive program of audits, evaluations, and investigations relating to the SSA's programs and operations.

The SSA/OIG understands the central role the social security number (SSN) plays in U.S. society as well as the critical need to protect its integrity. OIG investigators work daily on individual SSN misuse cases, bringing to justice scam artists, identity thieves, counterfeit document vendors, and other criminals whose tools of the trade are purloined SSNs. The SSA receives about 10,000 allegations of SSN misuse and investigates about 1,500 criminal cases of misuse annually.

In addition to the SSA's investigative efforts, auditors play a significant role in identifying vulnerabilities and suggesting ways the SSA can work with organizations and government entities to limit the use of SSNs and better protect this sensitive information. Audit and investigative experiences have taught the administration that the more SSNs are used unnecessarily, the higher the probability that these numbers will be improperly disclosed and used to commit crimes throughout society.

Schools, businesses, and state and local governments request SSNs for a multitude of purposes—very few of which are recognized by law. Rather, many of these organizations use SSNs as identifiers simply for convenience. For example, SSA auditors have looked at the use of SSNs by universities and hospitals as student and patient identifiers, respectively. Although both of these types of organizations may have had some reason for collecting SSNs, such as financial aid or Medicare coverage, it was found that once collected, SSNs were used frequently for other purposes and were not always sufficiently protected.

A recent SSA/OIG audit revealed a troubling practice by primary and secondary schools in 43 states. Namely, the schools collect students' SSNs at registration and often use the SSNs as primary student identifiers to help in record keeping and identifying students when they transfer to another school or apply for college. The No Child Left Behind Act of 2001 requires that each state implement a statewide accountability program that measures the progress of students and schools through data collection and analysis. However, this law does not require that states use SSNs to identify and track students. Rather, it appears that many primary and secondary schools use SSNs as a matter of convenience.

For the 2004–2005 school year, the National Education Association estimated that more than 15,000 school districts served more than 48 million students in kindergarten through 12th grade. The collection and use of SSNs without proper controls makes this population particularly vulnerable. According to information compiled by the Federal Trade Commission (FTC), recent data indicate that the number of children under the age of 18 whose identities have been stolen is growing. This is particularly troubling given that many of these individuals may not become aware of such activity until they apply for a credit card or student loan.[1]

Theft of Puerto Rican Identities

School districts' collection of student SSNs has not gone unnoticed by identity theft rings. Recently, the SSA/OIG's Strategic Research and Analysis Division noticed a troubling trend while conducting joint work site enforcement investigations with the U.S. Department of Homeland Security (DHS). Work site enforcement investigations focus on egregious employers involved in criminal activity or worker exploitation. This type of employer violation often involves alien smuggling, document fraud, identity theft, human rights abuses, and/or other criminal violations that have a direct link to the employment of unauthorized workers.[2]

To combat the hiring of unauthorized workers, the DHS and the SSA partnered to create the E-Verify Program (formerly known as the Basic Pilot/Employment Eligibility Verification Program), which allows participating employers to use telephone and Internet-based systems to verify newly hired employees' employment eligibility. E-Verify works by allowing employers to compare employee information taken from the Form 1-9 (the paper-based employment eligibility verification form used for all new hires) against more than 425 million SSA records and more than 60 million DHS records.[3] In addition, the SSA provides an additional service called the Social Security Number Verification Service (SSNVS), which allows companies to verify SSNs and names for the purpose of completing Internal Revenue Service (IRS) Form W-2.

E-Verify is particularly attractive to industries that historically employ a large percentage of non-U.S. citizens. E-Verify works extremely well in rejecting questionable identities when names, dates of birth (DOBs), and SSNs do not match. However, many unauthorized workers who previously obtained fraudulent work documents from counterfeit vendors containing invalid SSNs or SSNs that did not match the names and DOBs on the documents have begun turning to a new source to defeat the efficient screening systems contained within E-Verify and the SSNVS. Identity theft rings are now obtaining and selling entire identities of U.S. citizens with Hispanic names from either Puerto Rico or the southwestern United States. By purchasing entire identities—documents including names, DOBs, and SSNs—unauthorized workers can circumvent the SSNVS and E-Verify systems.

This particularly insidious form of identity theft has far-reaching implications for its victims, because wages will be reported to the IRS on their stolen SSNs, and they will be required to explain this income at tax time. In addition, unauthorized workers can use SSNs to obtain mortgages and loans, leading to credit report problems for the victims. The DHS reports that unauthorized workers who fraudulently purchase complete identities in this fashion often use these "breeder documents" as a stepping stone to obtaining valid state identity documents as a means to escape detection by law enforcement agencies and employers.[4] Adding to the problem are significant language barriers, as many of the victims speak little or no English, compounding the devastating impact of identity theft.

How does this relate to the practice of school districts collecting SSNs? In January 2008, the SSA/OIG became aware of a new crime wave in Puerto Rico involving the theft of student records at public schools. According to newspaper reports, there have been about 35 burglaries of Puerto Rico public schools since late 2007 where students' records have been stolen. The stolen records include original birth certificates, copies of social security cards, parents' names, and home addresses. Because the schools store records from previous years, identity thieves have been able to obtain student records dating back to the 1980s. The identities of between 7,000 and 10,000 Puerto Rican public school students are estimated to have been stolen in this manner.

The SSA/OIG is working with the FTC and the Puerto Rico Department of Education (PR-DOE) to facilitate victims' ability to file complaints with the FTC. As a result of these efforts, the PR-DOE website now includes a link to the FTC Identity Theft Data Clearinghouse, and the FTC shipped 5,000 copies of the FTC's Spanish-language Identity Theft Victim Assistance materials to the PR-DOE. The PR-DOE also committed to halting the practice of collecting student birth certificates and SSNs starting with the 2008–2009 school year.

Meanwhile, evidence that unauthorized workers in the United States are using stolen Puerto Rican identities continues to mount. A recent work site enforcement investigation by the DHS and the SSA/OIG at a company in Tennessee found that more than 700 unauthorized workers were using Puerto Rican identities for work purposes.

Phishing Schemes

Another prevalent identity theft scheme that has surfaced across the United States over the past year involves unscrupulous individuals and businesses who have used telemarketers claiming to be SSA employees when they initiate telephone calls to obtain personal information, including bank account numbers, from Social Security beneficiaries. The telemarketers are often outsourced from companies in foreign countries, who use voice over Internet protocol (VoIP) phone numbers to initiate the calls.

The telephone fraud scheme has several variations. In some instances, callers with foreign accents request bank account information to set up direct debit of Medicare premiums, claiming that the premiums will no longer be deducted from Social Security payments. In other versions, callers request bank account information to update Medicare cards, for direct deposit of the recent stimulus tax rebate payment, or to verify future entitlement to Social Security benefits. Another version has callers posing as SSA employees and asking for bank account information so that the SSA can deposit a tax credit amounting to $500 per month for a six-month period. In many cases where victims are duped into providing bank account information, funds are withdrawn from the bank accounts shortly after the phone calls are concluded.

This type of telemarketing scheme, which often preys on unsuspecting, elderly individuals, could lead to bank fraud or identity theft, in which personal information is misused to obtain credit, goods, or services. The SSA/OIG has responded by initiating an investigation into the individuals perpetrating this scheme. SSA inspector general Patrick P.O'Carroll Jr. has also issued numerous fraud advisories in various states affected by this form of telemarketing fraud. Citizens need to be educated to refrain from providing SSNs, bank account numbers, or other personal information over the phone or Internet unless they are extremely confident of the source.

Continuing the Fight

The SSA/OIG will continue to play an important role in the overall government effort to combat SSN misuse and identity theft. At this time, OIG investigators across the country are members of almost 200 task forces and work groups. These groups, comprising federal, state, and local law enforcement agencies, pool resources and, when permitted, share information to accomplish more than individual members could ever accomplish on their own.

For example, agents participating in the Central Florida Identity Theft Task Force, a group comprising 10 law enforcement agencies, recently arrested 15 members of an identity theft ring who obtained lists of individuals with good credit histories and used the personal information of those individuals to defraud a variety of commercial entities in the Orlando area. Twelve of the 15 individuals were sentenced to prison terms, and the total restitution ordered to victims exceeded $2 million. Through efforts like these, the SSA/OIG will continue to investigate vigorously and seek prosecution of individuals who commit identity theft crimes.

The SSN was never intended for anything but tracking workers' earnings and paying workers their accrued benefits. As the uses of SSNs have expanded over the decades, through acts of Congress as well as the adoption of the SSN by other entities simply as a matter of convenience, their value as a tool for criminals has increased accordingly. The SSA/OIG will continue its efforts to encourage the protection of SSNs by those who use them legitimately and to provide meaningful sanctions for those who fail to protect SSNs or who misuse this information themselves.

Notes

1. Social Security Administration, Office of the Inspector General, *State and Local Governments' Collection and Use of Social Security Numbers,* Audit Report A-08-07-17086, September 2007, http://www.ssa.gov/oig/ADOBEPDF/audittxt/A-08-07-17086.htm (accessed May 16, 2008).

2. U.S. Immigration and Customs Enforcement, "Worksite Enforcement," http://www.ice.gov/pi/worksite/ (accessed May 16, 2008).

3. U.S. Citizenship and Immigration Services, "E-Verify," http://www.uscis.gov/portal/site/uscis/menuitem.eb1d4c2a3e5b9ac89243c6a7543f6d1a/?vgnextoid=75bce2e261405110VgnVCM1000004718190aRCRD&vgnextchannel=75bce2e261405110VgnVCM1000004718190aRCRD (accessed May 16, 2008).

4. U.S. Immigration and Customs Enforcement, *Worksite Enforcement Advisory,* February 2008, http://www.ice.gov/doclib/pi/news/newsreleases/articles/wse_advisory_v27.pdf (accessed May 16, 2008), 2.

Violence and the Remaking of a Self

Susan J. Brison

On July 4, 1990, at 10:30 in the morning, I went for a walk along a country road in a village outside Grenoble, France. It was a gorgeous day, and I didn't envy my husband, Tom, who had to stay inside and work on a manuscript with a French colleague. I sang to myself as I set out, stopping along the way to pet a goat and pick a few wild strawberries. About an hour and a half later, I was lying face down in a muddy creek bed at the bottom of a dark ravine, struggling to stay alive.

I had been grabbed from behind, pulled into the bushes, beaten, and sexually assaulted. Helpless and entirely at my assailant's mercy, I talked to him, trying to appeal to his humanity, and, when that failed, addressing myself to his self-interest. He called me a whore and told me to shut up. Although I had said I'd do whatever he wanted, as the sexual assault began I instinctively fought back, which so enraged my attacker that he strangled me until I lost consciousness.

When I came to, I was being dragged by my feet down into the ravine. I had often thought I was awake while dreaming, but now I was awake and convinced I was having a nightmare. But it was no dream. After ordering me to get on my hands and knees, the man strangled me again. This time I was sure I was dying. But I revived, just in time to see him lunging toward me with a rock. He smashed it into my forehead, knocking me out. Eventually, after another strangulation attempt, he left me for dead.

After I was rescued and taken to the Grenoble hospital, where I spent the next 11 days, I was told repeatedly how "lucky" I was to be alive, and for a short while I even believed this myself. At the time, I did not yet know how trauma not only haunts the conscious and unconscious mind but also remains in the body, in each of the senses, in the heart that races and the skin that crawls whenever something resurrects the buried terror. I didn't know that the worst—the unimaginably painful aftermath of violence—was yet to come.

For the first several months after my attack, I led a spectral existence, not quite sure whether I had died and the world was going on without me, or whether I was alive but in a totally alien world. The line between life and death, once so clear and sustaining, now seemed carelessly drawn and easily erased. I felt as though I'd outlived myself, as if I'd stayed on a train one stop past my destination.

> **After I was rescued and taken to the hospital, I was told repeatedly how 'lucky' I was to be alive. For a short while I even believed this myself.**

My sense of unreality was fed by the massive denial of those around me—a reaction that is an almost universal response to rape, I learned. Where the facts would appear to be incontrovertible, denial takes the shape of attempts to explain the assault in ways that leave the observers' worldview unscathed. Even those who are able to acknowledge the existence of violence try to protect themselves from the realization that the world in which it occurs is their world. They cannot allow themselves to imagine the victim's shattered life, or else their illusions about their own safety and control over their lives might begin to crumble.

The most well-meaning individuals, caught up in the myth of their own immunity, can inadvertently add to the victim's suffering by suggesting that the attack was avoidable or somehow her fault. One victims'-assistance coordinator, whom I had phoned for legal advice, stressed that she herself had never been a victim and said I would benefit from the experience by learning not to be so trusting of people and to take basic safety precautions, like not going out alone late at night. She didn't pause long enough for me to point out that I had been attacked suddenly, from behind, in broad daylight.

I was initially reluctant to tell people (other than medical and legal personnel) that I had been raped. I still wonder why I wanted the sexual aspect of the assault—so salient to me—kept secret. I was motivated in part by shame, I suppose, and I wanted to avoid being stereotyped as a victim. I did not want the academic work I had already done on pornography and violence against women to be dismissed as the ravings of a "hysterical rape victim." And I felt that I had very little control over the meaning of the word "rape." Using the term denied the particularity of what I had experienced and invoked in other people whatever rape scenario they had already constructed. I later identified myself publicly as a rape survivor, having decided that it was ethically and politically imperative for me to do so.

But my initial wariness about the use of the term was understandable and, at times, reinforced by others' responses—especially by the dismissive characterization of the rape by some in the criminal-justice system. Before my assailant's trial, I heard my lawyer conferring with another lawyer on the question of victim's compensation from the state (to cover legal expenses and unreimbursed medical bills). He said, without irony, that a certain amount was typically awarded for "*un viol gentil*" ("a nice rape") and somewhat more (which they would request on my behalf) for "*un viol méchant*" ("a nasty rape").

Not surprisingly, I felt that I was taken more seriously as a victim of a near-fatal murder attempt. But that description of the assault provided others with no explanation of what had happened. Later, when people asked why this man had tried to kill me, I revealed that the attack had begun as a sexual assault, and most people were satisfied with that as an explanation. It made some kind of sense to them. But it made no sense to me.

A few months after the assault, I sat down at my computer to write about it for the first time, and all I could come up with was a list of paradoxes. Just about everything had stopped making sense. I thought it was quite possible that I was brain-damaged as a result of the head injuries I had sustained. Or perhaps the heightened lucidity I had experienced during the assault remained, giving me a clearer, though profoundly disorienting, picture of the world. I turned to philosophy for meaning and consolation and could find neither. Had my reasoning broken down? Or was it the breakdown of Reason? I couldn't explain what had happened to me. I

was attacked for no reason. I had ventured outside the human community, landed beyond the moral universe, beyond the realm of predictable events and comprehensible actions, and I didn't know how to get back.

As a philosopher, I was used to taking something apparently obvious and familiar—the nature of time, say, or the relation between words and things—and making it into something quite puzzling. But now, when I was confronted with the utterly strange and paradoxical, philosophy was, at least initially, of no use in helping me to make sense of it. And it was hard for me, given my philosophical background, to accept that knowledge isn't always desirable, that the truth doesn't always set you free. Sometimes, it fills you with incapacitating terror, and then uncontrollable rage.

I was surprised, perhaps naively, to find that there was virtually nothing in the philosophical literature about sexual violence; obviously, it raised numerous philosophical issues. The disintegration of the self experienced by victims of violence challenges our notions of personal identity over time, a major preoccupation of metaphysics. A victim's seemingly justified skepticism about everyone and everything is pertinent to epistemology, especially if the goal of epistemology is, as Wilfrid Sellars put it, that of feeling at home in the world. In aesthetics, as well as in the philosophy of law, the discussion of sexual violence in—or as—art could use the illumination provided by a victim's perspective. Perhaps the most important questions that sexual violence poses are in social, political, and legal philosophy. Insight into those areas, as well, requires an understanding of what it's like to be a victim of such violence.

It occurred to me that the fact that rape has not been considered a properly philosophical subject—unlike war, for example—resulted not only from the paucity of women in the profession but also from the disciplinary biases against thinking about the "personal" or the particular, and against writing in the form of narrative. (Of course, the avowedly personal experiences of *men* have been neglected in philosophical analysis as well. The study of the ethics of war, for example, has dealt with questions of strategy and justice as viewed from the outside, not with the wartime experiences of soldiers or with the aftermath of their trauma.) But first-person narratives, especially ones written by those with perspectives previously excluded from the discipline, are essential to philosophy. They are necessary for exposing previously hidden biases in the discipline's subject matter and methodology, for facilitating understanding of (or empathy with) those different from ourselves, and for laying on the table our own biases as scholars.

When I resumed teaching at Dartmouth, the first student who came to my office told me that she had been raped. Since I had spoken out publicly several months earlier about my assault, I knew that I would be in contact with other survivors. I just didn't realize that there would be so many—not only students, but also female colleagues and friends, who had never before told me that they had been raped. I continued to teach my usual philosophy courses, but, in some ways philosophy struck me as a luxury when I knew, in a more visceral way than before, that people were being brutally attacked and killed—all the time. So I integrated my work on trauma with my academic interests by teaching a course on global violence against women. I was still somewhat afraid of what would happen if I wrote about my assault, but I was much more afraid of what would continue to happen if I, and others with similar experiences, didn't make them public.

It was one thing to have decided to speak and write about my rape, but another to find the voice with which to do it. Even after my fractured trachea had healed, I frequently had trouble speaking. I lost my voice, literally, when I lost my ability to continue my life's narrative, when things stopped making sense. I was never entirely mute, but I often had bouts of what a friend labeled "fractured speech," during which I stuttered and stammered, unable to string together a simple sentence without the words scattering like a broken necklace. During the assault itself, my heightened lucidity had seemed to be accompanied by an unusual linguistic fluency—in French, no less. But being able to speak quickly and (so it seemed to me) precisely in a foreign language when I felt I had to in order to survive was followed by episodes, spread over several years, when I couldn't, for the life of me, speak intelligibly even in my mother tongue.

The fact that rape has not been considered a properly philosophical subject results in part from disciplinary biases against thinking about the 'personal.'

For about a year after the assault, I rarely, if ever, spoke in smoothly flowing sentences. I could sing, though, after about six months, and, like aphasics who cannot say a word but can sing verse after verse, I never stumbled over the lyrics. I recall spending the hour's drive home from the weekly meetings of my support group of rape survivors singing every spiritual I'd ever heard. It was a comfort and a release. Mainly, it was something I could do, loudly, openly (by myself in a closed car), and easily, accompanied by unstoppable tears.

Even after I regained my ability to speak, more or less reliably, in English, I was unable to speak, without debilitating difficulty, in French. Before my ill-fated trip in the summer of 1990, I'd never have passed for a native speaker, but I'd visited France many times and spent several summers there. I came of age there, intellectually, immersing myself in the late 1970s in research on French feminism, which had led to my interviewing Simone de Beauvoir (in Rome) one summer. Now, more than 10 years after the assault, I still almost never speak French, even in Francophone company, in which I often find myself, given my husband's interests.

After regaining my voice, I sometimes lost it again—once for an entire week after my brother committed suicide on Christmas Eve, 1995. Although I'd managed to keep my speech impairment hidden from my colleagues and students for five and a half years, I found that I had to ask a colleague to take over a class I'd been scheduled to teach the day after the funeral. I feared that I'd suffer a linguistic breakdown in front of a lecture hall full of students.

I lost my voice again, intermittently, during my tenure review, about a year after my brother's death. And, although I could still write (and type) during this time, I can see now that my writing about violence had become increasingly hesitant and guarded, as I hid behind academic jargon and excessive citations of others' work. Not only had my brother's suicide caused me to doubt whether I, who had, after all, survived, was entitled to talk about the trauma I'd endured, but now I could not silence the internalized voices of those who had warned me not to publish my work on sexual violence before getting tenure. In spite of the warm reception my writing on the subject was receiving in the larger academic community—from feminist philosophers and legal theorists, people in women's studies, and scholars from various disciplines who were interested in trauma—I stopped writing in the personal voice and slipped back into the universal mode, thinking that only writing about trauma in general was important enough to justify the academic risks I was taking. And I took fewer and fewer risks.

After getting tenure, I was given sanctuary, for nearly two years, at the Institute for Advanced Study, in Princeton. There I gradually came to feel safe enough to write, once again, in my own voice, about what I considered to be philosophically important. It helped to be surrounded by a diverse group of scholars who, to my initial amazement and eternal gratitude, simply assumed that whatever

I was working on must be of sufficient intellectual interest to be worth bothering about.

My linguistic disability never resurfaced in my many conversations at the institute, although it returned later, after a particularly stressful incident at Dartmouth. That episode, more than eight and a half years after the assault, forced me to accept that I have what may well be a permanent neurological glitch resulting from my brain's having been stunned into unconsciousness four times during the attack. Although I had spoken out as a rape survivor at a Take Back the Night rally nine months after the event, it took me nearly nine years to acknowledge, even to myself, that the assault had left me neurologically disabled—very minimally, to be sure, in a way that I could easily compensate for, by avoiding extremely stressful situations, but disabled nonetheless.

People ask me if I'm recovered now, and I reply that it depends on what that means. If they mean, am I back to where I was before the attack? I have to say no, and I never will be. I am not the same person who set off, singing, on that sunny Fourth of July in the French countryside. I left her in a rocky creek bed at the bottom of a ravine. I had to in order to survive. The trauma has changed me forever, and if I insist too often that my friends and family acknowledge it, that's because I'm afraid they don't know who I am.

But if recovery means being able to incorporate this awful knowledge of trauma and its aftermath into my life and carry on, then, yes, I'm recovered. I don't wake each day with a start, thinking: "This can't have happened to me!" It happened. I have no guarantee that it won't happen again. I don't expect to be able to transcend or redeem the trauma, or to solve the dilemmas of survival. I think the goal of recovery is simply to endure. That is hard enough, especially when sometimes it seems as if the only way to regain control over one's life is to end it.

A few months after my assault, I drove by myself for several hours to visit my friend Margot. Though driving felt like a much safer mode of transportation than walking, I worried throughout the journey, not only about the trajectory of every oncoming vehicle but also about my car breaking down, leaving me at the mercy of potentially murderous passersby. I wished I'd had a gun so that I could shoot myself rather than be forced to live through another assault. Later in my recovery, as depression gave way to rage, such suicidal thoughts

were quickly quelled by a stubborn refusal to finish my assailant's job for him. I also learned, after martial-arts training, that I was capable, morally as well as physically, of killing in self-defense—an option that made the possibility of another life-threatening attack one I could live with.

Some rape survivors have remarked on the sense of moral loss they experienced when they realized that they could kill their assailants, but I think that this thought can be seen as a salutary character change in those whom society does not encourage to value their own lives enough. And, far from jeopardizing their connections with a community, this newfound ability to defend themselves—and to consider themselves worth fighting for—enables rape survivors to move once more among others, free of debilitating fears. It gave me the courage to bring a child into the world, in spite of the realization that doing so would, far from making me immortal, make me twice as mortal, doubling my chances of having my life destroyed by a speeding truck.

But many trauma survivors who endured much worse than I did, and for much longer, found, often years later, that it was impossible to go on. It is not a moral failing to leave a world that has become morally unacceptable. I wonder how some people can ask of battered women, Why didn't they leave? while saying of those driven to suicide by the brutal and inescapable aftermath of trauma, Why didn't they stay? Jean Améry wrote, "Whoever was tortured, stays tortured," and that may explain why he, Primo Levi, Paul Celan, and other Holocaust survivors took their own lives decades after their physical torture ended, as if such an explanation were needed.

Those who have survived trauma understand the pull of that solution to their daily Beckettian dilemma—"I can't go on, I must go on"—for on some days the conclusion "I'll go on" can be reached by neither faith nor reason. How does one go on with a shattered self, with no guarantee of recovery, believing that one will always stay tortured and never feel at home in the world? One hopes for a bearable future, in spite of all the inductive evidence to the contrary. After all, the loss of faith in induction following an unpredictable trauma has a reassuring side: Since inferences from the past can no longer be relied upon to predict the future, there's no more reason to think that tomorrow will bring agony than to think that it won't. So one makes a wager, in which nothing is certain and the odds change daily, and sets about willing to believe that life, for all its unfathomable horror, still holds some undiscovered pleasures. And one remakes oneself by finding meaning in a life of caring for and being sustained by others.

While I used to have to will myself out of bed each day, I now wake gladly to feed my son, whose birth gave me reason not to have died. Having him has forced me to rebuild my trust in the world, to try to believe that the world is a good enough place in which to raise him. He is so trusting that, before he learned to walk, he would stand with outstretched arms, wobbling, until he fell, stiff-limbed, forward, backward, certain the universe would catch him. So far it has, and when I tell myself it always will, the part of me that he's become believes it.

SUSAN J. BRISON is an associate professor of philosophy at Dartmouth College and a visiting associate professor of philosophy at Princeton University. She is the author of *Aftermath: Violence and the Remaking of a Self,* published by Princeton University Press.

Understanding Stockholm Syndrome

NATHALIE DE FABRIQUE, PSYD ET AL.

Men, when they receive good from whence they expect evil, feel the more indebted to their benefactor.

—Niccolo Machiavelli

The world watched as Elizabeth Smart's family, both panicked and heartbroken, desperately cried out to news cameras and begged for their teenager's safe return. Viewers saw haunting images from a home movie that featured a beautiful young girl playing the harp like an angel. The terror of this 14-year-old snatched from her bed captivated the hearts and minds of millions.

So, when authorities rescued and safely returned her home, people questioned how, in 9 months, she could not escape or ask someone—anyone—for help. But, her abductors did not hold her captive, as initially believed. In fact, she walked in public, attended parties, and even refused to reveal her true identity when first approached by police. Perhaps, even more puzzling than her initial reluctance to escape was her apparent concern upon rescue about the fate of her captors. "What's going to happen to them? Are they in trouble?" she asked. When informed by officers that they likely would face punishment, she started to cry and sobbed the whole way to the station.[1]

This high-profile kidnapping generated a lot of scrutiny. In attempting to explain her reluctance to be rescued and her compassion toward the perpetrators, some mistakenly have suggested that Elizabeth Smart serves as yet another example of Stockholm syndrome and that her captors must have "brainwashed" her.[2] However, compassion alone does not define the condition, and this situation did not feature all elements necessary for development to truly occur. Instead, the case demonstrates the difficulty of gaining a true understanding of the phenomenon. Although scenarios resulting in the condition are rare, crisis negotiators must have a clear understanding of the psychological processes related to Stockholm syndrome to recognize and successfully address hostage and barricade-with-victim situations where it manifests.

Stockholm Syndrome Defined
Background

The term *Stockholm syndrome* was coined after the 1973 robbery of Kreditbanken in Stockholm, Sweden, in which two robbers held four bank employees hostage from August 23 to 28. During this time, the victims shared a vault and became very familiar with their captors—in fact, they wound up emotionally attached and even defended them after the ordeal. Today, people view Stockholm syndrome as a psychological response of a hostage or an individual in a similar situation in which the more dominant person has the power to put the victim's life in danger. Perpetrators occasionally use this advantage to get victims to comply with their demands.[3]

Disagreement exists over the identification of which factors characterize incidents that contribute to the development of Stockholm syndrome. Research has suggested that hostages may exhibit the condition in situations that feature captors who do not abuse the victim, a long duration before resolution, continued contact between the perpetrator and hostage, and a high level of emotion. In fact, experts have concluded that the intensity, not the length of the incident, combined with a lack of physical abuse more likely will create favorable conditions for the development of Stockholm syndrome. Apparently, a strong emotional bond develops between persons who share these life-threatening experiences.

The 1985 hijacking of TWA Flight 847 showcases these factors and demonstrates the variability among me hostages' responses. Shortly after takeoff from Athens, Greece, two terrorists armed with guns stormed the cockpit and demanded the diversion of the flight to Beirut, Lebanon. After capturing the plane, the perpetrators released the women and children. Two sailors and a group of wealthy American businessmen remained on the aircraft, and the captors held them for 10 days. During the incident, the terrorists threatened the hostages with guns to their heads and in their mouths. They also beat one of the victims to death and dumped his body out of the tail section of the plane.

After the eventual rescue, reporters interviewed the captives as they disembarked. When asked to describe the captors, one hostage stated, "They weren't bad people; they let me eat, they let me sleep, they gave me my life."[4] However, while one victim did display feelings of compassion for the perpetrators, most of the hostages showed no evidence of Stockholm syndrome. On the contrary, because of the violent manner in which the terrorists treated nearly all of the victims, most of the captives expressed fear that their captors would kill them and understood that their greatest chance for survival lay in the authorities' hands.

Crisis negotiators . . . encourage its development because it improves the chances of hostage survival. . . .

Characteristics

Stockholm syndrome is a paradoxical psychological phenomenon wherein a positive bond between hostage and captor occurs that appears irrational in light of the frightening ordeal endured by the victims. In essence, eventually, the hostage views the perpetrator as giving life by simply not taking it. Individuals involved in situations resulting in Stockholm syndrome display three characteristics, although these do not always exist together. Law enforcement officers must encourage and tolerate the first two components to, hopefully, induce the third, which preserves life.

1. Hostages have positive feelings for their captors.
2. Victims show fear, distrust, and anger toward the authorities.
3. Perpetrators display positive feelings toward captives as they begin to see them as human beings.

Frequency of the Phenomenon

According to the FBI's Hostage Barricade Database System, which contains data pertaining to over 4,700 reported federal, state, and local hostage/barricade incidents, 73 percent of captives show no evidence of Stockholm syndrome. And, while victims can display negative feelings toward law enforcement (usually out of frustration with the pace of negotiations), most do not develop the condition.[5]

One of the authors, a retired FBI expert, stated that in a career of over 30 years in law enforcement, he rarely witnessed behavior indicative of the development of Stockholm syndrome.[6] "I've seen the reluctance on the part of some hostages who refuse to come out without the hostage taker less than a handful of times." His explanation rests on the approximation that nearly 96 percent of hostage and barricade situations in the United States are domestic in nature; involve suicide, attempted suicide, and domestic violence; and include subjects with an existing relationship. He reports that for Stockholm syndrome

to occur, the incident must take place between strangers, and the hostage must come to fear and resent law enforcement as much as or more than the perpetrators.

The Psychological Process

Fully comprehending Stockholm syndrome requires an understanding of the process that leads to its development. Most important, this condition does not result from a conscious decision or a rational choice to befriend a captor. From a psychological perspective, the ego, described by Sigmund Freud as the "personality core," is responsible for providing people with defense mechanisms—ways for them to guard or distance themselves from and remain consciously unaware of unpleasant thoughts, feelings, and desires—and also helps individuals avoid hurt and disorganization.[7]

In hostage situations, the healthy ego seeks a means to achieve survival. In cases where Stockholm syndrome has occurred, the captive is in a situation where the captor has stripped nearly all forms of independence and gained control of the victim's life, as well as basic needs for survival. Some experts say that the hostage regresses to, perhaps, a state of infancy; the captive must cry for food, remain silent, and exist in an extreme state of dependence. In contrast, the perpetrator serves as a mother figure protecting her child from a threatening outside world, including law enforcement's deadly weapons. The victim then begins a struggle for survival, both relying on and identifying with the captor. Possibly, hostages' motivation to live outweighs their impulse to hate the person who created their dilemma.[8]

The Importance of Understanding

Crisis negotiators no longer consider the bonding that occurs between captive and captor in cases of Stockholm syndrome detrimental. They encourage its development because it improves the chances of hostage survival, despite the fact that it sometimes means authorities no longer can count on the cooperation of victims in working for their release or later prosecuting the perpetrators.[9] As such, individuals working as crisis negotiators must understand how the phenomenon unfolds, as well as ways to promote the psychological process, thus increasing the likelihood of a successful outcome.

Comprehending how Stockholm syndrome develops requires an understanding of the mind-set of the captive. Hostages have to concentrate on survival, requiring avoidance of direct, honest reactions to destructive treatment.[10] They must become highly attuned to the pleasure and displeasure reactions of their captors. As a result, victims seem more concerned about the perpetrator's feelings than their own. Hostages are encouraged to develop psychological characteristics pleasing to hostage takers, such as dependency; lack of initiative; and an inability to act, decide, or think. The captive actively devises strategies for staying alive, including denial, attentiveness to the captor's wants, fondness (and fear) of the perpetrator, apprehension toward interference by authorities, and adoption of the hostage taker's perspective. Victims are overwhelmingly grateful to captors for giving them life and focus on their acts of kindness, rather than their brutality.[11]

Law enforcement and psychology professionals have offered several opinions concerning the development of Stockholm syndrome. However, most agree on the conditions necessary for it to occur.

- A person held in captivity cannot escape and depends on the hostage taker for life. The captor becomes the person in control of the captive's basic needs for survival and the victim's life itself.
- The hostage endures isolation from other people and has only the captor's perspective available. Perpetrators routinely keep information about the outside world's response to their actions from captives to keep them totally dependent.
- The hostage taker threatens to kill the victim and gives the perception as having the capability to do so. The captive judges it safer to align with the perpetrator, endure the hardship of captivity, and comply with the captor than to resist and face murder.
- The captive sees the perpetrator as showing some degree of kindness. Kindness serves as the cornerstone of Stockholm syndrome; the condition will not develop unless the captor exhibits it in some form toward the hostage. However, captives often misinterpret a lack of abuse as kindness and may develop feelings of appreciation for this perceived benevolence. If the captor is purely evil and abusive, the hostage will respond with hatred. But, if perpetrators show some kindness, victims will submerge the anger they feel in response to the terror and concentrate on the captors' "good side" to protect themselves.[12]

Humanization of the Captive

While many experts consider encouraging the development of Stockholm syndrome to increase hostage survival difficult, crisis negotiators can attempt to humanize the captive in the mind of the perpetrator, thereby stimulating the emergence of the critical, third characteristic in the hostage taker—positive feelings toward the captive. To this end, determining the number of people involved, as well as their names, is paramount.

Another way negotiators can attempt to personalize the hostage is to ask the subject to pass on a personal message to the victim (e.g., "Tell Mark that his children love him very much and will be there to meet him when he comes out."). This type of dialogue reminds the perpetrator of the hostage's name and that the victim is a real person with a family. It also inserts a suggestibility statement ("when he comes out") that implies a peaceful resolution.

Trying to initiate Stockholm syndrome in the perpetrator involves a delicate blend of personalizing captives without overhauling them. "Most hostage takers want it to be all about them. If the negotiator asks too many questions about the hostages, he may begin to feel ignored and discounted. If you want to solve the hostage's problems, you need to solve the hostage taker's problems."[13] To strike the balance necessary for successful negotiations, asking about the welfare of the captor first, and the captive later, is key.

Using those simple strategies may assist in formulating a bond between the victim and perpetrator. That being said, law enforcement personnel must be aware that although they are attempting to maintain the "balancing act" of increasing rapport with the hostage taker and influencing the safety of the hostages, the ultimate goal is to peacefully resolve the crisis for all involved. If achieving that result involves manipulating hostage takers' belief that the focus remains on them, then negotiators must be willing to understand the rationale behind the maneuver and learn the skills necessary to employ it.

Conclusion

The subject of Stockholm syndrome, fueled, in part, by a number of high-profile cases, has generated a lot of discussion and opinions. Many people find the phenomenon as difficult to understand as it is fascinating.

. . . this condition does not result from a conscious decision or a rational choice to befriend a captor.

Although, at first, this psychological process may appear complex and uncontrollable, further exploration with those experienced in the area of crisis negotiation revealed that the condition and its effects can serve as a useful tool in successful outcomes. In understanding the basis behind the mental state and behavior of both the hostage taker and the captive, law enforcement agencies can place Stockholm syndrome in the appropriate perspective and see it as a catalyst in improving the training of hostage negotiators and encouraging peaceful resolutions.

Notes

1. Maggie Haberman and Jeane MacIntosh, *Held Captive: The Kidnapping and Rescue of Elizabeth Smart* (New York, NY: Avon Books, 2003).
2. Paul Wong, "Elizabeth Smart and Stockholm Syndrome"; retrieved from http://www.meaning,calarticles/stockholm_syndrome.htm.
3. http://en.wikipedia.org/wiki/Stockholm_syndrome
4. Pete Williams, "Twenty Years Later, Stethems Still Seek Justice"; retrieved from http://www.msnbc.msn.com/id/8219264.

5. G. Dwayne Fuselier, "Placing the Stockholm Syndrome in Perspective," *FBI Law Enforcement Bulletin,* July 1999, 22–25.

6. Stephen J. Romano served as chief of the Crisis Negotiation Unit of the Critical Incident Response Group at the FBI Academy.

7. Sigmund Freud, *The Ego and the Id: The Standard Edition* (New York, NY: W.W. Norton and Company, 1960).

8. Thomas Strentz, "Law Enforcement Policy and Ego Defenses of the Hostage," *FBI Law Enforcement Bulletin,* April 1979, 2–12.

9. Edna Rawlings, Dee Graham, and Roberta Rigsby, *Loving to Survive: Sexual Terror, Men's Violence, and Women's Lives* (New York, NY: New York University Press, 1994).

10. Ibid.

11. Anne Jones, "Post-Traumatic Stress Disorder, Rape Trauma Syndrome, and Battering"; retrieved from http://www.ojp.usdoj.gov/ovc/new/victempow/student/postram.htm.

12. Ibid.

13. Supra note 6.

DR. DE FABRIQUE is involved with clinical work in psychology and is an adjunct faculty member at Nova Southeastern University in Davie, Florida. **MR. ROMANO,** a retired FBI special agent, operates a consulting/training firm in Greenville, South Carolina, servicing corporate and law enforcement clients. **DR. VAN HASSELT** is a professor of psychology at Nova Southeastern University in Davie, Florida, and a part-time officer with the Plantation Police Department. **DR. VECCHI** serves as a special agent in the Behavioral Science Unit at the FBI Academy.

Judge Steven Leifman Advocates for the Mentally Jee

Susan L. Clayton

"When I became a judge I had no idea that I was becoming a gatekeeper to the largest psychiatric facility in the state of Florida—the Miami-Dade Jail," said Miami-Dade County Judge Steven Leifman, keynote speaker at the H-PIS Special Session and Luncheon. Since April 2007, Leifman has served as special advisor on criminal justice and mental health for the Florida Supreme Court.

Leifman began his address by sharing *The Forgotten Floor,* a video that was filmed by local Miami-Dade media in 2006. It highlighted some of the challenges faced by the Miami-Dade Jail in dealing with mentally ill offenders and the unfavorable conditions that these offenders lived in at the time of their convictions. Although the video was disturbing in spots, Leifman noted that "If we don't look at what is really going on out there we will never be able to fix it." He said the video was an example of the difficult and complex problems facing the justice system.

Leifman stressed the need to decrease inappropriate and costly involvement of people with mental illnesses in the criminal justice system by increasing access to comprehensive and cost-effective community-based services that target specialized treatment needs.

Leifman, who also serves as chair of the 11th Judicial Circuit of Florida's Mental Health Committee, created the 11th Judicial District Criminal Mental Health Project. This initiative, which includes both prearrest and post-arrest diversion programs, brings together justice system, law enforcement and community resources to divert low-level offenders with mental illnesses away from incarceration. Miami-Dade County has seen reductions in arrests and recidivism rates among people with mental illnesses; the burden of providing psychiatric services through the jail has decreased; and the county is saving money.

Leifman became involved with mentally ill offenders about eight years ago when he promised a couple that he would help obtain treatment for their son who was mentally ill and had been convicted of a low-level crime. As a county court judge at the time he could not involuntarily hospitalize someone. Leifman realized there was nothing he could do and he would not be able to keep his promise to the offender's parents. From this experience, Leifman said, he learned three important things. The first is that Miami-Dade has the largest percentage of people with mental illness of any urban area in the U.S. In fact, 9.1 percent (more than 210,000 people) of the general population in Miami-Dade County have a serious mental illness. Because the state is only treating 13 percent of them, many others end up in jail, Leifman said. "On any given day we have approximately 1,200 people on psychotropic medication, making us the largest psychiatric warehouse in the state of Florida occupying nine floors of our main jail. And because conditions are not conducive for treatment, people with mental illness in jails are staying eight times longer than those without mental illness."

Second, Leifman learned that this is not a local problem; it is a local, state and national problem. Finally, he learned that Florida's mental health system and crisis care system, like in most states, were developed more than 40 years ago when most people with serious mental illnesses were still in state hospitals. "They [state hospitals] were never developed and designed to handle the most acute population among people with mental illnesses. And we have the most fragmented, inadequate, antiquated systems of care for people with mental illness that is in need of great reform."

According to Leifman, there are less than 40,000 hospital beds for the mentally ill in the U.S. Ninety percent of the country's hospital beds have been closed and the nation has experienced a 400 percent increase in the mentally ill offenders entering the criminal justice system. Last year, 1.1 million people with severe mental illnesses were arrested, Leifman said. He added that on any given day, there are about 500,000 people with mental illnesses in the nation's jails and prisons, and about another 500,000 on probation. Leifman noted that in the late 1970s, the Supreme Court came out with an order for the deinstitutionalization of state mental hospitals. But because there was no community mental health system at the time, the country never deinstitutionalized, Leifman said. "Instead we transferred people from hospitals to jails giving them criminal records and making it much more difficult for them to go into recovery." And having a criminal record makes it harder to obtain housing and employment. Leifman noted that jails are now the primary place to house people with severe mental illnesses. "This is one area of civil rights we have gone backward on and it certainly speaks more about us as a society than it does about people with mental illnesses." The consequences of this failed policy, Leifman said, include an increase of homelessness, police injuries, police shootings of people with mental illnesses, and wasted tax dollars. "We have made mental illness a crime in this country," he said.

Last year, Florida initiated more involuntary hospitalizations than the number of arrests for robbery, burglary and grand-theft auto combined, Leifman said. He noted that the fastest growing public mental health dollars are going to a forensic hospital, where people go after they have committed a felony. Funding for this has increased 72 percent. Florida's forensic hospital houses about 3,000 people a year (1,700 beds) and costs the state more than $200 billion a year, meaning one-third of its mental health budget is dedicated to 1,700 beds. It is projected that in the next eight years the number of beds and the cost to the state will double, Leifman said. He also pointed out that in the last 10 years there has been a 145 percent increase in the number of people with mental illnesses entering the prison system. "One hundred eighty percent of people with moderate or severe mental illness—8,000 to 17,000 people—will grow to about 35,000 in the next 8 to 10 years . . . Florida needs 10 new prisons over the next five to six years just to house people with mental illnesses. The cost to the taxpayers will be $3.6 billion, which is more than our existing budget today."

Leifman noted that it is the people with the highest need and the least access to services who end up in the criminal justice system.

Leifman told attendees that there was a crisis in Florida that led to the state chief justice appointing him to his current advisory position. Florida law states that once one is found competent to stand trial, he or she must be moved to a forensic hospital within 15 days of the finding. Because this issue had been ignored for so many years, the hospital ran out of beds. So, according to Leifman, as the numbers continued to grow, people with mental illnesses got stuck in jails. Lawsuits resulted and the public defenders and sheriffs came together and sued the state of Florida and the secretary of the Department of Children and Families. A judge found the secretary in criminal contempt of court, fined her $80,000 and was on the verge of putting her in jail. The state took an appeal and lost. In an effort to rid the backlog, the Legislature and the governor allocated $48 million to rent 300 beds. "They did nothing to resolve the underlying problem that caused this in the first place," Leifman said. "We could have provided mental health care for more than 260,000 children or 60,000 adults. Instead we rented 300 beds which will be full by this summer." Leifman said Florida is now on the course for another constitutional crisis. In an effort to avoid this, the chief judge ordered a bipartisan multibranch task force to try to come up with a plan to resolve this problem. Leifman thinks they have.

The task force began by examining as much data and research as possible. Its members found that most people with mental illness in Florida have never come into contact with the system, but a small group of people keep recycling again and again. Leifman noted that it is the people with the highest need and the least access to services who end up in the criminal justice system. Leifman said that the problem should be looked at not as a criminal justice issue but as a medical one. With physical illness, Leifman said, "When we catch people early, they go into treatment, then go into recovery and most do fairly well." When people with a physical illness get sicker they see a doctor, however, when people with mental illness get sicker they go to the one institution that cannot say no—jails and prisons.

Leifman said the task force found a huge gap between how science dictates how mental illness is treated and how it is actually delivered to communities. He pointed out that 50 percent of people with bipolar disorder are not only on the wrong medication, but the medication they take actually exacerbates their mental illness. He also noted that almost 100 percent of women in jails and prisons with mental illness were sexually abused as children and now suffer from severe post-traumatic stress. Yet most communities do not offer trauma-related services to mentally ill people coming out of jail. According to Leifman, almost 75 percent of men in jails and prisons with severe mental illnesses suffer trauma. "As we continued to look at the system we realized that the case management services at the community level were inadequate. There was a lack of day activities, a lack of affordable housing and a lack of employment opportunities, and very little coordination between the criminal justice system and the local community."

In response, the task force created a document that serves as a guideline and blueprint for Florida and other states that focuses in on the problem and creates an appropriate level of services in the community for this population. This is also tied into a reentry plan. "We will intercede and try to provide an entire level of services so you don't continue to recycle," Leifman said. "If you don't have housing on the day you leave jail and you have a severe mental disorder it's almost impossible that you will succeed."

Leifman said that Florida has created a program based on one in Tennessee called Crisis Intervention Policing, which trains local law enforcement on how to identify people who are in crisis situations, how to deescalate the situation and where to take them as opposed to arresting them. In Miami-Dade County alone there are more than 1,800 police officers trained. Correctional officers are also trained. This along with diversion programs help to keep people with mental illnesses out of the criminal justice system whenever possible. "The guiding light for us is if you are in jail because of your mental illness we want to get you out. If you are in jail in spite of your mental illness you need to serve," Leifman said.

According to Leifman, the task force's work and recommendations have been turned into legislation. "We got very close last session with approval in the Florida House of Representatives and it barely failed in the Senate. We are very hopeful that we'll make some adjustments and we'll be able to get it passed," he said. The legislation will help someone with mental illnesses as he or she goes through prearrest diversion, is found incompetent to stand trial or is released from jail or prison. "We take you and wrap our arms around you and we build the system that provides six essential elements: good diagnosis and medication, intensive case management services, day activities, trauma-related services, support for housing, and support for employment," Leifman said. If you offer these things "You can save the states billions of dollars in unnecessary spending to keep people out of the system or to take care of them when they come out." For example, Leifman said, 50 percent of the people with mental illnesses who go back to prison go back not for committing a new offense but for some kind of technical violation. According to Leifman, Florida has to build a prison a year just to house people who are violating the terms of their probation. "We have a long way to go but we do think we have figured it out. I'm very hopeful that at the end of the day this legislation passes and we will finally succeed in what the Supreme Court was trying to do in the 1970s when it ordered the deinstitutionalization."

Victim Satisfaction with the Criminal Justice System

New research suggests that victims of domestic violence who initially turn to the criminal justice system for intervention may be so dissatisfied with the outcome that they do not call the police the next time they need help.

Researchers Eve Buzawa and the late Gerald Hotaling asked women in 353 domestic violence cases in the Quincy District Court (QDC) in Quincy, Massachusetts, to assess the role of the police, prosecutors, victim advocates, and judges and to rate their level of satisfaction.[1] They found that in 55 percent of the cases, women were generally satisfied with the outcome. In 17 percent, victims were dissatisfied.

The researchers found several common variables in the satisfied cases: the incidents were less serious, the offender was less dangerous, the victim said she felt some control and wanted the case to go forward, and the victim reported experiencing less violence in her past.

Dissatisfied victims appeared to have been involved in more serious incidents with highly dangerous offenders and were more likely to have disagreed with the police about the offender's arrest. These victims were also 16 times more likely than satisfied victims to report that they had experienced both sexual and severe physical abuse before the age of 18. As a group, dissatisfied victims appeared to be more willing to leave offenders or unwilling (or afraid) to directly confront the abuser, even if they were separated.

For the researchers, the bottom line was that victim satisfaction in domestic violence cases appeared to hinge on the extent to which the victim felt control over ending the violence in the incident, control over her offender's future conduct—and even over the criminal justice system. When the victim had a low sense of control, satisfaction with the system decreased significantly.

Consequences of Victim Dissatisfaction

Having identified the common variables in cases of satisfied and dissatisfied victims, Buzawa and Hotaling then examined what, if any, consequences flowed from dissatisfaction. The second stage of the study focused on the connection between victim dissatisfaction and willingness to report future victimizations. The researchers tracked 118 women for a year after the original study to see if they reported any new incidents or sought civil restraining orders.

Of the 118 women, 49 percent admitted that they had been revictimized. Of these, 22 percent reported the incidents to the police. Contrary to the presumption that "more serious" offenses get reported to the police, victims who reported the new incident were more likely to report less serious offenses, like violations of restraining orders, than they were to reach out for assistance due to a physical assault. Women who reported new abuse to the police also generally reported that the abuse was becoming more serious.

Women who chose not to report new incidents of abuse were:

- The least likely to have resisted the arrest of the offender during the first incident.
- The least likely to have been dissatisfied with how the police initially handled the incident.
- The most likely, by the conclusion of the case, to feel that the actions of the police negatively affected their safety and to complain that they wanted the prosecutor to make charges against the offender more severe.

Women who chose not to report new incidents of abuse also were likely to have experienced sexual abuse as a child. This finding coincides with other research that suggests a link between a woman's history of abuse and her likelihood of reporting revictimization to police. The researchers theorize that "for an individual who has experienced abuse through the 'life course,' reporting this latest incident to the police may be viewed as a useless ritualism."[2]

Balancing Different Perspectives

In the past, victims of domestic violence often expressed dissatisfaction with the lack of aggressive response to domestic assault by police, prosecutors, and the courts. Now, researchers have discovered, the pendulum may have swung the other way.

Mandatory arrest policies in many jurisdictions and implementation of "full enforcement" protocols have resulted in more cases being prosecuted whether the victim wants to proceed or not.

Women who are the victims of domestic abuse usually want to enhance their own safety, maintain economic viability, protect their children, and have an opportunity to force an abuser to participate in batterers' counseling programs. They are less concerned about upholding the law or deterring future abuse—the main objectives of the police, prosecutor, and judge.

Victim Services Increase Positive Experiences

Women who take advantage of victim service programs tend to have more positive outcomes and are more likely to report satisfaction, according to one study.[3] Researchers found that women benefit the most when the criminal justice system and nonprofit and community-based agencies collaborate and coordinate their efforts. Such cooperation results in more positive outcomes and greater victim satisfaction. Treating victims with respect, offering them positive encouragement, refraining from engaging in negative interactions, and most importantly, creating a sense of control increased the odds of positive outcomes in the victim's view.

Researchers concluded that the most positive outcomes occur when the staff at service agencies listen to women, carefully explain the options, and then take action. "Women know best about their own safety and well-being, and when they have a greater sense of control while working with agencies, they find the services more helpful and effective."[4]

Ensuring that victim service programs work in conjunction with the legal system and community agencies and that staff address victims' needs in a positive manner will encourage victims to turn to the criminal justice system for assistance and may maximize the potential to break the cycle of violence.

Notes

1. QDC was chosen as a data collection site because it is an acknowledged leader in implementing strategies that favor criminal justice intervention in domestic violence cases. Over a 7-month period in 1999, researchers interviewed victims to obtain their assessments of the role of police, prosecutors, victim advocates, and judges. Researchers also studied victims' satisfaction with various sectors of the criminal justice system.

2. Hotaling, Gerald T., and Eve S. Buzawa, *Forgoing Criminal Justice Assistance: The Non-Reporting of New Incidents of Abuse in a Court Sample of Domestic Violence Victims,* Washington, DC: U.S. Department of Justice, National Institute of Justice, 2003: 25 (NCJ 195667).

3. Zweig, Janine, Martha R. Burt, and Ashley Van Ness, *Effects on Victims of Victim Service Programs Funded by the STOP Formula Grants Program,* Washington, DC: U.S. Department of Justice, National Institute of Justice, 2003: 16 (NCJ 202903).

4. Ibid., 19.

From *National Institute of Justice Journal*, January 2006.

UNIT 3
The Police

Unit Selections

Key Points to Consider

- Can racial or ethnic profiling ever be a legitimate police tactic? Explain.

- Is police work the cause of suicides among officers, or does the availability of a gun just make it easier?

- Are civilian complaint review boards effective in combating police abuses?

Student Website
www.mhhe.com/cls

Internet References

ACLU Criminal Justice Home Page
   http://www.aclu.org/CriminalJustice/CriminalJusticeMain.cfm
Law Enforcement Guide to the World Wide Web
   http://leolinks.com/
Violent Criminal Apprehension Program (VICAP)
   http://www.state.ma.us/msp/unitpage/vicap.htm

Police officers are the guardians of our rights under the Constitution and the law, and as such they have an awesome task. They are asked to prevent crime, protect citizens, arrest wrongdoers, preserve the peace, aid the sick, control juveniles, control traffic, and provide emergency services on a moment's notice. They are also asked to be ready to lay down their lives, if necessary.

In recent years, the job of the police officer has become even more complex and dangerous. Illegal drug use and trafficking are still major problems; racial tensions are explosive; and terrorism is now an alarming reality. As our population grows more numerous and diverse, the role of the police in America becomes ever more challenging, requiring skills that can only be obtained by greater training and professionalism.

The lead article in this section, "Policing in Arab-American Communities after September 11," examines how the terrorist attacks of September 11 changed the face of law enforcement in the United States, including the effect on Arab-American communities brought about by these changes. The typical offender in violent crime categories is white, as pointed out by Tim Wise in "Racial Profiling and Its Apologists."

In the next article, "Our Oath of Office, A Solemn Promise", Rudd focuses on the oath of office that law enforcement officers take, in order to illuminate the purpose and history of the oath and to show its relevance to our Constitution. In "Stress Management . . . and the Stress-Proof Vest," the question of whether the police environment is responsible for the large number of police suicides is looked at by Robert Fox. Next, Benedict Carey writes about research on police interrogation in "Judging Honesty by Words, Not Fidgets." Finally, Pinizzotto, et al. write about a project that aimed at placing prosecutors in the shoes of police officers who may become involved in shooting incidents.

Policing in Arab-American Communities after September 11

Nicole J. Henderson et al.

For the past 20 years, local police agencies have worked to build stronger ties with the communities they serve. These "community policing" efforts have increased public safety and security as partnerships between law enforcement agencies and community groups have been effective at identifying and defusing community disputes.

However, the Sept. 11 terrorist attacks have led to a host of new concerns about public safety. Communities across the nation—from small towns to sprawling cities—are wrestling with security issues that did not exist a decade ago. These issues are especially complex for communities with significant Arab-American populations.

After Sept. 11, law enforcement agencies on both the local and federal levels experienced great pressure to prevent further attacks. Some researchers and law enforcement officials suggested that local law enforcement agencies should play a greater role in intelligence-gathering and immigration enforcement. In addition, the FBI began to stress counterterrorism efforts, with Joint Terrorism Task Forces working in concert with local law enforcement agencies. Often, these efforts focused on Arab-American communities.

At the same time, local law enforcement agencies were called on to protect the Arab-American community. After the attacks, some people of Arab descent said they experienced increased levels of harassment, ranging from workplace discrimination to verbal abuse and vandalism to severe hate crimes such as assault and homicide. To ensure the safety of Arab-Americans, some local law enforcement agencies felt it necessary to step up their outreach efforts.

Finally, some Arab-Americans and law enforcement officers said that public suspicion of Arab-Americans had led to an increase in false reporting. As one FBI special agent said, "The general public calls in some ridiculous stuff—it's really guilt by being Muslim." Because officers have to look into all reports, false reporting can be a significant strain on law enforcement agencies.

Arab-American communities have been deeply affected by the events of Sept. 11 in other ways. Before the attacks, many Arab-Americans were well assimilated into the American mainstream.[2] But after Sept. 11, some members of Arab-American

Study Methods

The study was conducted in 16 sites across the country, each of which is home to a geographically concentrated Arab-American community. For each site, researchers did telephone interviews with people from three groups: local law enforcement officers, FBI agents assigned to local field offices, and members of the Arab-American community. Researchers then held focus group discussions and in-person interviews at four sites.

What Were the Study's Limitations?

This study focused on Arab-American communities that are concentrated in specific regions, and the law enforcement agencies that serve them. However, such concentrated communities are not necessarily representative of the Arab-American population as a whole. In addition, although researchers interviewed FBI agents from local field offices at each site, they did not interview agents from other federal law enforcement agencies, such as Immigration and Customs Enforcement or the U.S. Attorney's Offices.

communities came to believe that many of their fellow citizens—not to mention some in the media and government—regarded them with suspicion. Although Arab-Americans report a fair amount of goodwill towards local law enforcement agencies, some Arab-Americans said these developments have strained relations between their communities and those agencies. Also, some members of Arab-American communities said they fear federal policies and practices more than violence.

Researchers from the Vera Institute of Justice, examining how post-Sept. 11 law enforcement changes have affected policing in Arab-American neighborhoods (see "Study Methods"), identified four primary and interrelated obstacles to improved relations between law enforcement and the Arab-American community:

- Distrust between Arab-American communities and law enforcement.
- Lack of cultural awareness.

- Language barriers.
- Concerns about immigration status and fear of deportation.

Fortunately, many law enforcement officials and community leaders generally agree on how to address these obstacles.

Distrust

Distrust between Arab-American communities and law enforcement was by far the most commonly cited barrier to improved relations. Although most respondents stressed distrust of law enforcement by the local Arab-American community, a few officers mentioned that the distrust is reciprocal.

Although much of the distrust in Arab-American communities stems from post-Sept. 11 developments, not all of it does. Recent immigrants often feel uncomfortable about approaching law enforcement.[3] This is especially true of immigrants from countries with brutal governments or widespread police corruption. As one local business leader explained, "[Many] Arabs come from [countries with] very authoritarian, dictatorial regimes. The police are run by the state. So from [their] perspective, [approaching law enforcement] is bad news."

The surveys suggest a number of practices that can help:

Begin or improve communication. Reaching out to the local community is the key to building trust. As one sergeant in the public affairs division of a department with an active outreach program noted, "Having a good relationship with the community helps patrol officers do their jobs." In setting up an outreach effort, law enforcement agencies will want to consider the following points:

- *Reach out in person.* Several people stressed the importance of face-to-face meetings as opposed to phone or e-mail contact. One community leader pointed out that "fliers aren't enough," while another explained that the Arab-American community has a strong "oral culture." Outreach efforts were most successful when they used a three-pronged approach: first send a letter, then make a phone call and finally follow up with a personal visit.
- *Meet with the community regularly.* Regular contact between the community and law enforcement agencies is important, and helps break down misconceptions and build trust. At one site, a potentially volatile instance of miscommunication was resolved by discussions in a series of regularly scheduled community forums.
- *Use community contacts to set up meetings.* When arranging meetings, it can help to have a member of the Arab-American community set up the contact: "A non-Arab who invites [members of the Arab-American] community to dinner or to a function will not have the same turnout as if someone from the Arab-American community invites them on [law enforcement's] behalf."

- *Hold meetings in the community as opposed to the precinct headquarters.* This is an effective way to address the fear and hesitation that community members may feel about contacting the police.
- *Include patrol officers in community meetings.* Patrol officers said that community meetings are important. However, some felt that they should play a larger role in these events. One patrol officer described a meeting in which he and his colleagues "were sent in at the beginning to show our faces and meet and greet, but when the meeting started they sent us on our way." Including patrol officers in community meetings gives them a stake in building stronger relations between law enforcement and the community.
- *Set up an open-door policy.* At one site, the chief of police held office hours for community members once a week. He said this policy allowed him to engage community members in "one-on-one dialogue."
- *Schedule community meetings for suitable times.* Often, certain times—such as Friday prayer for Arab-Muslim communities—are not suitable for community meetings.

Create a police-community liaison position. By registering complaints, giving advice or just meeting with community members, liaison officers can address potential problems before they intensify and require the intervention of patrol officers. The status of liaison officers varies from one location to another. Some are appointed by the chief of police or another administrator, while others assume the role on their own initiative and work in a more informal capacity. In creating a liaison position, agencies will want to consider the following points:

- *Get institutional support and backing of the police chief.* Liaison officers who report directly to the police chief and enjoy the institutional support of the department are the most effective in building trust between law enforcement and the Arab-American community. Because these officers are freed from their regular duties, they can focus all of their time and energy on community concerns.
- *Promote visibility and accessibility.* A successful liaison officer is accessible to the community. One effective liaison officer gave out his cell phone number, home number and e-mail address, and set up a website where the community could learn about the police department and send questions to the department. Holding office hours in the community is another way to increase accessibility.
- *Foster a connection to the community.* The liaison officer needs to be culturally competent. Most of the liaison officers interviewed for this study either spoke Arabic or were of Arab descent.

Recruit within Arab-American communities. Officers and community members agreed that having more Arab-Americans on the police force would help overcome fear of law enforcement. In jurisdictions with little precedent for cooperation between law enforcement and the community, recruitment efforts are likely to be greeted with suspicion. "I've seen ads for officer recruitment in our local Arabic newspapers," one community member told researchers. "Why didn't they want to recruit us before?"

The following measures are likely to boost recruitment among Arab-Americans:

- *Focus on young people.* Because young people are less likely to have had negative experiences with law enforcement, reaching out to them by having officers work in schools can help break down barriers.
- *Translate recruiting materials into Arabic.* At one site, the police department translated recruiting materials into Arabic and gave them out at police-community forums.

Be aware that officers may face skepticism when they first reach out to communities. Cultural training programs, advisory councils, regular meetings with the community and other outreach efforts all help build trust. However, officers should be prepared to face some skepticism when they first reach out to the Arab-American community. If their commitment is genuine, even skeptics can be won over.

Lack of Cultural Awareness

Many community leaders stressed the need for improved cultural awareness among law enforcement personnel. Police officers also felt that a deeper knowledge of Arab-American culture would make it easier to respond to calls and mediate disputes.

Setting up cultural awareness training and education is one promising practice. Law enforcement agencies have traditionally responded to their officers' changing vocational needs by offering comprehensive training programs. Such programs are well-suited to educating officers about Arab-American culture. When asked what makes a cultural awareness program effective, officers stressed that it must be both practical and relevant to their everyday work. In particular, officers wanted to learn more about the following topics:

- Islam and religious practices.
- Arab culture.
- Basic Arabic words and phrases.
- Cultural considerations when questioning someone.
- Cultural considerations when arresting someone.

The most successful training programs set the following goals:

Collaborate with the community. Leaders from the local Arab-American community played a role in developing the training programs that were most effective. Programs that are developed this way are better equipped to address a community's specific needs. Because many community leaders are eager and willing to teach others about Islam and Arab culture, they are valuable partners.

Reach rank-and-file officers. Cultural awareness programs need to target the patrol officers who work with the Arab-American community regularly. At one site, an officer remarked that relations between law enforcement administrators and the community were good, but that "among the rank and file there are serious problems . . . local police officers do not know the community."

Bring training sessions into the community. In one innovative training program, officers left the classroom to visit local Arab-American and American Muslim communities. Officers met with community members and visited a mosque.

Language Barriers

Reaching out to those with limited knowledge of English is important, especially for agencies that serve communities with large immigrant populations. Although language barriers can significantly undermine police-community relations, most barriers can be effectively broken down through simple measures.[4] Community leaders are often willing to help out with translation or language training. Inviting them to do so strengthens relations between the local community and law enforcement.

Offer basic language training. For officers working in Arab-American neighborhoods, basic language training is essential. As one community member explained, "The new immigrant hardly speaks any English. When they encounter an officer, they cannot understand them and that causes a problem."

Encourage officers to learn Arabic. Some police departments offer incentives (such as compensatory time) for officers who enroll in Spanish classes. It makes sense to do the same for those who study Arabic.

Provide incentives for Arabic-speaking officers. In police departments across the country, Spanish-speaking officers receive pay bonuses. However, none of the police departments under study offered bonuses for Arabic speakers.

Translate written materials and provide interpreters. Having Arabic interpreters at community meetings and providing Arabic translations of commonly used forms and informational pamphlets is helpful.

Concerns about Immigration Status and Fear of Deportation

Many community leaders expressed concern about the involvement of local law enforcement agencies in immigration enforcement. They noted that threats of deportation or other forms of pressure related to immigration status have been used to seek information. As a result, they said, some members of the community hesitate to report crimes.

Survey responses favored one practice: set up clear and consistent policies. Because immigration and counterterrorism enforcement practices vary from one police department to another, and even from one FBI field office to another, many Arab-Americans are unclear about the enforcement practices of their local police. This lack of clarity can significantly undermine a department's ability to build strong community ties. As one community leader explained, "The police need to establish ground rules. We don't know what the local and federal police will and won't do." Local police departments should carefully consider whether to engage in immigration enforcement, and then communicate their policies to the community. They should also develop policies against racial profiling or, if they already have such policies, reinforce them.

What Can Communities Do?

Efforts by law enforcement organizations are unlikely to succeed without active involvement from the community itself. Law enforcement agencies and communities need to work together. As one community leader put it, "We have to educate [the police] about our culture, and they have to educate us about [police] culture." The research suggests several activities for community leaders who want to reach out to local law enforcement agencies:

Start making contacts with law enforcement. Community leaders can invite police officials to events in the community and attend precinct or station meetings in the neighborhood.

Offer cultural and linguistic support services. Leaders can offer to help develop culturally suitable training materials for police officers. They can help lead training sessions that focus on cultural awareness and offer translation services.

Help with recruiting efforts. Leaders can work with law enforcement on recruiting initiatives in their communities.

Promote community awareness about police practices. Leaders can take part in training sessions the police department offers for community members. They can tell the community about such topics as local laws and codes, and how and when to contact the police.

Lobby for a liaison position. Leaders can let their local police department know that a liaison officer would help build trust, and identify community leaders who might fill such a role informally.

Strengthen community organization within and across communities. Leaders can build community solidarity and reach out to other communities in their area. Law enforcement agencies look for strong community leaders who are easily identifiable.

Renewed dedication to the principles of community policing can lead to positive, trusting relations between law enforcement and the Arab-American community—even in the current environment of concern about national security. Both groups want improved relations, and both groups agree that the practices outlined here are a good place to start.

Notes

1. Henderson, Nicole J., Christopher W. Ortiz, Naomi F. Sugie, and Joel Miller, *Law Enforcement & Arab American Community Relations After September 11, 2001: Engagement in a Time of Uncertainty.* New York: Vera Institute of Justice, 2006. Available online at http://www.vera.org/publication_pdf/353_636.pdf.

2. Naber, N., "Ambiguous Insiders: An Investigation of Arab American Invisibility," *Ethnic and Racial Studies* 23 (2000): 37–61.

3. See Davis, Robert C., and Nicole J. Henderson, "Willingness to Report Crimes: The Role of Ethnic Group Membership and Community Efficacy," *Crime and Delinquency* 49 (4) (October 2003): 564–580; Pogrebin, M.A., and E.D. Poole, "Culture Conflict and Crime in the Korean-American Community," *Criminal Justice Policy Review* 4 (1990): 69–78; Song, J., "Attitudes of Chinese Immigrants and Vietnamese Refugees Toward Law Enforcement in the United States," *Justice Quarterly* 9 (1992): 703–719.

4. Shah, Susan, Insha Rahman, and Anita Khashu, *Overcoming Language Barriers: Solutions for Law Enforcement,* New York: Vera Institute of Justice, and Washington: U.S. Department of Justice, Office of Community Oriented Policing Services, 2007. Available online at http://www.vera.org/ publication_pdf/ 382_735.pdf.

NICOLE J. HENDERSON, CHRISTOPHER W. ORTIZ, and **NAOMI F. SUGIE** were with the Vera Institute of Justice when this research was conducted. **JOEL MILLER** is currently with the Vera Institute of Justice.

From *National Institute of Justice*, July 2008.

Racial Profiling and Its Apologists

Racist law enforcement is rooted in deceptive statistics, slippery logic, and telling indifference.

TIM WISE

"It's just good police work." So comes the insistence by many—usually whites—that concentrating law enforcement efforts on blacks and Latinos is a perfectly legitimate idea. To listen to some folks tell it, the fact that people of color commit a disproportionate amount of crime (a claim that is true for some but not all offenses) is enough to warrant heightened suspicion of such persons. As for the humiliation experienced by those innocents unfairly singled out, stopped, and searched? Well, they should understand that such mistreatment is the price they'll have to pay, as long as others who look like them are heavily represented in various categories of criminal mischief.

Of course, the attempt to rationalize racism and discriminatory treatment has a long pedigree. Segregationists offer up many "rational" arguments for separation and even slaveowners found high-minded justifications for their control over persons of African descent. In the modern day, excuses for unequal treatment may be more nuanced and couched in calm, dispassionate, even academic jargon; but they remain fundamentally no more legitimate than the claims of racists past. From overt white supremacists to respected social scientists and political commentators, the soft-pedaling of racist law enforcement is a growing cottage industry: one rooted in deceptive statistics, slippery logic, and telling indifference to the victims of such practices.

As demonstrated convincingly in David Harris's new book *Profiles in Injustice: Why Racial Profiling Cannot Work* (New Press, 2002), racial profiling is neither ethically acceptable nor logical as a law enforcement tool. But try telling that to the practice's apologists.

According to racial separatist Jared Taylor of American Renaissance—a relatively highbrow white supremacist organization—black crime rates are so disproportionate relative to those of whites that it is perfectly acceptable for police to profile African Americans in the hopes of uncovering criminal activity. His group's report "The Color of Crime"—which has been touted by mainstream conservatives like Walter Williams—purports to demonstrate just how dangerous blacks are, what with murder, robbery, and assault rates that are considerably

higher than the rates for whites. That these higher crime rates are the result of economic conditions disproportionately faced by people of color Taylor does not dispute in the report. But he insists that the reasons for the disparities hardly matter. All that need be known is that one group is statistically more dangerous than the other and avoiding those persons or stopping them for searches is not evidence of racism, but rather the result of rational calculations by citizens and police.

Although in simple numerical terms, whites commit three times more violent crimes each year than blacks, and whites are five to six times more likely to be attacked by another white person than by a black person, to Taylor, this is irrelevant. As he has explained about these white criminals: "They may be boobs, but they're our boobs."

Likewise, Heather MacDonald of the conservative Manhattan Institute has written that racial profiling is a "myth." Police, according to MacDonald—whose treatment of the subject was trumpeted in a column by George Will last year—merely play the odds, knowing "from experience" that blacks are likely to be the ones carrying drugs.

Michael Levin, a professor of philosophy at the City College of New York, argues it is rational for whites to fear young black men since one in four are either in prison, on probation, or on parole on any given day. According to Levin, the assumption that one in four black males encountered are therefore likely to be dangerous is logical and hardly indicates racism. Levin has also said that blacks should be treated as adults earlier by the justice system because they mature faster and trials should be shorter for blacks because they have a "shorter time horizon."

Conservative commentator Dinesh D'Souza says that "rational discrimination against young black men can be fully eradicated only by getting rid of destructive conduct by the group that forms the basis for statistically valid group distinctions. It is difficult to compel people to admire groups many of whose members do not act admirably."

Even when the profiling turns deadly, conservatives show little concern. Writing about Amadou Diallo, recipient of 19 bullets (out of 41 fired) from the NYPD Street Crimes Unit, columnist Mona Charen explained that he died for the sins of his black brethren, whose criminal proclivities gave the officers good reason to suspect that he was up to no good.

Putting aside the obvious racial hostility that forms the core of many if not all of these statements, racial profiling cannot be justified on the basis of general crime rate data showing that blacks commit a disproportionate amount of certain crimes, relative to their numbers in the population. Before making this point clear, it is worth clarifying what is meant by racial profiling.

Racial profiling means one of two things. First, the over-application of an incident-specific criminal description in a way that results in the stopping, searching, and harassment of people based solely or mostly on skin color alone. An example would be the decision by police in one upstate New York college town a few years ago to question every black male in the local university after an elderly white woman claimed to have been raped by a black man (turns out he was white).

So while there is nothing wrong with stopping black men who are 6'2", 200 pounds, driving Ford Escorts, if the perp in a particular local crime is known to be 6'2", 200 pounds, and driving a Ford Escort, but when that description is used to randomly stop black men, even who aren't 6'2", aren't close to 200 pounds, and who are driving totally different cars, then that becomes a problem.

The second and more common form of racial profiling is the disproportionate stopping, searching, frisking, and harassment of people of color in the hopes of uncovering a crime, even when there is no crime already in evidence for which a particular description might be available. In other words: stopping black folks or Latinos and searching for drugs.

This is why general crime rates are irrelevant to the profiling issue. Police generally don't randomly stop and search people in the hopes of turning up last night's convenience store hold-up man. They tend to have more specific information to go on in those cases. As such, the fact that blacks commit a higher share of some crimes (robbery, murder, assault) than their population numbers is of no consequence to the issue of whether profiling them is legitimate. The "crime" for which people of color are being profiled mostly is drug possession. In that case, people of color are not a disproportionate number of violators and police do not find such contraband disproportionately on people of color.

All available evidence indicates that whites are equally or more likely to use (and thus possess at any given time) illegal narcotics. This is especially true for young adults and teenagers, in which categories whites are disproportionate among users.

Although black youth and young adults are more likely than white youth to have been approached by someone offering to give them or sell them drugs during the past month, they are less likely to have actually used drugs in the last 30 days. Among adults, data from California is instructive: although whites over the age of 30 are only 36 percent of the state's population, they comprise 60 percent of all heavy drug users in the state.

Although blacks and Latinos often control large drug sale networks, roughly eight in ten drug busts are not for dealing, but for possession. Drug busts for narcotics trafficking rarely stem from random searches of persons or vehicles—the kind of practice rightly labeled profiling—but rather, tend to take place after a carefully devised sting operation and intelligence gathering, leading to focused law enforcement efforts. As such, the usage numbers are the more pertinent when discussing the kinds of police stops and searches covered by the pejorative label of "profiling."

A Department of Justice study released in 2001 notes that although blacks are twice as likely as whites to have their cars stopped and searched, police are actually twice as likely to find evidence of illegal activity in cars driven by whites.

In New Jersey, for 2000, although blacks and Latinos were 78 percent of persons stopped and searched on the southern portion of the Jersey Turnpike, police were twice as likely to discover evidence of illegal activity in cars driven by whites, relative to blacks, and whites were five times more likely to be in possession of drugs, guns, or other illegal items relative to Latinos. In North Carolina, black drivers are two-thirds more likely than whites to be stopped and searched by the State Highway Patrol, but contraband is discovered in cars driven by whites 27 percent more often.

In New York City, even after controlling for the higher crime rates by blacks and Latinos and local demographics (after all, people of color will be the ones stopped and searched most often in communities where they make up most of the residents), police are still two to three times more likely to search them than whites. Yet, police hunches about who is in possession of drugs, guns, other illegal contraband, or who is wanted for commission of a violent crime turn out to be horribly inaccurate. Despite being stopped and searched more often, blacks and Latinos are less likely to be arrested because they are less likely to be found with evidence of criminal wrongdoing.

So much for MacDonald's "rational" police officers, operating from their personal experiences. Despite police claims that they only stop and search people of color more often because such folks engage in suspicious behavior more often, if the "hit rates" for such persons are no higher than, and even lower than the rates for whites, this calls into question the validity of the suspicious action criteria. If blacks seem suspicious more often, but are actually hiding something less often, then by definition the actions deemed suspicious should be reexamined, as they are not proving to be logical at all, let alone the result of good police work. Indeed, they appear to be proxies for racial stops and searches.

Nor can the disproportionate stopping of black vehicles be justified by differential driving behavior. Every study done on the subject has been clear: there are no significant differences between people of color and whites when it comes to the commission of moving or other violations. Police acknowledge that virtually every driver violates any number of minor laws every time they take to the road. But these violations are not enforced equally and that is the problem.

In one New Jersey study, for example, despite no observed differences in driving behavior, African Americans were 73 percent of all drivers stopped on the Jersey Turnpike, despite being less than 14 percent of the drivers on the road: a rate that is 27 times greater than what would be expected by random chance. Similar results were found in a study of stops in Maryland. On a particular stretch of Interstate 95 in Florida, known for being a drug trafficking route, blacks and Latinos comprise only 5 percent of drivers, but 70 percent of those stopped by members of the Highway Patrol. These stops were hardly justified, as only nine drivers, out of 1,100 stopped during the study, were ever ticketed for any violation, let alone arrested for possession of illegal contraband.

As for Levin's claim that whites should properly consider one in four black males encountered to be a threat to their personal safety, because of their involvement with the criminal justice system, it should be remembered that most of these have been arrested for non-violent offenses like drug possession. Blacks comprise 35 percent of all possession arrests and 75 percent of those sent to prison for a drug offense, despite being only 14 percent of users.

When it comes to truly dangerous violent crime, only a miniscule share of African Americans will commit such offenses in a given year and less than half of these will choose a white victim.

With about 1.5 million violent crimes committed by blacks each year (about 90 percent of these by males) and 70 percent of the crimes committed by just 7 percent of the offenders—a commonly accepted figure by criminologists—this means that less than 2 percent of blacks over age 12 (the cutoff for collecting crime data) and less than 3.5 percent of black males over 12 could even theoretically be considered dangerous. Less than 1.5 percent of black males will attack a white person in a given year, hardly lending credence to Levin's claim about the rationality of white panic.

The fact remains that the typical offender in violent crime categories is white. So even if black rates are disproportionate to their population percentages, any "profile" that tends to involve a black or Latino face is likely to be wrong more than half the time. Whites commit roughly 60 percent of violent crimes, for example. So if 6 in 10 violent criminals are white, how logical could it be to deploy a profile—either for purposes of law enforcement or merely personal purposes of avoiding certain people—that is only going to be correct 40 percent of the time? So too with drugs, where any profile that involves a person of color will be wrong three out of four times?

Additionally, the apologists for profiling are typically selective in terms of the kinds of profiling they support. Although whites are a disproportionate percentage of all drunk drivers, for example, and although drunk driving contributes to the deaths of more than 10,000 people each year, none of the defenders of anti-black or brown profiling suggests that drunk driving roadblocks be set up in white suburbs where the "hit rates" for catching violators would be highest.

Likewise, though white college students are considerably more likely to binge drink (often underage) and use narcotics than college students of color, no one suggests that police or campus cops should regularly stage raids on white fraternity houses or dorm rooms occupied by whites, even though the raw data would suggest such actions might be statistically justified.

Whites are also nearly twice as likely to engage in child sexual molestation, relative to blacks. Yet how would the Heather MacDonalds and Dinesh D'Souzas of the world react to an announcement that adoption agencies were going to begin screening out white couples seeking to adopt, or subjecting them to extra scrutiny, as a result of such factual information?

Similarly, those seeking to now justify intensified profiling of Arabs or Muslims since September 11 were hardly clamoring for the same treatment of white males in the wake of Oklahoma City. Even now, in the wake of anthrax incidents that the FBI says have almost certainly been domestic, possibly white supremacist in origin, no one is calling for heightened suspicion of whites as a result.

The absurdity of anti-Arab profiling is particularly obvious in the case of trying to catch members of al-Qaeda. The group, after all, operates in 64 countries, many of them non-Arab, and from which group members would not look anything like the image of a terrorist currently locked in the minds of so many. Likewise, Richard Reid, the would-be shoe bomber recently captured was able to get on the plane he sought to bring down precisely because he had a "proper English name," likely spoke with a proper English accent, and thus, didn't fit the description.

The bottom line is that racial profiling doesn't happen because data justifies the practice, but rather because those with power are able to get away with it, and find it functional to do so as a mechanism of social control over those who are less powerful. By typifying certain "others" as dangerous or undesirable, those seeking to maintain divisions between people whose economic and social interests are actually quite similar can successfully maintain those cleavages.

No conspiracy here, mind you: just the system working as intended, keeping people afraid of one another and committed to the maintenance of the system, by convincing us that certain folks are a danger to our well-being, which then must be safeguarded by a growing prison-industrial complex and draconian legal sanctions; or in the case of terrorist "profiles," by the imposition of unconstitutional detentions, beefed-up military and intelligence spending, and the creation of a paranoiac wartime footing.

Until and unless the stereotypes that underlie racial profiling are attacked and exposed as a fraud, the practice will likely continue: not because it makes good sense, but because racist assumptions about danger—reinforced by media and politicians looking for votes—lead us to think that it does.

TIM WISE is a Nashville-based writer, lecturer and antiracist activist. Footnotes for this article can be obtained at tjwise@mindspring.com.

Our Oath of Office: A Solemn Promise

JONATHAN L. RUDD

Early in the morning, on their first full day at the FBI Academy, 50 new-agent trainees, dressed in conservative suits and more than a little anxious about their new careers, stand as instructed by the assistant director of the FBI and raise their right hands. In unison, the trainees repeat the following words as they are sworn in as employees of the federal government:

> I [name] do solemnly swear (or affirm) that I will support and defend the Constitution of the United States against all enemies, foreign and domestic; that I will bear true faith and allegiance to the same; that I take this obligation freely, without any mental reservation or purpose of evasion; and that I will well and faithfully discharge the duties of the office on which I am about to enter. So help me God.

At the end of their academy training, and as part of the official graduation ceremony, these same new-agent trainees once again will stand, raise their right hands, and repeat the same oath. This time, however, the oath will be administered by the director of the FBI, and the trainees will be sworn in as special agents of the Federal Bureau of Investigation.[1] Similar types of ceremonies are conducted in every state, by every law enforcement agency, for every officer across the country. And, each officer promises to do one fundamentally important thing—support and defend the Constitution of the United States.

All too often in our culture, we participate in ceremonies and follow instructions without taking the time to contemplate and understand the meaning and significance of our actions. This article attempts to shed some light on the purpose and history of the oath and to further enhance our understanding of the Constitution that we as law enforcement officers solemnly swear to uphold.

Origins of the Oath

The idea of taking an oath in support of a government, ruler, or cause was not new to the founding fathers. The practice stems from ancient times and was common in England and in the American colonies. "During the American Revolution, General George Washington required all officers to subscribe to an oath renouncing any allegiance to King George III and pledging their fidelity to the United States."[2]

When asked where the requirement that all law enforcement officers take an oath to support and defend the Constitution comes from, some have speculated that it is linked to the presidential oath found in the Constitution.[3] They reason that because the president is the chief executive and law enforcement officers are generally seen as members of the executive branch of government, the requirement to take an oath is inferred from Article II of the Constitution. Others assume that it comes from statutes enacted by Congress and the various state legislatures. Most are surprised to learn that the requirement to take an oath is found in the Constitution itself. Article VI mandates that both federal and state officers of all three branches of government (legislative, executive, and judicial) take an oath to support the Constitution of the United States.

> The Senators and Representatives [. . .], and the Members of the several State Legislatures, and all executive and judicial Officers, both of the United States and of the several States, shall be bound by Oath or Affirmation, to support this Constitution [. . .].[4]

Wording of the Oath

Unlike the presidential oath, the particular wording of this oath is not delineated in the Constitution, merely the requirement that an oath be taken. As suspected, the wording of the oath has been formulated by the federal and state legislatures.

The significance the founding generation placed on the requirement to take an oath as mandated in Article VI is highlighted by the fact that the very first act of the first Congress of the United States was to establish a simple 14-word oath: "I do solemnly swear (or affirm) that I will support the Constitution of the United States."[5]

From the founding of our new government until the Civil War era, this simple oath adequately served its intended purpose. However, in April 1861, in light of the conflicts surrounding the Civil War, President Abraham Lincoln demanded that all federal, executive branch employees take an expanded oath in support of the Union. Shortly thereafter, at an emergency session of Congress, legislation was enacted requiring all employees to take the expanded oath. By the end of the year, Congress had revised the expanded oath and added a new section, creating what came to be known as the Ironclad Test Oath or Test Oath.[6] "The war-inspired Test Oath, signed into law on July 2, 1862, required 'every person elected or appointed to any office . . . under the Government of the United States . . . excepting the President of the United States' to swear or affirm that they had never previously engaged in criminal or disloyal conduct."[7]

As early as 1868, Congress created an alternative oath for individuals unable to take the Test Oath "on account of their participation in the late rebellion."[8] Nearly two decades later, Congress repealed the Test Oath and mandated the federal oath of office we have today.[9] This oath, taken by most federal employees, can be found in Title 5, U.S. Code, § 3331.[10]

State officers, on the other hand, are required by federal statute to take the original oath first promulgated in 1789.[11] In addition to this requirement, state constitutions and legislatures have generally added words and sentiments appropriate to their respective states. One obvious addition is the dual requirement to support and defend not only the federal Constitution but also the constitution and laws of the individual state.[12]

Meaning of the Oath

At the core of each of these oaths, whether the federal oath in its current form or the various state oaths with their additional obligations, lies the simple language put forth by our first Congress: "I do solemnly swear that I will support and defend the Constitution of the United States."

A brief analysis of these words and their meanings may help to solidify their significance. "I . . . "—an individual, person, citizen, one member of the whole, officer; "do"—perform, accomplish, act, carry out, complete, achieve, execute; "solemnly"—somberly, gravely, seriously, earnestly, sincerely, firmly, fervently, with thought and ceremony; "swear (or affirm)[13]"—vow, pledge, promise, guarantee; "that I will"—a positive phrase confirming present and future action, momentum, determination, resolve, responsibility, willpower, and intention; "support"—uphold, bear, carry, sustain, maintain; "and defend"—protect, guard, preserve, secure, shield, look after; "the Constitution of the United States."

The Constitution of the United States

It is significant that we take an oath to support and defend the Constitution and not an individual leader, ruler, office, or entity. This is true for the simple reason that the Constitution is based on lasting principles of sound government that provide balance, stability, and consistency through time. A government based on individuals—who are inconsistent, fallible, and often prone to error—too easily leads to tyranny on the one extreme or anarchy on the other. The founding fathers sought to avoid these extremes and create a balanced government based on constitutional principles.

The American colonists were all too familiar with the harmful effects of unbalanced government and oaths to individual rulers. For example, the English were required to swear loyalty to the crown, and many of the early colonial documents commanded oaths of allegiance to the king.[14] The founding fathers saw that such a system was detrimental to the continued liberties of a free people. A study of both ancient and modern history illustrates this point. One fairly recent example can be seen in the oaths of Nazi Germany. On August 19, 1934, 90 percent of Germany voted for Hitler to assume complete power. The very next day, Hitler's cabinet decreed the Law On the Allegiance of Civil Servants and Soldiers of the Armed Forces. This law abolished all former oaths and required that all soldiers and public servants declare an oath of unquestioned obedience to "Adolf Hitler, Fuhrer of the German Reich and people."[15] Although many of the officers in Hitler's regime came to realize the error of his plans, they were reluctant to stop him because of the oath of loyalty they had taken to the Fuhrer.[16]

The founding fathers diligently sought to avoid the mistakes of other nations and, for the first time in history, form a balanced government where freedom could reign. To appreciate this ideal, we first must acknowledge what some have called the preface or architectural blueprint to the Constitution—the Declaration of Independence.[17] "While the Declaration of Independence, as promulgated on July 4, 1776, did not bring this nation into existence or establish the government of the United States of America, it magnificently enunciated the fundamental principles of republican or constitutional government—principals that are not stated explicitly in the Constitution itself."[18] The essence of these fundamental principles were memorialized when Thomas Jefferson penned the famous words

> We hold these truths to be self-evident, that all men are created equal, that they are endowed by their Creator with certain unalienable Rights, that among these are Life, Liberty and the pursuit of Happiness. That to secure these rights, Governments are instituted among Men, deriving their just powers from the consent of the governed. . . .[19]

Once the colonists declared their independence from Great Britain, they knew they needed a form of government that would keep the 13 colonies united. However, many were skeptical of creating a central government that would destroy their independence as separate and sovereign states. The result was the creation of the Articles of Confederation and Perpetual Union, which lasted only 7 years. This document provided for a weak legislative body and no judicial or executive branch.

Although some have referred to the Articles of Confederation as America's first constitution, it never was given that status by the colonists. American colonists were familiar with, and placed great emphasis on, the supremacy of written constitutions. Immediately following the Declaration of Independence, in addition to creating the Articles of Confederation, 11 of the 13 colonies drafted and ratified state constitutions. The inferiority of the Articles of Confederation can be seen by the fact that "[m]ost of the new state constitutions included elaborate oaths that tied allegiance to and provided a summary of the basic constitutional principles animating American constitutionalism. There was no oath in the Articles of Confederation."[20]

> The Articles of Confederation provided the Federal Government with too little authority to maintain law, order and equality among the new states. So America's best minds came together once again in Philadelphia, where they had declared their independence from Britain 11 years before, and hammered together a far better government for themselves, creating a Constitution that has served Americans well for more than 200 years now.[21]

The Constitution was not miraculously formulated by ideas invented by the founding fathers during the Constitutional Convention. To the contrary, in the years preceding the "Miracle at Philadelphia," Thomas Jefferson, James Madison, Benjamin Franklin, Samuel Adams, John Adams, John Jay, Alexander Hamilton, George Wythe, James Wilson, and others made every effort to study and comprehend the nature and politics of truly free government.[22] During the Revolutionary War, John Adams wrote the following to his wife:

> The science of government is my duty to study, more than all other sciences; the arts of legislation and administration and

negotiation ought to take [the] place of, indeed to exclude, in manner, all other arts. I must study politics and war, that my sons may have liberty to study mathematics and philosophy. My sons ought to study mathematics and philosophy, geography, natural history and naval architecture, navigation, commerce, and agriculture, in order to give their children the right to study painting, poetry, music, architecture, statuary, tapestry, and porcelain.[23]

Based on these studies and the collective wisdom of these men, the Constitution our founding fathers created was an amazingly concise, yet comprehensive, document. Comprising a mere seven articles, it embodies the fundamental principles of popular sovereignty, separation of powers, and federalism, allows for a process of amendment, and provides a system of checks and balances. A closer look at these principles and how they apply to law enforcement today may be instructive.

The Preamble and Popular Sovereignty

It has been said that the Preamble sets forth the goals or purposes of the Constitution.[24] When read from the perspective of a law enforcement officer, the purposes described therein could be seen as a mission statement for today's law enforcement community.

> . . . in Order to form a more perfect Union, establish Justice, insure domestic Tranquility, provide for the common defense, promote the general Welfare, and secure the Blessings of Liberty to ourselves and our Posterity. . . .

The opening and closing words of the Preamble—"We the people of the United States [. . .] do ordain and establish this Constitution for the United States of America"—embrace the idea of "popular sovereignty," a government ordained and established by the consent of the people. From the outset, then, we see that this new government was to be different from any government then in existence. It was not a monarchy where the rule of one could easily lead to tyranny; it was not an aristocracy where the rule of a privileged few could descend into oligarchy, nor was it even to be a pure democracy where mob rule could slip into anarchy.[25] The American dream was to be founded on a constitutional republic where elected representatives swear to uphold the Constitution as they serve at the will and by the consent of the people. This was something "[s]o rare that some historians maintain it has been accomplished only three times during all of human history: Old Testament Israel, the Golden Age of Greece, and the era of emergence of the United States of America."[26]

Separation of Powers and Federalism

The structure of the Constitution itself emphasizes the principle of separation of powers. Article I established the legislative branch with the power to make laws; Article II, the executive branch with the authority to enforce the laws; and Article III, the judicial branch with jurisdiction over legal disputes. "It is important to note that the Constitution in no way granted the federal courts the power of judicial review, or an ultimate interpretive power over the constitutional issues. Modern federal courts possess this

huge power thanks to a long series of precedents beginning with the 1803 case of Marbury v. Madison."[27] Under the doctrine of separation of powers, each branch of government specializes in its particular area of expertise with no one branch having ultimate power over the whole.

Another aspect of the separation of powers, which is of significance to law enforcement today, is the principle of federalism. Federalism is a legal and political system where the national or federal government shares power with the state governments while each maintains some degree of sovereignty.[28] The Constitution helps to delineate the roles of the federal government by spelling out, to some degree, its limited powers, which are outlined in the first three Articles. Section 10 of Article I also places specific, limited restrictions on the states; however, these restrictions actually serve to emphasize the powers reserved exclusively to the federal government (e.g., the power to make treaties with other nations). Article IV delineates a few fundamental requirements incumbent upon state governments, as well as guaranteeing to each state a republican form of government. Other than the limited guidance given to the states, the Constitution does not direct the states on the establishment and functions of state governments. The idea is that there are certain limited activities the federal government is best situated to handle; there are other activities that are best left to the states; and still others best dealt with by counties, cities, families, and individuals.

Under this system of government, the founding fathers realized that conflicts between state and federal jurisdiction would arise. Accordingly, in Article VI of the Constitution, they designated the Constitution itself and other federal laws as "the supreme Law of the Land."[29] This clause (known as the supremacy clause) serves as a "conflict-of-laws rule specifying that certain national acts take priority over any state acts that conflict with national law."[30]

The Bill of Rights and the Fourteenth Amendment

Although the federal government was intended to be a government of limited powers, there were many who feared the inevitable expansion of those powers, particularly in light of the supremacy clause. Without the promise of a Bill of Rights limiting the power of the federal government, the Constitution never would have been ratified. Accordingly, "a total of 189 suggested amendments were submitted to [the first] Congress. James Madison boiled these down to 17, but the Congress approved only 12 of them."[31] The states ended up ratifying 10 as amendments to the Constitution, which became known as the Bill of Rights.

Included within the Bill of Rights are a number of provisions that have had a great impact on criminal law enforcement. In particular, the First Amendment freedoms of religion, speech, press, and assembly; the Fourth Amendment restrictions on unreasonable searches and seizures; the Fifth Amendment protection against compelled self-incrimination; and the Sixth Amendment guarantee of the right to counsel in all criminal prosecutions. The Bill of Rights, however, initially served only as a limitation on the federal government and did not apply to the states. While states had their own state constitutions with their own bills of rights, individual state officers were not bound to provide the protections afforded the people under the federal Constitution. This changed, however, with the adoption of the Fourteenth Amendment in 1868, just 3 years after the end of the Civil War.[32]

Over time, via the Fourteenth Amendment's due process clause, the Supreme Court has selectively incorporated most of the provisions of the Bill of Rights and applied them to the states, thereby unifying fundamental criminal procedure law throughout the United States.

> Today, every law enforcement academy in America provides training in constitutional law, because virtually every aspect of an officer's job touches that area where the authority of government and the liberty of the individual meet. Arrests, searches and seizures, investigative detentions, eyewitness identification, interrogations—all of these everyday law enforcement tasks, and more, are governed by the Federal Constitution. Under their own constitutions, the States may provide greater protections to their people; but by virtue of the Due Process Clause of the 14th amendment, they cannot provide less.[33]

Due, in part, to major paradigm shifts regarding the rights and freedoms of individuals, which gained momentum during the Civil War, the enactment of the Fourteenth Amendment and the Supreme Court's interpretation of its due process clause, and the many advances in the area of technology, communication, and transportation, the federalism that prevailed in the first half of our country's existence is very different from the federalism of today. "Since the New Deal of the 1930s, more and more areas of American law, government, and life have crossed an invisible line from state responsibility into the federal domain."[34] While some lament the far-reaching power of today's federal government, in the area of law enforcement, most of these changes have been welcome, particularly when they have allowed local, state, and federal law enforcement agencies to pool their resources and fight crime, which itself continues to defy jurisdictional boundaries.

Checks and Balances

Finally, the founding fathers built a system of checks and balances into the Constitution, whereby the executive, legislative, and judiciary would check and balance each other and state governments would balance the federal while it, in turn, would maintain a check on the states.[35] When considering our system of checks and balances, obvious examples surface, such as when the president (executive) nominates judges to serve on the Supreme Court (judicial) with the advice and consent of the Senate (legislative). However, nowhere is the use and effect of checks and balances more poignantly illustrated than in the everyday lives of today's law enforcement officers. For example, when officers determine that they have enough probable cause to search a home or make an arrest, barring special limited circumstances, they do not execute the search or arrest of their own accord and based on their singular authority as members of the executive branch. To the contrary, they seek the review and approval of a neutral and detached magistrate—a member of the judicial branch. Even though they may not realize it, every time officers prepare an affidavit and request approval of a warrant, they are engaging in the process of checks and balances so painstakingly advanced by our founding fathers over two centuries ago.

While debates were raging among colonists over whether or not to ratify the Constitution, which had recently been adopted by the Constitutional Convention, the father of the Constitution, James Madison, wrote the following insightful words:

> Ambition must be made to counteract ambition. The interest of the man must be connected with the constitutional rights of the place. . . . If men were angels, no government would be necessary. If angels were to govern men, neither external nor internal controls on government would be necessary. In framing a government which is to be administered by men over men, the great difficulty lies in this: you must first enable the government to control the governed; and in the next place oblige it to control itself.[36]

The most fundamental of the many checks and balances in our system of government is the power to control oneself. At no time is a commitment to this principle more eloquently expressed than when individual officers raise their hands and solemnly swear to support and defend the Constitution of the United States. May all of us do so with a firm understanding of the principles we have determined to defend and a clear recognition of the people we promise to protect.

Conclusion

We owe an incomparable debt of gratitude to the men and women who fought to bring us the Constitution, and those who have fought to preserve it to this day. In memory of the federal, state, and local law enforcement officers who have made the ultimate sacrifice in the service of this country, may we read the words of President Lincoln anew and rededicate our lives to the privilege of protecting and defending the Constitution of the United States.

> Four score and seven years ago our fathers brought forth on this continent a new nation, conceived in liberty and dedicated to the proposition that all men are created equal.
>
> Now we are engaged in a great civil war, testing whether that nation, or any nation so conceived and so dedicated, can long endure. We are met on a great battlefield of that war. We have come to dedicate a portion of that field as a final resting place for those who here gave their lives that that nation might live. It is altogether fitting and proper that we should do this.
>
> But in a larger sense, we cannot dedicate—we cannot consecrate—we cannot hallow—this ground. The brave men, living and dead, who struggled here have consecrated it far above our poor power to add or detract. The world will little note nor long remember what we say here, but it can never forget what they did here. It is for us the living, rather, to be dedicated here to the unfinished work which they who fought here have thus far so nobly advanced.
>
> It is rather for us to be here dedicated to the great task remaining before us—that from these honored dead we take increased devotion to that cause for which they gave the last full measure of devotion; that we here highly resolve that these dead shall not have died in vain; that this nation, under God, shall have a new birth of freedom; and that government of the people, by the people, for the people shall not perish from the earth.[37]

Notes

1. 5 U.S.C. § 3331, infra at endnote 10. See also 5 U.S.C. § 2905 (a) which leaves the decision of whether or not to renew the oath due to a change in status to the discretion of the head of the executive agency.

2. Edwin Meese III et al. eds., 2005, *The Heritage Guide to the Constitution*, Article VI, Oaths Clause by Matthew Spalding, 294–295.

3. *U.S. Const.*, art. II, § 1, cl. 8, which states

   Before he enter on the Execution of his Office, he shall take the following Oath or Affirmation:—"I do solemnly swear (or affirm) that I will faithfully execute the Office of President of the United States, and will to the best of my ability, preserve, protect and defend the Constitution of the United States."

   (For insight regarding whether or not George Washington added the words so help me God to the end of the oath of office he took in 1789, see Forrester Church, *So Help Me God: The Founding Fathers and the First Great Battle Over Church and State*, 2007, 445.).

4. *U.S. Const.*, art. VI, cl. 3.

5. *United States Statutes at Large*, Vol. I, Statute I, Chapter 1, §§ 1–5, June 1, 1789, which, in pertinent part reads

   STATUTE I.
   Chapter I.—An Act to regulate the Time and Manner of administering certain Oaths.

   Sec. 1. Be it enacted by the Senate and [House of] Representatives of the United States of America in Congress assembled. That the oath or affirmation required by the sixth article of the Constitution of the United States, shall be administered in the form following, to wit: "I, A.B. do solemnly swear or affirm (as the case may be) that I will support the Constitution of the United States." [. . .]

   Sec. 3. And be it further enacted, That the members of the several State legislatures [. . .], and all executive and judicial officers of the several States, who have been heretofore chosen or appointed, or who shall be chosen or appointed [. . .] shall, before they proceed to execute the duties of their respective offices, take the foregoing oath or affirmation [. . .].

   Sec. 4. And be it further enacted, That all officers appointed, or hereafter to be appointed under the authority of the United States, shall, before they act in their respective offices, take the same oath or affirmation [. . .].

6. *Revised Statutes of the United States: First Session of the 43rd Congress*, 1873–74, Part 1, 1st Edition, 1875, Title XIX, Section 1756, which states the July 2, 1862, statute as follows:

   Every person elected or appointed to any office of honor or profit, either in the civil, military, or naval service, excepting the President [. . .], shall, before entering upon the duties of such office, and before being entitled to any part of the salary or other emoluments thereof, take and subscribe the following oath: "I, AB, do solemnly swear (or affirm) that I have never voluntarily borne arms against the United States since I have been a citizen thereof; that I have voluntarily

   given no aid, countenance, counsel, or encouragement to persons engaged in armed hostility thereto; that I have neither sought, nor accepted, nor attempted to exercise the functions of any office whatever, under any authority, or pretended authority, in hostility to the United States; that I have not yielded a voluntary support to any pretended government, authority, power, or constitution within the United States, hostile or inimical thereto. And I do further swear (or affirm) that, to the best of my knowledge and ability, I will support and defend the Constitution of the United States against all enemies, foreign and domestic; that I will bear true faith and allegiance to the same; that I take this obligation freely, without any mental reservation or purpose of evasion, and that I will well and faithfully discharge the duties of the office on which I am about to enter, so help me God."

7. U.S. Senate: Oath of Office (http://www.senate.gov/ artandhistory/history/common/briefing/Oath_Office.htm).

8. *Revised Statutes of the United States: First Session of the 43rd Congress*, 1873–74, Part 1, 1st Edition, 1875, Title XIX, Section 1757, which states the July 11, 1868, statute as

   Whenever any person who is not rendered ineligible to office by the provisions of the Fourteenth Amendment to the Constitution is elected or appointed to any office of honor or trust under the Government of the United States, and is not able, on account of his participation in the late rebellion, to take the oath prescribed in the preceding section, he shall, before entering upon the duties of his office, take and subscribe in lieu of that oath the following oath: "I, AB, do solemnly swear (or affirm) that I will support and defend the Constitution of the United States against all enemies, foreign and domestic; that I will bear true faith and allegiance to the same; that I take this obligation freely, without any mental reservation or purpose of evasion, and that I will well and faithfully discharge the duties of the office on which I am about to enter. So help me God."

9. *United States Statutes at Large*, Vol. 23, p. 22, Chapter 46, Sec. 2 (May 13, 1884).

10. 5 U.S.C. § 3331, which states

    An individual, except the President, elected or appointed to an office of honor or profit in the civil service or uniformed services, shall take the following oath: "I, AB, do solemnly swear (or affirm) that I will support and defend the Constitution of the United States against all enemies, foreign and domestic: that I will bear true faith and allegiance to the same; that I take this obligation freely, without any mental reservation or purpose of evasion, and that I will well and faithfully discharge the duties of the office on which I am about to enter. So help me God." This section does not affect other oaths required by law.

11. 4 U.S.C. § 101 (July 30, 1947), which states

    Every member of a State legislature, and every executive and judicial officer of a State, shall, before he proceeds to execute the duties of his office, take an oath in the following form, to wit: "I, AB, do solemnly swear that I will support the Constitution of the United States."

12. For example, see *Constitution of Kentucky* § 228 Oath of Officers [. . .] as ratified and revised 1891

    Members of the General Assembly and all officers, before they enter upon the execution of the duties of their respective offices [. . .], shall take the following oath or affirmation: I do solemnly swear (or affirm, as the case may be) that I will support the Constitution of the United States, and the Constitution of this Commonwealth, and be faithful and true to the Commonwealth of Kentucky so long as I continue a citizen thereof, and that I will faithfully execute, to the best of my ability, the office of_____according to law: and I do further solemnly swear (or affirm) that since the adoption of the present Constitution. I, being a citizen of this State, have not fought a duel with deadly weapons within this State nor out of it. Nor have I sent or accepted a challenge to fight a duel with deadly weapons, nor have I acted as second in carrying a challenge, nor aided or assisted a person thus offending, so help me God.

13. The delegates to the first Congress allowed for the word affirm to be used instead of swear to appease those whose religious beliefs forbid them from taking oaths. See *Heritage Guide*, 295.

14. *Heritage Guide*, 294.

15. William Shirer, *The Rise and Fall of the Third Reich*. New York, NY: Simon & Schuster, 1990, 226–230.

    Service oath for soldiers of the armed forces: "I swear by God this sacred oath that I shall render unconditional obedience to Adolf Hitler, the Fuhrer of the German Reich and people, supreme commander of the armed forces, and that I shall at all limes be ready, as a brave soldier, to give my life for this oath." Service oath for public servants: "I swear: I will be faithful and obedient to Adolf Hitler, Fuhrer of the German Reich and people, to observe the law, and to conscientiously fulfil, my official duties, so help me God."

16. Id.

17. Mortimer J. Adler, *We Hold These Truths: Understanding the Ideas and Ideals of the Constitution*, Collier Books. Macmillan Publishing Company (1987).

18. Id. at 7.

19. *The Declaration of Independence* (July 4, 1776).

20. *Heritage Guide*, 295.

21. *The Making of America: Life, Liberty and the Pursuit of a Nation*, by the Editors of Time, vi.

22. W. Cleon Skousen, *The Making of America: The Substance and Meaning of the Constitution*, The National Center For Constitutional Studies (1986). 41.

23. W. Cleon Skousen, *The Five Thousand Year Leap: 28 Great Ideas that Changed the World* (1981, 2009), p. 146, quoting from Adrienne Koch, ed., *The American Enlightenment*, George Braziller, New York, 1965, 163.

24. "The Preamble was placed in the Constitution more or less as an afterthought. It was not proposed or discussed on the floor of the Constitution. Rather, Gouverneur Morris, a delegate from Pennsylvania who as a member of the Committee of Style actually drafted the near-final text of the Constitution, composed it at the last moment. It was Morris who gave the considered purposes of the Constitution coherent shape, and the Preamble was the capstone of his expository gift. The Preamble did not. in itself, have any substantive legal meaning." *Heritage Guide*, 43.

25. Referencing the teachings of the Greek Historian Polybius who lived from 204 to 122 B.C. as quoted in Skousen, *The Five Thousand Year Leap*, 142.

26. Floyd G. Cullop, *The Constitution of the United States: An Introduction*, Mentor (1999), preface to the third edition. (The United States is the oldest continuous government based on a written constitution in the world.)

27. Larry Schweikart and Michael Allen, *A Patriot's History of the United States: From Columbus's Great Discovery to the War on Terror*, Sentinel, Penguin Group (2004), 117.

28. Lawrence M. Friedman, *American Law: An Introduction*, Second Edition, W. W. Norton & Company (1998), 146.

29. *U.S. Const.*, art. VI, cl. 2.

30. *Heritage Guide*, 291.

31. Skousen, *The Making of America*. 673.

32. John C. Hall, "The Constitution and Criminal Procedure," FBI Law Enforcement Bulletin, September 1986. 24–30.

33. Id. at 30.

34. Friedman. *American Law*, 160.

35. Id, at 161.

36. Charles R. Kesler ed., *The Federalist Papers*, No. 51: The Structure of the Government Must Furnish the Proper Checks and Balances Between the Different Departments (Madison).

37. *The Gettysburg Address*, by President Abraham Lincoln, November 19, 1863.

Law enforcement officers of other than federal jurisdiction who are interested in this article should consult their legal advisors. Some police procedures ruled permissible under federal constitutional law are of questionable legality under state law or are not permitted at all.

Stress Management . . . and the Stress-Proof Vest

DR. ROBERT A. FOX

Police commit suicide at up to three times the national average and are eight times more likely to kill themselves than to become a victim of a homicide. They divorce at double the national average, and up to 25% have alcohol abuse problems. By profession, police officers are at high risk for stress disorders.

It would be convenient to dismiss this data by saying that high-risk individuals select law enforcement as a career, but research suggests otherwise. Most data indicates that the personality profiles of police officers entering the academy differ little from those of the population as a whole.

A survey of more than 10,000 law enforcement officers revealed that more than 90% said their major reason for becoming a cop was "to make a difference." This suggests a desire to help rather than to engage in risky scenarios. So what is wrong with the law enforcement environment?

The answer, in short, is loss of identity. The police officer is a standardized uniform with hat and a stern visage. How many of us really see the face of the officer who has vowed to protect our homes and families? Cops know that they are often dehumanized by the citizenry. They know they are expected to put their lives on the line if necessary. This kind of pressure requires strong support, yet many police officers voice the fear that the department might not back them up if they get into trouble.

While law enforcement spends millions of dollars on body armor, nothing protects the officer from two internal bullets—loss of identity and cynicism. Against these lethal weapons, cops need a "stress vest."

A Paradigm for Stress

Stress is a force that necessitates change. Neither good nor bad, it is simply the energy that presses upon us as we struggle to survive. How we use this energy determines the quality of our lives.

Such energy, used productively, is called eustress, or "good stress;" energy used destructively is termed distress or "bad stress." Burning the midnight oil to study for exams is an example of eustress; staying out all night drinking and partying when you have to get up and go to work the next day is distress. Whether we are happy or unhappy depends on the kinds of stress in our lives, and whether the level of that stress is within our comfort zones.

Eustress meets basic human needs and contributes to wellness, while distress jeopardizes human welfare. When you think of stress, think about the energy we use to enjoy and fulfill ourselves instead of the distress of fear and worry. A productive life is based on a positive outlook, good self-esteem, and discipline, where time and energy are invested in eustress to meet one's personal basic human needs.

The undisciplined person, characterized by low self-esteem and a negative outlook, is prone to gratification that often denies one's basic human needs. A life dominated by distress often leads to cynicism, loss of hope, and an attitude that whatever can go wrong, will.

It's all about outlook and attitude. One can focus on stress as a positive force, as the energy for accomplishment and the enjoyment of all life has to offer, or as a negative force, as the energy needed to combat fear and cynicism, where the only goal seems to be surviving another day. Understanding and fulfilling basic needs is the key. When one uses stress energy in the pursuit of becoming all that one can be, then life is good and fulfilling, and basic needs are met. But when one's needs are thwarted and go unfulfilled, that stress energy may become a destructive force.

Human Beings, Basic Needs and Stress

Every human being has personal, social, occupational and spiritual needs. While healthy human development requires a certain level of satisfaction in each of these areas, the level will differ from person to person. Some people are more social and family-oriented; some are more spiritual; some need greater career satisfaction. In a similar vein, the amount of stress that allows one to function best is highly individual. Let's look at these areas of basic human needs a little more closely.

Personal Wellness: Physical and psychological wellness-safety, security, self-esteem and identity. A healthy person eats right, exercises, gets proper rest, recreates, looks good, feels good, and is vital in every way.

Social Wellness: Family and friends-relationships, communication and intimacy. A socially healthy person is connected to other people and has satisfying relationships.

Occupational Wellness: Purpose and work-love what you do, and do what you love. An occupationally healthy person is capable of giving his best and receives the appreciation and satisfaction that is deserved.

Spiritual Wellness: Meaning of life beyond our understanding and control. A spiritually healthy person has a comfortable understanding of the greater meaning of life and his place in the world. This person lives according to that understanding.

Identity and Cynicism

Police officers rarely get to follow a case from start to finish, so they often feel disconnected and thwarted in terms of satisfaction. Shift work and arbitrary deployment, which are common in police work, further marginalize the individual. Marginalization is common in paramilitary organizations, highly structured, vertical bureaucracies in which orders become more impersonal as they drop from higher levels.

Most veteran police officers agree that it is hard to maintain an individual identity in a profession where one has to wear a uniform and be recognized more in terms of the profession than as an individual. Over time, the powerful "cop culture" tends to obliterate one's civilian identity, and many police officers find themselves becoming alienated from society.

As they lose their sense of identity and control, many become cynical, feeling that no one than other police officers can understand them; this creates an "us against them" mentality. In short, they have become police officers who happen to be human beings rather than human beings who happen to be police officers.

When this occurs, communication with one's spouse, family, and friends outside law enforcement becomes difficult. While the police officer still has personal, social, and spiritual needs as any human, these may be ignored or rationalized in favor of the police identity.

Social and esteem needs, including praise and acceptance, may now be sought from police management and colleagues instead of from family and friends. Cynicism may obliterate spiritual needs. For many, personal wellness may be ignored or even undercut by socially accepted—but often destructive—behaviors within the "cop culture," such as drinking together after hours.

Police officers with strong personalities can be hard to control. But police officers are not soldiers, even though law enforcement was largely based and modeled on military culture. Each police officer, after his shift, is expected to go back into that very community as one of its functioning members. And this is where identity conflicts will often occur.

How, then, can the job help people develop and maintain stronger personal identities? How can law enforcement managers encourage police officers to take care of their personal, social and spiritual wellness, as well as their careers? And what can management do to attenuate the forces within the paramilitary structure that erode personal identity, but without compromising the mission of policing?

From Industrial to Humanistic Management

Fifty years ago, most people considered themselves lucky to have a job, and autocratic management styles with little flexibility or sensitivity for the individual were commonly accepted. Households and businesses, schools and police departments were usually vertical hierarchies with little tolerance for diversity.

But times have changed, and many of today's enlightened leaders recognize that economic and social forces have necessitated accompanying changes in management styles. The ideas of psychologist Abraham Maslow and management guru Peter Drucker, for example, promote the importance of communication and good relations between management and workers for high morale and maximum performance.

In many organizations, autocratic leadership has given way to more sophisticated styles that work with instead of over workers. In sports, legendary, iron-fisted coaches like Woody Hayes, Vince Lombardi and Adolph Rupp have been replaced by those who relate more positively to their players. And it wasn't long ago that Sam Walton, the founder of Wal-Mart, revolutionized the business world by focusing on the needs of his employees—or associates, as he called them—instead of on the needs of his stockholders, thus pioneering a new concept of retail management.

Of course, not all institutions have thrived in this evolution of enlightenment. Some have still not learned the importance of employee morale and so continue to struggle with a high incidence of employee suicide, alcoholism, drug abuse, absenteeism, domestic violence, and divorce.

There are signs that many within law enforcement are seeking change. They are becoming aware that healthy, well-balanced people make the best police officers and that higher morale and less stress will improve the quality of law enforcement. But changing a culture is very difficult and takes time.

The complexity of this wellness challenge is not lost on former IACP President Joseph G. Estey, chief of the Hartford, VT Police Department. In a recent interview, Estey said law enforcement had come a long way in integrating the importance of individual officer wellness into management's priorities. But he was quick to add, "Change in large organizations is slow, and more needs to be done—and will be done, as these new ideas become more accepted."

Estey maintained that most chiefs are aware of and concerned with the stress that individual officers endure because police work is more complex today than ever before. But whether the job-related stresses are an outgrowth of increased scrutiny by the media and the public or ramped-up internal pressures, certain basic assumptions will be helpful in determining better policies.

Assumption 1: Higher morale and reduced stress will improve the quality of law enforcement. Low morale hinders law enforcement effectiveness and is detrimental to the personal lives of police officers. Assumption 2: The healthiest person makes the best police officer. Healthy police officers should see themselves as humans who happen to be police officers, not police officers who happen to be humans.

Outfitting Police Officers with a "Stress Vest"

Unlike standard issue Kevlar body wear, the "stress vest" comes in two distinct layers: the personal and the institutional. The personal "stress vest" is what every individual police officer must learn to acquire. Just like a healthy diet contains a variety of foods, a healthy identity requires personal, social, and spiritual wellness, as well as occupational wellness.

Every officer must 1) learn to wake up each morning with "an attitude of gratitude." Gratitude for life, family, friends, and the freedoms and opportunities we have. Feeling grateful is an important part of taking control of one's life and maintaining a positive identity. It combats cynicism, the emotional cancer that destroys hope. Every officer must 2) take care of his personal needs: exercise regularly, eat a balanced diet, and maintain good body composition; enjoy private time for hobbies and special interests; and get sufficient rest and relaxation.

Further, each officer must 3) have meaningful relationships outside of law enforcement. Good communication with family and friends is critical to a healthy identity and a happy life. And all the officers must 4) recognize that there is something in this world that is bigger than we are as individuals. Connect with your purpose and meaning in life and be honored and grateful that you have the opportunity to fulfill that higher purpose.

The Institutional "Stress Vest"

Help for police officers must come from the top. Not long ago, at the end of a course I taught on stress management in law enforcement, one student—a retired police officer—contributed to the class discussion with this lament: "The NYPD had my body for 25 years and made me feel insignificant when they could have had my mind for nothing and made me feel important." Perhaps this man's superiors would have been more helpful had they understood a point articulated by William James, the great American psychologist, who said: "The deepest principle in human nature is the craving to be appreciated." Indeed, one can imagine appreciation as one of the raw materials used to create the aforementioned "stress vest." How can law enforcement managers raise their consciousness and provide the help and appreciation needed by their officers?

Every police manager must 1) recognize and embrace the notion that individual police officers are suffering from stress-related problems exacerbated by the work environment. A chief must be a role model not only as a law enforcement officer but as a well-balanced human being who exemplifies personal, social, and spiritual wellness, and 2) be educated and trained in modern management theory that will equip him with more effective organizational, personnel and communication skills.

Further, 3) police academy training curricula should have a stress-management component, and should invite a spouse or significant other to participate in exercises that focus on communication skills and sensitivity to the demands of the job, 4) departments should develop opportunities for officers to exercise and recreate together by creating fitness centers and gymnasiums for law enforcement personnel, and 5) in-service sensitivity training should be required for all police officers.

Also, 6) workplace activities such as picnics and holiday parties should include and celebrate officers' families and 7) police officers must be recognized as people who have needs outside law enforcement. They should be given more individual recognition on the job, their professional opinions should be solicited and considered, and more consideration should be exercised for personal and family obligations such as children's birthdays and graduations.

In summary, the keys to the two-layer "stress vest" are simple. Each police officer must take personal responsibility to develop and maintain a balanced identity that begins with an "attitude out of gratitude," and where occupational wellness is only one part. And management, realizing that police officers are humans first, must create policies designed to show appreciation for individual accomplishments and positive contributions.

DR. ROBERT A. FOX is a professor at the John Jay College of Criminal Justice in New York City. Teaching at John Jay College for the past 10 years, he developed a course in stress management in law enforcement. He can be reached at rfox@jjay.cuny.edu.

Judging Honesty by Words, Not Fidgets

BENEDICT CAREY

Before any interrogation, before the two-way mirrors or bargaining or good-cop, bad-cop routines, police officers investigating a crime have to make a very tricky determination: Is the person I'm interviewing being honest, or spinning fairy tales?

The answer is crucial, not only for identifying potential suspects and credible witnesses but also for the fate of the person being questioned. Those who come across poorly may become potential suspects and spend hours on the business end of a confrontational, life-changing interrogation—whether or not they are guilty.

Until recently, police departments have had little solid research to guide their instincts. But now forensic scientists have begun testing techniques they hope will give officers, interrogators and others a kind of honesty screen, an improved method of sorting doctored stories from truthful ones.

The new work focuses on what people say, not how they act. It has already changed police work in other countries, and some new techniques are making their way into interrogations in the United States.

In part, the work grows out of a frustration with other methods. Liars do not avert their eyes in an interview on average any more than people telling the truth do, researchers report; they do not fidget, sweat or slump in a chair any more often. They may produce distinct, fleeting changes in expression, experts say, but it is not clear yet how useful it is to analyze those.

Nor have technological advances proved very helpful. No brain-imaging machine can reliably distinguish a doctored story from the truthful one, for instance; ditto for polygraphs, which track changes in physiology as an indirect measure of lying.

"Focusing on content is a very good idea," given the limitations of what is currently being done, said Saul Kassin, a professor of psychology at John Jay College of Criminal Justice.

One broad, straightforward principle has changed police work in Britain: seek information, not a confession. In the mid-1980s, following cases of false confessions, British courts prohibited officers from using some aggressive techniques, like lying about evidence to provoke suspects, and required that interrogations be taped. Officers now work to gather as much evidence as possible before interviewing a suspect, and they make no real distinction between this so-called investigative interview and an interrogation, said Ray Bull, a professor of forensic psychology at the University of Leicester.

"These interviews sound much more like a chat in a bar," said Dr. Bull, who, with colleagues like Aldert Vrij at the University of Portsmouth, has pioneered much of the research in this area. "It's a lot like the old 'Columbo' show, you know, where he pretends to be an idiot but he's gathered a lot of evidence."

Dr. Bull, who has analyzed scores of interrogation tapes, said the police had reported no drop-off in the number of confessions, nor major miscarriages of justice arising from false confessions. In one 2002 survey, researchers in Sweden found that less-confrontational interrogations were associated with a higher likelihood of confession.

Still, forensic researchers have not abandoned the search for verbal clues in interrogations. In analyses of what people say when they are lying and when they are telling the truth, they have found tantalizing differences.

Kevin Colwell, a psychologist at Southern Connecticut State University, has advised police departments, Pentagon officials and child protection workers, who need to check the veracity of conflicting accounts from parents and children. He says that people concocting a story prepare a script that is tight and lacking in detail.

"It's like when your mom busted you as a kid, and you made really obvious mistakes," Dr. Colwell said. "Well, now you're working to avoid those."

By contrast, people telling the truth have no script, and tend to recall more extraneous details and may even make mistakes. They are sloppier.

Psychologists have long studied methods for amplifying this contrast. Drawing on work by Dr. Vrij and Dr. Marcia K. Johnson of Yale, among others, Dr. Colwell and Dr. Cheryl Hiscock-Anisman of National University in La Jolla, Calif., have developed an interview technique that appears to help distinguish a tall tale from a true one.

The interview is low-key but demanding. First, the person recalls a vivid memory, like the first day at college, so researchers have a baseline reading for how the person communicates. The person then freely recounts the event being investigated, recalling all that happened. After several pointed questions ("Would a police officer say a crime was committed?" for example), the interviewee describes the event in question again, adding sounds, smells and other details. Several more stages follow, including one in which the person is asked to recall what happened in reverse.

In several studies, Dr. Colwell and Dr. Hiscock-Anisman have reported one consistent difference: People telling the truth tend to add 20 to 30 percent more external detail than do those who are lying. "This is how memory works, by association," Dr. Hiscock-Anisman said. "If you're telling the truth, this mental reinstatement of contexts triggers more and more external details."

Not so if you've got a concocted story and you're sticking to it. "It's the difference between a tree in full flower in the summer and a barren stick in winter," said Dr. Charles Morgan, a psychiatrist at the National Center for Post-Traumatic Stress Disorder, who has tested it for trauma claims and among special-operations soldiers.

In one recent study, the psychologists had 38 undergraduates enter a professor's office and either steal an exam or replace one that had been stolen. A week later, half told the truth in this structured interview, and the other half tried not to incriminate themselves by lying in the interview. A prize of $20 was offered to the most believable liars.

The researchers had four trained raters who did not know which students were lying analyze the transcripts for response length and richness of added detail, among other things. They correctly categorized 33 of the 38 stories as truthful or deceitful.

The study, whose co-authors were Amina Memon, Laura Taylor and Jessica Prewett, is one of several showing positive results of about 75 percent correct or higher.

This summer, Dr. Colwell and Dr. Hiscock-Anisman are scheduled to teach the technique at the San Diego Police Department, which has a force of some 2,000 officers. "You really develop your own antenna when interviewing people over the years," said Chris Ellis, a lieutenant on the force who invited the researchers to give training. "But we're very open to anything that will make our jobs easier and make us more accurate."

This approach, as promising as it is, has limitations. It applies only to a person talking about what happened during a specific time— not to individual facts, like, "Did you see a red suitcase on the floor?" It may be poorly suited, too, for someone who has been traumatized and is not interested in talking, Dr. Morgan said. And it is not likely to flag the person who changes one small but crucial detail in a story—"Sure, I was there, I threw some punches, but I know nothing about no knife"—or, for that matter, the expert or pathological liar.

But the science is evolving fast. Dr. Bull, Dr. Vrij and Par-Anders Granhag at Goteborg University in Sweden are finding that challenging people with pieces of previously gathered evidence, gradually introduced throughout an investigative interview, increases the strain on liars.

And it all can be done without threats or abuse, which is easier on officers and suspects. Detective Columbo, it turns out, was not just made for TV.

Law Enforcement Perspective on the Use of Force

Hands-On, Experiential Training for Prosecuting Attorneys

ANTHONY PINIZZOTTO, PhD ET AL.

In 1998, Washington, D.C., experienced a period of high crime and violence with a number of incidents involving officers who used deadly force. These cases generated media attention concerning alleged abuse of deadly force by members of the police department. Citizens began demanding a judicial review of these shootings. At the same time, the city selected a new police chief from an outside agency. The new chief requested assistance from the U.S. Attorney's Office of the District of Columbia to review these use-of-force cases, as well as any subsequent ones that might occur. To this end, the U.S. attorney requested assistance from the director of the FBI to create a training program for senior prosecutors of the newly established Civil Rights Unit responsible for investigating the use of deadly force by law enforcement officers. The goal of the training was to give these attorneys a realistic experience that would help them gain a better understanding of the use of force from a law enforcement perspective.[1]

The authors developed an initiative that included collaborative efforts by both firearms training and behavioral science personnel at the FBI Academy. The main intention of the project centered on placing prosecuting attorneys in the shoes of officers on the street who may become involved in deadly force incidents.

The authors based the program on a variety of factors, such as law enforcement experience and training, the interrelated aspects of research, and case consultation. Together, they had a combined amount of law enforcement service equaling more than 100 years that included actually employing deadly force, investigating such actions, and extensive training in the use of firearms. Their research focused not only on the use of deadly force against law enforcement but also by officers themselves. It involved numerous in-depth interviews with officers who had survived critical incidents where subjects had used force against them, as well as with offenders convicted of murdering law enforcement officers or feloniously assaulting them. The resulting publications detailed the varying perspectives of these officers and offenders.[2] The authors also consulted with members of local, state, and federal law enforcement on the aspects of perception, memory, and recall during a critical incident; wound ballistics; action-reaction models; sensory distortion; and facing edged and other weapons, including hands and feet.[3]

The Program

To give attorneys the perspective of an officer, the authors employed an interactive video simulator that played scenarios requiring the participants to decide whether to engage the use of deadly force. Some of these allowed such action and others presented a no-shoot situation. The different scenarios enabled the attorneys to describe and justify their actions in a particular set of circumstances and generated discussion from other attorneys in the classroom who witnessed the events.

The main intention of the project centered on placing prosecuting attorneys in the shoes of officers . . . who may become involved in deadly force incidents.

These discussions, held prior to replaying the particular scenario, had the attorneys who acted as officers describe in detail as much as they could recall concerning the circumstances of the incident, including descriptions and actions of the alleged offenders; activity of any partners present; number of shots fired, if any; who fired the shots; and justification for the use of force, if used. The attorneys who played the role of witnesses then had to describe what they saw at the scene. After these exchanges, the authors replayed the specific scenario. The results and highlights of the discussions that emanated from this hands-on training follow.

Justification of Action

After each scenario, the attorneys had to explain their actions as officers. In a large segment of the cases, most of the attorneys fired their weapons *only* after being shot at. They based their justification for shooting on the fact that their lives were in clear and present danger. They identified this threat not only as the presence of a weapon but because the suspect had fired at them first.

Ballistic Issues

While many attorneys did shoot and could justify their actions, most fired only one or two rounds and, in many cases, did not incapacitate their assailants. When questioned, the attorneys stated that they believed only one or two shots would disable someone. Additionally, they assumed that their shots actually hit the subjects. In some instances, however, this proved incorrect as some of their shots clearly missed their intended targets.

Subsequent instruction to the attorneys included dispelling the "one shot drop" myth. The authors explained that a person, upon being shot, generally does not become immediately powerless, unlike many portrayals in television shows and movies.[4] Experts agree that the only true instant incapacitation is caused either by the disruption of the central nervous system or from significant blood loss wherein individuals lose 20 percent of the volume of their blood, which can take 8 to 10 seconds to accomplish.[5] In situations where officers must fire their handguns, considered as defensive weapons, these rarely result in the instantaneous debilitation of their assailants. This is why officers are taught to continue to shoot until the threat ceases or is eliminated.

Perception, Memory, and Recall

During initial discussions of the scenarios, the attorneys acting as officers and those cast as witnesses disagreed on several important issues: what occurred on the scene, how many shots were fired, and who shot first. Only after the class reviewed each scenario did the participants reach an agreement as to what had happened and the number and origin of shots fired.

The attorneys also achieved a better understanding as to why witnesses often contradict each other. They came to realize that witnesses can differ slightly or even profoundly about what took place, and their recollections may change over time. Memory, in most situations, is constructive; it does not operate as a videotape recorder. Under critical or traumatic circumstances, perception, memory, and retrieval have a greater likelihood of being affected by the intensity and duration of the event.[6]

Action Versus Reaction

The two-phase model of action versus reaction demonstrates why, in some instances, officers are killed or debilitated without returning fire with their service weapons. In the action phase of one scenario, the attorneys saw the offender draw a handgun and point it at the officer who is taken by surprise. Then, in the reaction phase, they witnessed the officer attempt to draw and fire *quicker* than the offender who can simply pull the trigger. Because this is not possible in most situations, officers are killed or wounded before they can react to the threat.

This model also explains why officers sometimes have shot someone in the back while both consciously and truthfully believing that they shot the person in the chest. In these cases, the individuals turned and ran as the officers drew their weapons. Because of the time lag between the officer's decision to draw and fire the weapon and the physical completion of the act, the person had the opportunity to change position. Action versus reaction is linear and compatibility dependant; that is, action does not always beat reaction.[7]

Myths and Misconceptions

As the attorneys participated in the interactive video scenarios, some made comments and statements that often appeared founded in myths from television shows and movies. As one attorney noted, "The major benefit is educating us about the realities of a shoot. I had no idea that things really went down as they did. I bought into the Hollywood mythology entirely."

Edged Weapons

Collectively, the attorneys reported that they did not view edged weapons to be as great a threat to their safety as firearms. However, edged weapons are the second leading cause of homicides in the United States behind handguns.[8] Assailants continue to kill more people with edged weapons than with rifles and shotguns combined. As such, law enforcement officers follow the safety rule of 21 feet: if a subject armed with an edged weapon comes within 21 feet before an officer can draw and fire a weapon, the officer could be seriously injured or even killed.[9]

Other Weapons

The attorneys thought that a person without any visible weapon was not a threat. But, in fact, if officers are incapacitated by a punch or a kick, their own service weapons can be taken and used against them.

Decision Making

Another myth held by the attorneys involved the decision-making process. When an officer in a movie decides to shoot someone, it often is portrayed in slow motion, appearing to give the officer more than enough time. In fact, officers have only a split second to decide whether to shoot. Moreover, they often must form this crucial decision based on limited information.

Subjects Killed

Many of the attorneys believed that law enforcement officers kill a much greater number of subjects than can be substantiated by facts. In reality, officers often refrain from the use of deadly force. Several studies have demonstrated that the majority of officers had many more opportunities to use justifiable deadly force than actually did. "After all, in more simplistic terms, it often is not the officer's *decision* to use deadly force but the suspect's *actions* that require it."[10]

During initial discussions of the scenarios, the attorneys acting as officers and those cast as witnesses disagreed on several important issues. . . .

The Findings

This first training effort was well received by the attorneys who attended. They offered positive feedback, expressed an appreciation of the insights and materials presented, and recommended expanding the training to other attorneys within the U.S. Department of Justice. Comments from the attorneys included—

- "Very helpful, informative, eye-opening, at times even moving."
- "Thanks for giving the course. It sure has made me rethink deadly force cases."
- "I have a newfound respect for law enforcement training and decision-making processes."
- "I learned a lot about action/reaction and how most deadly force scenarios happen much faster than one would think."

The authors eventually expanded the course in both time and content. Most important, they added a live-fire exercise so the attorneys could experience actually using a firearm. Attendees at these subsequent classes included attorneys for state and local governments, trial attorneys from the U.S. Department of Justice, Civil Rights Division, as well as general counsel for large police departments. Commanders of units within these law enforcement agencies charged with the responsibility of investigating deadly force incidents also attended these additional classes.

The training proved a learning experience for both the attorneys and the instructors. The attorneys willingly participated and raised many issues. The authors instructed them to question everything they encountered in the training, and they did. From their inquiries and comments, several important issues arose. One student approached two of the authors and expressed the need for expanded training on perception, memory, and recall. She told them that prior to this training, she thought all officers involved in a deadly force incident should report exactly the same story. But, after attending the training, she realized that individuals can view similar circumstances in different ways, and those specific memories, in fact, may change over time.

As for the authors, they fully recognized that the attorneys never could experience certain realities firsthand. These obviously would include the actual consequences of using deadly force, such as post-traumatic stress disorder, media scrutiny, excessive legal review prior to the return to duty, stress placed on family members, and peer pressure. Losing a gunfight in a simulator never can compare with losing one on the street. But, giving prosecuting attorneys the experience of making a decision in the use of deadly force—with limited information and in a fraction of a second—can have far-reaching effects long after they complete the training.

The Recommendations

The authors recommend that local and state law enforcement agencies consider developing training programs for attorneys charged with reviewing the use of deadly force by their officers. These departments should take into account several issues when developing this type of training. Using scenarios that are simple, slow moving, and with obvious choices will cause participants to believe that the decision-making process is easy. They may not fully understand and appreciate the complexities and difficulties of the issues being taught. Conversely, fast-paced, high-speed, and complicated scenarios tend to overwhelm attendees. They may believe that the instructors are trying to make them fail. After all, this training should be difficult and challenging but obtainable.

Losing a gunfight in a simulator never can compare with losing one on the street.

Law enforcement agencies also may want to offer a similar course for those outside the criminal justice system, such as members of the media, civic organizations, seated grand juries, and human-interest groups. Many departments conduct citizen academies and could include this training in the existing curriculum.[11]

Conclusion

The goal of this hands-on, experiential training was to place U.S. attorneys in the shoes of objective, reasonable law enforcement officers who must use deadly force. The attorneys experienced anxiety in reporting the decisions they made during these high-stress but nonthreatening scenarios. It gave them some insight into what officers may experience when their lives and those of the citizens they have sworn to protect are in jeopardy. While remaining objective and emotionally distant in each investigation, these attorneys now have additional information to make clear, equitable reviews. They also have gained a significant understanding of the effects of these agonizing events on those law enforcement officers compelled to use deadly force.

Notes

1. For additional information on legal issues surrounding the use of force by law enforcement officers, see Thomas D. Petrowski, "Use-of-Force Policies and Training (Parts One and Two)," *FBI Law Enforcement Bulletin,* October and November 2002; and "When Is Force Excessive? Insightful Guidance from the U.S. Supreme Court," *FBI Law Enforcement Bulletin,* September 2005, 27–32.

2. Three FBI studies comprise research on officer safety conducted over nearly a 20-year span. The researchers, Anthony J. Pinizzotto, Edward F. Davis, and Charles E. Miller III, interviewed surviving officers and the offenders who assaulted them, as well as those felons who killed officers. They presented their findings in *Killed in the Line of Duty: A Study of Selected Felonious Killings of Law Enforcement Officers* (1992); *In the Line of Fire: Violence Against Law Enforcement* (1997); and *Violent Encounters: A Study of Felonious Assaults on Our Nation's Law Enforcement Officers* (2006). All are available from the Uniform Crime Reporting Program Office at 888-827-6427.

3. These consultations came about from a variety of sources, including students the authors taught at the FBI's National Academy. The FBI hosts four 10-week sessions each year during which national and international law enforcement executives, along with officers from street level to supervisory positions, come together to attend classes in various criminal justice subjects.

4. For additional information, see Anthony J. Pinizzotto, Harry A. Kern, and Edward F. Davis, "One-Shot Drops: Surviving the Myth," *FBI Law Enforcement Bulletin,* October 2004, 14–21.

5. "Physiologically, a determined adversary can be stopped reliably and immediately only by a shot that disrupts the brain or upper spinal cord. Failing a hit to the central nervous system, massive bleeding from holes in the heart, or major blood vessels of the torso causing circulatory collapse is the only way to force incapacitation upon an adversary, and this takes time. For example, there is sufficient oxygen within the brain to support full, voluntary action for 10 to 15 seconds after the heart has been destroyed." See U.S. Department of Justice, Federal Bureau of Investigation, Firearms Training Unit, FBI Academy, *Handgun Wounding Factors and Effectiveness* (Quantico, VA, July 14, 1989), 8.

6. For additional information, see Alexis Artwohl, "Perceptual and Memory Distortion During Officer-Involved Shootings," *FBI Law Enforcement Bulletin,* October 2002, 18–24; Anthony J. Pinizzotto, Edward F. Davis, and Charles E. Miller III, "Officers' Perceptual Shorthand: What Messages Are Offenders Sending to Law Enforcement Officers?" *FBI Law Enforcement Bulletin,* July 2000, 1–6; and Anthony J. Pinizzotto and Edward F. Davis, "Offenders' Perceptual Shorthand: What Messages Are Law Enforcement Officers Sending to Offenders?" *FBI Law Enforcement Bulletin,* June 1999, 1–4.

7. For additional information, see Richard A. Schmidt, *Motor Learning and Performance* (Champaign, IL: Human Kinetics, 1991), 19–26.

8. U.S. Department of Justice, Federal Bureau of Investigation, *Crime in the United States, 2006;* accessible at *http://www.fbi.gov/ucr/cius2006/index.html.*

9. For additional information on edged weapons, see Frank Thompson and Charlie Mesloh, "Edged Weapons: Traditional and Emerging Threats to Law Enforcement," *FBI Law Enforcement Bulletin,* March 2006, 14–19.

10. Shannon Bohrer, Harry A. Kern, and Edward F. Davis, "The Deadly Dilemma: Shoot or Don't Shoot?" *FBI Law Enforcement Bulletin,* March 2008, 7–12.

11. For additional information about citizen academies, see Giant Abutalebi Aryani, Terry D. Garrett, and Carl L. Alsabrook, "The Citizen Police Academy: Success Through Community Partnerships," *FBI Law Enforcement Bulletin,* May 2000, 16–21; and Elizabeth M. Bonello and Joseph A. Schafer, "Citizen Police Academies: Do They Do More Than Entertain?" *FBI Law Enforcement Bulletin,* November 2002, 19–23.

Dr. Pinizzotto, a retired FBI senior scientist, is a clinical forensic psychologist who privately consults for law enforcement and other criminal justice agencies. **Mr. Davis**, a retired police lieutenant and FBI Academy instructor, currently owns a private consulting company in Virginia. **Mr. Bohrer**, a retired Maryland State Police sergeant, is the range master for the Maryland Police and Correctional Training Commissions in Sykesville. **Mr. Chaney**, a retired homicide detective, staff assistant to the deputy attorney general, and chief of the Criminal Investigations Unit, U.S. Attorney's Office in Washington, D.C., currently owns a security consulting firm in Virginia.

Acknowledgements—The authors thank all of the attorneys who participated in the training for their candid and insightful evaluations. They also invite readers interested in discussing or obtaining additional information about this training to contact Anthony Pinizzotto at ajp1818@msn.com, Edward Davis at efdllc@aol.com, or Robert Chaney at rchaney@aol.com.

UNIT 4

The Judicial System

Unit Selections

Key Points to Consider

- Do you believe that restricting where convicted sex offenders may live helps to protect communities?

- Does a poor person get treated fairly by the criminal justice system?

- Do you think prosecutors should receive some sort of discipline when they cause an innocent person to be convicted of a crime?

Student Website

www.mhhe.com/cls

Internet References

Center for Rational Correctional Policy
    http://www.correctionalpolicy.com
Justice Information Center (JIC)
    http://www.ncjrs.org
National Center for Policy Analysis (NCPA)
    http://www.public-policy.org/~ncpa/pd/law/index3.html
U.S. Department of Justice (DOJ)
    http://www.usdoj.gov

The courts are an equal partner in the American justice system. Just as the police have the responsibility of guarding our liberties by enforcing the law, the courts play an important role in defending these liberties by applying and interpreting the law. The courts are the battlegrounds where civilized "wars" are fought without bloodshed, to protect individual rights and to settle disputes.

The articles in this unit discuss several issues concerning the judicial process. Ours is an adversary system of justice, and the protagonists—the state and the defendant—are usually represented by counsel.

In the opening article of this section, Adam Liptak informs us that in England and Canada, posting bail for people accused of crimes in exchange for a fee is a crime, as he examines the uniquely American system of bail in "Illegal Globally, Bail for Profit Remains in U.S." Following is "Avoiding Sixth Amendment Suppression: An Overview and Update," in which Myers discusses the sixth amendment right to counsel.

In "When Our Eyes Deceive Us" the problem of wrongful convictions as a result of eyewitness identifications by victims is looked at by Dahlia Lithwick. Jayme Holcomb deals with the issue of a person's reasonable expectation of privacy under the fourth amendment, as it relates to police searches.

Next, Tewksbury and Levenson argue in "When Evidence Is Ignored: Residential Restrictions for Sex Offenders" that no

© ThinkStock/SuperStock

empirical data exist to support the belief that residence restrictions reduce sex offense recidivism. "When the Poor Go to Court" shows how being poor can affect the treatment one receives in court. This unit concludes with "Justice & Antonin Scalia: The Supreme Court's Most Strident Catholic," in which the author sketches a picture of the provocative Supreme Court Justice Antonin Scalia.

Illegal Globally, Bail for Profit Remains in U.S.

Adam Liptak

Wayne Spath is a bail bondsman, which means he is an insurance salesman, a social worker, a lightly regulated law enforcement agent, a real estate appraiser—and a for-profit wing of the American justice system.

What he does, which is posting bail for people accused of crimes in exchange for a fee, is all but unknown in the rest of the world. In England, Canada and other countries, agreeing to pay a defendant's bond in exchange for money is a crime akin to witness tampering or bribing a juror—a form of obstruction of justice.

Mr. Spath, who is burly, gregarious and intense, owns Brandy Bail Bonds, and he sees his clients in a pleasant and sterile office building just down the street from the courthouse here. But for the handcuffs on the sign out front, it could be a dentist's office.

"I've got to run, but I'll never leave you in jail," Mr. Spath said, greeting a frequent customer in his reception area one morning a couple of weeks ago. He turned to a second man and said, "Now, don't you miss court on me."

Other countries almost universally reject and condemn Mr. Spath's trade, in which defendants who are presumed innocent but cannot make bail on their own pay an outsider a nonrefundable fee for their freedom.

"It's a very American invention," John Goldkamp, a professor of criminal justice at Temple University, said of the commercial bail bond system. "It's really the only place in the criminal justice system where a liberty decision is governed by a profit-making businessman who will or will not take your business."

Although the system is remarkably effective at what it does, four states—Illinois, Kentucky, Oregon and Wisconsin—have abolished commercial bail bonds, relying instead on systems that require deposits to courts instead of payments to private businesses, or that simply trust defendants to return for trial.

Most of the legal establishment, including the American Bar Association and the National District Attorneys Association, hates the bail bond business, saying it discriminates against poor and middle-class defendants, does nothing for public safety, and usurps decisions that ought to be made by the justice system.

Here as in many other areas of the law, the United States goes it alone. American law is, by international standards, a series of innovations and exceptions. From the central role played by juries in civil cases to the election of judges to punitive damages to the disproportionate number of people in prison, the United States has charted a distinctive and idiosyncratic legal path.

Bail is meant to make sure defendants show up for trial. It has ancient roots in English common law, which relied on sworn promises and on pledges of land or property from the defendants or their relatives to make sure they did not flee.

America's open frontier and entrepreneurial spirit injected an innovation into the process: by the early 1800s, private businesses were allowed to post bail in exchange for payments from the defendants and the promise that they would hunt down the defendants and return them if they failed to appear.

Commercial bail bond companies dominate the pretrial release systems of only two nations, the United States and the Philippines.

The flaw in the system most often cited by critics is that defendants who have not been convicted of a crime and who turn up for every court appearance are nonetheless required to pay a nonrefundable fee to a private business, assuming they do not want to remain in jail.

"Life is not fair, and I probably would feel the same way if I were a defendant," said Bill Kreins, a spokesman for the Professional Bail Agents of the United States, a trade group. "But the system is the best in the world."

The system costs taxpayers nothing, Mr. Kreins said, and it is exceptionally effective at ensuring that defendants appear for court.

Mr. Spath's experience confirms that.

If Mr. Spath considers a potential client a good risk, he will post bail in exchange for a nonrefundable 10 percent fee. In a 35-month period ending in November, his records show, Mr. Spath posted about $37 million in bonds—7,934 of them. That would suggest revenues of about $1.3 million a year, given his fee.

Mr. Spath, who is 62, has seven bail agents working for him, including his daughters Tia and Mia. "It probably costs me 50 grand a month to run this business," he said.

Mr. Spath hounds his clients relentlessly to make sure they appear for court. If they do not, he must pay the court the full amount unless he can find them and bring them back in short order.

Only 434 of his clients failed to appear for a court date over that period, and Mr. Spath straightened out 338 of those cases within the 60 days allowed by Florida law. In the end, he had to pay up only 76 times.

That is a failure rate of less than 1 percent.

But he had just taken a $100,000 hit. "Everything I worked for this year, I lost because of that one guy," he said. "If I write a bad bond, it takes me 17 to make it right."

Mr. Spath had thought the defendant, accused of drug trafficking, was a good bet because he had been cooperating with the government. The defendant is in Brazil now, but Mr. Spath is very good at finding people, and he is not giving up. He is working travel records, phone companies and a former girlfriend, and he is getting closer.

He sometimes requires collateral in addition to his fee, and has accepted rugs, an airplane and a winning Rhode Island lottery ticket. But mostly he is interested in houses.

"In this business, you have to understand real estate," Mr. Spath said. When the real estate market goes south, he said, bail bondsmen get hurt.

According to the Justice Department and academic studies, the clients of commercial bail bond agencies are more likely to appear for court in the first place and more likely to be captured if they flee than those released under other forms of supervision.

That may be because bail bond companies have financial incentives and choose their clients carefully. They also have more power. In many states, bond enforcement agents, sometimes called bounty hunters, may break into homes of defendants without a warrant, temporarily imprison them and move them across state lines without entering into the extradition process.

Still, critics say, efficiency and business considerations should not trump the evenhanded application of justice.

The experiences in states that have abolished commercial bail bonds, prosecutors say, have been mixed.

"The bail bond system is rife with corruption," said Joshua Marquis, the district attorney in Clatsop County, Ore. Since bond companies do not compete on price, they have every incentive to collude with lawyers, the police, jail officials and even judges to make sure that bail is high and that attractive clients are funneled to them.

Mr. Kreins, the industry spokesman, acknowledged scandals in Illinois, where "basically all the agents were in collusion with the judges," and in Louisiana, where sheriffs were also in the mix.

"We have acted responsibly every time an incident has occurred to seek stronger legislation," Mr. Kreins said. Mr. Marquis, the Oregon prosecutor, said doing away with commercial bonds had affected the justice system in a negative way as well. "The fact of the matter is," he said, "that in states like Oregon the failure-to-appear rate has skyrocketed." Oregon uses a combination of court deposits, promises to appear and restrictions on where defendants can live and work.

The rest of the world considers the American system a warning of how not to set up a pretrial release system, F. E. Devine wrote in "Commercial Bail Bonding," a 1991 book that remains the only comprehensive international survey of the subject.

He said that courts in Australia, India and South Africa had disciplined lawyers for professional misconduct for setting up commercial bail arrangements.

Other countries use a mix of methods to ensure that defendants appear for trial.

Some simply keep defendants in jail until trial. Others ask defendants to promise to turn up for trial. Some make failure to appear a separate crime. Some impose strict conditions on release, like reporting to the police frequently. Some make defendants liable for a given sum should they fail to appear but do not collect it up front. Others require a deposit in cash from the defendant, family members or friends, which is returned when the defendant appears.

But injecting money into the equation, even without the bond company's fee, is the exception. "Even purged of commercialism, most countries avoid a bail system based chiefly on financial security deposits," Mr. Devine wrote.

In the United States, the use of commercial bail bonds is rising, and they became the most popular form of pretrial release in 1998. More than 40 percent of felony defendants released before trial paid a bail bond company in 2004, up from 24 percent a decade earlier, according to the Justice Department.

Forty percent of people released on bail are eventually acquitted or have the charges against them dropped. Quite a few of them paid a substantial and nonrefundable fee to remain free in the meantime.

Kate Santana, a 20-year-old waitress, had spent eight days in jail when she found her way to Mr. Spath.

"Me and my husband got into a fight," Ms. Santana explained, "and the cops were called and I was arrested because there was a bite mark on his shoulder."

Mr. Spath took her $200 and posted her $2,000 bail. "I checked her criminal history out," he said. "I found out she was a mother and really she shouldn't be in jail."

But when a friend of a man accused of identity theft and perjury turned up seeking a $16,000 bond, Mr. Spath took a different attitude. "You bet your fanny I'm going to take collateral," he said. "I'll take his firstborn."

Mr. Spath is not much concerned with how the rest of the world views commercial bail bonds, but he was worked up about recent talk of a greater government role in pretrial release here in Broward County.

"Here's what everybody forgets," he said. "The taxpayers have to pay for these programs. Why should they pay for them? Why should they? When we can provide the same service for free. I'd rather see the money spent in parks, mental health issues, the homeless. Let the private sector do it. We do it better."

Avoiding Sixth Amendment Suppression
An Overview and Update

KENNETH A. MYERS, JD

T he impact of a defendant's confession in a criminal prosecution cannot be overstated. As described by the U.S. Supreme Court

A confession is like no other evidence. Indeed, "the defendant's own confession is probably the most probative and damaging evidence that can be admitted against him. . . . [T]he admissions of a defendant come from the actor himself, the most knowledgeable and unimpeachable source of information about his past conduct."[1]

Because confessions are such powerful evidence, defense attorneys will aggressively challenge their admissibility through a variety of legal avenues. These challenges may include one or more of the following: 1) the confession violates the Fourth Amendment in that it is the direct result of an unreasonable search or seizure;[2] 2) the confession violates due process in that it was involuntarily obtained through improper police coercion;[3] 3) the confession violates the defendant's Fifth Amendment privilege against self-incrimination (alleged violation of *Miranda v. Arizona*);[4] and 4) the confession violates the defendant's Sixth Amendment right to counsel.[5] This article provides an overview of the Sixth Amendment right to counsel, including a discussion of recent Supreme Court cases addressing this right, and briefly compares and contrasts this protection with the right to counsel under the Fifth Amendment's privilege against self-incrimination (*Miranda*).[6]

> **When analyzing Sixth Amendment right to counsel protection, one of the first concepts to be understood is the point at which an accused may assert this right.**

Attachment of the Right

According to the Sixth Amendment, "[i]n all criminal prosecutions, the accused shall enjoy the right . . . to have the assistance of counsel for his defense."[7] This Sixth Amendment right applies to both federal and state criminal prosecutions, inasmuch as the Supreme Court has incorporated this right

to the states through the due process clause of the Fourteenth Amendment.[8] The Supreme Court has limited this right, however, to all felony prosecutions and those misdemeanor cases where actual imprisonment is imposed.[9]

When analyzing Sixth Amendment right to counsel protection, one of the first concepts to understand is the point at which an accused may assert this right. In other words, when does the Sixth Amendment right to counsel attach? In *Rothgery v. Gillespie County, Texas*,[10] the Supreme Court recently reaffirmed[11] that the Sixth Amendment right to counsel attaches when criminal prosecution is commenced, that is at "the initiation of adversary judicial criminal proceedings—whether by way of formal charge, preliminary hearing, indictment, information, or arraignment."[12] The rationale behind this rule is "not mere formalism" but "a recognition of the point at which 'the government has committed itself to prosecute,' 'the adverse positions of government and defendant have solidified,' and the accused 'finds himself faced with the prosecutorial forces of organized society, and immersed in the intricacies of substantive and procedural criminal law.' "[13] By this definition of criminal prosecution, the Sixth Amendment right to counsel does not attach at the time of a warrantless, probable cause arrest or at the time of an arrest based upon warrant, complaint, and affidavit.[14] However, in such circumstances, the Sixth Amendment right to counsel later attaches at the earliest of a formal charge (indictment or information) or the defendant's initial appearance. The initial appearance is the first appearance before a judicial officer, where defendants learn the charge against them and that their liberty is subject to restriction.[15] The Sixth Amendment right to counsel attaches at the initial appearance, even if the prosecutor is not aware of or does not participate in this initial judicial proceeding.[16] In simplest terms, the Sixth Amendment right to counsel attaches at criminal prosecution, which is the earliest of indictment, information, or initial appearance.

Critical Stage

Once the Sixth Amendment right to counsel has attached, a defendant is entitled to the assistance of counsel at all "critical stages" of that criminal prosecution.[17] According to the Supreme Court, critical stages include any proceedings between the defendant and the prosecution (or agents thereof), whether the proceeding is "formal or informal, in court or out," where counsel would help the accused "in coping with legal problems or . . . meeting his adversary."[18]

Recognizing the important role of counsel in ensuring fairness in criminal prosecutions, the Supreme Court applies a "deliberate elicitation" standard to capture a broad range of conduct deemed to be critical stages in a criminal prosecution.[19] Under this standard, the Sixth Amendment is implicated when the government attempts to deliberately elicit incriminating statements from the accused once the right to counsel has attached. Government action deemed to be a critical stage includes direct interrogation,[20] words or action tantamount to interrogation (e.g., the infamous "Christian burial speech"),[21] and use of confidential human sources or undercover employees to intentionally elicit incriminating statements.[22] In this regard, the use of a cellblock informant to elicit incriminating statements from an incarcerated defendant would be considered a critical stage[23] unless the informant merely serves as a "listening post" and makes no effort to stimulate conversation involving the charged offense.[24]

In addition to that conduct described as deliberate elicitation, the Supreme Court also has found that a physical lineup for the charged offense is a critical stage in a prosecution because the attorney's presence at a lineup can help avert prejudice and ensure a meaningful confrontation at trial.[25] Police conduct not deemed to be a critical stage for Sixth Amendment right to counsel purposes includes the taking of handwriting exemplars,[26] fingerprints, blood samples, clothing, or hair;[27] the showing of a photo display;[28] and requests for consent to search.[29] Other critical stages (but of more significance to prosecutors than to law enforcement officers) include preliminary hearings,[30] plea hearings,[31] and competency hearings.[32]

> **. . . the Sixth Amendment right to counsel attaches at criminal prosecution, which is the earliest of indictment, information, or initial appearance.**

Warnings and Waivers

If a defendant's Sixth Amendment right to counsel has attached and there is a critical stage, then the defendant's attorney must be present or the defendant must knowingly, intelligently, and voluntarily waive the right for the incriminating evidence to be admissible.[33] The warnings that suffice for waiver of *Miranda* rights also are sufficient to waive the defendant's Sixth Amendment right to counsel.[34] Defendants do not have to be specifically advised that they are waiving the Sixth Amendment right to counsel, inasmuch as the sum and substance of the Sixth Amendment protection is set forth in the traditional *Miranda* warnings.[35]

Invocation of Right

As set forth above, once the Sixth Amendment right to counsel has attached, a defendant must be provided assistance of counsel or knowingly, intelligently, and voluntarily waive the

right for every critical stage of the charged criminal proceeding. If defendants invoke their Sixth Amendment right to counsel instead of waiving the right, the government may not initiate contact with the defendants regarding the charged offense for the remainder of the criminal prosecution outside the presence of counsel.[36] If the government initiates the contact with the defendants, any subsequent waiver during a police-initiated interrogation (or other critical stage) is ineffective.[37] Assuming that a defendant's Sixth Amendment right to counsel has attached by way of formal charge, one direct way that a defendant may invoke the Sixth Amendment right to counsel is to request assistance of counsel at the time that law enforcement provides the required warnings prior to attempted interrogation (or other critical stage). However, there also is a less obvious way that a criminal defendant may invoke the Sixth Amendment right to counsel. This would occur at the defendant's initial appearance when the defendant is advised by the magistrate or judge of the nature of the charges and applicable constitutional rights, including the right to assistance of counsel. If the defendant requests assistance of counsel for the charged offense after such an admonition, the Sixth Amendment right to counsel is invoked. Such an invocation precludes any police-initiated interrogation or other conduct deemed to be a critical stage with the defendant for the charged offense for the duration of the prosecution unless counsel is present.[38]

For example, a defendant is charged with drug trafficking and arrested by law enforcement based on a warrant, complaint, and affidavit. If the defendant requests the assistance of counsel at the initial appearance, the Sixth Amendment right to counsel is now invoked. If the defendant, thereafter, is released on bail and no charge (indictment or information) has been filed, law enforcement would not be able to initiate an interrogation or engage in any other conduct deemed a critical stage with this defendant without the presence of counsel in regard to the charged offense without violating the Sixth Amendment right to counsel. Even if the defendant was provided the advice of rights and waived these rights, a subsequent confession would be inadmissible because law enforcement could not initiate the contact after the defendant invoked the Sixth Amendment right to counsel at the initial appearance. Instead, a post-invocation confession would only be admissible if the defendant initiated the contact (and was properly warned of and waived these rights) or the defendant's attorney was present for the interrogation. The invocation of the Sixth Amendment right to counsel is a separate legal event from that of attachment of the right.[39] When the right has attached, a defendant is entitled to assistance of counsel at all critical stages of that prosecution. However, if the Sixth Amendment right to counsel has attached but the defendant has not yet invoked the right, law enforcement may still approach the defendant and obtain a lawful waiver of the right. On the other hand, if the Sixth Amendment right to counsel has attached and the defendant has invoked this right by refusing to waive the right or accepting the appointment of counsel at the initial appearance,[40] law enforcement may not initiate contact with the defendant regarding the charged offense for the duration of the prosecution outside the presence of counsel.

> **The warnings that suffice for waiver of *Miranda* rights also are sufficient to waive the defendant's Sixth Amendment right to counsel.**

Offense Specific

While the Supreme Court has interpreted the Sixth Amendment right to counsel in broad fashion by including within its scope conduct that amounts to the deliberate elicitation of information, being "offense specific" narrows the application.[41] In *Texas v. Cobb,*[42] the Supreme Court defined the meaning of the term *offense specific*, and ruled that it does not necessarily extend to uncharged offenses factually related to the charged offense.[43] The Supreme Court ruled that although the term *offense* for Sixth Amendment right to counsel purposes is "not necessarily limited to the four corners of the charging instrument,"[44] it is synonymous with the same term as applied under the Fifth Amendment's double jeopardy clause.[45] Accordingly, "where the same act or transaction constitutes a violation of two distinct statutory provisions, the test to be applied to determine whether there are two offenses or only one is whether each provision requires proof of fact which the other does not."[46] In *Texas v. Cobb,*[47] Raymond Levi Cobb was indicted for a local burglary and represented by counsel for this charge. Prior to the indictment, Cobb had confessed to committing the burglary but had denied any involvement in the disappearance of a woman and her infant daughter who lived at the burglarized residence. While out on bail, Cobb confessed to his father about murdering the missing mother and girl. The father notified police, and law enforcement obtained a warrant to arrest Cobb for the murders. Prior to the custodial interrogation, the police administered warnings pursuant to *Miranda*. Cobb waived his *Miranda* rights and confessed to both murders.

Cobb sought to have his confession suppressed, claiming that law enforcement violated his Sixth Amendment right to counsel by deliberately eliciting information about criminal activity factually related to that for which he previously invoked his Sixth Amendment right to counsel. The Texas Court of Appeals agreed, holding that the Sixth Amendment right to counsel attaches not only to the offense charged but to other offenses "closely related factually."[48] The Supreme Court agreed to hear the case. The Court concurred that Cobb's Sixth Amendment right to counsel for the burglary offense had attached at the time he was indicted. Moreover, he invoked this right by requesting assistance of counsel for the burglary charge. However, the Supreme Court held that even though the burglary and murder charges arose from the same factual situation, the charges involved different elements of proof and were separate offenses for Sixth Amendment right to counsel purposes. Therefore, an invocation of the Sixth Amendment right to counsel for the burglary charge did not bar police from interrogating Cobb about the murders, even though they were factually related. According to the Supreme Court, Cobb's Sixth Amendment right to

counsel had not yet attached to the murders. Therefore, Cobb's confession about the murders was admissible.[49]

After the holding in *Texas v. Cobb,* lower courts have found the following matters to be separate offenses for Sixth Amendment purposes (and thus no Sixth Amendment violation for law enforcement conduct following the attachment or invocation of the Sixth Amendment right to counsel for the initial charges): kidnapping and murder charges factually related;[50] immigration fraud and witness tampering charges arising in the same fraud prosecution;[51] and federal and state prosecutions, even if identical in the elements of their respective offenses (recognizing the dual sovereign doctrine).[52]

Comparison of Rights to Counsel

This article discusses the applicability and scope of the Sixth Amendment right to counsel. However, there is a separate and distinct right to counsel arising from the Fifth Amendment's privilege against self-incrimination. In *Miranda v. Arizona,*[53] the Supreme Court "established a number of prophylactic rights to counteract the 'inherently compelling pressures' of custodial interrogation, including the right to have counsel present."[54] Therefore, there is a Fifth Amendment right to counsel, as well as a Sixth Amendment right to counsel. It is important to recognize the existence of these two rights to counsel and to compare and contrast their respective applicability and scope.[55]

> **Apart from the purposes and triggering events for the two rights of counsel, another difference between the rights is the scope of their protections.**

The Fifth Amendment right to counsel is designed to protect individuals from police-dominated atmospheres and attaches at the time of custodial interrogation.[56] Accordingly, custody is one of the two triggering events (along with interrogation) for purposes of Fifth Amendment right to counsel analysis. Once attached, the Fifth Amendment right to counsel remains in effect as long as there is continuous custody.[57] On the other hand, the purpose of the Sixth Amendment right to counsel is to "'protect the unaided layman at critical confrontations' with his 'expert adversary,' the government, after 'the adverse positions of government and defendant have solidified' with respect to a particular alleged crime."[58] For Sixth Amendment right to counsel purposes, custody is irrelevant. Instead, as discussed, the Sixth Amendment right to counsel attaches at criminal prosecution (the earliest of indictment, information, or initial appearance) and remains throughout the prosecution, regardless of custody.

Apart from the purposes and triggering events for the two rights of counsel, another difference between the rights is the scope of their protections. As set forth, the Sixth Amendment right to counsel is crime specific. However, the Fifth Amendment right to counsel is not. Once a subject invokes the Fifth Amendment right to counsel and remains in continuous custody, the subject "may not be reapproached regarding any offense unless counsel is present."[59]

Another difference between the two rights of counsel is law enforcement's ability to use undercover officers or confidential human sources once the respective right has attached. The use of undercover officers or confidential human sources to deliberately elicit incriminating statements from an accused about a charged offense is considered a critical stage for Sixth Amendment right to counsel purposes.[60] On the other hand, the Supreme Court has ruled that as the government's identity is not known to the subject, such covert activity does not create a coercive, police-dominated atmosphere, which is the heart of the protection afforded by the Fifth Amendment right to counsel. Accordingly, police may use an undercover officer or cellmate informant to elicit incriminating statements when an individual is in custody and not be in violation of the Fifth Amendment right to counsel.[61]

Although significant differences exist between the two rights of counsel, there also are some similarities. Once either right to counsel has attached (but not yet been invoked), police may warn individuals of their rights and obtain a lawful waiver.[62] However, whenever an individual invokes either right to counsel, police generally may not reinitiate contact with the individual outside the presence of counsel.[63] Of course, once the right to counsel has attached and the individual has invoked, the person may initiate contact with law enforcement and elect to proceed without the assistance of counsel.[64] Moreover, while a confession obtained in violation of either right to counsel may not be used in the prosecution's chief case, such a confession may be used to impeach a defendant's false or inconsistent testimony.[65]

Conclusion

The Sixth Amendment right to counsel is just one of several constitutional protections afforded to individuals when dealing with police and prosecutors in criminal matters. As described, this right attaches once the government commits itself to prosecuting an individual, and it affords an accused the right to counsel at all critical stages of the prosecution relating to the charged offense. Once the right has attached, police must advise the individual of this right and obtain a lawful waiver prior to eliciting information about the charged criminal activity from the subject. If the Sixth Amendment right to counsel is invoked, police may not initiate any activity considered to be a critical stage with that individual for the charged offense unless that person's attorney is present. Law enforcement officers must understand the nature and scope of this Sixth Amendment right to counsel and recognize that it is a different protection from the right to counsel afforded under the Fifth Amendment's privilege against self-incrimination. Once understood, law enforcement officers will be better equipped to deal with this challenge to the admissibility of a confession and, hopefully, avoid Sixth Amendment suppression.

> **Another difference between the two rights of counsel is law enforcement's ability to use undercover officers or confidential human sources once the respective right has attached.**

Notes

1. *Arizona v. Fulminante*, 499 U.S. 279, 296, 111 S. Ct. 1246, 1257 (1991); citing *Bruton v. United States*, 391 U.S., at 139–140, 88 S. Ct. at 1630 (White, J. dissenting).

2. *See, for example, Brown v. Illinois*, 422 U.S. 590, 95 S. Ct. 2254 (1975) (in-custody statements that stemmed from an illegal arrest were not rendered admissible merely because defendant had been given *Miranda* warnings prior to making the statements); *Dunaway v. New York*, 442 U.S. 200, 99 S. Ct. 2248 (1979) (Confession following arrest made without probable cause was inadmissible); *Kaup v. Texas*, 538 U.S. 626. 123 S. Ct. 1843 (2003).

3. *See, for example, Arizona v. Fulminante*, 499 U.S. 279, 111 S. Ct. 1246 (1991).

4. *Miranda v. Arizona*, 384 U.S. 436, 86 S. Ct. 1602 (1966).

5. *Powell v. State of Alabama*, 287 U.S. 45, S. Ct. 55 (1932); *Massiah v. U.S.*, 377 U.S. 201, 84 S. Ct. 1199 (1964).

6. This topic was addressed in previous *FBI Law Enforcement Bulletin* articles and is being reemphasized inasmuch as the protection afforded by the Sixth Amendment right to counsel often is misunderstood by law enforcement, the consequences of which may be devastating to the admissibility of a confession and overall success of a criminal prosecution. *See*, Kimberly A. Crawford, "The Sixth Amendment Right to Counsel Applications and Limitations," *FBI Law Enforcement Bulletin*, July 2001; and "Constitutional Rights During Interrogation, Comparing Rights Under the Fifth and Sixth Amendments," *FBI Law Enforcement Bulletin*, September 2002.

7. The Sixth Amendment provides that "[i]n all criminal prosecutions, the accused shall enjoy the right to a speedy trial, by an impartial jury of the State and district wherein the crime shall have been committed, which district shall have been previously ascertained by law, and to be informed of the nature and cause of the accusation; to be confronted with the witnesses against him; to have compulsory process for obtaining witnesses in his favor, and to have the assistance of counsel for his defense." U.S. CONST. amend. VI.

8. *Gideon v. Wainwright*, 372 U.S. 335, 83 S. Ct. 792 (1963).

9. *Argersinger v. Hamlin*, 407 U.S. 25, 92 S. Ct. 2006 (1972); *Scott v. Illinois*, 440 U.S. 367, 99 S. Ct. 1158 (1979).

10. 128 S. Ct. 2578 (2008).

11. *See, for example, Michigan v. Jackson*, 475 U.S. 625, 106 S. Ct. 1404 (1986); *Brewer v. Williams*, 430 U.S. 387, 97 S. Ct. 1232 (1977).

12. *Supra* note 10, at 2583.

13. *Id., quoting Kirby v. Illinois*, 406 U.S. 682, 689, 92 S. Ct. 1877, 1882 (1972).

14. *See, for example, United States v. Gouveia,* 467 U.S. 180, 190, 104 S. Ct. 2292, 2298 (1984) ("... [W]e have never held that the right to counsel attaches at the time of arrest."); *United States v. Alvarado,* 440 F.3d 191,. 200 (4th Cir. 2006), cert, denied; 549 U.S. 817 (2006) ("The filing of a federal complaint does not commence a formal prosecution. . . . The filing of a federal complaint, therefore, can no more be characterized as 'the initiation of adversary judicial proceedings against the defendant' . . . than can the filing of an affidavit in support of a search warrant."); *United States v. Boskic,* 545 F.3d 69, 83 (1st Cir. 2008) ("The Supreme Court has never elaborated on what instruments beyond indictment and information would constitute a 'formal charge' for purposes of the Sixth Amendment. However, every circuit that has considered the issue has concluded that a federal complaint does not qualify as such, primarily because of its limited role as the precursor to an arrest warrant. . . . We agree with these courts.")

15. *Supra* note 10, at 2592.

16. *Id.* at 2584.

17. *Id.* at 2591.

18. *Id.*

19. *See, for example, Fellers v. United States,* 540 U.S. 519., 124 S. Ct. 1019 (2004).

20. *Michigan v. Jackson,* at 630.

21. *Brewer v. Williams,* at 399. In *Brewer,* two police officers were responsible for transporting the defendant, who was accused of murdering a young girl, by automobile approximately 160 miles from the location of his arrest to the location of the crime. While en route, the officers sought to obtain incriminating statements from the defendant (contrary to an agreement made with the defendant's attorney) by exploiting the fact that he was a former mental patient and was deeply religious. The police encouraged the defendant to show them the location of the victim's body, stating that her parents were entitled to a Christian burial for the young murder victim. Based on their prompting, the defendant led the police to the victim's body, which was used as evidence in his murder prosecution. The Supreme Court found this activity to be a deliberate attempt by police to elicit incriminating statements from a defendant tantamount to formal interrogation. Because the defendant's Sixth Amendment right to counsel had attached and had been invoked (and the defendant had not waived the right), this evidence was obtained in violation of the Sixth Amendment right to counsel and was suppressed.

22. *Massiah v. United States,* at 206; *see also Maine v. Moulton,* 474 U.S. 159, 106 S. Ct. 477 (1985).

23. *United States v. Henry,* 447 U.S. 264, 100 S. Ct. 2183 (1980).

24. *Kuhlmann v. Wilson,* 477 U.S. 436, 106 S. Ct. 2616 (1986).

25. *United States v. Wade,* 388 U.S. 218, 87 S. Ct. 1926 (1967).

26. *Gilbert v. California,* 388 U.S. 263, 87 S. Ct. 1951 (1967).

27. *United States v. Wade,* 388 U.S. 218, 227, 87 S. Ct. 1926, 1933 (1967).

28. *United States v. Ash,* 413 U.S. 300, 321, 93 S. Ct. 2568, 2579 (1973).

29. *United States v. Kon Yu-Leung,* 910 F.2d 33 (2nd Cir. 1990).

30. *United States v. Lott,* 433 F.3d 718, 723 (10th Cir. 2006), cert. denied, 549 U.S. 851 (2006).

31. *Iowa v. Tovar,* 541 U.S. 77, 87, 124 S. Ct. 1379, 1387 (2004).

32. *Appel v. Horn,* 250 F.3d 203, 215 (3rd Cir. 2001).

33. *Patterson v. Illinois,* 487 U.S. 285, 108 S. Ct. 2389 (1988).

34. *Id.* at 298.

35. *Id.* at 299.

36. *Michigan v. Jackson,* at 635.

37. *Id.* at 636; *see also McNeil v. Wisconsin,* 501 U.S. 171, 111 S. Ct. 2204 (1991).

38. *Id.*

39. *See, for example, Michigan v. Jackson,* 475 U.S. 625, 106 S. Ct. 1404 (1986); *Maine v. Moulton,* 474 U.S. 159, 106 S. Ct. 477 (1985).

40. *See also United States v. Harrison,* 213 F.3d 1206 (9th Cir. 2000) where the Ninth Circuit Court of Appeals held that in limited and well-defined circumstances, a defendant invokes the Sixth Amendment right to counsel as a matter of law when (1) the defendant retains counsel on an ongoing basis to assist with a pending investigation, (2) the government knows, or should know, that the defendant has ongoing legal representation relating to the subject of that investigation, and (3) the eventual indictment brings charges precisely anticipated by the scope of the pre-indictment investigation.

41. *Texas v. Cobb,* 532 U.S. 162, 121 S. Ct. 1335 (2001).

42. *Id.*

43. *Id.* at 168–175.

44. *Id.* at 173.

45. *Id.*

46. *Id., citing Blockburger v. United States,* 284 U.S. 299, 304, 52 S. Ct. 180 (1932)

47. 532 U.S. 162, 121 S. Ct. 1335 (2001).

48. *Cobb v. State,* 93 S.W.3d 1 (2000).

49. *Id.* at 173–174.

50. *Henderson v. Quarterman,* 460 F.3d 654 (5th Cir. 2006), cert. denied, 127 S. Ct. 1383 (2007).

51. *United States v. Mir,* 535 F.3d 351 (4th Cir. 2008).

52. *See, for example, United States v. Alvarado,* 440 F.3d 191 (4th Cir. 2006), cert. denied, 549 U.S. 817 (2006); *United States v. Avants,* 278 F.3d 510 (5th Cir. 2002), cert. denied, 22 S. Ct. 2683 (2002); *United States v. Coker,* 433 F.3d 39 (1st Cir. 2005); *but see United States v. Mills,* 412 F.3d 325 (2nd Cir. 2005) (rejecting dual sovereignty doctrine as applied in the Sixth Amendment right to counsel context); *United States v. Bird,* 287 F.3d 709 (8th Cir. 2002) (separate sovereignty does not necessarily mean separate offense for purposes of the Sixth Amendment).

53. 384 U.S. 436, 86 S. Ct. 1602 (1966).

54. *McNeil v. Wisconsin,* 501 U.S. 171, 176, 111 S. Ct. 2204, 2208 (1991).

55. "It is necessary to treat the *Miranda* and Sixth Amendment versions of the right to counsel separately. They attach at different times, under different circumstances, for different reasons, and with different effects." Dressler and Michaels, *Understanding Criminal Procedure,* 4th ed., Vol. 1: Investigation, page 417.

56. *Miranda v. Arizona,* 384 U.S. 436, 444, 86 S. Ct. 1602, 1612 (1966).

57. *McNeil v. Wisconsin,* 501 U.S. 171, 177, 111 S. Ct. 2204, 2208 (1991) 1; *See also U.S. v. Harris,* 221 F.3d 1048, 1051–1052 (8th Cir. 2000).

58. *McNeil v. Wisconsin,* at 177–178, *quoting United States v. Gouveia,* 467 U.S. 180, 189 (1984).

59. *Id.* at 177; *see also Arizona v. Roberson,* 486 U.S. 675, 108 S. Ct. 2093 (1988).

60. *United States v. Henry,* 447 U.S. 264, 100 S. Ct. 2183 (1980).

61. *Illinois v. Perkins,* 496 U.S. 292, 110 S. Ct. 2394 (1990).

62. *See, for example, Miranda v. Arizona,* 384 U.S. 436, 86 S. Ct. 1602 (1966); *Patterson v. Illinois,* 487 U.S. 285, 108 S. Ct. 2389 (1988).

63. For Fifth Amendment right to counsel purposes, this applies to contact about any offense as long as the individual remains in continuous custody. For Sixth Amendment right to counsel purposes, this applies to any critical stage regarding the charged offense(s) only.

64. *Michigan v. Harvey,* 494 U.S. 344, 352, 110 S. Ct. 1176, 1181 (1990).

65. *Id.* at 350–353.

Acknowledgements—Law enforcement officers of other than federal jurisdiction who are interested in this article should consult their legal advisors. Some police procedures ruled permissible under federal constitutional law are of questionable legality under state law or are not permitted at all.

When Our Eyes Deceive Us

Dahlia Lithwick

Describe the last person who served you coffee. What if I helped refresh your memory? Showed you some photos of local baristas? Pulled together a helpful lineup? Cheered exuberantly when you picked the "right" one? Now imagine that instead of identifying the person who made your venti latte last week, we had just worked together to nail a robber or a rapist. Imagine how good we would feel. Now imagine what would happen if we were wrong.

Last month, a Texas judge cleared Timothy Cole of the aggravated-sexual-assault conviction that sent him to prison in 1986. Although his victim positively identified him three times—twice in police lineups and again at trial—Cole was ultimately exonerated by DNA testing. The real rapist, Jerry Wayne Johnson, had been confessing to the crime since 1995. Unfortunately for Cole, he died in prison in 1999, long before his name was cleared.

Our eyes deceive us. Social scientists have insisted for decades that our eyewitness-identification process is unreliable at best and can be the cause of grievous injustice. A study published last month by Gary Wells and Deah Quinlivan in Law and Human Behavior, the journal of the American Psychology-Law Society, reveals just how often those injustices occur: of the more than 230 people in the United States who were wrongfully convicted and later exonerated by DNA evidence, approximately 77 percent involved cases of mistaken eyewitness identification, more than any other single factor.

Wells has been studying mistaken identifications for decades, and his objection to the eyewitness-identification system is not that people make mistakes. In an interview, he explains that eyewitness evidence is important, but should be treated—like blood, fingerprints and fiber evidence—as trace evidence, subject to contamination, deterioration and corruption. Our current criminal-justice system allows juries to hear eyewitness-identification evidence shaped by suggestive police procedures. In a 1977 case, *Manson v. Braithwaite,* the Supreme Court held that such evidence could be used if deemed "reliable." Today we know you can have a good long look, be certain you have the right guy and also be wrong. But Manson is still considered good law.

Jennifer Thompson was 22 the night she was raped in 1984. Throughout the ordeal, she scrupulously studied her attacker, determined to memorize every detail of his face and voice so that, if she survived, she could help the police catch him. Thompson soon identified Ronald Cotton in a photo lineup. When she—after some hesitation—again picked Cotton out of a physical lineup a few days later, a detective told her she'd picked the same person in the photo lineup.

But in this case Thompson got it wrong, although Cotton served 10 years before DNA evidence exonerated him and decisively implicated another man, Bobby Poole. The curious part of the story is that despite Thompson's determination to memorize every detail, when she first saw Poole in court she was certain she had never seen him before. Indeed, according to Wells and Quinlivan, "even after DNA had exonerated Cotton and Thompson herself had accepted the fact that Poole was her attacker, she had no memory of Poole's face and, when thinking back to the attack, she says, 'I still see Ronald Cotton'."

In their paper, Wells and Quinlivan suggest a host of tricks the mind can play, ranging from incorporating innocent "feedback" from police investigators to increasing certainty in one's shaky memories that become reinforced over time. Add to that Thompson's determination to regain control over her life, and her need to believe that the justice system was just, and it would have been doubly hard for her to look at a police lineup that, as it happened, did not include an image of the real rapist, and walk away. To hear Thompson and other victims tell it, being part of a system that identified and ultimately convicted the wrong man became another form of victimization, and for that reason alone the system needs to be reformed.

Being part of a system that identified and ultimately convicted the wrong man became another form of victimization.

The problems with the eyewitness-identification system cannot be laid at the feet of crime victims any more than they can be blamed on police investigators. Wells's argument for reforming our eyewitness-identification system is that the incentive for the police to subtly nudge our memories is not only uncorrected by the justice system, but also sometimes rewarded by it. Wells wants the Supreme Court to revisit the scientific basis for its 1977 decision. Whether or not the John Roberts court wishes to take up the issue of innocent prisoners—there is one test case percolating through the New Jersey courts—a few states and cities have used innocent-exoneration scandals to rethink their eyewitness-identification practices. Proposed changes include showing victims photos sequentially and explaining that the perpetrator may not be included in the lineup, and ensuring that whoever conducts the lineup has no knowledge of which person is the actual suspect.

This is not an issue that tracks the usual left-right divide. Some of the most zealous reformers of the eyewitness-identification process are lifelong conservatives who recognize that the credibility of the whole justice system is on the line each time an innocent man goes to jail and a guilty one walks free.

LITHWICK is a *Newsweek* contributing editor and a senior writer for *Slate*. A version of this column also appears on Slate.com.

Abandoning Places

JAYME W. HOLCOMB, JD, EdD

Abandonment is defined in Black's Law Dictionary as "[t]he surrender, relinquishment, disclaimer, or cession of property or of rights. Voluntary relinquishment of all right title, claim and possession, with the intention of not reclaiming it."[1] Abandonment issues commonly arise[2] in search and seizure situations involving trash,[3] vehicles,[4] locations, and items. A prior *FBI Law Enforcement Bulletin* article titled, "Abandonment of Items Associated with the Person"[5] focused on abandonment of items. This article examines the legal issues associated with the abandonment of locations, such as homes,[6] apartments,[7] hotel rooms,[8] and storage lockers.[9] It also addresses the Fourth Amendment concept of a reasonable expectation of privacy and the issues of disclaimer of association with a particular location and the physical relinquishment of a location.

Reasonable Expectation of Privacy

The Fourth Amendment to the Constitution provides that "[t]he right of the people to be secure in their persons, houses, papers, and effects, against unreasonable searches and seizures, shall not be violated, and no warrants shall issue, but upon probable cause. . . ."[10] The U.S. Supreme Court has stated, "[a] 'search' occurs when an expectation of privacy that society is prepared to consider reasonable is infringed. A 'seizure' of property occurs when there is some meaningful interference with an individual's possessory interests in that property."[11]

When an individual abandons a location, the individual's Fourth Amendment rights and protections in relation to that location no longer exist.[12] The Fourth Amendment protections cease to exist because the person has given up his reasonable expectation of privacy in the location.[13] This is important because if an individual has no reasonable expectation of privacy in the location, then an intrusion by the police into that location is not a search under the Fourth Amendment.[14]

The burden rests on the government to prove that the location was abandoned and, therefore, an individual had no reasonable expectation of privacy in the area.[15] As courts have noted, "the critical inquiry is 'whether the person prejudiced by the search . . . voluntarily discarded, left behind, or otherwise relinquished his interest in the property in question so that he could no longer retain a reasonable expectation of privacy with regard to it at the time of the search.'"[16]

To demonstrate that an individual had no reasonable expectation of privacy in an abandoned location, courts will look to the intent of the individual "which may be inferred from acts, words and 'other objective facts.'"[17] In undertaking this analysis, courts will look to the totality of the circumstances and, particularly, to the words and acts of the individual regarding the abandonment.[18] As in abandonment situations regarding the abandonment of items of property associated with the person, location abandonment situations involve close examination of the two primary issues of disclaimers and the physical relinquishment of a location.[19]

Disclaimers

An individual's statement that he does not own or has not rented a particular location can provide strong evidence of abandonment. Such disclaimers may be written, verbal, or nonverbal in nature. Because the government has the burden of proving that an individual disclaimed a particular location, law enforcement officers should be very clear regarding the exact location they asked about and exactly how the individual disclaimed or denied association with the location.

In abandonment of location cases, a person may abandon the actual location or both the location and the items within it. The U.S. Court of Appeals for the Eighth Circuit decision *United States v. Caballero-Chavez*[20] involved assessment of disclaimers and abandonment of both a location and specific items. In *Caballero-Chavez*, the defendants hired a 70-year-old woman to transport seven kilograms of cocaine from El Paso, Texas, to Omaha, Nebraska. In Omaha, the woman rented rooms 123 and 222 under her name. The defendants arrived at the hotel and paid the woman. She then gave them the keys to the car she had driven and the key to room 222.

When an individual abandons a location, the individual's Fourth Amendment rights and protections in relation to that location no longer exist.

The next day, officers working on a large drug investigation learned from an intercepted call that a Hispanic man staying in room 222 of the hotel would be involved in a drug delivery at 8:00 that evening. When the officers went to the hotel to investigate, they received information that a woman had rented rooms 123 and 222. The officers then watched both rooms. They saw two Hispanic males through the window to room 222 but observed no other activity at either room. The officers later observed two Hispanic males leaving the hotel in the car that the woman had driven, but the officers had not seen anyone leave room 222. The two males in the car returned to the hotel about 35 minutes later and went to the hotel restaurant.

A short time later, the officers decided to contact the occupants of rooms 123 and 222. At room 222, no one responded. At room 123, the officers identified themselves to the woman and obtained consent to search both rooms 123 and 222. The officers found a large roll of cash in room 123 and 7 kilograms of cocaine in the unoccupied room 222. At the hotel restaurant, the officers spoke to the two Hispanic males they had seen earlier in the car. The men denied that they were guests at the hotel and said that they were at the hotel to meet a woman named Maria. The men agreed to show the officers Maria's room at the hotel. On the way to room 123 they agreed to follow the officers to room 222. Outside of room 222 the men "denied that room 222 was theirs, denied they had ever been in the room, and said they did not care whether the officers searched the room because it was not their room."[21] The men also denied ownership of the bags in the room, including the bag in which the cocaine was hidden.

> **. . . if an individual has no reasonable expectation of privacy in the location, then an intrusion by the police into that location is not a search under the Fourth Amendment.**

The court examined the totality of the circumstances surrounding the abandonment and took particular note of "two factors: whether the suspect denied ownership of the property and whether he physically relinquished the property."[22] The court affirmed the trial court's denial of the defendants' motion to suppress, holding that the defendants had abandoned any interest in room 222 because of their repeated denials that the room was theirs, that they had ever been in the room, and that anything in the room was theirs. The court also concluded that the abandonment was voluntary and untainted by the initial search of the room and duffle bag based upon the earlier consent from the renter of room 222.[23]

Physical Relinquishment

Courts have frequently stated that the Fourth Amendment analysis within the context of abandonment cases is not driven by property law rules.[24] However, the status of any lease or rental agreement associated with the location is important because, as noted by the U.S. Court of Appeals for the Second Circuit in *United States v. Parizo,*[25] "[p]reliminary to the inquiry into intentional abandonment by the defendant, it must be shown that the defendant had sufficient control over the premises to establish a right to privacy therein."[26]

The U.S. Supreme Court has ruled that under ordinary circumstances, a landlord may not consent to a search of a tenant's property.[27] The Court also has specifically held that hotel employees do not have the authority to consent to police searches of hotel rooms.[28] The general rule in cases involving hotel rooms is that after the room rental period has expired, the hotel guest no longer has a reasonable expectation of privacy in the room.[29] After the rental period, hotel personnel have the authority to give consent to search the room or items within or that have been taken from the room.[30]

In *United States v. Croft,*[31] the defendant rented a room at a motel on July 8 for 2 days. On July 10, shortly after the noon checkout time, the owner of the motel allowed the local county attorney and county sheriff to search the room the defendant had rented. The lower court did not suppress the evidence discovered during the warrantless search of the room. The U.S. Court of Appeals for the Tenth Circuit found that "after the rental period expires a guest has no right of privacy, there can be no invasion thereof."[32]

At first glance, the general rule as stated above appears to be simple to understand and easy to apply. However, there are nuanced issues that frequently arise in abandonment of location cases that officers need to know, including whether a lease or rental agreement has expired, an abandonment occurred before the expiration of a lease or rental agreement, and, if the subject has been arrested.

Lease Expiration

In cases involving the expiration of leases or rental agreements, the nature of the property involved,[33] the lease terms,[34] the timeliness of rent or lease payment,[35] the practice of a business,[36] the condition of the property,[37] the actions taken by the renter,[38] the actions taken by the property owner,[39] and any statements made in relation to the location[40] are all important factors to consider in determining when a lease actually has expired.[41] This article focuses on examples involving hotels because the most frequently litigated scenarios involve whether abandonment of a hotel room occurred.[42] However, law enforcement officers must be aware that the issues are different than in hotel room situations, and potentially more complex, in cases involving alleged abandonment of homes, condominiums, and apartments because an individual has a significantly higher expectation of privacy.[43] At least one court has held law enforcement to a higher standard of proof of abandonment because the renter's privacy interests are greater in more permanent housing.[44]

In *United States v. Parizo,*[45] a man and his companion checked into a hotel on April 22. They paid for one night at the hotel in advance in accordance with hotel policy. The desk clerk told them that checkout time was 2:00 P.M. The man subsequently mentioned to both a busboy and a maid that he would be staying at the hotel for a few days; however, neither employee told hotel management of the man's intention to stay beyond the 2:00 P.M., checkout time. At 2:30 P.M., a maid entered the man's room to clean, found a hidden marijuana pipe and marijuana,[46] and informed hotel management of the discovery. The manager ordered the man to be checked out of the hotel and then called the police. In the meantime, the man returned to the hotel and, upon the arrival of law enforcement, was asked to go with the police to the police station. The manager then went to the empty room and found a gun, which the police removed without a search warrant. The U.S. Circuit Court of Appeals for the Second Circuit affirmed the trial court's decision that the defendant had no expectation of privacy in the room. The court stated

> [t]he appellant had not communicated to the front desk or to the management any desire to stay beyond checkout time. The room was cleaned and readied for new occupancy. After discovery of the marijuana, the manager attempted to regain his exclusive possession of the room by checking out the appellant, by calling the police, and, subsequently, by searching the room. On the other hand, the appellant on his return to the room may have thought that his conversations with the employees were sufficient to extend his stay and that his term of occupancy had not expired. . . . Thus, the facts as found indicate that even if the defendant had not completely vacated the room, the motel manager had the right to enter and examine the room as if it had been relinquished.[47]

In *United States v. Owens,*[48] the defendant checked into a hotel and paid $28.45 in advance for a 1-night stay. The defendant failed to check out by the usual noon checkout time. Shortly thereafter, hotel employees called the defendant's room to find out if he intended to extend his stay. At approximately 3:00 P.M., and apparently in response to that call, the defendant's companion deposited $100 with the front desk as advanced payment for the room rental. There was a dispute regarding whether the defendant was being charged a weekly or daily rental rate and how phone charges were calculated. If the defendant were a weekly renter, his room would have been paid for through noon on September 13; however, if he were a daily renter, his room would have been paid for through noon on September 12.

An individual's statement that he does not own or has not rented a particular location can provide strong evidence of abandonment.

On September 11, hotel personnel noticed a large number of calls to the defendant's room and advised hotel security. Shortly after noon on September 12, the defendant was arrested in the hotel parking lot for receiving stolen property. Officers who arrested the defendant called the hotel front desk and told an employee about the arrest and that there was a second person still in the room. The hotel manager told the police that the room had been rented for one person only and that the term of paid occupancy had expired. The defendant, who was

handcuffed to a railing outside of the hotel, urged the officers not to enter the room because his girlfriend was sleeping there naked. The officers entered the room, saw the girlfriend in bed; observed marijuana cigarettes, white powder, and drug paraphernalia in plain view; and found 2 ounces of cocaine in a bag in a drawer.

The officers never obtained an arrest or search warrant during their investigation. The U.S. Court of Appeals for the Tenth Circuit addressed the issue of whether the defendant had abandoned his reasonable expectation of privacy in the hotel room by staying in the room after noon on September 12. The court stated that the defendant "testified that he believed his $100 deposit had converted his status to that of a weekly rate tenant. His vigorous attempts to persuade the police not to enter his room further demonstrated that he held a subjective expectation of privacy."[49] The court found this expectation to be reasonable, noting that

> a reasonable person in Owens' situation might well have expected a weekly rental rate in exchange for a $128.45 advance deposit. All motel guests cannot be expected to be familiar with the detailed internal policies and bookkeeping procedures of the inns where they lodge. Even assuming that Owens was renting on a day-to-day basis, his reasonable expectation of privacy continued past check-out time for at least the short period in question here. On September 9, Owens had remained in his room past checkout time without consequence. Some time after noon, on the 9th, the Inn merely had inquired politely whether he planned to stay an extra day. Eventually, after 3:00 P.M., he had paid in advance for continued occupancy.[50]

The court held that "Owens had a reasonable expectation of privacy in his hotel room and in the contents of the closed bag inside the dresser drawer. For that reason a warrant was required to justify the search, absent application of some exception to the warrant requirement."[51] Officers should be aware that in another case, a court noted that "[a] guest may still have a legitimate expectation of privacy even after his rental period has terminated if there is a pattern or practice which would make that expectation reasonable."[52]

Physical Relinquishment Prior to Lease Expiration

Sometimes, it can be difficult to determine whether an individual has relinquished a reasonable expectation of privacy in a location. It may be hard to determine how long a lease lasts or what the practice is of the hotel, storage area, or other location. Where there is enough evidence that an individual has physically relinquished a location, some courts have found that the location can be considered abandoned even if an existing lease or rental agreement has not yet expired at the time of the search,[53] while other courts have concluded the opposite.[54] Courts have considered the following factors in analyzing whether an area has been physically relinquished: the type of location in question;[55] statements made or actions taken by individuals involved with the location, including making payment;[56] observations made by individuals familiar with the location;[57] and law enforcement officer observations of the location.[58]

The most notable example of the U.S. Supreme Court's analysis of the issue of abandonment is *Abel v. United States.*[59] In *Abel,* the FBI was investigating Abel's involvement in espionage. FBI agents accompanied Immigration and Naturalization Service agents when they executed an administrative deportation warrant and order to show cause on Abel at his hotel. Abel was arrested in the hotel room. He was allowed to dress and gather his belongings from the room. He then checked out of the hotel and turned in his room key. The bill the defendant paid entitled him to occupy the room until 3:00 P.M. that day. However, the hotel's practice was that once a guest turned in the key and took his luggage, the room was considered vacated. In *Abel,* FBI agents searched the defendant's vacated room without a warrant for approximately 3 hours after he had checked out. The agents found a hollowed-out pencil and a block of wood containing a "cipher pad" the defendant had put in the garbage can while packing his things. With respect to these items, the Court stated

> it [the search] was entirely lawful, although undertaken without a warrant. This is so for the reason that at the time of the search petitioner had vacated the room. The hotel then had the exclusive right to its possession, and the hotel management freely gave its consent that the search be made. . . . There can be nothing unlawful in the Government's appropriation of such abandoned property.[60]

In the U.S. Court of Appeals for the Fifth Circuit case *United States v. Hunter,*[61] personnel at an airfield found a general aviation aircraft on a grassy area about 20 feet off the airport runway at approximately 7:00 A.M. The plane had a flat tire. Airport personnel went to the plane, opened the unlocked door, and found that it contained large plastic covered bales that smelled like marijuana. Law enforcement officers called to the scene at 7:30 A.M. moved the plane and found that it contained 2,081 pounds of marijuana.

At 6:00 A.M., the defendant had called for a hotel courtesy van to pick him up at a restaurant approximately 2.5 miles from the airport. The defendant told the desk clerk at the hotel that his car had broken down. The defendant, who had no luggage, checked in and paid for a room at 6:25 A.M. He made a long distance call between 7:00 A.M. and 7:30 A.M. After paying for the phone call in cash and eating breakfast, the defendant was told that checkout time was at noon. The defendant told the desk clerk he would be out around noon. DEA agents went to the hotel that morning and spoke to the assistant manager. They asked the manager to have the housekeeper find out if the defendant was still in his room. The housekeeper knocked on the door to the room at 11:00 A.M. After receiving no reply to the knock, the housekeeper entered the room where she found a disarrayed bed and the room key on the night stand. She also found two keys on a chain and a single key in the toilet. The agents then entered the room and seized the keys, which later were determined to fit the

master lock on the airplane. They also found a fingerprint that matched the defendant's.

. . . under ordinary circumstances, a landlord may not consent to a search of a tenant's property.

The court rejected the defendant's argument that he had not abandoned either the plane or the hotel room and that, therefore, the searches by law enforcement officers were unlawful. With respect to the hotel room, the court stated

> [i]t also appears clear that the appellant had given up his rental interest in the motel room. He had paid his bill in full, indicated that he was departing by checkout time that day and left the motel with the room key locked inside the room. The mere fact that the room was entered prior to checkout time to ascertain whether it was occupied, and then searched, does not aid appellant's arguments.[62]

Impact of Arrest

There are a number of reported cases involving searches of hotel rooms rented by people arrested during the course of the rental period. In these cases, the arrestee has failed to pay for the continued rental of the room because of his arrest. Some courts have found such rooms abandoned by the occupant at the end of the time through which the rent had been paid. In those cases, courts have generally found that the defendant's own actions caused the situation to arise, but that did not change the finding that the location was abandoned.[63]

In *United States v. Ramirez,*[64] DEA agents arrested multiple defendants who had completed a series of cocaine transactions. During the arrests, another DEA agent went to a motel where several of the defendants had been staying. The agent set up surveillance on the room registered to one of the defendants that had been rented through noon the next day. No one was seen either going in or out of the room by either the agent or hotel staff during the evening. Upon returning to the hotel on the checkout day, the agent told the hotel manager that "if the room were later determined to be abandoned, he [the agent] would like to view any personal property."[65] When no one returned to the room and the rental period expired, the manager followed his usual procedure with an abandoned room by examining the property in the room and readying the room for new occupants. The manager notified the agent the following day about the property. The agent retrieved suitcases containing nondrug evidence in the room.

The defendant argued that the DEA agent "improperly exploited an exception to the exclusionary rule" by waiting for the rental period to expire and not getting a search warrant.[66] The court rejected the defendant's argument and found that

> [b]ecause the hotel room was abandoned, appellants had forfeited their reasonable expectation of privacy in it, and a search by the hotel manager did not trespass on appellants' fourth amendment rights. An equally compelling refutation of appellants' position, as will be discussed

below, is that the hotel manager was not acting in the capacity of a government agent, and his independent conduct implicated no Fourth Amendment concerns.[67]

Conclusion

This article has explored Fourth Amendment issues in cases involving the abandonment of locations. To determine whether an individual has abandoned a location, courts will look at whether an individual disclaimed any interest in or physically relinquished the location.

In cases involving the denial or disclaimer of a location, officers should carefully document the disclaimer. Because the government has the burden of proving that an abandonment occurred, officers should clarify exactly what is being disclaimed. The disclaimer should be specific and, if possible, in writing.

In cases involving physical relinquishment of a location, officers always should consider the totality of the circumstances in determining whether a location has been abandoned. Significant factors to consider could include, but are not limited to, the existence of a lease, the type of location, the practice of a lessor, statements made by the defendant, statements made by other people with knowledge of the property, and the condition of the location.

When individuals abandon a location, the protections afforded by the Fourth Amendment no longer apply because they have given up their reasonable expectation of privacy. Such an abandonment must not be the result of improper police behavior.[68] Officers should obtain search warrants whenever possible prior to the search of a location. In situations where obtaining a search warrant is not possible but a location has been abandoned, officers need to remain alert and focused on the details determining that the location is abandoned. Officers also must be aware of other related Fourth Amendment issues that exist in these cases but are beyond the scope of this article. Such issues include, but are not limited to, consent searches, private searches, protective sweeps, and exigent circumstances. As in all situations, officers need to be conscientious, diligent, and thorough in documenting the facts that led them to conclude that a location has been abandoned.

. . . hotel employees do not have the authority to consent to police searches of hotel rooms.

Notes

1. Black's Law Dictionary 2 (6th ed. 1990).
2. Additional information regarding the different contexts in which abandonment issues can arise involving the Fourth Amendment are addressed in John P. Ludington, Annotation, *Search and Seizure: What Constitutes Abandonment of Personal Property Within the Rule that Search and Seizure of Abandoned Property Is Not Unreasonable—Modern Cases*, 40 A. L. R. 4th 381 (1985).
3. *See* T. Kukura, "Trash Inspections and the Fourth Amendment," *FBI Law Enforcement Bulletin*. February 1991. p. 27–32.
4. *See. e.g., United States v. Hunter*, 647 F.2d 566 (5th Cir. 1981) (airplane).
5. *See* J. W. Holcomb, "Abandonment of Items Associated with the Person," *FBI Law Enforcement Bulletin*, August 2007. p. 23–32.
6. *See. e.g., United States v. Winchester*, 916 F.2d 601 (11th Cir. 1990); *United States v. Sellers*, 667 F.2d 1123 (4th Cir. 1981); *United States v. Haynie*, 637 F.2d 227 (4th Cir. 1980).
7. *See, e.g., United States v. Stevenson*, 39 F.3d 538 (4th Cir. 2005); *United States v. Ramos*, 12 F.3d 1019 (11th Cir. 1994); *United States v. Hoey*, 983 F.2d 890 (8th Cir. 1993); *United States v. Lavasseur*, 816 F.2d 37 (2d Cir. 1987); *United States v. De Parias*, 805 F.2d 1447 (11th Cir. 1986); *United States v. Wilson*, 472 F.2d 901 (9th Cir. 1972); *United States v. Kress*, 466 F.2d 358 (9th Cir. 1971); *United States v. Hocker*, 450 F.2d 490 (9th Cir. 1971); *United States v. Robinson*, 430 F.2d 1141 (6th Cir. 1970); *United States v. Parkman*, 399 F.2d 559 (D.C. Cir. 1968); *United States v. Jordan*, 399 F.2d 610 (2d Cir. 1968); *United States v. Friedman*, 347 F.2d 697 (8th Cir. 1965); *United States v. Minker*, 312 F.2d 632 (3d Cir. 1963); *United States v. Feguer*, 302 F.2d 214 (8th Cir. 1962).
8. *See, e.g., United States v. Caballero-Chavez*, 260 F.3d 863 (8th Cir. 2001); *United States v. Bond*, 77 F.3d 1009 (7th Cir. 1996); *United States v. Alvarez*, 6 F.3d 257 (5th Cir. 1993); *United States v. Huffhines*, 967 F.2d 314 (9th Cir. 1992); *United States v. Rahme*, 813 F.2d 31 (2d Cir. 1987); *United States v. Ramirez*, 810 F.2d 1338 (5th Cir. 1987); *United States v. Mulder*, 808 F.2d 1346 (9th Cir. 1987); *United States v. Rambo*, 789 F.2d 1289 (8th Cir. 1986); *United States v. Larson*, 760 F.2d 852 (8th Cir. 1985); *United States v. Rackley*, 742 F.2d 1266 (11th Cir. 1984); *United States v. Garcia*, 741 F.2d 363 (11th Cir. 1984); *United States v. Lee*, 700 F.2d 424 (10th Cir. 1983); *United States v. Sledge*, 650 F.2d 1075 (9th Cir. 1981); *United States v. Diggs*, 649 F.2d 731 (9th Cir. 1981); *United States v. Hunter*, 647 F.2d 566 (5th Cir. 1981); *United States v. Callabrass*, 607 F.2d 559 (2d Cir. 1979); *United States v. Jackson*, 585 F.2d 653 (4th Cir. 1978); *United States v. Cella*, 568 F.2d 1266 (9th Cir. 1978); *United States v. Savage*, 564 F.2d 728 (5th Cir. 1977); *United States v. Akin*, 562 F.2d 459 (7th Cir. 1977); *United States v. Haddad*, 558 F.2d 968 (9th Cir. 1977); *United States v. Parizo*, 514 F.2d 52 (2d Cir. 1975); *United States v. West*, 453 F.2d 1351 (3d Cir. 1972); *United States v. Edwards*, 441 F.2d 749 (5th Cir. 1971); *United States v. Croft*, 429 F.2d 884 (10th Cir. 1970); *United States v. Cowan*, 396 F.2d 83 (2d Cir. 1968); *United States v. Granza*, 377 F.2d 746 (5th Cir. 1967); *United States v. Dargento*, 353 F.2d 327 (9th Cir. 1965); *United States v. Frank*, 347 F.2d 486 (D.C. Cir. 1965).
9. *See, e.g., United States v. Poulsen*, 41 F.3d 1330 (9th Cir. 1994); *United States v. Reyes*, 980 F.2d 281 (8th Cir. 1990).
10. U.S. Const. amend. IV.
11. *United States v. Jacobsen*, 466 U.S. 109, 113 (1984).
12. Some courts also address the related issue of standing in abandonment cases. However, the first question to be asked in abandonment cases is whether the individual abandoned the property. If the individual is found to have abandoned the property, the court then may find that he has no standing to challenge a search of the property. *See, e.g., United States v. Gilman*, 684 F.2d 616, 619 (9th Cir. 1982).
13. *See, e.g., United States v. Thomas*, 451 F.3d 543, 545 (8th Cir. 2006) ("Abandoned property is outside the scope of Fourth

Amendment protection because its owner has forfeited any expectation of privacy in it.").

14. *See, e.g., United States v. Hoey,* 983 F.2d 890, 892 (8th Cir. 1993) ("It is well established that the warrantless search of abandoned property does not constitute an unreasonable search and does not violate the Fourth Amendment."); *United States v. Levasseur,* 816 F.2d 37, 44 (2d Cir. 1987) ("Since one forfeits any reasonable expectation of privacy upon abandoning one's property, a warrantless search or seizure of abandoned property does not violate the fourth amendment.").

15. *See, e.g., United States v. Ramos,* 12 F.3d 1019, 1023 (11th Cir. 1994).

16. *United States v. Winchester,* 916 F.2d 601, 603 (11th Cir. 1990) (quoting *United States v. Pirolli,* 673 F.2d 1200, 1204 (11th Cir. 1982)). *See also United States v. Diggs,* 649 F.2d 731, 735 (9th Cir. 1981); *United States v. Wilson,* 472 F.2d 901, 902 (9th Cir. 1973) ("The proper test for abandonment is not whether all formal property rights have been relinquished, but whether the complaining party retains a reasonable expectation of privacy in the articles alleged to be abandoned.").

17. *See, e.g., United States v. Ramos,* 12 F.3d 1019, 1023 (11th Cir. 1994) ("Whether abandonment occurred is a question of intent which may be inferred from acts, words and 'other objective facts.'"); *United States v. Sampol,* 636 F.2d 621, 683 (D.C. Cir. 1980) ("Abandonment is primarily a question of intent, and intent may be inferred from words, acts, and other objective facts."); *United States v. Cowan,* 396 F.2d 83, 87 (2nd Cir. 1968) ("Abandonment does not require performing a ritual; rather, it is a question of intent.").

18. *United States v. Levasseur,* 816 F.2d 37, 44 (2d Cir. 1987).

19. *See e.g., United States v. Cabballero-Chavez,* 260 F.3d 863, 866–67 (8th Cir. 2001) ("we 'look to the totality of the circumstances, noting in particular two factors: whether the suspect denied ownership of the property and whether he physically relinquished the property.'").

20. 260 F.3d 863 (8th Cir. 2001).

21. *Id.* at 866.

22. *Id.* at 867.

23. *Id.*

24. *See, e.g., United States v. Levasseur,* 816 F.2d 37, 44 (2d Cir. 1987); *United States v. Haynie,* 637 F.2d 227, 237 (4th Cir. 1980); *United States v. Wilson,* 472 F.2d 901, 902 (9th Cir. 1973) ("The proper test for abandonment is not whether all formal property rights have been relinquished, but whether the complaining party retains a reasonable expectation of privacy in the articles alleged to be abandoned."); *Paraman v. United States,* 399 F.2d 559, 565 (D.C. Cir. 1968) ("We are, of course, mindful of the admonition that it is not necessary to import the subtle refinements of property law into the law surrounding search and seizure.").

25. 514 F.2d 52 (2d Cir. 1975).

26. *Id.* at 55.

27. *Chapman v. United States,* 365 U.S. 610 (1961).

28. *Stoner v. California,* 376 U.S. 483 (1964).

29. *See, e.g., United States v. Huffines,* 967 F.2d 314, 318 (9th Cir. 1992); *United States v. Rahme,* 813 F.2d 31, 34 (2d Cir. 1987); *United States v. Ramirez,* 810 F.2d 1338, 1341 n. 3 (5th Cir. 1987); *United States v. Rambo,* 789 F.2d 1289,

1296 n. 7 (8th Cir. 1986); *United States v. Larson,* 760 F.2d 852, 854–55 (8th Cir. 1985); *United States v. Lee,* 700 F.2d 424, 425-26 (10th Cir. 1983); *United States v. Jackson,* 585 F.2d 653, 658 (4th Cir. 1978); *United States v. Savage,* 564 F.2d 728. 733 (5th Cir. 1977); *United States v. Akin,* 562 F.2d 459, 464 (7th Cir. 1977); *United States v. Haddad,* 558 F.2d 968, 975 (9th Cir. 1977); *United States v. Parizo,* 514 F.2d 52, 54-55 (2d Cir. 1975); *United States v. Croft,* 429 F.2d 884, 887 (10th Cir. 1970); *United States v. Collins,* 515 F. Supp. 2d 891 (N.D. Ind. 2007).

30. A complete discussion of the authority to consent to a search is beyond the scope of this article.

31. 429 F.2d 884 (10th Cir. 1970).

32. *Id.* at 887. *See also United States v. Parizo,* 514 F.2d 52, 54 (2d Cir. 1975) ("when the term of a guest's occupancy of a room expires the guest loses his exclusive right to privacy in the room").

33. *See, e.g., United States v. Thomas,* 451 F.3d 543 (8th Cir. 2006) (rented mailbox store); *United States v. Ramos,* 12 F.3d 1019 (11th Cir. 1994) (condo); *United States v. Hoey,* 983 F.2d 890 (8th Cir. 1993) (apartment); *United States v. Mulder,* 808 F.2d 1346 (9th Cir. 1987) (hotel room); *United States v. Larson,* 760 F.2d 852 (8th Cir. 1985) (hotel room); *United States v. Gilman,* 684 F.2d 616 (9th Cir. 1982) (storage locker); *United States v. Haynie,* 637 F.2d 227, 237 (4th Cir. 1980); *United States v. Wilson,* 472 F.2d 901 (9th Cir. 1973) (apartment).

34. *See, e.g., United States v. Thomas,* 451 F.3d 543 (8th Cir. 2006); *United States v. Ramos,* 12 F.3d 1019 (11th Cir. 1994).

35. *See. e.g., United States v. Hoey,* 983 F.2d 890 (8th Cir. 1993) (apartment rent 6 weeks overdue); *United States v. Mulder,* 808 F.2d 1346 (9th Cir. 1987); *United States v. Sellers,* 667 F.2d 1123, 1125 (4th Cir. 1981) (defendant 5 months delinquent paying house rent); *United States v. Wilson,* 472 F.2d 901 (9th Cir. 1973) (rent 2 weeks late); *United States v. Jordan,* 399 F.2d 610. 614 (2d Cir. 1968); *United States v. Watson,* 783 F. Supp. 258, 263 (E.D. Va. 1992); *United States v. Wyler,* 502 F. Supp. 959, 967 (S.D.N.Y. 1980).

36. *See, e.g., United States v. Kitchens,* 114 F.3d 29, 32 (4th Cir. 1997); *United States v. Ramos,* 12 F.3d 1019 (11th Cir. 1994); *United States v. Larson,* 760 F.2d 852 (8th Cir. 1985); *United States v. Jordan,* 399 F.2d 610, 614 (2d Cir. 1968); *United States v. Watson,* 783 F. Supp. 258, 263 (E.D. Va. 1992) ("The presence in the room of many personal items in addition to the hotel's lax enforcement of its check-out policy and Mr. Watson's prior payment history suggest that Mr. Watson intended to continue his stay at the hotel and that it was reasonable for him to intend to continue his stay. The court finds that he did not abandon his room and that, at the time of the search, he had a reasonable expectation of privacy in the room and the personal things he had left in the room.").

37. *See, e.g., United States v. Hoey,* 983 F.2d 890 (8th Cir. 1993); *United States v. Larson,* 760 F.2d 852 (8th Cir. 1985) (assistant hotel manager enters room after checkout time and observes empty liquor bottles, prescription pills, keys, and grocery bags containing plastic bags with white powder in them); *United States v. Haynie,* 637 F.2d 227, 237 (4th Cir. 1980); *United States v Wilson,* 472 F.2d 901 (9th Cir. 1973); *United States v. Watson,* 783 F. Supp. 258, 263 (E.D. Va. 1992); *United States v. Wyler,* 502 F. Supp. 959, 967 (S.D.N.Y. 1980).

38. *See e.g., United States v. Hoey,* 983 F.2d 890 (8th Cir. 1993) (defendant has a moving sale and is seen by neighbor leaving apartment); *United States v. Larson,* 760 F.2d 852 (8th Cir. 1985) (defendant stays in room after extended checkout time, leaves, and then returns to room 5 hours later without paying for next day's rent); *United States v. Sellers,* 667 F.2d 1123, 1125 (4th Cir. 1981) (defendant who was 5 months delinquent paying house rent left a note in the house saying that he was "sorry he could not pay his rent but he told her he was leaving everything in the house and that she could have them" found to have abandoned house); *United States v. Wilson,* 472 F.2d 901 (9th Cir. 1973) (defendant leaves apartment door open); *United States v. Jordan,* 399 F.2d 610, 614 (2d Cir. 1968); *United States v. Wai-Keung,* 845 F. Supp. 1548, 1563 (S.D. Fla. 1994); *United States v. Wyler,* 502 F. Supp. 959, 967 (S.D.N.Y. 1980).

39. *See, e.g., United States v. Hoey,* 983 F.2d 890 (8th Cir. 1993); *United States v. Mulder,* 808 F.2d 1346 (9th Cir. 1987); *United States v. Larson,* 760 F.2d 852 (8th Cir. 1985); *United States v. Gilman,* 684 F.2d 616 (9th Cir. 1982); *United States v. Wilson,* 472 F.2d 901 (9th Cir. 1973).

40. *See, e.g., United States v. Haynie,* 637 F.2d 227, 237 (4th Cir. 1980); *United States v. Mourning,* 716 F. Supp. 279, 290 (W.D. Tex. 1989) ("Certain vague statements that the Defendant did not go around the warehouse anymore, whether before or after the search, are insufficient to show an abandonment of the Defendant's interest in that property, particularly when the defendant is the lessee and the rent-payer for that property.").

41. Many of these factors were present in *United States v. Olsen,* 245 F. Supp. 641 (D. Mont. 1965). In *Olsen,* the court found that the tenant had not abandoned the house he rented and that, therefore, agents had not lawfully searched the house with the landlord's consent but without a search warrant. Of particular import in the case was the fact that "both the landlord and the defendant considered the tenancy to be still in effect on February 10th [the day of the search] despite the nonpayment of rent on February 9th." *Id.* at 644. Additionally, the defendant had paid the utilities through March 8th, retained a key to the house, and still had many personal belongings in the house. The court stated that the failure of the agents "to obtain a search warrant in this case is beyond the court's comprehension." *Id.* at 645.

42. *United States v. Wyler,* 502 F. Supp. 959, 967 (S.D.N.Y. 1980) ("The majority of the precedents in the area of abandonment have arisen in the context of a search of a hotel room.").

43. In a case involving an apartment, the U.S. Circuit Court of Appeals for the Eighth Circuit stated, "[t]his court has held that an individual has no reasonable expectation of privacy after the expiration of the rental period for a storage locker. In addition, this court has held that one does not have a legitimate expectation of privacy in a hotel room after the rental term has expired. This court does not suggest that there are equivalent privacy interests in storage lockers, hotel rooms, and apartments." *United States v. Hoey,* 983 F.2d 890, 892 (8th Cir. 1993) (citations omitted).

44. In *United States v. Wyler,* 502 F. Supp. 959, 967 (S.D.N.Y. 1980), the court stated, "the premises involved in this case were the defendants' home where it is reasonable for one to expect the maximum degree of privacy. Accordingly, a very heavy burden of justification must be placed upon officials who enter a house or dwelling without authorization. . . ." The court later noted "[t]hus, while the transiently occupied hotel room cases may provide guidance by analogy, stricter scrutiny must be applied when the government seeks to demonstrate that a defendant has abandoned his home. In this Court's view, the government has not met its burden here."

45. 514 F.2d 52 (2d Cir. 1975).

46. A complete discussion of the legal issues associated with searches conducted by private parties is beyond the scope of this article.

47. *Id.* at 55.

48. 782 F.2d 146 (10th Cir. 1986).

49. *Id.* at 150.

50. *Id.*

51. *Id.*

52. *United States v. Kitchens,* 114 F.3d 29, 32 (4th Cir. 1997) (citing *United States v. Watson,* 783 F. Supp. 258, 263 [E.D. Va. 1992]). *See also United States v. Owens,* 782 F.2d 146, 150 (10th Cir. 1986); *United States v. Wai-Keung,* 845 F. Supp. 1548, 1563 (S.D. Fla. 1994).

53. *See, e.g., United States v. Akin,* 562 F.2d 459, 464 (7th Cir. 1977) (agents walked through room prior to checkout time but waited to search room until checkout time passed to get management consent to search room); *United States v. Feguer,* 302 F.2d 214, 249 (8th Cir. 1962) ("Abandonment is not foreclosed here until the paid rent period ran out. . . .").

54. *See, e.g., United States v. Hossbach,* 518 F. Supp. 759 (E.D. Pa. 1980) (court found there was no abandonment of office suite and that landlord had no right to permit DEA agents to search rented office without a warrant even though rent was in arrears when mail was being received at the office, the phone worked, and there were files and filing cabinets in good order in the business [apartment similarly not held abandoned but storage locker held to have been abandoned]).

55. *See, e.g., United States v. Binder,* 794 F.2d 1195 (7th Cir. 1986) (office); *United States v. Sledge,* 650 F.2d 1075 (9th Cir. 1981) (apartment); *United States v. Hunter,* 647 F.2d 566, 568 (5th Cir. 1981) (hotel room).

56. *See, e.g., United States v. Winchester,* 916 F.2d 601 (11th Cir. 1990); *United States v. Binder,* 794 F.2d 1195 (7th Cir. 1986); *United States v. Sledge,* 650 F.2d 1075 (9th Cir. 1981); *United States v. Hunter,* 647 F.2d 566, 568 (5th Cir. 1981) (stated he was leaving by checkout time); *United States v. Akin,* 562 F.2d 459, 464 (7th Cir. 1977) (there was no luggage or suits in the room, the rent had not been paid, and no arrangements had been made to extend stay).

57. *See. e.g., United States v. Binder,* 794 F.2d 1195 (7th Cir. 1986); *United States v. Sledge,* 650 F.2d 1075 (9th Cir. 1981); *United States v. Akin,* 562 F.2d 459, 464 (7th Cir. 1977); *United States v. Feguer,* 302 F.2d 214, 249 (8th Cir. 1962).

58. *See, e.g., United States v. Akin,* 562 F.2d 459, 464 (7th Cir. 1977).

59. 362 U.S. 217 (1960).

60. *Id.* at 241.

61. 647 F.2d 566 (5th Cir. 1981).

62. *Id.* at 568.

63. *See, e.g., United States v. Huffhines,* 967 F.2d 314, 318 (9th Cir. 1992) ("[I]t was Huffhines's own conduct in giving a false name to the police that precipitated his arrest and prevented him from returning to the motel to renew the rental period. He cannot rely on his own misconduct to extend the period of his expectation of privacy in the motel room.") (citing *United States v. Croft,* 429 F.2d 884, 887 (10th Cir. 1970); *United States v. Reyes,* 908 F.2d 281, 285–86 (8th Cir. 1990)); *United States v. Rahme,* 813 F.2d 31, 35 (2d Cir. 1987); *United States v. Haddad,* 558 F.2d 968 (9th Cir. 1977). However, in at least one case, a court found that the government failed to meet its burden of proving abandonment when the defendant had not paid rent in over a month and was in jail at the time agents searched his apartment without a warrant. *See United States v. Robinson,* 430 F.2d 1141 (6th Cir. 1970).

64. 810 F.2d 1338 (5th Cir. 1987).

65. *Id.* at 1340.

66. *Id.* at 1341.

67. *Id.*

68. *United States v. Alvarez,* 6 F.3d 287, 289 (5th Cir. 1993).

Acknowledgements—Law enforcement officers of other than federal jurisdiction who are interested in this article should consult their legal advisors. Some police procedures ruled permissible under federal constitutional law are of questionable legality under state law or are not permitted at all.

When Evidence Is Ignored: Residential Restrictions for Sex Offenders

RICHARD TEWKSBURY AND JILL LEVENSON

The use of evidence-based practices in corrections and public policy is now considered the gold standard for policy and program development. Numerous examples (as discussed throughout this edition of *Corrections Today*) are available to show the importance and benefits of such an approach. In the practice of both institutional and community corrections, scientific evidence is important in formulating foundations for the operation of policies and programs. It identifies which are most likely to yield the desired results and where decisions can be guided to facilitate the achievement of safe, secure and humane institutions as well as enhanced community safety. Some observers criticize correctional policies and programs for contributing to high rates of recidivism, institutional violence, and the general failure of offenders to transform into productive and law-abiding citizens. It is therefore critical for correctional policies and practices to adhere to an evidence-based approach.

However, many of the ways that correctional facilities and programs operate are determined not by informed correctional administrators but instead by decision-makers outside the correctional enterprise. There are several obvious downfalls to this procedure. First, when decisions are made outside the correctional realm, these policies either may impose restrictions on corrections officials in being able to do what they know is in the best interests of offenders and society, or the policies may compel them to implement practices that differ from recognized best practices. Second, sizeable costs may not always achieve the most efficient distribution of resources. If increased resources do not accompany new public policies, corrections officials may be forced to reallocate funding away from well-informed and beneficial programs and practices. Third, when those outside the correctional industry develop policies, corrections officials can end up (inappropriately) bearing the brunt of public disparagement for ill-advised decisions.

The value of an evidence-based approach to policy development and program implementation is best realized when decisions are made by individuals who are educated in the extensive research literature and experienced in translating scientific data into correctional practices and programs. The focus of this article is on the effect of the misguided and detrimental development of a community corrections practice that ignores existing research evidence. Residential restrictions for registered sex offenders is a clear example of how criminal re-integration, and potentially public safety, are negatively impacted by the failure of policymakers to draw on research evidence in establishing crime prevention policy.

Sex Offender Registration and Residential Restrictions

The registration of sex offenders has been a prominent part of the American criminal justice landscape since 1994 when Congress enacted the Jacob Wetterling Act that required convicted sex offenders to record their addresses with local law enforcement agencies. Megan's Law amended the Wetterling Act in 1996 by allowing the dissemination of registry information directly to the public. In 2006, the Adam Walsh Sex Offender Registration and Notification Act facilitated the creation of a national, Internet-based searchable sex offender database; increased registration and notification requirements; and enhanced penalties for crimes against children and for failure to register.

As a result of increased awareness of sex offenders living in the nation's communities, approximately one-half of the states and hundreds of local municipalities have also enacted laws that impose restrictions on where registered sex offenders may reside. Explicitly intended to enhance the safety of children, these laws prohibit registered sex offenders from living within specified distances (usually one-quarter to one-half mile) of places where children are likely to congregate. Various state laws and local ordinances identify protected zones around entities such as schools, daycare centers, public playgrounds and swimming pools, libraries, and school bus stops. On the surface, such laws are both politically and socially attractive, as they appear to be intuitively logical and well-intentioned public policies.

However, although residence restrictions appear to be rational and valid social policy, there are numerous problems with both their design and implementation. Making communities safer for children is a laudable goal, but these laws do not achieve that goal because they are fundamentally flawed for several important reasons. First, these laws are based upon the widespread beliefs that sex offenders have extremely high recidivism rates, sex-crime rates are on the rise and sex offenders often kill their victims. Second, there is an assumption that sex offenders are a homogeneous group and that all pose equal risk. Residence laws usually apply to all registered sex offenders, regardless of whether an individual is a predatory pedophile or whether his (or her) victims of choice are adults, the elderly or family members. Finally, the myth of stranger danger assumes that sex offenders frequently make contact with potential child victims in public locations and that they entice or abduct unsupervised children from such places.

Flaw No. 1. Media attention of sex crimes, especially random and lethal acts of sexual violence against children, gives the impression that sex-crime rates are higher than ever. In actuality, sexual assaults, like most crimes, have been on the decline for 15 years. According to the U.S. Department of Health and Human Services, rates of substantiated sexual abuse of children have dropped by 51 percent since 1991. These declines are consistently seen in data from child protective services, law enforcement and victim surveys. Media coverage tends to portray sexually motivated child abductions as a real threat to children, but the Center for Missing and Exploited Children estimates that only approximately 100 such cases occur in the United States each year. Sex offenders also are reputed to have exceedingly high recidivism rates, inciting fear of inevitable re-offending. Large sophisticated studies following nearly 30,000 sex offenders from North America and Europe have found that, on average, only about 14 percent of convicted sex offenders are rearrested for new sex crimes within four to six years after release.[1]

Flaw No. 2. Recidivism rates differ based on the offense type and risk factors such as offender age, pattern of sexual deviance, criminal history and victim preferences. Pedophiles who molest boys have the highest probability of re-offense (but fewer than 40 percent of sex offenders are diagnosed with pedophilia), while rapists of adults have the next highest probability of re-offending. Though often thought of as the most relentless and dangerous of offenders, sex offenders are in fact among the least likely offenders to re-offend or to murder their victims.[2]

Flaw No. 3. Laws restricting where sex offenders may live have been inspired by crimes committed by perpetrators who were strangers to their victims. However, a well-established body of research has clearly demonstrated that such cases are the rare exception, not the typical way children come to be sexually victimized. Children are much more likely to be molested by trusted caretakers and relatives. The Bureau of Justice Statistics reported that 34 percent of sexually abused minors were assaulted by family members and 59 percent by acquaintances.[3] In addition, about 49 percent of victims under the age of six are abused by people related to them, and it is estimated that less than 7 percent of sex crimes against juveniles are committed by strangers. Similarly, about three-fourths of sex crimes against adults are perpetrated by known assailants, BJS reports.

Furthermore, children are not in schools and daycare centers by themselves, but instead are under the constant supervision of teachers, care providers and other adults. Even if one presumes that children at times play outside unsupervised, they are statistically unlikely to be approached or harmed by a registered sex offender. Such laws fail to acknowledge that the vast majority of child-victimizing sex offenders are not strangers who make contact with youngsters in public settings. One of the most conspicuous ironies of residence laws is that they control where sex offenders sleep, but do little to prevent a motivated predator from visiting places where he or she can cultivate relationships with children and groom them for sexual abuse.

The problems with residence laws extend to the authorities that are charged with enforcing them. As many communities have already experienced, when restrictions are imposed, many registered sex offenders "disappear" and go underground. Some offenders may be attempting to avoid overly harsh residential restriction laws, but others, who are having difficulty securing housing, may simply not have an address to register. This imposes serious (and costly) problems for law enforcement officials who have to allocate additional resources to track down missing sex offenders, and it also damages the validity of sex offender registries. As a result, communities may actually be less safe rather than more safe.

What the Evidence Says

No empirical data exist to support the belief that residence restrictions reduce sex offense recidivism. A 2004 Colorado study found that sex offense re-offenders were randomly located and did not live closer to schools and parks than those who did not re-offend.[4] In Minnesota, a 2003 study failed to find a relationship between proximity to schools and re-offending.[5] A subsequent Minnesota study concluded that "there is very little support for the notion that residency restriction laws would lower the incidence of sexual recidivism, particularly among child molesters," and that "rather than lowering sexual recidivism, housing restrictions may work against this goal by fostering conditions that exacerbate [problems with] sex offenders' reintegration."[6] Reinforcing this view, a California Research Bureau report, prepared for the Assembly Public Safety Committee, determined that "there is little research regarding the effectiveness of restricting the housing locations available to sex offenders, but the few studies available find they have no impact on re-offense rates."[7]

An emerging body of research is uncovering many unintended consequences of residential restrictions. Florida researchers found that the state's requirement that child molesters on probation live 1,000 feet from a school, park, playground, daycare center or other place where children congregate led to displacement and transience for many sex offenders.[8] About one-half were unable to live with family and found affordable housing less accessible. Many also described increased isolation and stress. These data were collected in 2004, prior to the explosion of municipal ordinances throughout Florida in 2005. Since that time, 24 of the 30 cities in Broward County (the Fort Lauderdale metropolitan area) have passed sex offender zoning laws requiring a buffer zone of 2,500 feet. A more recent study of 109 sex offenders in Broward County found that 39 percent reported a period of homelessness, and 22 percent said they were forced to relocate two or more times.[9] Almost one-half experienced a landlord refusing to rent to them, and 13 percent had been jailed for a residence violation.

In Indiana, one-fourth of sex offenders reported being unable to return to their homes after release from prison; more than one-third could not live with family members; and almost one-third said that a landlord refused to rent to them or to renew a lease.[10] As a result, offenders were forced to live farther away from employment opportunities, social services and mental health treatment programs. Young adults were especially affected, and age was significantly inversely correlated with being unable to live with family and with difficulties obtaining and maintaining affordable housing.

Geographical information system research, using mapping technology, has confirmed that residence restrictions gravely diminish housing availability. In Orange County (Orlando), Fla., researchers found that 64 percent of the residential properties are located within 2,500 feet of schools, and 99 percent are within 2,500 feet of bus stops.[11] When considering the locations of dwellings located within 2,500 feet of a variety of types of restricted locales (schools, parks, daycare centers and bus stops), only 37 residential properties remained available where sex offenders could live. Likewise, in Miami, sex offenders are living under bridges because the county's 2,500-foot restrictions leave virtually nowhere for them to live. Still, lawmakers are hesitant to repeal these laws.

Residence restrictions, which lead to instability, transience and hopelessness, contradict decades of criminological research identifying factors associated with successful offender re-integration. Sex offenders and other offenders with positive support systems are less likely to re-offend and violate probation than those who lack support. Stable employment and relationships make it less likely that offenders reentering the community will resume a life of crime.[12] Conversely, lifestyle instability and negative moods are associated with increased sexual recidivism. Social stigma and economic hardships resulting from conviction can preclude involvement in pro-social roles and activities, including employment, education, parenting and property ownership.[13] Social and economic marginalization is especially pronounced for registered sex offenders who are publicly identified.[14] Desistance from crime, however, is facilitated by reinforcing the offender's identity as a conforming and invested citizen, not by preventing the ability to meet basic needs.

It is important to note that corrections professionals, law enforcement agents, prosecutors and victim advocates generally believe that laws and policies restricting where registered sex offenders may live are ill-advised and ineffective. This can perhaps most clearly be seen in the fact that at the American Correctional Association's 2007 Winter Conference in Tampa, Fla., the association's Delegate Assembly passed the Resolution on Neighborhood Exclusion of Predatory Sex Offenders. This resolution calls for "all legislative bodies to take into consideration the unintended consequences of statutes intended to exclude these offenders from neighborhoods or locations." It goes on to state that ACA "supports legislation which is reasonably related to the ability of community corrections agencies to afford proper supervision and oversight to predatory sex offenders and which is practical, enforceable and likely to result in the protection of children and others in the community from sexual predators."

It is the responsibility of corrections professionals—through both rigorous empirical evaluation and the sharing of experiential knowledge—to identify correctional practices and policies that work to achieve goals of public safety and those that impede such goals. When well-intentioned but flawed policies create administrative and programmatic problems, it behooves those who are directly affected to communicate these deficiencies to lawmakers. In doing so, correctional administrators, practitioners and researchers need to collaborate with policymakers and support their arguments with scientific evidence. Using existing research to demonstrate the unintended adverse consequences of policies such as sex offender residential restrictions is one means to construct the argument. However, corrections officials need not rely solely on the evidence gathered by others. Rather, corrections officials need to apply their existing resources to assess externally imposed policies and practices—such as residential restrictions for sex offenders—and thereby accumulate evidence for what does work. Evaluation research, using state-of-the-art methodologies and conducted by credible and disinterested parties, is the key to collecting evidence designed to inform the development and modification of crime prevention policy, while facilitating desired outcomes of improved community safety as well as successful offender reentry.

Notes

1. Hanson, R.K. and M.T. Bussiere. 1998. Predicting relapse: A meta-analysis of sexual offender recidivism studies. *Journal of Consulting and Clinical Psychology,* 66(2):348–362.

    Hanson, R.K. and K. Morton-Bourgon. 2005. The characteristics of persistent sexual offenders: A meta-analysis of recidivism studies. *Journal of Consulting and Clinical Psychology,* 73(6):1154–1163.

2. Bureau of Justice Statistics. 2003. *Recidivism of sex offenders released from prison in 1994.* Washington, D.C.: U.S. Department of Justice.

Sample, L.L. 2006. An examination of the degree to which sex offenders kill. *Criminal Justice Review,* 31(3):230–250.

Sample, L.L. and T.M. Bray. 2003. Are sex offenders dangerous? *Criminology and Public Policy,* 3(1):59–82.

Sample, L.L. and T.M. Bray. 2006. Are sex offenders different? An examination of rearrest patterns. *Criminal Justice Policy Review,* 17(1):83–102.

3. Bureau of Justice Statistics. 2000. *Sexual assault of young children as reported to law enforcement: Victim, incident and offender characteristics.* Washington, D.C.: U.S. Department of Justice.

4. Colorado Department of Public Safety. 2004. *Report on safety issues raised by living arrangements for and location of sex offenders in the community.* Denver: Sex Offender Management Board.

5. Minnesota Department of Corrections. 2003. *Level three sex offenders residential placement issues.* St. Paul, Minn.: Minnesota DOC.

6. Minnesota Department of Corrections. 2007. *Residential proximity and sex offense recidivism in Minnesota.* St. Paul, Minn.: Minnesota DOC.

7. Nieto, M. and D. Jung. 2006. *The impact of residency restrictions on sex offenders and correctional management practices: A literature review.* Sacramento, Calif.: California Research Bureau.

8. Levenson, J.S. and L.P. Cotter. 2005. The impact of sex offender residence restrictions: 1,000 feet from danger or one step from absurd? *International Journal of Offender Therapy and Comparative Criminology,* 49(2):168–178.

9. Levenson, J.S. 2007. Collateral consequences of sex offender residence restrictions. Manuscript submitted for publication.

10. Levenson, J.S. and A. Hern. 2007. Sex offender residence restrictions: Unintended consequences and community re-entry. *Justice Research and Policy,* 9(1):60–73.

11. Zandbergen, P.A. and T.C. Hart. 2006. Reducing housing options for convicted sex offenders: Investigating the impact of residency restriction laws using GIS. *Justice Research and Policy,* 8(2):1–24.

12. Laub, J.H. and R.J. Sampson. 2001. Understanding desistance from crime. *Crime and Justice,* vol. 28:1–69.

13. Uggen, C., J. Manza and A. Behrens. 2004. Less than the average citizen: Stigma, role transition, and the civic reintegration of convicted felons. In *After crime and punishment: Pathways to offender reintegration,* eds. S. Maruna and R. Immarigeon, 258–290. Devon, United Kingdom: Willan Publishing.

14. Tewksbury, R. 2005. Collateral consequences of sex offender registration. *Journal of Contemporary Criminal Justice,* 21(1):67–82. Tewksbury, R. and M. Lees. 2006. Consequences of sex offender registration: Collateral consequences and community experiences. *Sociological Spectrum,* 26(3):309–334.

RICHARD TEWKSBURY is a professor of justice administration at the University of Louisville Department of Justice Administration. **JILL LEVENSON** is an assistant professor of human services at Lynn University in Florida.

When the Poor Go to Court

Across the nation, many indigents wind up being sentenced to jail time without ever seeing a lawyer.

KIT R. ROANE

L ast July, a homeless man named Hubert Lindsey was stopped by police officers in Gulfport, Miss., for riding his bicycle without a light. The police soon discovered that Lindsey was a wanted man. Gulfport records showed he owed $4,780 in old fines. So, off to jail he went.

Legal activists now suing the city in federal court say it was pretty obvious that Lindsey couldn't pay the fines. According to their complaint, he lived in a tent, was unemployed, and appeared permanently disabled by an unseeing eye and a mangled arm. But without a lawyer to plead his case, the question of whether Lindsey was a scofflaw or just plain poor never came up. Nor did the question of whether the fines were really owed, or if it was constitutional to jail him for debts he couldn't pay. Nobody, the activists say, even bothered to mention alternatives like community service. The judge ordered Lindsey to "sit out" the fine in jail. That took nearly two months.

Lindsey isn't the only poor American to face a judge on dubious charges without adequate legal representation. Far from it. More than 40 years after the Supreme Court ruled that competent counsel was a fundamental right of all Americans accused of crimes, the American Bar Association says thousands of indigent defendants still navigate the court system each year without a lawyer, or with one who doesn't have the time, resources, or interest to provide effective representation. Whether they face serious felony charges or misdemeanors, the poor often find themselves alone in a sometimes-Kafkaesque system where they have little, if any, voice.

Without advocates, some poor defendants serve jail time longer than the law requires or plead guilty to crimes they didn't commit just to get out of jail. A few, as has been documented, receive the death penalty or life in prison because their court-appointed lawyers were incompetent, lazy, or both. Most shocking, says Norman Lefstein, who chaired the American Bar Association's Indigent Defense Advisory Group, "is the lack of overall real success, the lack of progress" given the overwhelming evidence that inadequate counsel often leads to wrongful conviction. The many cases we know about "likely are only the tip of the iceberg," he says. "This is an enormous problem."

Kicking and screaming. It's also quite a complicated one. The federal government has been slow to the game, both in

providing funds or setting rules. That means that each state, and often each county, is left to its own devices on deciding how to fund and institute indigent-defense programs. Funding is a perpetual problem. In New York alone, there are more than 95 different systems. Sometimes, representation is determined by whichever lawyer bills taxpayers the least, no matter that the lawyer could have a full load of other pending cases.

It's not hard to see why the bottom line has such pull. Most states have a hard time coming up with the necessary dollars for indigent-defense programs, and only 27 attempt to provide full funding. That leaves already-strapped cities and counties on the hook for most of the costs—costs that must be weighed against local needs, from new roads to sewer upgrades and firehouses.

Shortfalls in some places are acute. In Alabama, pay cuts have caused lawyers representing indigent death penalty clients to flee the system. In New Mexico, a lack of funds to hire lawyers for indigent defendants caused the court of appeals there to place an ad for lawyers willing to work free.

While several states have enacted some reforms in recent years, most have been dragged kicking and screaming to the table, often on the heels of civil rights lawsuits, court orders, or striking examples of injustice made public. And while such reforms are welcome, critics say the jury is still out on how well they are implemented. In Georgia, for instance, new public defenders are required to contact their clients within 72 hours of their arrest, but there is no requirement that they do much else until a defendant has his day in court. In one case, a public defender representing a severely mentally ill woman facing a parole violation had contacted his client only once after her arrest and was not scheduled to see her again until a bond hearing set for nearly two months later. John Cole Vodicka, director of the Prison and Jail Project, a watchdog group active in southern Georgia, says the public defender didn't even meet with the woman personally on the first occasion; he sent her a form letter. Cole Vodicka left several messages for the lawyer, saying that he knew the woman from his church and that he could help get in touch with character witnesses with knowledge of her troubles and her mental illness. The lawyer failed to call him back, Cole Vodicka says. The woman's case is pending. Asked about the case, Samuel Merritt, the head of the public defender's office in that circuit, said his office should have fought more aggressively to schedule the woman's bond hearing for an earlier date, but he says the new system is generally working very well.

At least Georgia is trying. In many cities and states, advocates say, it appears officials have just ignored the law. The New York Civil Liberties Union has threatened to file suit against New York State. While New York City, which has a well-funded legal-aid office, is in many ways a model for other locales, the rural counties upstate are another story. In Schuyler County, lawyers for the National Association for the Advancement of Colored People's legal defense fund say an investigation they conducted revealed a system where indigent defendants routinely sat in jail for weeks or months without seeing a lawyer. Often they went through the entire court process, from arrest, to arraignment, on through bail hearings and even through plea bargains, without ever consulting an attorney. One public defender, they say, deliberately kept his phone off the hook.

Then there's Gulfport, the second largest city in Mississippi, which, up until Hurricane Katrina hit, was beating the pavement looking for those who owed fines for things like public profanity—at $222 a pop. The result of Gulfport's fine-reclamation project was that while it collected modest sums of money, it also packed the county jail with hundreds of people who couldn't pay. The Southern Center for Human Rights filed a federal civil rights lawsuit against Gulfport last July. Attorney Sarah Geraghty says that before bringing the case against the city, she witnessed hundreds of court adjudications involving Gulfport's poor in which no defense attorney was present or even offered. Many defendants, Geraghty said, were obviously indigent, mentally ill, or physically disabled, like Hubert Lindsey; some had been jailed for fines they had already paid. One mentally ill woman attempted suicide by jumping from an elevated cell in the county jail after she was picked up for having failed to pay several city fines; the lawsuit alleges that police then grabbed her again on the same charge a few months later, causing her to miss the surgery scheduled to fix the broken bones in her feet.

The city says it is still reviewing the lawsuit, but there is talk of a settlement. And Geraghty, who recently sat in on the court's proceedings again, says judges are now advising indigent defendants of their rights. But it never should have taken a lawsuit, adds Geraghty, noting that the problem with the city's actions was clear: "It's illegal. Period."

Justice & Antonin Scalia
The Supreme Court's Most Strident Catholic

JULIA VITULLO-MARTIN

After being nominated as a Supreme Court Justice by President Ronald Reagan in 1986, Antonin Scalia faced down the Democratic-controlled Senate Judiciary Committee by refusing to discuss his views on any question likely to come before him as a sitting justice. Yet his confirmation hearings became a virtual lovefest. Scalia handled his interrogation so engagingly that the Senate voted ninety-eight to zero to confirm him. Reagan was said to have danced around the Oval Office, singing "Scalia/I've just picked a judge named Scalia," to the tune of *West Side Story's* "Maria."

Reagan knew what he was getting. Scalia would soon establish himself as one of the most brilliant and belligerent conservatives ever to sit on the high court. The late Justice William Brennan's reputation as the most influential Supreme Court justice of his generation would shortly pass to Scalia, asserted Michael Greve, cofounder of the libertarian Center for Individual Rights, a public-interest law firm in Washington, D.C.

From today's perspective, in which Scalia has emerged as a reliable proponent of hard-right views on issues from property rights to the death penalty, his confirmation hearings seem to have happened in a parallel universe. Some senators even called Scalia by his nickname, Nino. It became clear that Nino was a man of many parts—Nino, the tennis player, opera singer, pianist, poker player, raconteur, man about town, father of nine. Potential enemies were declawed by his accomplishments and affability. Howard Metzenbaum, for example, an outspokenly liberal Ohio Democrat, announced that Scalia's conservatism was irrelevant and that all that mattered was his "fitness." Senator Edward Kennedy worried that Scalia might be "insensitive" on women's rights, but concluded that one could hardly "maintain that Judge Scalia is outside the mainstream."

His immigrant saga—the only child of a Sicilian father and a first-generation Italian-American mother—was lavishly praised. Born in 1936, he spent his early childhood in Trenton, New Jersey, before the family moved to New York, when his father became a professor of Romance languages at Brooklyn College. He graduated first in his class from Saint Francis Xavier, a Jesuit high school in Manhattan, first in his class from Georgetown University, and cum laude from Harvard Law School. He went on to practice law from 1961 to 1967 with Cleveland's most prestigious firm, Jones, Day, Cockley, and Reavis—named after the city's first family of Virginia, became general counsel to the White House Office Telecommunications Policy, chaired the Administrative Conference of the United States, and became assistant attorney general in the U.S. Department of Justice's Office of Legal Counsel. In 1977, he joined the law faculty at the University of Chicago, from which he was appointed in 1982 to the nation's second most important court, the U.S. Court of Appeals for the D.C. Circuit.

Even the legal press was effusive about Scalia's Supreme Court confirmation. Tony Mauro in the *Legal Times* predicted that Scalia would become the court's "intellectual lodestar."

How, then, did this exemplar of charm and learning become what he is today—the scourge of the country's liberal establishment? FindLaw columnist Edward Lazarus, for example, recently questioned Scalia's integrity, arguing that his reputation as "a rigorous and thoroughly principled jurist" has always seemed to him "largely a myth." (Lazarus's own moral claim to fame: he betrayed the ethics of his Supreme Court clerkship by publishing the first and only insider account of the workings of the Court. But that's another story.) Ex-prosecutor and best-selling legal commentator Vincent Bugliosi's inflammatory charge is that "having Justice Antonin Scalia speak on ethics is like having a prostitute speak on sexual abstinence." Peter Laarman, minister at New York's Judson Memorial Church, gave a sermon naming Justices Scalia and Clarence Thomas as members of the "scary lunatic fringe occupying most of the seats of power."

Scoffing at the idea that our "maturing" society's "evolving standards of decency" might in and of themselves make the death penalty unconstitutional, Scalia said that the Constitution he interprets and applies is not living but dead.

But the pièce de résistance of liberal loathing can be found in a July 8, 2002, OpEd in the *New York Times* by Princeton professor Sean Wilentz. Wilentz attacked a speech Scalia had given at the University of Chicago Divinity School (and reworked for the conservative journal, *First Things*), arguing that the Eighth Amendment's prohibition of cruel and unusual punishment does not proscribe the death penalty. Scalia's remarks, wrote Wilentz, "show bitterness against democracy, strong dislike for the Constitution's approach to religion, and eager advocacy for the submission of the individual to the state. It is a chilling mixture for an American."

More important for Wilentz and his political allies, this is a chilling mixture for a chief justice—a job Scalia is rumored to want and that President George W. Bush is rumored to want him to have. While the chief is only first among equals, he has the crucial task of assigning opinions in which he is in the majority. A powerful, congenial chief such as Chief Justice Earl Warren—or William Rehnquist, for that matter—can mold the court in his image through persuasive deliberations and adept assignments. Scalia puts little effort into winning over those who disagree with him. Harvard Professor Lawrence Tribe once pointed out that Scalia's "vigor and occasional viciousness" in his written opinions may "alienate people who might be his allies in moving the Court to the right. I therefore hope he will keep it up." There's little reason to think that as chief Scalia wouldn't keep it up. After all, he recently attacked all his colleagues, asserting that the justices on the Court were no better qualified to rule on the right to die than nine people selected at random from a Kansas City phone book. He also took them on individually. He ridiculed Justice Stephen Breyer, for example, for writing a decision so vague that it gave trial courts "not a clue" as to how to carry it out. He mocked Justice David Souter for resorting "to that last hope of lost interpretive causes, that Saint Jude of the hagiography of statutory construction, legislative history."

Scalia can be particularly provocative, even shocking, on race. In a majority opinion on racially based jury selection, he attacked Justice Thurgood Marshall, saying that his dissent "rolls out the ultimate weapon, the accusation of insensitivity to racial discrimination—which will lose its intimidating effect if it continues to be fired so randomly." Given that Marshall knew far better than Scalia the reality of racial discrimination when he saw it—he was surely the only justice in the history of the Supreme Court to have once been dragged to a river by a lynch mob—even years later Scalia's words seem intemperate and misplaced.

He can also be combative on issues that usually call for compassion. He says that the death penalty, for example, is not a "difficult, soul-wrenching question." Scoffing at the idea that our "maturing" society's "evolving standards of decency" might in and of themselves make the death penalty unconstitutional, Scalia said that the Constitution he interprets and applies is not living but dead. Or, as he prefers to put it, "enduring." It means today not what current society (much less the Court) thinks it ought to mean, but what it meant when it was adopted. Scalia has even affronted his conservative Catholic supporters. He's argued (correctly) that the pope's opposition to the death penalty expressed in *Evangelium vitae* is not "binding teaching" requiring adherence by all Catholics—though they must give it

thoughtful and respectful consideration. When Cardinal Avery Dulles said he agreed with the pope's position, Scalia answered that this was "just the phenomenon of the clerical bureaucracy saying, 'Yes, boss.'"

What the pope has to say is irrelevant to him as a judge, says Scalia, since his own views on the morality of the death penalty have nothing to do with how he votes judicially. However, one's moral views do govern whether or not one can or should be a judge at all. "When I sit on a Court that reviews and affirms capital convictions," said Scalia, "I am part of 'the machinery of death.'" The Supreme Court's ruling is often the last step that permits an execution to proceed. Any judge who believes the death penalty immoral should resign, he says, rather than "simply ignoring duly enacted, constitutional laws and sabotaging death-penalty cases."

How, then, can Scalia continue to serve as a judge in a court that has repeatedly upheld abortion, which he regards as immoral? Capital cases, argues Scalia, are different from the other life-and-death issues the Court might hear, like abortion or legalized suicide. In these instances, it is not the state that is decreeing death, but private individuals whom the state has decided not to restrain. One may argue (as many do) that society has a moral obligation to interfere. That moral obligation may weigh heavily upon the voter, and upon the legislator who enacts the laws, Scalia argues, but a judge "bears no moral guilt for the laws society has failed to enact."

Ironically, despite Scalia's carefully drawn, if dubious, distinctions, Scalia's antagonist Wilentz accuses him of believing that Catholics, as citizens, would be unable to uphold views that contradict church doctrine. A shocked Wilentz says that Scalia "sees submission as desirable." This, Wilentz continues, is "exactly the stereotype of Catholicism as papist mind-control that Catholics have struggled against, and that John F. Kennedy did so much to overcome."

Obedience, for good or ill, is indeed an ongoing Scalia theme. He has joked more than once that the keys to being a good Catholic and a good jurist are the same: being strong enough to obey the relevant law. Still, he has not urged submission on American Catholic citizens.

Wilentz also writes that despite calling himself a strict constructionist—actually, he doesn't—Scalia wants to impose "a religious sense that is directly counter to the abundantly expressed wishes of the men who wrote the Constitution." This is not strict constructionism, says Wilentz. It "is opportunism, and it threatens democracy."

Is Wilentz right? Is Scalia an opportunist who threatens the very democracy whose Constitution he has sworn to uphold? Or is he a brave originalist, seeking to return to the principles of the American Founding Fathers that the Court discarded in the last fifty years?

The answer is not yet clear. Part of the anger Scalia arouses is a result of how successful he has been in restoring respect for the Constitution's actual words. Calling his approach textualism, Scalia argues that primacy must be given to the text, structure, and history of any document—Constitution or statute—being interpreted. Judges, he says, are to eschew their own "intellectual, moral, and personal perceptions." Scalia says he takes the Constitution as it is, not as he wants it to be.

In effect, of course, this is an attack on much of twentieth-century jurisprudence, which has created a host of new constitutional rights by embracing such Holmesian ideas as the "balancing of competing interests" and Justice William Brennan's "living Constitution." This expanded vision of the Constitution gave judges enormous power to assert that their individual policy preferences and social goals—however unpopular—were also the law. As Scalia wrote in his solo, and prescient, dissent in the case recognizing the constitutionality of the now notorious Office of the Special Prosecutor: "Evidently, the governing standard is to be what might be called the unfettered wisdom of a majority of this Court, revealed to an obedient people in a case-by-case basis. This is not only not the government of laws that the Constitution established, it is not a government of laws at all."

Larry Kramer, a law professor at New York University, calls Scalia's belief that judges should renounce their own desires when interpreting the law "judicial asceticism." He argues that Scalia's "formalism, textualism, and originalism are only means: denial and self-control are the reasons."

If Scalia's first sin in the eyes of doctrinaire liberals is his textualism, make no mistake about the fact that his second sin is that he is a practicing Catholic—or, as commentators repeatedly mention, a "devout" Catholic. (How the devotion is known is not clear.) Of course, the sins of textualism and Catholicism are not unrelated—both reflect respect for the written word, an ordered universe, and an attachment to tradition. And both have a long contentious relationship with liberalism. Wilentz probably put his finger on something important when he wrote, "One senses that Mr. Scalia's true priority is to get secular humanists off the federal bench."

Certainly, there is something admirable in Scalia's allegiance to tradition and his stubborn refusal to pander on moral issues—both of which predictably incite his critics to excess. Harvard Law Professor Alan Dershowitz, for example, calls Scalia the "voice of Spanish clerical conservatism." The liberal *American Prospect* magazine scathingly refers to Scalia's "Jesuitical" logic. The editor of Salon.com wrote that defenders of the Bush v. Gore decision, in which Scalia played such a large role, "would have to perform feats of casuistry unseen since the days when Ignatius Loyola strode the earth to do so." Calling Scalia a cheap-shot artist, *Washington Post* columnist Richard Cohen maintains that the justice's mind is rigid on constitutional issues between church and state: "Anyone who thinks Scalia will give First Amendment issues a fair and reasoned hearing is, it seems, proceeding in a way Scalia would appreciate: solely on faith."

These knee-jerk liberal denunciations are appalling in a way, but while some of these comments might set off alarms for William Donohue and his Catholic League cohorts, they do not represent a revival of pure, nineteenth-century anti-Catholicism.

No respectable attack was ever leveled at the Catholicism of Scalia's nemesis, Justice William Brennan. Generally thought by legal scholars (including Scalia) to have been the twentieth century's most influential justice, Brennan may well have also been the most loved. He was a brilliant, strategic, persuasive conciliator who more often than not won the day. He once said, "With five votes you can do anything around here." His "living Constitution" is both the dominant liberal constitutional concept and the polar opposite of Scalia's textualism.

Scalia, in contrast, goes out of his way to give speeches like his provocative 1996 "Fools for Christ's Sake" address at the Mississippi College of Law, a Baptist school. Most (perhaps all) of his critics missed the reference to Saint Paul and therefore misinterpreted the speech, but then Scalia pretty much knew they would. Baiting the opposition—whether outside or inside the Court—is basic to his temperament.

As a Catholic who grew up in working-class neighborhoods (even though his father was an academic), Scalia often reveals a different sensibility from his Brahmin peers. In a 1979 law review article he denounced "the Wisdoms and the Powells and the Whites," whose ancestors participated in the oppression of African Americans, and who as justice sought to correct the effects of that ancestral oppression at the expense of newer immigrants. In a 1987 dissent he defended the "unknown, unaffluent, and unorganized" workers ignored by proponents of affirmative action.

And, then, of course, there's abortion, by far the most divisive social issue of our time, and one that Scalia argues should be settled legislatively rather than judicially. Yet the conservative Rehnquist Court has signaled more than once that it's not going to reverse *Roe v. Wade*. It doesn't really matter to a majority of the Court that Scalia was probably correct when he said, "I do not believe—and for two hundred years, no one believed—that the Constitution contains a right to abortion." In *A Matter of Interpretation* (Princeton), his Tanner Lectures at Princeton, he cautions that creating new constitutional rights may trigger a majoritarian reaction. "At the end of the day," he notes, "an evolving Constitution will evolve the way the majority wishes." One has to wonder whether the 2002 elections giving the House, Senate, and (by extension, the Supreme Court) to the Republicans reflect, in part, this prediction come true.

Scalia's third sin is his shockingly bad temper, in print, toward his intellectual opponents. Some of his harshest language concerning his colleagues came in his criticism of *Roe*: "The emptiness of the 'reasoned judgment' that produced *Roe* is displayed in plain view by the fact . . . that the best the Court can do to explain how it is that the word 'liberty' must include the right to destroy human fetuses is to rattle off a collection of adjectives that simply decorate a value judgment and conceal a political choice."

That temper has regularly been directed at centrist Justice Sandra Day O'Connor, who often must be wooed as the crucial fifth vote in a conservative coalition. In dissenting from *Planned Parenthood v. Casey* (1992), Scalia questioned O'Connor's intelligence. "Reason finds no refuge in this jurisprudence of confusion," he wrote.

Such outbursts have been costly. For many years, O'Connor avoided signing majority opinions authored by Scalia, which meant that Chief Justice Rehnquist—who needed her vote—avoided assigning controversial opinions to Scalia.

Perhaps Scalia's most troubling sin is that he does not always hold himself to his own principles. He explains his judicial rigidity by saying that when "I adopt a general rule, and say 'This is the basis of our decision,' I not only constrain lower courts, I constrain myself as well. If the next case should have such different facts that my political or policy preferences regarding the outcome are quite opposite, I will be unable to indulge those preferences; I have committed myself to the governing principle." Such rules can embolden judges to be courageous when having to issue an unpopular ruling, such as one protecting a criminal defendant's rights. All around, an admirable position.

How then to explain *Bush v. Gore*, the 5-4 ruling that effectively handed the presidency to George W. Bush in 2000? Bush may well have won the election fair and square, but we'll never know for sure. This was the first time in American history that the Court decided a presidential election, and it did so by improbably concluding that Florida's diverse standards for counting votes constituted an equal protection violation under the Fourteenth Amendment. Scalia's respect for established precedents and his disdain for catchall uses of the equal protection clause suddenly didn't seem to apply here—nor did his reverence for the separation of powers. As if the decision weren't mischievous enough, the Court also pronounced—amazingly—that "our consideration is limited to the present circumstances, for the problem of equal protection in election processes generally presents many complexities." Since when does the Supreme Court limit its rulings to present circumstances?

Ironically, Scalia's tightly argued dissent in *Casey* eerily foreshadows his own lead role in the scandal of *Bush v. Gore*: "The Imperial Judiciary lives," Scalia wrote. "It is instructive to compare this Nietzschean vision of us unelected, life-tenured judges—leading a Volk who will be 'tested by following,' and whose very 'belief in themselves' is mystically bound up in their 'understanding' of a Court that 'speak[s] before all others for their constitutional ideals'—with the somewhat more modest role envisioned for these lawyers by the Founders."

How can Scalia reconcile his principled views with his vote in *Bush v. Gore*? There aren't many convincing answers. His opponents claim Scalia acted as a ruthless, self-serving politician who put his own boy in power when it looked like the other side might win. Another possible explanation is that Scalia believes deeply something else he said in his *Casey* dissent, which is that *Roe* "fanned into life an issue that has inflamed our national politics in general, and has obscured with its smoke the selection of justices to this Court, in particular, ever since." In other words, the Court has embroiled itself in political issues that should be left to the people and their representatives—and that only a Republican administration would set the Court back on its right course. (It is not at all clear that this will happen.) Thus Scalia saw nothing wrong with the

language he used in concurring with the Court's stay (by definition an emergency measure) halting the Florida vote recount. Continuing the manual count, wrote Scalia, would "threaten irreparable harm" to Bush "and to the country, by casting a cloud upon what he claims to be the legitimacy of his election." He may never have written a less convincing justification of one of his positions, but it makes some sense if understood in light of how far wrong he thinks the Court has gone.

Scalia has spent most of his career captivating others, who often let their affection for him overcome their distaste for some of his ideas. He is a social animal, and it is possible that his fury about being correct yet alone over several momentous issues has warped his judgment on others—on which he is probably not right. His wrath is born of his self-confidence in the face of universal opposition. Take two 1988 dissents, *Morrison* and *Mistretta*, which, in the words of Northwestern University Law Professor Thomas Merrill, showed Scalia to be "completely isolated" on the Court. Isolated he may have been, but he was also completely right.

Morrison v. Olson was the decision upholding the Independent Counsel Act. Scalia's colleagues thought he had pretty much lost it when he ferociously wrote, "The institutional design of the Independent Counsel is designed to heighten, not to check, all of the institutional hazards of the dedicated prosecutor; the danger of too narrow a focus, of the loss of perspective, of preoccupation with the pursuit of one alleged suspect to the exclusion of other interests." With unchecked discretionary powers and unlimited funds, the independent counsel would be accountable to no one and would be entirely focused on a single target. The office would encourage the worst tendencies in American democracy. "The context of this statute is acrid with the smell of threatened impeachment," wrote Scalia. Indeed.

The history of the Independent Counsel Act is replete with examples of prosecutorial abuse that would have made the Founders recoil. Scalia accurately predicted, "If the prosecutor is obliged to choose his case, it follows that he can choose his defendants. Therein is the most dangerous power of the prosecutor: that he will pick people that he thinks he should get, rather than cases that need to be prosecuted. . . . It is not a question of discovering the commission of a crime and then looking for the man who has committed it, it is a question of picking the man and then searching the law books, or putting investigators to work, to pin some offense on him."

Mistretta v. U.S., the other dissent that isolated Scalia, concerned a revolution in criminal sentencing that has gone almost unnoticed by most Americans. In 1984, Congress established the U.S. Sentencing Commission as an independent rule-making body to promulgate mandatory guidelines for every federal criminal offense. The act specifically rejected rehabilitation as a goal of imprisonment, and mandated instead "that punishment should serve retributive, educational, deterrent, and incapacitative goals." All sentences would become determinate (fixed), with no parole other than a small credit that could be earned by good behavior.

Indeed, the country has grappled with the gross injustices of federal sentencing. In the past, judges were able to use their discretion to minimize inequities in the law. No longer. Now judges are governed by this new branch of government, by what Scalia mockingly calls "a sort of junior-varsity Congress."

Scalia lost on *Mistretta*, but he eventually won on another crucial sentencing issue—victim impact statements. In the mid-1970s, the Supreme Court had begun requiring that defendants in capital cases be allowed to present "mitigating circumstances" during the sentencing phase of capital trials. Yet while defendants in particularly heinous crimes could present evidence about an abusive childhood, victims and their families had no standing to speak. The Supreme Court repeatedly said victim-impact statements created a constitutionally unacceptable risk of arbitrary and capricious decisions by juries. Worse, they would focus attention not on the moral guilt of the defendant's alleged harms to society but on the emotions and opinions of persons who were not parties to the crime. Scalia dissented, attacking the "recently invented" requirement of mitigating circumstances, asking why the jury could not also take into account "the specific harm visited upon society by a murderer." In 1991, in *Payne v. Tennessee*, the Court finally agreed and overturned the ban on victim-impact statements. Justice Marshall announced his retirement the same day—some said because his heart was broken.

This term the Court has ruled 5 to 4 on another sentencing issue—California's three-strikes law. Like victim-impact statements, added punishment for multiple offenses has a long tradition in the common law. Adopted by referendum in 1994, California's harsh law permits judges to treat crimes that would ordinarily be considered misdemeanors as third felonies. (Most states with three-strikes laws require the third strike to actually be a felony, usually a violent one.) The particular cases before the Court involved life sentences for two men whose third crimes were shoplifting—$1,200 worth of golf clubs in one case, and $154 worth of children's videotapes in the other.

Here was a case with Scalia's favorite elements: the direct voice of the majority expressed via referendum, state sovereignty via its law, and centuries of Anglo-Saxon tradition. All of these considerations were to be weighed in determining the punishment of two career criminals who had led astonishingly unproductive lives. What should society do with such people? It is a testament to the revolution Scalia has wrought that this case even came before the Court, much less that the Court upheld three strikes. No longer do courts cavalierly assume that the Constitution prevents Americans from protecting themselves against known repeat predators. We are reminded, again, that in most matters of criminal justice, Scalia is the people champion— even if this decision was written by his protagonist, Justice O'Connor, leaving him to concur. This, in turn, reminds us of the conundrum of his role in *Bush v. Gore*. There he seemed to place the "irreparable harm" that a Florida recount would do to petitioner George W. Bush above the irreparable harm to citizens whose votes would not even be counted. Is Antonin Scalia an opportunist or an originalist? Perhaps he is both.

JULIA VITULLO-MARTIN writes frequently for *Commonweal,* the *Wall Street Journal,* and other publications. She is working on a book on the American Jury and Criminal Law.

UNIT 5

Juvenile Justice

Unit Selections

Key Points to Consider

- What reform efforts are currently under way in the juvenile justice system?

- What are some recent trends in juvenile delinquency? In what ways will the juvenile justice system be affected by these trends?

- Is the departure of the juvenile justice system from its original purpose warranted? Why or why not?

Student Website
www.mhhe.com/cls

Internet References

Gang Land: The Jerry Capeci Page
http://www.ganglandnews.com
Institute for Intergovernmental Research (IIR)
http://www.iir.com
National Criminal Justice Reference Service (NCJRS)
http://virlib.ncjrs.org/JuvenileJustice.asp
Partnership Against Violence Network
http://www.pavnet.org

Although there were variations within specific offense categories, the overall arrest rate for juvenile violent crime remained relatively constant for several decades. Then, in the late 1980s, something changed; more and more juveniles charged with a violent offense were brought into the justice system. The juvenile justice system is a twentieth-century response to the problems of dealing with children in trouble with the law, or children who need society's protection.

Juvenile court procedure differs from the procedure in adult courts because juvenile courts are based on the philosophy that their function is to treat and to help, not to punish and abandon the offender. Recently, operations of the juvenile court have received criticism, and a number of significant Supreme Court decisions have changed the way that the courts must approach the rights of children. Despite these changes, however, the major thrust of the juvenile justice system remains one of diversion and treatment, rather than adjudication and incarceration, although there is a trend toward dealing more punitively with serious juvenile offenders.

In this unit's opening article, "America's Imprisoned Kids," Ari Paul reports that there are some signs of change in the way the United States detains and sentences juvenile offenders.

In the next article of this unit, "The 21st Century Juvenile Justice Work Force," the authors examine the difficulty corrections departments face in recruiting for positions in juvenile corrections. "Teens Caught in the Middle: Juvenile Justice System and Treatment" shows the frustrations and inadequacies of the justice system in dealing with teen crime. Nelson and Olcott report in "Jail Time Is Learning Time" about the efforts of New York State's Onondaga County Justice Center

© BananaStock/PunchStock

in rehabilitating its inmates by offering them valuable classroom instruction. In "Lifers as Teenagers, Now Seeking Second Chance," Adam Liptak writes about the unique American practice of convicting young adolescents as adults and sentencing them to live their lives in prison.

Studies that look at adolescent dating violence are the subject of the article by Jouriles, et al. Concluding this section, Moore describes what happens to young people with mental illness who find themselves in the juvenile justice system.

America's Imprisoned Kids

The United States is an outlier in the world when it comes to detaining and sentencing juvenile offenders as adults. But there are finally signs of change.

ARI PAUL

There can only be a few issues where government policies in countries like Libya and Burma appear more progressive than those in the United States. Juvenile sentencing is one of them.

The United States currently imprisons 2,270 people who have life sentences without the chance for parole for crimes they committed when they were minors, according to both Human Rights Watch and Amnesty International; in all other nations on Earth, there are a combined total of only 12 such prisoners, HRW says. These are grim figures to prison reform advocates in the United States, who have long battled with the punitive, get-tough ethos that dominates American political discussion about criminal justice issues. But there are notable signs of a turn in the political winds.

Alison Parker, a researcher for HRW, has documented this kind of sentencing, and the United States is far behind the curve when it comes to the rights of child prisoners. The United Nation's Convention on the Rights of the Child provides that children may not receive life sentences without parole or the death penalty. All member states have ratified the CRC—except Somalia and the United States. (Both have signed the treaty but have not ratified it.)

The reality, she maintains, is that most countries do not even contemplate sanctioning this kind of punishment. (This isn't to say that the rest of the world is perfect on the matter. "Israel, South Africa and Tanzania reported that they were in violation of the treaty," Parker says.) Domestically, what is just as disturbing for Parker is that her research has found that African American criminal youths in California receive life without parole at a rate 22 times that for their white counterparts.

For Babe Howell, a law professor at New York University and a former criminal defense attorney, this is a symptom of something larger in the United States. "I think we are so punitive in terms of juvenile sentencing for the same reasons why we are so punitive in terms of all other sentencing," she says. "The reason why we are so punitive otherwise is the harder question, although I think it may have to do with how diverse our society is and that criminal sentences generally fall on people regarded as 'other.' I also think that politics have a lot to do with it. Being

soft on crime is untenable and voting for sentencing increases is just so easy."

Indeed, the trend in trying juveniles as adults started in earnest in the 1980s, when homicide rates in the nation started to soar. (Those rates have come down dramatically since.) By the late 1990s most states had made reforms to make the trial of juveniles as adults easier. And it was at this time that Senator Orrin Hatch of Utah introduced the get-tough Violent and Repeat Juvenile Offender Act, which passed in 1999.

But there are some signs of a potential shift in that prevailing political culture. To take one of the most notable examples, a bill in the California Senate that would make it impossible for the state's judges to sentence criminals younger than 18 to life without the chance of parole is now moving forward. In April 2007 the California Senate Committee on Public Safety passed the Juvenile Life Without Parole Reform Act. The state senator behind it is Leland Yee, a Democrat who has a doctorate in child psychology. He says that the human brain is still maturing during adolescence, and therefore minors are more likely to rehabilitate. "We should always sentence kids a little differently," says Adam Keigwin, a spokesperson for Sen. Yee.

A vote before the full state Senate should take place by mid-May. Some of the bill's supporters are hopeful about its eventual passage. In fact, Republican Governor Arnold Schwarzenegger has made at least some efforts to refocus the state's prison system towards rehabilitation. But Keigwin knows the supporters have to win over conservatives in the legislature, especially those allied with the Christian right. "The message of redemption is very important to them," Parker says. Meanwhile, to appeal to fiscally conservative lawmakers, Yee and the bill's supporters are arguing that it will cost the state $500 million to imprison the current population of minors sentenced without the chance of parole until their deaths.

But it remains the case that any such attempt to reform aspects of America's prison-industrial complex will involve tussling with powerful and entrenched interests. Moreover, the culture of excessive punishment pervades all parts of the American political spectrum.

For example, while the Supreme Court, in the 2005 case *Roper v. Simmons*, ended by a vote of 5–4 the practice of putting to death inmates for crimes committed when they were minors, the written dissents are telling. Sandra Day O'Connor, then the court's famed moderate, said that a difference in maturity levels was not a compelling enough reason to rob the state's ability of executing such convicts. Antonin Scalia scoffed at the majority opinion's comparison to what other countries do. "'Acknowledgement' of foreign approval has no place in the legal opinion of this Court," he wrote. Rhetoric like that is an attempt to neuter the ability of attorneys to use an international standard in charging that specific punishments are 'cruel and unusual' and thus unconstitutional.

While many are hopeful about Yee's proposed legislation in California, if it too fails to pass, it will serve as an all-too-typical illustration of the shame that is America's sentencing policy.

"Given current politics it is not clear to me that there are any promising arguments against these sentencing norms but human rights law," says Howell. "International embarrassment may someday put us in a position where life sentences for juveniles become as embarrassing as Jim Crow did in the 1950s and 1960s."

ARI PAUL is a reporter for *The Chief-Leader,* a weekly newspaper covering municipal labor unions in New York City. He has also written for *Z, In These Times,* and many other publications.

The 21st Century Juvenile Justice Work Force

Meghan Howe, Elyse Clawson, and John Larivee

Corrections is facing a work force crisis, as are many other fields in the public sector. Changing demographics are leading to a dwindling number of motivated, qualified workers entering and remaining in the corrections field. This reduction of potential employees is coupled with the challenges that agencies face in a dynamic field, where the number of clients is increasing and policy and practice are continuously evolving. The field is facing a serious question of how to keep up.

The American Correctional Association is meeting this challenge with its Building a Correctional Workforce for the 21st Century project. This includes both adult and juvenile corrections, and has begun to identify the work force needs and concerns regarding front-line workers in both arenas. This begs the question: Is it appropriate to consider juvenile and adult correctional workers as one work force? While both groups fulfill a critical public safety role, juvenile justice is additionally charged with a child welfare role. The potential of the work force to nurture the positive growth and development of children, or conversely to place children in harm's way, adds another dimension to the consequences of a work force crisis in juvenile justice. Thus, it is worthwhile to consider this work force as a separate entity.

Juvenile Justice Workers

There is little specific information available on the juvenile justice work force. Aggregate data on the number of workers in the field, their education and experience levels, average salary, and demographic information are generally best-guess estimates. This is the case for several reasons. Juvenile justice often is not considered a field on its own, which discourages the collection and tracking of data on the work force. The Bureau of Labor Statistics[1] does not maintain a job classification for juvenile detention workers or juvenile probation officers, so no specific trend or forecasting data are available at the national level. In many cases, individual agencies maintain work force data for their own population, but no comprehensive efforts have been undertaken to compile and analyze this information.

However, three initiatives have shed some light on the state of the juvenile justice work force. The first is ACA's 21st century work force effort, which is aimed at developing a strategic plan for the correctional work force and draws predominantly from data on the adult correctional work force. The second is the Human Services Workforce Initiative, funded by the Annie E. Casey Foundation (of which the authors are grantees) and administered through Cornerstones for Kids. This initiative is attempting to improve outcomes for children and families by improving the quality of the human services work force, including juvenile justice. The third initiative relies on data compiled by the National Center on Juvenile Justice, such as state profiles that include some training, caseload and salary information for probation officers. In addition, some of these data are confounded with information from adult correctional departments.

Together, these initiatives describe several characteristics of the work force, as well as several areas for further research:

- According to the Annie E. Casey Foundation, the juvenile justice work force comprises approximately 300,000 workers earning an average of $30,000 per year.[2]
- Several studies[3] indicate that workers remain in the field because they enjoy working with children and families, and they want to help children achieve meaningful outcomes.
- Workers leave the field because of long hours, insufficient support from supervisors, low pay, lack of a career ladder and high stress.[4]
- Workers perceive that they are managing more high-need children than in the past, such as those with substance abuse or mental health disorders, and that they are not trained to manage this population.[5]
- Working conditions vary widely between agencies, but many workers feel that they work in unsafe conditions.[6]

Though this information is not representative, it paints a picture of many employees who are dedicated to the needs of children but often frustrated with stressful working conditions and a lack of recognition and opportunities for advancement.

The Human Services Workforce Initiative also sought to identify the competencies (i.e., the knowledge, skills and attributes) that make an effective juvenile justice worker. Both front-line staff and managers listed similar competencies, including good communication skills, patience, creativity, respect, motivation, compassion and commitment to youths. However, many workers also agreed that these attributes were not necessarily reflected in job descriptions and that agencies do not always know how to hire for those competencies.

Role Duality in Juvenile Justice

Juvenile justice workers fulfill a dual role: a public safety and accountability role, which involves the management of youths' behavior, and a rehabilitation and youth development role, which involves mentoring and coaching youths in pro-social skill development. This duality is a source of frustration as well as opportunity among the juvenile justice workers.

A source of frustration is that the field is not well defined for potential and current employees. This results in confusion for workers who are not well prepared for their role[7] and difficulty in recruiting workers who are appropriately educated and trained. Many juvenile justice positions now require a bachelor's degree. However, degrees in the social sciences or social work do not prepare candidates for the public safety aspect of the job, and programs in criminal justice do not address the youth development role of the juvenile justice worker. In both cases, it is possible to complete a degree without ever taking a course specifically related to juvenile justice; such courses may not even be offered for interested students. As a result, students may leave college without considering juvenile justice as an option, without an understanding of what the work entails or with the idea that juvenile justice is simply a stepping stone to a career in adult corrections.

For entry-level employees, role duality can be especially frustrating because the job is not what they expected, because they see inconsistency within the organization or because they do not see their colleagues as supportive. For example, corrections-minded individuals may not perceive their treatment-minded colleagues as supportive in maintaining safety and holding youths accountable for their behavior, while treatment-minded workers may feel that corrections-minded workers treat children too much like adult offenders. These are generalities, of course, and most employees fall on a continuum rather than at the extremes of these perceptions. However, the attempt to blend these two mindsets is a source of frustration for juvenile justice workers.

The opportunity of this duality lies in the fact that juvenile justice falls into the realm of corrections and human services work. Juvenile justice can take advantage of work force development efforts in both arenas. In addition, potential juvenile justice workers can be drawn from the applicant pool for both sectors, thereby increasing the likelihood of recruiting candidates with required competencies. If social work and criminal justice students are given opportunities for informational sessions, coursework and internships in juvenile justice, they may find that the mix of competencies required in juvenile justice is an excellent match to their skills.

Unique Concerns

Several issues in juvenile justice differ from adult corrections and human services, and require attention. The results of a 2003 ACA work force study[8] emphasize the need to market juvenile justice as a viable career option and to work with educational institutions to ensure that new workers are prepared for the challenges of the job.

According to the survey, 24 percent of respondents from juvenile correctional facilities reported that recruitment was "extremely difficult," compared with only 10 percent of those from adult institutions.

In addition, juvenile facilities were more likely to cite a "shortage of applicants" (42 percent juvenile vs. 33 percent adult), "too few applicants that meet job requirements" (24 percent vs. 13 percent) and "young people lack knowledge of profession" (21 percent vs. 12 percent).

Data from a Brookings Institution survey[9] of students pursuing Bachelor of Arts and social work degrees at top colleges support ACA's findings:

- When asked whether they had considered working in juvenile justice, 86 percent answered "not too seriously" or "not seriously at all."
- When asked how informed they were about career opportunities in juvenile justice, 73 percent were "not too informed" or "not informed at all."

These data point to a marketing crisis in juvenile justice. To increase the potential applicant pool, the field must engage in a public relations campaign to improve understanding of what juvenile justice work entails. This lack of public awareness could intensify the work force crisis if other fields start to vigorously recruit available workers. Many juvenile justice employees report that they came to juvenile justice as a stepping stone to other jobs and discovered that they loved the work. If in-demand workers no longer need the juvenile justice stepping stone, juvenile justice may be bypassed as a career option.

Where to Go from Here

As the demand for correctional and human service workers grows, juvenile justice agencies will face competition from both fronts in hiring and retaining a qualified work force. Juvenile justice agencies, in partnership with their human services and adult corrections counterparts, can take several steps to ameliorate a juvenile justice work force crisis.

Collect more data on the work force. A dearth of information is available on work force demographics, working conditions and, most notably, the pathways by which individuals enter and leave the field. Without more primary research, the unique needs of the juvenile justice work force cannot be completely understood.

Tailor promising practices to the needs of the juvenile justice work force. Juvenile justice work is unique among both corrections and human services professions, combining elements of youth development, child welfare, education and public safety. Many work-force-related promising practices put forth in corrections and human services are relevant to juvenile justice but must be tailored to attract the right people for the job. This should include raising the profile of juvenile justice as a career option.

Address adult and juvenile justice work force in tandem. Unless jurisdictions' work force issues are addressed simultaneously in the adult and juvenile systems, an improvement in one will likely be at the expense of the other. If both adult and juvenile corrections increase their desirability as employers, then employees can self-select the workplace that best suits them, and agencies can more carefully match employees to their population.

Increase public perception of juvenile justice as a desirable career choice. Qualified individuals are not going to enter juvenile justice without an awareness of what the work entails and the opportunity to access appropriate education and training. Unless the field increases the visibility of the unique aspects of juvenile justice work and facilitates opportunities for education and training, other more visible fields will lure away qualified applicants.

Increase the diversity of the work force. Though juvenile justice is increasingly employing more women, individuals of color and bilingual/bicultural staff, much more must be done to align staff demographics with client demographics. Targeted recruitment of a more diverse work force serves the dual purpose of increasing the available applicant pool while reflecting the diversity of the community and the client population.

Engage in a comprehensive work force planning process. Work force planning is a systematic approach to assessing the condition of the current work force, as well as an agency's future needs, and then creating a plan to address gaps. Many government agencies require a work force planning approach, and private and nonprofit agencies are beginning to follow suit. Many resources are available to assist agencies with this process.[10] Unless the "big picture" of current and future work force needs is considered, agencies will be continually playing catch-up with their work force and likely falling short of meeting the needs of youths and the community.

A reduction in the number of working-age Americans is inevitable, but this reduction does not need to translate into a work force crisis. Agencies must plan ahead in order to identify their staffing needs and to create a plan for recruiting and retaining employees with the desired competencies. Juvenile justice settings require employees with a unique blend of correctional and human services mindsets; therefore, identifying these workers may require a specialized approach. Juvenile justice agencies must get on board with the work force planning efforts under way in human services and corrections. Otherwise, the field will have its potential work force lured away. However, juvenile justice also must differentiate itself, so that its opportunities and needs are not subsumed under those of other organizations.

Notes

1. Bureau of Labor Statistics. 2006. *Occupational outlook handbook 2006–2007.* Available at www.bls.gov/oco.

2. Annie E. Casey Foundation. 2003. *The unsolved challenge of system reform: The condition of the frontline human services work force.* Annie E. Casey Foundation: Baltimore.

3. Annie E. Casey Foundation. 2003.

   Light, P.C. 2003. *The health of the human services work force.* Washington, D.C.: The Brookings Institution.

   Howe, M., C. Champnoise, E. Clawson, I. Cutler and S. Edwards. 2006. *The Juvenile Justice work force—Status and the challenge of reform.* Houston: Cornerstones for Kids.

   National Council on Crime and Delinquency. 2005a. *Exploring the effect of juvenile justice system functioning and employee turnover on recidivism rates.* Houston: Cornerstones for Kids.

4. National Council on Crime and Delinquency. 2005b. *Job turnover in child welfare and Juvenile Justice: The voices of former frontline workers.* Houston: Cornerstones for Kids.

   National Council on Crime and Delinquency. 2005a.

5. Howe, M. et al. 2006.

   National Council on Crime and Delinquency. 2005a.

6. National Council on Crime and Delinquency. 2005b.

   Light, P.C. 2003.

7. Liou, K.T. 1995. Role stress and job stress among detention care workers. *Criminal Justice and Behavior,* 22(4):425–436.

8. Workforce Associates. 2004. *A 21st century work force for America's correctional profession.* Indianapolis: Workforce Associates.

9. Light, P.C. 2003.

10. Barlow, E.D. and J.G. Fogg. 2004. Building a strategic work force plan for the correctional organization. *Corrections Today,* 66(5):110–115.

    International Personnel Management Association. 2002. *Workforce planning resource guide for public sector human resources professionals.* Alexandria, Va: International Personnel Management Association.

MEGHAN HOWE is senior project manager at the Crime and Justice Institute. **ELYSE CLAWSON** is executive director of the Crime and Justice Institute. **JOHN LARIVEE** is chief executive officer of Community Resources for Justice.

Teens Caught in the Middle
Juvenile Justice System and Treatment

Substance abuse treatment for adults in the criminal justice system is seriously inadequate, causing recidivism and other problems. But the situation is even worse in the juvenile system, according to a new report from Drug Strategies, a research institute based in Boston, Mass. The report, "Bridging the Gap: A Guide to Drug Treatment in the Juvenile Justice System," was released December 6, and focuses on the conflicts between treatment, on the one hand, and criminal justice, on the other. Nobody likes to use the word "punitive" to describe the criminal justice system, but compared to treatment, that's what it is, sources agree.

"The primary goal of drug treatment for adolescents is rehabilitation," Mathea Falco, president of Drug Strategies, told CABL. "But for the juvenile justice system, control is often the dominant concern."

However, the fact that juvenile justice is connected to substance abuse treatment also works in favor of these adolescents. If it were not for juvenile justice referrals, and treatment programs like those profiled in the Drug Strategies report, many of these teens would not be able to access treatment at all.

Best Interests?

In most states, according to the report, the goals of the 51 different juvenile court systems are threefold: to protect public safety, reduce recidivism, and act in the "best interests" of the child. How a child's best interests are defined is up to interpretation, the report notes. But it adds that the juvenile justice goals and the goals of treatment are "not necessarily mutually exclusive" because teens who are not abusing substances are less likely to be rearrested.

In some areas, getting involved in the criminal justice system can be almost a guarantee of substance abuse treatment—for adults. In California, for example, Proposition 36 mandates treatment instead of incarceration for adults. "If we had that for adolescents, we'd have much better services," says Elizabeth Stanley-Salazar, director of public policy for Phoenix Houses of California, whose Phoenix Academy of Los Angeles is profiled in the Drug Strategies report.

"Kids who are at high risk—such as in foster care—simply don't have access to treatment," Stanley-Salazar told CABL. "We know we should be using evidence based practices, but there's only a veneer of funding for substance abuse services." Because of the lack of funding, even teens in the juvenile justice system

---

Eleven Elements of Effective Drug Treatment in Juvenile Justice System

1. Systems integration
2. Assessment and treatment matching
3. Comprehensive, integrated treatment approach
4. Staff who are trained to recognize psychiatric problems
5. Developmentally appropriate program
6. Family involvement in treatment
7. A way to engage and retain teens in treatment
8. Qualified staff who have experience in diverse areas, such as delinquency, adolescent development, depression, or attention deficit disorder
9. Staff with gender and cultural competence
10. Process of continuing care that includes relapse prevention training
11. A way to measure treatment outcomes

Source: Drug Strategies.

---

who need treatment have a hard time getting it in California, she says, but she adds that the courts provide one of the few "on-ramps" for treatment. "Most of the kids who come to us come through the court system—a kid almost has to get tied up in the criminal justice system before they can access treatment."

Are there differences between adolescents in treatment because of juvenile justice referrals, and other adolescents in treatment? "The ones in the juvenile justice system are more severe, because their drug use has reached a higher threshold," says Stanley-Salazar. "So at Phoenix House we're receiving kids who have very serious substance abuse problems." However, she says that "many of the kids who are not on probation look similar to kids who have been picked up by probation."

Some of the teens at Phoenix House are on "home probation" or "informal probation." According to Stanley-Salazar, what they have in common with those on formal probation are "very disordered lives." And for those on probation, those lives are more likely to have histories of violence and abuse and neglect.

Programs Profiled in Drug Strategies Report

Travis County Juvenile Justice Integrated Network
(Austin, Tex.)
Tampa Juvenile Assessment Center (Tampa, Fla.)
King County Juvenile Treatment Court
(Seattle, Wash.)
Adolescent Portable Therapy (New York, N.Y.)
Thunder Road Adolescent Treatment Center
(Oakland, Calif.)
Chestnut Health Systems (Bloomington, Ill.)
Multidimensional Family Therapy (Miami, Fla.)
Multisystemic Therapy (Mount Pleasant, S.C.)
Phoenix Academy of Los Angeles
La Bodega de la Familia (New York, N.Y.)

Multiple Agencies

The report builds on an earlier one from Drug Strategies called Treating Teens: A Guide to Adolescent Drug Programs, published in 2003. This report identified 9 key elements of treatment programs for adolescents (see box); this new report adds two elements that are specific to people coming through the juvenile justice system: (1) juvenile offenders are more likely to have co-occurring disorders, and (2) it's important to integrate functions of agencies.

Integrating agency functions is essential but often not done. One of the biggest challenges for a family in the juvenile justice system anywhere is navigating the bureaucracy. And this bureaucracy is particularly daunting in New York City. But this is the focus of Adolescent Portable Therapy (APT), a program of the Vera Institute, which acts as "a liaison" for people in the juvenile justice system, according to Evan Elkin, APT director. "You need to have a cultural understanding of the multiple agencies, of their fiscal, operational, and philosophical constraints, to make treatment work," Elkin told CABL. "You can't just ask for access, and come in and do treatment."

The New York City Department of Juvenile Justice does assessment and pretrial detention but does not house adolescents when they are "placed" or sentenced, as it is called in the adult system—the state does, says Elkin. "Given how briefly a kid can be in the city's custody, it's impressive that the city agency has wanted to be involved in funding drug treatment for a kid who may quickly leave and enter the state system for placement." The city Department of Juvenile Justice, among others, funds APT.

Clinic without Walls

APT remains involved with an adolescent who is arrested, goes to court, and is sent to placement, as well as with the one who the judge allows to go home. The screening and assessment is integrated into the city's booking process, says Elkin. Then,

during the first days of detention, APT assigns a therapist to him. "The kid may go to a residential placement facility for a year, but APT stays with the kid," says Elkin. "Then, they get four months of intensive home services when they get home." If the child is not placed, but returns home with services—which is happening more and more as New York State sends the message that it wants to rely less on institutional placement and more on home-based services—APT will treat that child as well. The key is portability. "We're a clinic without walls," says Elkin.

However, there's one down side to portability: payment. "The agencies who establish the standards of practice for alcohol and drug treatment do not yet recognize the reimbursability of portable home-based services," Elkin told CABL. "We would not get Medicaid reimbursement." APT is, however, licensed by the state Office of Alcoholism and Substance Abuse Services to provide this kind of treatment. "We are the only body that holds a license for this from OASAS," Elkin said proudly. "They created a special category for us 5 years ago."

Thanks to a grant from the Substance Abuse and Mental Health Administration (SAMHSA) for community-based adolescent drug treatment providers, APT was able to expand its services by over 50 percent for a four-year period. Under the SAMHSA grant, APT sees 90 additional teens a year returning home from state custody with the Office of Children and Family Services (OCFS). And under the Department of Juvenile Justice funding, they see 150 a year. That's about 250 families a year treated by APT. "We could triple in size and still not meet the need," says Elkin. The good news is that in recognition of the successful collaboration between APT and OCFS, the program is in the State's 2006 proposed budget for further expansion. "We hope also to remain in the City's budget in 2006."

The Role of the Family

LaBodega de la Familia, a spinoff from the Vera Institute's pre-APT days, is another program profiled in the Drug Strategies report. This New York City-based program focuses on the family as a unit. "Some families come in and say, 'My kid is smoking pot, what should I do,'" says Carol Shapiro, founder and director of Family Justice, of which LaBodega is a direct service. "In other cases, the teen was arrested, but it's a family member with a drug problem." It's important to engage the whole family, Shapiro, who started LaBodega 10 years ago, told CABL.

By working with the government and families in tandem, LaBodega promotes the notion of family case management. This is an example of the juvenile justice system helping the treatment process, says Shapiro. "The escalation and the hammers of the justice system are an advantage," she says.

Unlike the "clinic without walls" concept of APT, LaBodega is "place-based," says Shapiro. "We have a storefront and a satellite in public housing in a neighborhood that is affected by drugs. We'll do home visits too." And LaBodega's services integrate into the community. "We engage in a lot of things that have nothing to do with drug treatment," says Shapiro. "We help with gardening, poetry, photography, we work with the housing police and the people who are the natural leaders, the social fabric of the neighborhood."

Getting judges to understand that the community, home, and home-based treatment might be in the child's "best interests" is an uphill battle. "We have a problem with getting the justice system to understand that if you match these kids to treatment, using the American Society of Addiction Medicine (ASAM) criteria, you'd be putting them in variable lengths of stay," says Stanley-Salazar, noting that the average stay at Phoenix House is 9 to 12 months. "But corrections doesn't always look through the lens of treatment. They place them because of their offense, but there's not enough capacity to provide the services."

Ideally, she adds, these patients should be treated earlier, before their problems get so severe. "But if they weren't in the justice system, who would pay for their treatment?"

From *The Brown University Child and Adolescent Behavior Letter,* January 2006, pp. 4–6. Copyright © 2006 by John Wiley & Sons. Reprinted by permission.

Jail Time Is Learning Time

Signe Nelson and Lynn Olcott

There is excitement in the large, well-lit classroom. Student work, including history posters and artwork, adorn the walls. A polite shuffling of feet can be heard, as names are called and certificates presented. It is the graduation ceremony at the Onondaga County Justice Center in Syracuse, N.Y. The ceremony is held several times a year, recognizing inmates in the Incarcerated Education Program who have passed the GED exam or completed a 108-hour vocational program. The courses in the Incarcerated Education Program are geared to prepare inmates to transition successfully to several different settings.

The Incarcerated Education Program is a joint effort by the Syracuse City School District and the Onondaga County Sheriff's Office, and is housed inside the nine-story Onondaga County Justice Center in downtown Syracuse. The Justice Center is a 250,000 square-foot maximum-security, nonsentenced facility, completed and opened in 1995. The facility was built to contain 616 beds, but currently houses 745 inmates. Between 13,000 and 14,000 inmates passed through booking during 2004. About 2,500 of them were minors.

The Justice Center

The Justice Center is a state-of-the-art facility, designed for and operating on the direct supervision model. Direct supervision is a method of inmate management developed by the federal government in 1974 for presentenced inmates in the Federal Bureau of Prisons. There are about 140 such facilities operating throughout the United States and a few hundred currently under construction. Direct supervision places a single deputy directly in a "housing pod" with between 32 and 64 inmates. Maximum pod capacity in the Onondaga County Justice Center is 56 inmates. Inmates are given either relative freedom of movement within the pod or confined to their cells based on their behavior.

The program has been providing courses and classes at the Justice Center for 10 years, but this partnership between the school district and the sheriff's office began almost 30 years ago with the provision of GED instruction. The Incarcerated Education Program was originally conceived to ensure education for inmates who are minors. The program has grown tremendously and now has more than 20 offerings in academic, vocational and life management areas.

The Syracuse City School District professional staff includes six full-time and 18 part-time teachers and staff members. The program is unique in that there are three Onondaga County Sheriff's sergeants who hold New York State Adult Education certification and who teach classes in the vocational component. An average of 250 inmates, or about one-third of the Justice Center's incarcerated population, are enrolled in day and/or evening classes. There are about 250 hours of class time in the facility per week.

Varied Educational and Training Opportunities

As in the public education sector, vocational programs have evolved with the times. The Basic Office Skills class now offers two sections, and includes computer repair and office production skills. A course in building maintenance can be complemented by a course in pre-application to pre-apprenticeship plumbing, or in painting and surface preparation, a class that includes furniture refinishing. A baking class and nail technology have been added in the past few years. All vocational courses, before implementation, are approved by the New York State Education Department and are designed to be consistent with New York State Department of Labor employment projections for Onondaga County. No vocational programming is implemented without first identifying whether the occupation is an area of growth in the community.

Additionally, a broadly inclusive advisory board, made up of community representatives who are stakeholders in the local economy and in the quality of life in the Syracuse metropolitan area has been established. The Incarcerated Education Advisory Board meets approximately three times a year to discuss the perceived needs of the community and to address strategies for transitioning students into employment. Ongoing topics of study are issues surrounding employment, continuing education and housing.

Incarcerated Education Program planners are very aware that job skills are ineffective without proper work attitudes. Job Readiness Training addresses work ethic, proper work behavior, communication and critical behavior skills. Vocational classes are voluntary for the nonsentenced population. However, because of their popularity, a waiting list is maintained for several courses. Among these popular courses are Basic Office Skills and Small Engine Repair. An additional section of Small Engine Repair has been added for female inmates in the class to ensure gender equity in this training opportunity.

New York State law requires that incarcerated minors continue their education while incarcerated. The Incarcerated Education Program enrolls inmates, ages 16 to 21, in Adult Basic Education/GED classes and addresses students with special needs. Other adult inmates attend on a voluntary basis. Inmates are given an initial placement test to determine math and reading skill levels. Because inmates work at a wide range of ability levels, instruction is individualized and materials are geared to independent work. English as a second Language and English Literacy/Civics are complementary offerings for inmates who are in need of assistance in English language proficiency and knowledge of American culture and history.

The GED exam is given at the Justice Center every 60 days or more often as needed. In the past three years, 225 students have taken the exam. Passing rates fluctuate between 63 percent and 72 percent. The average passing rate for correctional institutions in New York is about 51 percent. The state average passing rate for the general public in community-based courses is fairly stable at 50 percent.[1]

Of course, not everyone will take the GED. Student turnover is high, as inmates are released, bailed out, sent to treatment centers, or sentenced to county, state and federal correctional facilities. Judy Fiorini is a GED teacher who has been with the program for more than 10 years. "Many go back out into our community. We try to teach them something useful for their lives," Fiorini explains.

Transition services form an integral part of the program. The focus is on minors, but help is available for everyone. Two fulltime staff members assist people upon release, with such important tasks as acquiring a driver's license, seeking housing, reenrolling in high school or preparing for job interviews. A very important part of transition services is helping people acquire birth certificates, social security cards and other documents crucial for identification.

Tackling Cognitive Issues

Corrections professionals and educators are aware that it is not enough to improve the skill base of an inmate. There must be cognitive changes as well. The justice center is not a treatment facility, but it has been evolving into a therapeutic community. As the Incarcerated Education Program has grown, there has been the flexibility to add several important courses dealing with life issues, attitude and decision-making. According to data provided by the justice center, about 80 percent of inmates have substance abuse-related issues at the time of their arrest. To support desired cognitive changes, the justice center began establishing "clean and sober" pods in 2002. Currently, there

are several clean and sober pods, including pods for adult men, women and youths. There are waiting lists for placement in the clean and sober pods.

The Incarcerated Education Program has been offering anger management groups for several years. Anger management helps group members deal with compulsive behavior and focus on long-term goals. Other life management offerings include family education, action for personal choice and a course called Parent and Child Together. Most courses of study are developed inhouse by experienced professional faculty. Additionally, the program established gender-specific courses, Men's Issues and Women's Issues, to help inmates become more directly aware of their own responsibilities, separate from the role of a partner or significant other in their lives. The Men's Issues class is led by certified professionals and focuses on actions and their consequences. As in most jails, male inmates significantly outnumber female inmates. Courses and groups continue to be added, though it is sometimes difficult to find space for the abundance of activity in the program.

The program is financially supported, using state and federal funds, via nine carefully coordinated grants. Also significant for the success of the program has been ongoing encouragement and technical assistance from the New York State Education Department, the New York State Association of Incarcerated Education Programs and support from the New York State Sheriffs' Association.[2]

The Incarcerated Education Program continues to encounter challenges. It takes energy and dedication to keep the varied curricula substantial and cohesive, despite high student turnover and complex student needs. With a large civilian staff, the program requires close coordination between security and civilian concerns to help civilian staff work most effectively within the safety and security priorities of the facility. Biweekly meetings facilitate ongoing communication.

Making the Most of Time

Every available square inch of classroom space is in constant use. Classes have exceeded available space and some classes meet in core areas of the justice center as well. Several classes are held in the residence pods, where heavy, white tables are pulled together and portable white-boards are erected to create nomadic classrooms. Overall, the program is succeeding in several ways. Incarcerated minors are directly and meaningfully involved in high school equivalency classes, and inmates older than 21 receive academic and vocational services on a voluntary basis. All inmates are offered the opportunity for life-skills classes and for transitional services upon release. Time served at the Onondaga County Justice Center can also be time used for valuable academic, vocational and life management achievements.

Notes

1. New York State Department of Education maintains statistics for educational activities at correctional facilities in New York state. Patricia Mooney directs the GED Program for the state

through the GED Testing Office in the State Department of Education. Greg Bayduss is the State Department of Education coordinator in charge of Incarcerated Education Programs throughout New York state.

2. State Professional Organizations: The New York State Association of Incarcerated Education Programs Inc. is a professional organization for teachers, administrators and security personnel (www.nysaiep.org). Its mission is to promote excellence in incarcerated education programs in the state, support research in this field and advocate for incarcerated education initiatives through collaboration with other professional organizations. The authors must mention the valuable assistance of the New York State Sheriffs' Association, supporting each county sheriff, as the chief law enforcement officer in his or her county (www.nyssheriffs.org). The association provides valuable information and technical assistance to county sheriffs to help implement programs in their jails.

SIGNE NELSON is the coordinator of the Incarcerated Education Program, and LYNN OLCOTT is a teacher at Auburn Correctional Facility in New York, formerly with the Incarcerated Education Program. The program could not have attained its present strength without the vision and support of law enforcement officials Sheriff Kevin Walsh, Chief Anthony Callisto, and Syracuse City School District administrator Al Wolf. Special thanks to Capt. John Woloszyn, commander of Support Services; Sgt. Joseph Powlina, administrative compliance supervisor; and Deputy Joseph Caruso, photographer. Their assistance in the production of this article was crucial and much appreciated.

Lifers as Teenagers, Now Seeking Second Chance

Adam Liptak

In December, the United Nations took up a resolution calling for the abolition of life imprisonment without the possibility of parole for children and young teenagers. The vote was 185 to 1, with the United States the lone dissenter.

Indeed, the United States stands alone in the world in convicting young adolescents as adults and sentencing them to live out their lives in prison. According to a new report, there are 73 Americans serving such sentences for crimes they committed at 13 or 14.

Mary Nalls, an 81-year-old retired social worker here, has some thoughts about the matter. Her granddaughter Ashley Jones was 14 when she helped her boyfriend kill her grandfather and aunt—Mrs. Nalls's husband and daughter—by stabbing and shooting them and then setting them on fire. Ms. Jones also tried to kill her 10-year-old sister.

Mrs. Nalls, who was badly injured in the rampage, showed a visitor to her home a white scar on her forehead, a reminder of the burns that put her into a coma for 30 days. She had also been shot in the shoulder and stabbed in the chest.

"I forgot," she said later. "They stabbed me in the jaw, too."

But Mrs. Nalls thinks her granddaughter, now 22, deserves the possibility of a second chance.

"I believe that she should have gotten 15 or 20 years," Mrs. Nalls said. "If children are under age, sometimes they're not responsible for what they do."

The group that plans to release the report on Oct. 17, the Equal Justice Initiative, based in Montgomery, Ala., is one of several human rights organizations that say states should be required to review sentences of juvenile offenders as the decades go by, looking for cases where parole might be warranted.

But prosecutors and victims' rights groups say there are crimes so terrible and people so dangerous that only life sentences without the possibility of release are a fit moral and practical response.

"I don't think every 14-year-old who killed someone deserves life without parole," said Laura Poston, who prosecuted Ms. Jones. "But Ashley planned to kill four people. I don't think there is a conscience in Ashley, and I certainly think she is a threat to do something similar."

Specialists in comparative law acknowledge that there have been occasions when young murderers who would have served life terms in the United States were released from prison in Europe and went on to kill again. But comparing legal systems is difficult, in part because the United States is a more violent society and in part because many other nations imprison relatively few people and often only for repeat violent offenses.

"I know of no systematic studies of comparative recidivism rates," said James Q. Whitman, who teaches comparative criminal law at Yale. "I believe there are recidivism problems in countries like Germany and France, since those are countries that ordinarily incarcerate only dangerous offenders, but at some point they let them out and bad things can happen."

The differences in the two approaches, legal experts said, are rooted in politics and culture. The European systems emphasize rehabilitation, while the American one stresses individual responsibility and punishment.

Corrections professionals and criminologists here and abroad tend to agree that violent crime is usually a young person's activity, suggesting that eventual parole could be considered in most cases. But the American legal system is more responsive to popular concerns about crime and attitudes about punishment, while justice systems abroad tend to be administered by career civil servants rather than elected legislators, prosecutors and judges.

In its sentencing of juveniles, as in many other areas, the legal system in the United States goes it alone. American law is, by international standards, a series of innovations and exceptions. From the central role played by juries in civil cases to the election of judges to punitive damages to the disproportionate number of people in prison, the United States is an island in the sea of international law.

And the very issue of whether American judges should ever take account of foreign law is hotly disputed. At the hearings on their Supreme Court nominations, both John G. Roberts Jr. and Samuel A. Alito Jr. said they thought it a mistake to consider foreign law in constitutional cases.

But the international consensus against life-without-parole sentences for juvenile offenders may nonetheless help Ms. Jones. In about a dozen cases recently filed around the country on behalf of 13- and 14-year-olds sentenced to life in prison, lawyers for the inmates relied on a 2005 Supreme Court decision that banned the execution of people who committed crimes when they were younger than 18.

That decision, Roper v. Simmons, was based in part on international law. Noting that the United States was the only nation in the world to sanction the juvenile death penalty, Justice Anthony M. Kennedy, writing for the majority, said it was appropriate to look to "the laws of other countries and to international authorities as instructive" in interpreting the Eighth Amendment's prohibition of cruel and unusual punishment.

He added that teenagers were different from older criminals—less mature, more susceptible to peer pressure and more likely to change for the better. Those findings, lawyers for the juvenile lifers say, should apply to their clients, too.

"Thirteen- and 14-year-old children should not be condemned to death in prison because there is always hope for a child," said Bryan Stevenson, the executive director of the Equal Justice Initiative, which represents Ms. Jones and several other juvenile lifers.

The 2005 death penalty ruling applied to 72 death-row inmates, almost precisely the same number as the 73 prisoners serving life without parole for crimes committed at 13 or 14.

The Supreme Court did not abolish the juvenile death penalty in a single stroke. The 2005 decision followed one in 1988 that held the death penalty unconstitutional for those who had committed crimes under 16.

The new lawsuits, filed in Alabama, California, Florida, Missouri, North Carolina and Wisconsin, seek to follow a similar progression.

"We're not demanding that all these kids be released tomorrow," Mr. Stevenson said. "I'm not even prepared to say that all of them will get to the point where they should be released. We're asking for some review."

In defending American policy in this area in 2006, the State Department told the United Nations that sentencing is usually a matter of state law. "As a general matter," the department added, juvenile offenders serving life-without-parole terms "were hardened criminals who had committed gravely serious crimes."

Human rights groups have disputed that. According to a 2005 report from Human Rights Watch and Amnesty International, 59 percent of the more than 2,200 prisoners serving life without parole for crimes they committed at 17 or younger had never been convicted of a previous crime. And 26 percent were in for felony murder, meaning they participated in a crime that led to a murder but did not themselves kill anyone.

The new report focuses on the youngest offenders, locating 73 juvenile lifers in 19 states who were 13 and 14 when they committed their crimes. Pennsylvania has the most, with 19, and Florida is next, with 15. In those states and Illinois, Nebraska, North Carolina and Washington, 13-year-olds have been sentenced to die in prison.

In most of the cases, the sentences were mandatory, an automatic consequence of a murder conviction after being tried as an adult.

A federal judge here will soon rule on Ms. Jones's challenge to her sentence. Ms. Poston, who prosecuted her, said Ms. Jones was beyond redemption.

"Between the ages of 2 and 3, you develop a conscience," Ms. Poston said. "She never got the voice that says, 'This is bad, Ashley.' "

"It was a blood bath in there," Ms. Poston said of the night of the murders here, in 1999. "Ashley Jones is not the poster child for the argument that life without parole is too long."

In a telephone interview from the Tutwiler Prison for Women in Wetumpka, Ala., Ms. Jones said she did not recognize the girl who committed her crimes. According to court filings, her mother was a drug addict and her stepfather had sexually molested her. "Everybody I loved, everybody I trusted, I was betrayed by," Ms. Jones said.

"I'm very remorseful about what happened," she said. "I should be punished. I don't feel like I should spend the rest of my life in prison."

Mrs. Nalls, her grandmother, had been married for 53 years when she and her husband, Deroy Nalls, agreed to take Ashley in. She was "a problem child," and Mr. Nalls was a tough man who took a dislike to Ashley's boyfriend, Geramie Hart. Mr. Hart, who was 16 at the time of the murders, is also serving a life term. Mrs. Nalls said he deserved a shot at parole someday as well.

Violence in Adolescent Dating Relationships

"The early-to mid-teenage years mark a time in which romantic relationships begin to emerge. From a developmental perspective, these relationships can serve a number of positive functions. However, for many adolescents, there is a darker side: dating violence."

ERNEST N. JOURILES, PhD, CORA PLATT, BA, AND RENEE MCDONALD, PhD

For many, the early- to mid-teenage years mark a time in which romantic relationships begin to emerge. From a developmental perspective, these relationships can serve a number of positive functions. However, for many adolescents, there is a darker side: dating violence. In this article, we discuss the definition and measurement of adolescent dating violence, review epidemiological findings regarding victimization, and describe correlates of victimization experiences. We end with a discussion of prevention and intervention programs designed to address adolescent dating violence and highlight important gaps in our knowledge.

Defining and Measuring Adolescent Dating and Dating Violence

"Dating" among adolescents is complicated to define and measure, in part because the nature of dating changes dramatically over the course of adolescence (Connolly et al., 1999; Feiring, 1996). In early adolescence, dating involves getting together with small groups of friends of both sexes to do things together as a group. From these group experiences, adolescents progress to going out with or dating a single individual. Initial single-dating relationships are typically casual and short-term; more serious, exclusive, and longer-lasting relationships emerge in mid- to late-adolescence.

"Dating" among adolescents is complicated to define and measure.

In research on adolescent dating violence, adolescents are often asked to respond to questions about a "boyfriend" or "girlfriend" or someone with whom they have "been on a date with or gone out with." However, what constitutes a boyfriend or girlfriend or a dating partner is not clear, and these judgments are likely to vary tremendously across adolescents. These judgments are probably also influenced by a number of factors including the amount of time spent with each other, the degree of emotional attachment, and the activities engaged in together (Allen, 2004). They are also likely to change over the course of adolescence, as youth mature and become more experienced with dating.

Most everyone has a general idea about what constitutes "violence" in adolescent dating relationships, but not everyone conceptualizes and defines it the same way. In the empirical literature, multiple types of dating violence have been studied, including physical, sexual, and psychological violence. Definitions for these different types of violence vary from study to study, but each is typically based on adolescents' reports of the occurrence of specific acts. For example, physical violence often refers to adolescents' reports of hits, slaps, or beatings; sexual violence refers to forced kissing, touching, or intercourse; and psychological violence to reports of insults, threats, or the use of control tactics. These different types of violence are sometimes further subdivided. For example, indirect aggression (also referred to as relational or social aggression), which includes spreading hurtful rumors or telling cruel stories about a dating partner, has recently begun to be conceptualized as a form of dating violence that may be distinct from more overt forms of psychological or emotional abuse (Wolfe, Scott, Reitzel-Jaffe et al., 2001). As another example, in a recent prevalence study, sexual assault was distinguished from drug- or alcohol-facilitated rape, with the latter defined as sexual assault that occurred while the victim was "high, drunk, or passed out from drinking or taking drugs" (Wolitzky-Taylor et al., 2008).

In the bulk of studies on adolescent dating violence, the youth are surveyed about the occurrence of specific acts of violence within a particular time period, for example, during the previous 12 months. These surveys are typically administered on a single occasion, in either a questionnaire or interview format. Some include only one or two questions about violence; others include comprehensive scales of relationship violence with excellent psychometric properties (e.g., Wolfe et al., 2001). A handful of investigators have attempted to study adolescent dating violence using other methods, such as laboratory observations (e.g., Capaldi, Kimm, & Shortt, 2007), and repeated interviews over a short, circumscribed period of time (e.g., Jouriles et al., 2005). However, studies using alternatives to one-time, self-report survey assessments are few and far between.

This first section highlights some of the complexities involved in conceptualizing adolescent dating violence and describes how different types of dating violence are often defined and measured, providing a backdrop for understanding and interpreting empirical findings in the literature. As illustrated in the section below, different conceptualizations and definitions of dating violence lead to different research findings and conclusions. Similarly, various data collection methods (such as using more questions and/or repeated questioning) also yield different results. At the present time, there is no gold standard with respect to defining or measuring adolescent dating violence; the field is still developing in this regard.

Prevalence of Adolescent Dating Violence

Over the past decade, data from several different national surveys have been used to estimate the prevalence of the various forms of adolescent dating violence. Surveys conducted by the Centers for Disease Control suggest that 9–10% of students in grades 9–12 indicate that a boyfriend or girlfriend has hit, slapped, or physically hurt them on purpose during the previous 12 months, and approximately 8% report having been physically forced to have sexual intercourse against their wishes (Howard, Wang, & Yan, 2007a, 2007b). The 2005 National Survey of Adolescents (NSA) indicates that 1.6% of adolescents between 12 and 17 years of age have experienced "serious dating violence" (Wolitzky-Taylor et al., 2008). Serious dating violence was defined as experiencing one or more of the following forms of violence from a dating partner: physical violence (badly injured, beaten up, or threatened with a knife or gun), sexual violence (forced anal, vaginal, or oral sex; forced penetration with a digit or an object; forced touching of genitalia), or drug/alcohol-facilitated rape.

Most studies in this area ask about male-to-female and female-to-male violence or include gender-neutral questions without assessing whether a respondent is in an opposite-sex or same-sex relationship. The National Longitudinal Study of Adolescent Health is unique in that it reports data on violence

Table 1 Prevalence of Dating Violence in Same-Sex and Opposite-Sex Romantic Relationships

Data from National Longitudinal Study of Adolescent Health		
In the previous 18 months partner had been:	Opposite-sex relationship	Same-sex relationship
Physically violent	12%	11%
Psychologically violent	29%	21%

Halpern, Oslak, Young, Martin, & Kupper, 2001; Halpern, Young, Waller, Martin, & Kupper, 2004.

in opposite-sex as well as same-sex romantic relationships. As can be seen in Table 1, prevalence rates for both physical and psychological violence are similar in opposite-sex and same-sex romantic relationships among adolescents in grades 7–12.

Prevalence rates for both physical and psychological violence are similar in opposite-sex and same-sex romantic relationships among adolescents in grades 7–12.

The prevalence of physical dating violence appears to be fairly similar across studies of national samples. Variation across estimates most likely reflects differences in how violence is defined, and perhaps differences in the samples from which the estimates were derived (e.g., different age ranges sampled). It should be noted that prevalence estimates based on smaller, less representative, localized samples tend to be higher than those based on national samples. In fact, a number of researchers have reported prevalence estimates for physical dating violence among adolescents (over a one-year period or less) to be over 40% (Hickman, Jaycox, & Aronoff, 2004). These elevated estimates might stem directly from sampling differences, but also perhaps from differences in the conceptualization and measurement of dating violence. For example, in many of the smaller samples, investigators assessed dating violence more extensively (such as using more questions and/or through repeated questioning), which might contribute to higher prevalence estimates.

Taken together, the results across studies yield some general conclusions about the nature and scope of adolescent dating violence. Regardless of how it is defined, it appears that a substantial number of United States youth are affected by dating violence. Even with very conservative definitions, such as the one used in the NSA, it was projected that approximately 400,000 adolescents have been victims, at some point in their lives, of serious dating violence (Wolitzky-Taylor et al., 2008).

Psychological violence appears to be much more common than either physical or sexual violence. Data are mixed on the relative prevalence of physical and sexual violence, but some of the national surveys suggest that they are approximately equal in prevalence.

Onset and Course

Dating violence appears to emerge well before high school. For example, cross-sex teasing and harassment, which involve behaviors often construed as either psychological or sexual violence, is evident among 6th graders and increases in prevalence over time (McMaster et al., 2002). One-third of a sample of 7th graders who indicated that they had started dating also reported that they had committed acts of aggression (physical, sexual, or psychological) toward a dating partner; in over half of these cases, physical or sexual aggression was involved (Sears et al., 2007). In the NSA, serious dating violence victimization was not reported by 12-year-olds, but it was by 13-year-olds (Wolitzky-Taylor et al., 2008).

Longitudinal data on the course of adolescent dating violence are scarce, but there is evidence that psychological aggression predicts subsequent physical aggression (O'Leary & Slep, 2003). In fact, different types of dating violence commonly co-occur within adolescent relationships, with the occurrence of one type of violence (physical, psychological, or sexual) associated with an increased likelihood of other types of violence (Sears, Byers, & Price, 2007). In research on interpersonal victimization in general, victims of violence are known to be at increased risk for subsequent victimization. This appears to be true for victims of adolescent dating violence as well (Smith, White, & Holland, 2003).

Demographics of Adolescent Dating Violence

Certain demographic variables including age, race and ethnicity, geographic location, and sex are associated with increased risk for victimization. Specifically, the risk for dating violence victimization increases with age, at least through the middle and high school years. This trend appears to be true for physical, psychological, and sexual violence (e.g., Halpern et al., 2001; Howard et al., 2007a, 2007b; Wolitzky-Taylor et al., 2008). This might be attributable to a number of things, including the changing nature of dating over the course of adolescence. Some evidence has emerged pointing to racial and ethnic differences in adolescents' experiences of dating violence, but other recent, large-scale studies call these findings into question. For example, a number of investigators have found Black adolescents to be more likely than their White counterparts to experience physical and sexual dating violence (e.g., Howard et al., 2007a, 2007b). However, these differences have sometimes disappeared when other variables, such as prior exposures to violence, are considered (Malik, Sorenson, & Aneshensel, 1997). Moreover, recent, well-designed studies of very large samples have found no evidence of racial or ethnic differences in adolescent victimization

(e.g., O'Leary et al., 2008; Wolitzky-Taylor et al., 2008). There do appear to be regional differences in dating violence, with adolescents in southern states at substantially greater risk for experiencing dating violence than adolescents in other regions of the U.S. (Marquart, et al., 2007). Although the reasons for regional differences are not known, it is interesting to note that the South has a higher prevalence rate of overall violence than other regions in the U.S. In short, there may be factors in the Southern U.S. that facilitate the promotion, acceptance, or tolerance of violent behavior.

When violence is defined broadly, prevalence rates for male and female victimization tend to be similar (e.g., Halpern et al., 2001). However, narrower definitions of violence point to some sex differences in the experience of violence. For example, female adolescents are more likely than males to experience severe physical violence (violent acts that are likely to result, or actually have resulted, in physical injuries) and sexual violence (e.g., Molidor & Tolman, 1998; Wolitzky-Taylor et al., 2008). Females are also more likely than males to experience fear, hurt, and the desire to leave the situation for self-protection (Molidor & Tolman, 1998; Jackson, Cram, & Seymour, 2000). In addition, females are more likely to report physical injuries and more harmful and persistent psychological distress after being victimized (O'Keefe, 1997).

Correlates of Adolescent Dating Violence

Most of the findings on the correlates of adolescent dating violence come from studies in which data were collected at a single point in time. Thus, it is difficult to discern if observed correlates are precursors or consequences of the violence, or if they are simply related to experiencing violence, but not in a cause-and-effect manner. Although it is tempting to interpret some of these associations in a causal, unidirectional manner, more often than not, alternative explanations can also be offered. For example, the documented association between dating violence and psychological distress is typically interpreted to mean that experiencing dating violence causes psychological distress (e.g., Howard et al., 2007a, 2007b; Molidor & Tolman, 1998). However, it is not too difficult to imagine how feelings of psychological distress might influence an adolescent's decision about whom to go out with (i.e., adolescents who are psychologically distressed, compared with those who are not, may make different choices about whom to date) and, perhaps, lead an adolescent to an abusive relationship.

Many adolescents engage in antisocial or illegal activities, but those who do so consistently and frequently are at increased risk of dating violence victimization (e.g., Howard et al., 2007a, 2007b). In addition, simply having antisocial friends increases risk for victimization. For example, females who associate with violent or victimized peers appear to be at increased risk for dating violence victimization (Gagne, Lavoie, & Hebert, 2005). Similarly, male and female adolescents exposed to peer-drinking activities within the past 30 days (e.g., "Hanging out with friends who drank") were victimized more often than their counterparts who were not exposed to such activities (Howard, Qiu, & Boekeloo, 2003).

Many other adolescent experiences have also been associated with dating violence victimization. For example, earlier exposures to violence, both within and outside of the family, are associated with victimization (e.g., Gagne et al., 2005; Malik et al., 1997). Negative parent-child interactions and parent-child boundary violations at age 13 predict victimization at age 21 (Linder & Collins, 2005). Trauma symptoms, which may result from violence exposure and untoward parent-child interactions, are posited to interfere with emotional and cognitive processes important in interpreting abusive behavior, and possibly to heighten tolerance for abuse (Capaldi & Gorman-Smith, 2003). Having had prior sexual relationships with peers increases adolescent females' risk for experiencing relationship violence (e.g., Howard et al., 2007a, 2007b). Also, the likelihood of victimization increases as the number of dating partners increases (Halpern et al., 2001).

Several different dimensions of adolescent relationships have been examined in relation to dating violence. For example, physical violence is often reciprocated within relationships, meaning that when dating violence is reported, both partners are typically violent toward one another (e.g., O'Leary, Slep, Avery-Leaf, Cascardi, 2008). Relationship violence is more likely to happen in serious or special romantic relationships, rather than more casual ones (O'Leary et al., 2008; Roberts, Auinger, & Klein, 2006). It is also more likely to occur in relationships with problems, conflict, and power struggles (Bentley et al., 2007; O'Keefe, 1997).

Relationship violence is more likely to happen in serious or special romantic relationships, rather than more casual ones.

Although there are many risk factors for adolescent dating violence, some protective factors have emerged as well. For instance, having high-quality friendships at age 16 is associated with reduced likelihood of experiencing dating violence in romantic relationships at age 21 (Linder & Collins, 2005). High-quality friendships are characterized by security, disclosure, closeness, low levels of conflict, and the effective resolution of conflict that does occur. Also, adolescents who do well in school and those who attend religious services are at decreased risk for experiencing dating violence (Halpern et al., 2001; Howard et al., 2003).

Prevention and Intervention

Much of the prevention research in this area is directed at an entire population (e.g., 9th grade at a school) with the goal of preventing violence from occurring. However, the prevalence data indicate that a sizable number of adolescents in high school, and even middle school, have already perpetrated and/or experienced dating violence. Thus, in most cases the research

is not technically universal prevention, from the standpoint of preventing violence before it ever occurs. Rather, it is an attempt to reduce dating violence, by preventing its initial occurrence as well as preventing its re-occurrence among those who have already experienced it.

A sizable number of adolescents in high school, and even middle school, have already perpetrated and/or experienced dating violence.

Many of the school-based prevention programs share a number of commonalities, in addition to the joint focus on prevention and intervention (Whitaker et al., 2006). Most are designed to address perpetration and victimization simultaneously. Many are incorporated into mandatory health classes in middle or high school. Most are based on a combination of feminist and social learning principles, and involve didactic methods to increase knowledge and change attitudes regarding dating violence. Despite these similarities, there are potentially important differences in the structure (e.g., duration) and content of these various programs. Unfortunately, most of these school-based programs have not undergone rigorous empirical evaluation to determine whether they actually reduce occurrences of violence.

A notable exception is Safe Dates, a program developed for 8th and 9th grade students (Foshee, Bauman, Arriaga et al., 1998) that has undergone a fairly rigorous evaluation. Safe Dates includes: (a) ten interactive classroom sessions covering topics such as dating violence norms, gender stereotyping, and conflict management skills, (b) group activities such as peer-performed theater productions and a poster contest, and (c) information about community resources for adolescents in abusive relationships. Evaluation results indicate that Safe Dates reduces psychological and physical violence perpetration, but not victimization, among the students who participated in the program. At first glance, this result might be puzzling: How can the perpetration of violence go down, without a commensurate reduction in victimization? This might be explained, in part, by the fact that not all individuals who participated in Safe Dates dated other Safe Date participants. Although the Safe Dates participants were less likely to commit acts of dating violence after completing the program, they were not necessarily less likely to date individuals who commit violent acts.

Evaluations of other school-based programs using techniques similar to those employed in Safe Dates have not had demonstrable effects on violence perpetration or victimization. Some of these evaluations simply did not include measures of perpetration or victimization as outcomes. Others, however, have attempted to measure intervention effects on violent behavior and victimization, but have found no effects (e.g., Avery-Leaf et al., 1997; Hilton et al., 1998). Many of these school-based programs, however, *have* achieved changes in knowledge or attitudes regarding dating violence (e.g., Avery-Leaf et al., 1997; Hilton et al., 1998; Krajewski et al., 1996; Weisz & Black, 2001).

Another program with demonstrated results is The Youth Relationships Project (YRP) (Wolfe et al., 2003). YRP is a community-based intervention designed for 14-16 year olds who were maltreated as children and were thus at increased risk of being in abusive relationships in the future. YRP is an 18-session, group-based program with three primary components: (a) education about abusive relationships and power dynamics within these relationships, (b) skills development, and (c) social action. The skills targeted in this program include communication skills and conflict resolution. The social action portion of the program includes, among other things, allowing program participants the opportunity to become familiar with and to practice utilizing resources for individuals in violent relationships, as well as the chance to develop a project to raise awareness of dating violence within the community. Sessions include skills practice, guest speakers, videos, and visits to relevant community agencies. Evaluation results indicate that YRP reduces physical dating violence perpetration and physical, emotional, and threatening abuse victimization.

It is encouraging that Safe Dates and the YRP have yielded promising results in reducing dating violence among adolescents. However, given the current state of the prevention literature in this area, it would be erroneous to suggest that we know how to prevent adolescent dating violence. Systematic reviews of this literature indicate that the vast majority of studies attempting to evaluate a dating violence prevention program have *not* found intervention effects on behavioral measures, and even though changes in knowledge and attitudes are often documented, it is not really clear if such changes lead to changes in either perpetration or victimization (Hickman et al., 2004; Whitaker et al., 2006). The promising findings of the Safe Dates and YRP programs require replication, and more information is needed on how these programs accomplished their positive effects. Researchers and practitioners can use these programs as a starting point in their own efforts at preventing relationship violence, but it is still important to continue exploring new ideas about prevention in this area.

Concluding Remarks

It is clear that violence in adolescent dating relationships is a prevalent problem with potentially devastating consequences. We also know a great deal about correlates of such violence. On the other hand, there are still important gaps in our knowledge. For example, longitudinal research on this topic is extremely scarce; thus, we know little about the emergence and unfolding of dating violence and victimization over time. This is particularly true for high-risk groups, such as children from violent homes and other groups potentially at risk. In addition, we know very little about how to address the problem of adolescent dating violence effectively. This might be due, in part, to the dearth of well-designed longitudinal studies on this topic, which are necessary to develop a solid knowledge base on the causes of relationship violence and targets for intervention. Although there are promising and notable efforts in the area of understanding and preventing violence in adolescent dating relationships, we still have much to learn.

Longitudinal research on this topic is extremely scarce; thus, we know little about the emergence and unfolding of dating violence and victimization over time.

References

Allen, L. (2004). "Getting off" and "going out": Young people's conceptions of (hetero) sexual relationships. *Health & Sexuality, 6,* 463–481.

Avery-Leaf, S., Cascardi, M., O'Leary, K.D., & Cano, A. (1997). Efficacy of a dating violence prevention program on attitudes justifying aggression. *Journal of Adolescent Health, 21,* 11–17.

Bentley, C.G., Galliher, R.V., & Ferguson, T.J. (2007). Associations among aspects of interpersonal power and relationship functioning in adolescent romantic couples. *Sex Roles, 57,* 483–495.

Capaldi, D.M., & Gorman-Smith, D. (2003). The development of aggression in young male/female couples. In P. Florsheim (Ed.), *Adolescent Romantic Relations and Sexual Behavior: Theory, Research, and Practical implications* (pp. 243–278). Lawrence Erlbaum Associates, Publishers.

Capaldi, D.M., Kim, H.K., & Shortt, J.W. (2007). Observed initiation and reciprocity of physical aggression in young, at risk couples. *Journal of Family Violence, 22,* 101–111.

Connolly, J., Craig, W., Goldberg, A., & Pepler, D. (1999). Conceptions of cross-sex friendships and romantic relationships in early adolescence. *Journal of Youth and Adolescence, 28,* 481–494.

Feiring, C. (1996). Concept of romance in 15-year-old adolescents. *Journal of Research on Adolescence, 6,* 181–200.

Foshee, V., Bauman, K.E., Arriaga, X.B., Helms, R.W., Koch, G.G., & Linder, G.F. (1998). An evaluation of safe dates, an adolescent dating violence prevention program. *American Journal of Public Health, 88,* 45–50.

Gagne, M., Lavoie, F., & Hebert, M. (2005). Victimization during childhood and revictimization in dating relationships in adolescent girls. *Child Abuse & Neglect, 29,* 1,155–1,172.

Halpern, C.T., Oslak, S.G., Young, M.L., Martin, S.L., & Kupper, L.L. (2001). Partner violence among adolescents in opposite-sex romantic relationships: Findings from the national longitudinal study of adolescent health. *American Journal of Public Health, 91,* 1,679–1,685.

Halpern, C.T., Young, M.L., Wallet, M.W., Martin S.L., & Kupper, L.L. (2004). Prevalence of partner violence in same-sex romantic and sexual relationships in a national sample of adolescents. *Journal of Adolescent Health, 35,* 131.

Hickman, L.J., Jaycox, L.H., & Aranoff, J. (2004). Dating violence among adolescents: Prevalence, gender distribution, and prevention program effectiveness. *Trauma, Violence, and Abuse, 5,* 123–142.

Hilton, N.Z., Harris, G.T., Rice, M.E., Krans, T.S., & Lavigne, S.E. (1998). Antiviolence education in high schools: Implementation and evaluation. *Journal of interpersonal Violence, 13,* 726–742.

Howard, D.E., Qiu, Y., & Boekeloo, B. (2003). Personal and social contextual correlates of adolescent dating violence. *Journal of Adolescent Health, 33,* 9–17.

Howard, D.E., Wang, M. Q., & Yan, F. (2007a). Psychosocial factors associated with reports of physical dating violence among U.S. adolescent females. *Adolescence, 42,* 311–324.

Howard, D.E., Wang, M.Q., & Yan, F. (2007b). Prevalence and psychosocial correlates of forced sexual intercourse among U.S. high school adolescents. *Adolescence, 42,* 629–643.

Jackson, S.M., Cram, F., & Seymour, F.W. (2000). Violence and sexual coercion in high school students' dating relationships. *Journal of Family Violence, 15,* 23–36.

Jouriles, E.N., McDonald, R., Garrido, E., Rosenfield, D., & Brown, A.S. (2005). Assessing aggression in adolescent romantic relationships: Can we do it better? *Psychological Assessment, 17,* 469–475.

Krajewsky, S.S., Rybarik, M.F., Dosch, M.F., & Gilmore, G.D. (1996) Results of a curriculum intervention with seventh graders regarding violence in relationships. *Journal of Family Violence, 11,* 93–112.

Linder, J.R., & Collins, W.A. (2005). Parent and peer predictors of physical aggression and conflict management in romantic relationships in early adulthood. *Journal of Family Psychology, 19,* 252–262.

Malik, S., Sorenson, S.B., & Aneshensel, C.S. (1997). Community and dating violence among adolescents: Perpetration and victimization. *Journal of Adolescent Health, 21,* 291–302.

Marquart, B.S., Nannini, D.K., Edwards, R.W., Stanley, L.R., & Wayman, J.C. (2007). Prevalence of dating violence and victimization: Regional and gender differences. *Adolescence, 42,* 645–657.

McMaster, L.E., Connolly, J., Pepler, D., & Craig, W.M. (2002). Peer to peer sexual harassment in early adolescence: A developmental perspective. *Development and Psychopathology, 14,* 91–105.

Molidor, C., & Tolman, R.M. (1998). Gender and contextual factors in adolescent dating violence. *Violence Against Women, 4,* 180–194.

O'Keefe. M. (1997). Predictors of dating violence among high school students. *Journal of Interpersonal Violence, 12,* 546–568.

O'Leary, K.D., & Slep, A.M.S. (2003). A dyadic longitudinal model of adolescent dating aggression. *Journal of Clinical Child and Adolescent Psychology, 32,* 314–327.

O'Leary, K.D., Slep, A.M., Avery-Leaf, S., & Cascardi, M. (2008). Gender differences in dating aggression among multiethnic high school students. *Journal of Adolescent Health, 42,* 473–479.

Roberts, T.A., Auinger, M.S., & Klein, J.D. (2006). Predictors of partner abuse in a nationally representative sample of adolescents involved in heterosexual dating relationships. *Violence and Victims, 21,* 81–89.

Sears, H.A., Byers, E.S., & Price, E.L. (2007). The co-occurrence of adolescent boys' and girls' use of psychologically, physically, and sexually abusive behaviours in their dating relationships. *Journal of Adolescence, 30,* 487–504.

Smith, P.H., White, J.W., & Holland, L.J. (2003). A longitudinal perspective on dating violence among adolescent and college-age women. *American Journal of Public Health, 93,* 1,104–1,109.

Weisz, A.N., & Black, B.M. (2001). Evaluating a sexual assault and dating violence prevention program for urban youths. *Social Work Research, 25,* 89–102.

Whitaker, D.J., Morrison, S., Lindquist, C., Hawkins, S.R., O'Neil, J.A., Nesius, A.M., Mathew, A., & Reese, L. (2006). A critical review of interventions for the primary prevention of perpetration of partner violence. *Aggression and Violent Behavior, 11,* 151–166.

Wolfe, D.A., Scott, K., Reitzel-Jaffe, D., Wekerle, C., Grasley, C., & Straatman, A.-L. (2001). Development and validation of the conflict in adolescent dating relationships inventory. *Psychological Assessment, 13,* 277–293.

Wolfe, D.A., Wekerle, C., Scott, K., Straatman, A. L., Grasley, C., & Reitzel-Jaffe, D. (2003). Dating violence prevention with at-risk youth: A controlled outcome evaluation. *Journal of Consulting and Clinical Psychology, 71,* 279–291.

Wolitzky-Taylor, M.A., Ruggiero, K.J., Danielson, C.K., Resnick, H.S., Hanson, R.F., Smith, D.W., Saunders, B.E., & Kilpatrick, D.G. (2008). Prevalence and correlates of dating violence in a national sample of adolescents. *Journal of the American Academy of Child and Adolescent Psychiatry, 47,* 755–762.

ERNEST N. JOURILES, PhD is Professor in the Department of Psychology and Co-Director of the Family Research Center at Southern Methodist University. **CORA PLATT** is a doctoral student in the Department of Psychology at Southern Methodist University. **RENEE MCDONALD,** PhD is Associate Professor in the Department of Psychology and Co-Director of the Family Research Center at Southern Methodist University.

Mentally Ill Offenders Strain Juvenile System

SOLOMON MOORE

The teenager in the padded smock sat in his solitary confinement cell here in this state's most secure juvenile prison and screamed obscenities.

The youth, Donald, a 16-year-old, his eyes glassy from lack of sleep and a daily regimen of mood stabilizers, was serving a minimum of six months for breaking and entering. Although he had received diagnoses for psychiatric illnesses, including bipolar disorder, a judge decided that Donald would get better care in the state correctional system than he could get anywhere in his county.

That was two years ago.

Donald's confinement has been repeatedly extended because of his violent outbursts. This year he assaulted a guard here at the prison, the Ohio River Valley Juvenile Correctional Facility, and was charged anew, with assault. His fists and forearms are striped with scars where he gouged himself with pencils and the bones of a bird he caught and dismembered.

As cash-starved states slash mental health programs in communities and schools, they are increasingly relying on the juvenile corrections system to handle a generation of young offenders with psychiatric disorders. About two-thirds of the nation's juvenile inmates—who numbered 92,854 in 2006, down from 107,000 in 1999—have at least one mental illness, according to surveys of youth prisons, and are more in need of therapy than punishment.

"We're seeing more and more mentally ill kids who couldn't find community programs that were intensive enough to treat them," said Joseph Penn, a child psychiatrist at the Texas Youth Commission. "Jails and juvenile justice facilities are the new asylums."

At least 32 states cut their community mental health programs by an average of 5 percent this year and plan to double those budget reductions by 2010, according to a recent survey of state mental health offices.

Juvenile prisons have been the caretaker of last resort for troubled children since the 1980s, but mental health experts say the system is in crisis, facing a soaring number of inmates reliant on multiple—and powerful—psychotropic drugs and a shortage of therapists.

In California's state system, one of the most violent and poorly managed juvenile systems in the country, according to federal investigators, three dozen youth offenders seriously injured themselves or attempted suicide in the last year—a sign, state juvenile justice experts say, of neglect and poor safety protocols.

In Ohio, where Gov. Ted Strickland, a former prison psychologist, approved a 34 percent reduction in community-based mental health services to reduce a budget deficit, Thomas J. Stickrath, the director of the Department of Youth Services, said continuing cuts would swell his youth offender population.

"I'm hearing from a lot of judges saying, 'I'm sorry I'm sending so-and-so to you, but at least I know that he'll get the treatment he can't get in his community,'" Mr. Stickrath said.

But youths are often subjected to neglect and violence in juvenile prisons, and studies show that mental illnesses can become worse there.

George, 17, an inmate at Ohio River Valley, detailed his daily cocktail of psychiatric medications, including Abilify and Seroquel. In addition to having bipolar disorder, he is a sex offender and is H.I.V. positive—severe stigmas in prison.

"I be getting punked," he said, using prison slang to describe how gang youths routinely humiliate him. He blinked, and his leg shook uncontrollably. "They take my food, they hit me, they make me do things."

Demetrius, 16, another inmate there, said he had received a diagnosis of bipolar disorder. Officials said he has *psychotic* episodes and attacks other inmates. In an interview in June, he said he was receiving no mental health counseling or medications. Andrea Kruse, a spokeswoman for Mr. Stickrath, said that since July 1, he has had more than 20 counseling sessions.

According to a Government Accountability Office report, in 2001, families relinquished custody of 9,000 children to juvenile justice systems so they could receive mental health services.

Donald has been in and out of mental health programs since he attacked a schoolteacher at age 5. As he grew older, he became more violent until he was eventually committed to the Department of Youth Services.

"I've begged D.Y.S. to get him into a mental facility where they're trained to deal with people like him," said his grandmother, who asked not to be identified because of the stigma of having a grandson who is mentally ill. "I don't think a lockup situation is where he should be, although I don't think he should be on the street either."

Lawsuits and federal civil rights investigations in Indiana, Maryland, Ohio and Texas have criticized juvenile corrections systems for failing to meet their obligation to prohibit cruel and unusual punishment of prisoners.

Despite downsizing to about 1,650 juvenile inmates from about 10,000 youth offenders in 1996, California's state system remains under a 2004 federal mandate to improve conditions, including mental health services—the result of a class-action lawsuit that documented the systematic physical and sexual abuse of wards.

Under a plan to reduce the state juvenile inmate population, many youths who once would have been held by the state are now detained by the Los Angeles County juvenile detention system. Los Angeles County is also under a federal mandate to improve psychiatric services for juvenile inmates, especially at the six camps at its Challenger Memorial Youth Center, which holds most of the county's medium- and high-risk offenders and most of its mentally ill ones.

"We were told that the Challenger camps are, paradoxically, the only camps at which staff are authorized to carry O.C. spray," wrote federal civil rights investigators in a 2008 report to county authorities, referring to oleoresin capsicum, known as pepper spray. "One supervisor told us that he believed that allowing staff to carry and use O.C. spray made sense given the 'mental health population.'"

The investigators also recounted how staff members body slammed unruly juveniles, often breaking their bones.

In May, a reporter toured the Los Angeles County Central Juvenile Hall with Eric Trupin, a consultant hired by the Department of Justice to monitor mental health services in California's juvenile justice system. Dr. Trupin, a psychologist, said some detainees appeared to be held there for no reason other than that they were mentally ill and the county had no other institution capable of treating them.

One inmate at the county's juvenile hall, Eric, 18, was given a diagnosis of bipolar disorder and prescribed Risperdal, a powerful antipsychotic, to help him avoid violent flashes of temper.

A public defender who specializes in juvenile mental health issues, said Eric had been arrested more than 20 times near his South Los Angeles home. Dr. Trupin worried that if Eric is released and arrested again, he will be charged as an adult and enter the Los Angeles County jail, the nation's largest residential mental institution, with 1,400 mentally ill inmates.

In the 1960s and '70s, the increasing availability of antipsychotic medications coincided with a national movement to close public mental hospitals. Many private hospitals barred psychotic patients, including juveniles. By the 1980s, juvenile justice systems had become the primary providers of residential psychiatric care for mentally ill youths.

But as cutbacks have worsened, the debate has intensified over what constitutes adequate mental health care. Often juvenile justice systems have very little to go on when attempting a diagnosis.

"Often Daddy is nowhere to be found, Mommy might be in jail," said Daniel Connor, a psychiatrist for the Connecticut juvenile corrections system. "The home phone is cut off. The parent speaks another language, so it's often hard to figure out exactly what's going on with each kid."

School records often do not arrive with arrested youths, nor do files often come from other corrections institutions. The lack of information is particularly problematic when psychiatrists try to prescribe medications. Joseph Parks, medical director for the Missouri Department of Mental Health and a national expert on pharmaceutical drug use in corrections facilities, said many juvenile offenders are prescribed multiple psychiatric drugs as they move from mental health clinics to detention halls to juvenile prisons.

A decade ago, it was rare to find juvenile offenders on two psychotropic drugs at once, Dr. Parks said. Now, many take three or four at a time, often for nonprescribed uses like helping the youths sleep.

"If you just give a kid a pill, the prison administration doesn't have to do anything differently," he said. "The staff doesn't have to do anything differently. The guards don't have to get more training."

Census studies of child mental health professionals show chronic shortages. A 2006 study estimated that for every 100,000 youths, there were fewer than nine child psychiatrists. Dr. Penn of Texas said the state youth prison system there recently instituted a system of telepsychiatry sessions, conducting videoconferences between mental health professionals and youths being detained hundreds of miles away.

Inadequate mental health services increases recidivism. In a February report on psychiatric services at the Ohio River Valley center, Dr. Cheryl Wills, an independent mental health expert, found that officials were unnecessarily extending incarceration for youths who acted out because of their mental illnesses.

Mr. Stickrath, the director of the Ohio Department of Youth Services, said that one challenge in dealing with large numbers of psychologically ill youths is determining who is "mad versus bad." He mentioned Donald, whose file he knew by heart.

"He's been in 130 fights since he's been with us, and there were no resources in the small county he's from to deal with him," Mr. Stickrath said. "Our staff worked to get him in a sophisticated psychiatric residential program, but they said he had to leave because he was attacking staff."

Mr. Stickrath shook his head. "He just wears you out."

UNIT 6

Punishment and Corrections

Unit Selections

Key Points to Consider

• How does probation differ from parole? Are there similarities?

• Discuss the points for and against the death penalty.

• Should the impact of incarceration on inmates' families be a consideration for parole boards?

Student Website
www.mhhe.com/cls

Internet References

American Probation and Parole Association (APPA)
   http://www.appa-net.org
The Corrections Connection
   http://www.corrections.com
Critical Criminology Division of the ASC
   http://www.critcrim.org/
David Willshire's Forensic Psychology & Psychiatry Links
   http://members.optushome.com.au/dwillsh/index.html
Oregon Department of Corrections
   http://egov.oregon.gov/DOC/TRANS/CC/cc_welcome.shtml

In the American system of criminal justice, the term "corrections" has a special meaning. It designates programs and agencies that have legal authority over the custody or supervision of people who have been convicted of a criminal act by the courts. The correctional process begins with the sentencing of the convicted offender. The predominant sentencing pattern in the United States encourages maximum judicial discretion and offers a range of alternatives, from probation (supervised, conditional freedom within the community) through imprisonment, to the death penalty.

Selections in this unit focus on the current condition of the U.S. penal system and the effects that sentencing, probation, imprisonment, and parole have on the rehabilitation of criminals.

This section begins with "Inmate Count in U.S. Dwarfs Other Nations," in which Liptak writes about the grim statistics that distinguish this country's incarceration rates from those of other countries. According to Alan Greenblatt in "Felon Fallout," the problems of overcrowded prisons and soaring costs are causing some states to take another look at the concept of rehabilitating our nation's convicts, rather than simply warehousing them.

According to diZerega and Shapiro in "Asking about Family Can Enhance Reentry," one simple idea could lead to considerable change in the search for innovative, effective ways to help prepare former inmates make the transition from prison back to the community. In the next article, "The Ex-Con Next Door," Alex Kingsbury writes about the problem of ending the cycle of recidivism. He says that community leaders and criminal justice experts are focusing on a fresh approach to help the offender make a healthy return to society.

Following is a commencement address given by Jablecki, entitled "Prison Inmates Meet Socrates" in which he spoke about the problems caused by public policy that ignores the benefits of attempting to rehabilitate offenders. In "One Clique," Campbell discusses how the issue of race is handled by prison inmates. In the next article, "The Professor was a Prison Guard," Jeffrey J. Williams writes about how the time he spent working in a prison compares with his present position as a college professor.

The following article, "Supermax Prisons," by Jeffrey Ian Ross is a warning about the possible constitutional and human rights violations occurring in these institutions. Any answer to the question: What do we get from imprisonment? has to recognize that U.S. imprisonment operates differently from that in

© Royalty-Free/Corbis

any other democratic state in the world. This point is made in Todd R. Clear's essay, "The Results of American Incarceration." A prison warden says that crime is a social disease that we cannot ignore in the hope it will go away. Finally, "Partnering with Law Enforcement" is an article that reports on some of the positive outcomes that have resulted from partnerships among probation and parole officers and police officers.

Inmate Count in U.S. Dwarfs Other Nations'

ADAM LIPTAK

The United States has less than 5 percent of the world's population. But it has almost a quarter of the world's prisoners.

Indeed, the United States *leads* the world in producing prisoners, a reflection of a relatively recent and now entirely distinctive American approach to crime and punishment. Americans are locked up for crimes—from writing bad checks to using drugs—that would rarely produce prison sentences in other countries. And in particular they are kept incarcerated far longer than prisoners in other nations.

Criminologists and legal scholars in other industrialized nations say they are mystified and appalled by the number and length of American prison sentences.

The United States has, for instance, 2.3 million criminals behind bars, more than any other nation, according to data maintained by the International Center for Prison Studies at King's College London.

China, which is four times more populous than the United States, is a distant second, with 1.6 million people in prison. (That number excludes hundreds of thousands of people held in administrative detention, most of them in China's extrajudicial system of re-education through labor, which often singles out political activists who have not committed crimes.)

San Marino, with a population of about 30,000, is at the end of the long list of 218 countries compiled by the center. It has a single prisoner.

The United States comes in first, too, on a more meaningful list from the prison studies center, the one ranked in order of the incarceration rates. It has 751 people in prison or jail for every 100,000 in population. (If you count only adults, one in 100 Americans is locked up.)

The only other major industrialized nation that even comes close is Russia, with 627 prisoners for every 100,000 people. The others have much lower rates. England's rate is 151; Germany's is 88; and Japan's is 63.

The median among all nations is about 125, roughly a sixth of the American rate.

There is little question that the high incarceration rate here has helped drive down crime, though there is debate about how much.

Criminologists and legal experts here and abroad point to a tangle of factors to explain America's extraordinary incarceration rate: higher levels of violent crime, harsher sentencing laws, a legacy of racial turmoil, a special fervor in combating illegal drugs, the American temperament, and the lack of a social safety net. Even democracy plays a role, as judges—many of whom are elected, another American anomaly—yield to populist demands for tough justice.

Whatever the reason, the gap between American justice and that of the rest of the world is enormous and growing.

It used to be that Europeans came to the United States to study its prison systems. They came away impressed.

"In no country is criminal justice administered with more mildness than in the United States," Alexis de Tocqueville, who toured American penitentiaries in 1831, wrote in "Democracy in America."

No more.

"Far from serving as a model for the world, contemporary America is viewed with horror," James Q. Whitman, a specialist in comparative law at Yale, wrote last year in *Social Research*. "Certainly there are no European governments sending delegations to learn from us about how to manage prisons."

Prison sentences here have become "vastly harsher than in any other country to which the United States would ordinarily be compared," Michael H. Tonry, a leading authority on crime policy, wrote in "The Handbook of Crime and Punishment."

Indeed, said Vivien Stern, a research fellow at the prison studies center in London, the American incarceration rate has made the United States "a rogue state, a country that has made a decision not to follow what is a normal Western approach."

The spike in American incarceration rates is quite recent. From 1925 to 1975, the rate remained stable, around 110 people in prison per 100,000 people. It shot up with the movement to get tough on crime in the late 1970s. (These numbers exclude people held in jails, as comprehensive information on prisoners held in state and local jails was not collected until relatively recently.)

The nation's relatively high violent crime rate, partly driven by the much easier availability of guns here, helps explain the number of people in American prisons.

"The assault rate in New York and London is not that much different," said Marc Mauer, the executive director of the Sentencing Project, a research and advocacy group. "But if you look at the murder rate, particularly with firearms, it's much higher."

Despite the recent decline in the murder rate in the United States, it is still about four times that of many nations in Western Europe.

But that is only a partial explanation. The United States, in fact, has relatively low rates of nonviolent crime. It has lower burglary and robbery rates than Australia, Canada and England.

People who commit nonviolent crimes in the rest of the world are less likely to receive prison time and certainly less likely to receive long sentences. The United States is, for instance, the only advanced country that incarcerates people for minor property crimes like passing bad checks, Mr. Whitman wrote.

Efforts to combat illegal drugs play a major role in explaining long prison sentences in the United States as well. In 1980, there were about 40,000 people in American jails and prisons for drug crimes. These days, there are almost 500,000.

Those figures have drawn contempt from European critics. "The U.S. pursues the war on drugs with an ignorant fanaticism," said Ms. Stern of King's College.

Many American prosecutors, on the other hand, say that locking up people involved in the drug trade is imperative, as it helps thwart demand for illegal drugs and drives down other kinds of crime. Attorney General *Michael B. Mukasey,* for instance, has fought hard to prevent the early release of people in federal prison on crack cocaine offenses, saying that many of them "are among the most serious and violent offenders."

Still, it is the length of sentences that truly distinguishes American prison policy. Indeed, the mere number of sentences imposed here would not place the United States at the top of the incarceration lists. If lists were compiled based on annual admissions to prison per capita, several European countries would outpace the United States. But

American prison stays are much longer, so the total incarceration rate is higher.

Burglars in the United States serve an average of 16 months in prison, according to Mr. Mauer, compared with 5 months in Canada and 7 months in England.

Many specialists dismissed race as an important distinguishing factor in the American prison rate. It is true that blacks are much more likely to be imprisoned than other groups in the United States, but that is not a particularly distinctive phenomenon. Minorities in Canada, Britain and Australia are also disproportionately represented in those nation's prisons, and the ratios are similar to or larger than those in the United States.

Some scholars have found that English-speaking nations have higher prison rates.

"Although it is not at all clear what it is about Anglo-Saxon culture that makes predominantly English-speaking countries especially punitive, they are," Mr. Tonry wrote last year in "Crime, Punishment and Politics in Comparative Perspective."

"It could be related to economies that are more capitalistic and political cultures that are less social democratic than those of most European countries," Mr. Tonry wrote. "Or it could have something to do with the Protestant religions with strong Calvinist overtones that were long influential."

The American character—self-reliant, independent, judgmental—also plays a role.

"America is a comparatively tough place, which puts a strong emphasis on individual responsibility," Mr. Whitman of Yale wrote. "That attitude has shown up in the American criminal justice of the last 30 years."

French-speaking countries, by contrast, have "comparatively mild penal policies," Mr. Tonry wrote.

Of course, sentencing policies within the United States are not monolithic, and national comparisons can be misleading.

"Minnesota looks more like Sweden than like Texas," said Mr. Mauer of the Sentencing Project. (Sweden imprisons about 80 people per 100,000 of population; Minnesota, about 300; and Texas, almost 1,000. Maine has the lowest incarceration rate in the United States, at 273; and Louisiana the highest, at 1,138.)

Whatever the reasons, there is little dispute that America's exceptional incarceration rate has had an impact on crime.

"As one might expect, a good case can be made that fewer Americans are now being victimized" thanks to the tougher crime policies, Paul G. Cassell, an authority on sentencing and a former federal judge, wrote in *The Stanford Law Review.*

From 1981 to 1996, according to Justice Department statistics, the risk of punishment rose in the United States and fell in England. The crime rates predictably moved in the opposite directions, falling in the United States and rising in England.

"These figures," Mr. Cassell wrote, "should give one pause before too quickly concluding that European sentences are appropriate."

Other commentators were more definitive. "The simple truth is that imprisonment works," wrote Kent Scheidegger and Michael Rushford of the Criminal Justice Legal Foundation in *The Stanford Law and Policy Review*. "Locking up criminals for longer periods reduces the level of crime. The benefits of doing so far offset the costs."

There is a counterexample, however, to the north. "Rises and falls in Canada's crime rate have closely paralleled America's for 40 years," Mr. Tonry wrote last year. "But its imprisonment rate has remained stable."

Several specialists here and abroad pointed to a surprising explanation for the high incarceration rate in the United States: democracy.

Most state court judges and prosecutors in the United States are elected and are therefore sensitive to a public that is, according to opinion polls, generally in favor of tough crime policies. In the rest of the world, criminal justice professionals tend to be civil servants who are insulated from popular demands for tough sentencing.

Mr. Whitman, who has studied Tocqueville's work on American penitentiaries, was asked what accounted for America's booming prison population.

"Unfortunately, a lot of the answer is democracy—just what Tocqueville was talking about," he said. "We have a highly politicized criminal justice system."

Felon Fallout

Overcrowding and soaring corrections costs are pushing prison reform to the top of states' policy agendas.

ALAN GREENBLATT

A couple of years ago, the state of California did something surprising. It changed the name of its Department of Corrections, tacking on the words "and Rehabilitation" to the agency's title. It was a small step—the modification wasn't accompanied by any sudden surge in funding for rehabilitation programs. But it was symbolically important nonetheless. Thirty years ago, the state officially recast the department's mission from rehabilitation to incarceration and punishment. Since then, the idea of rehabilitating prisoners has been a much lower priority than locking up more of them. Now, with the state's prisons bursting at the bars, that may be about to change.

California's prison system houses more than 170,000 inmates, roughly double the number it was designed to hold. Overcrowding has precipitated riots and viral outbreaks, as well as straining basic services such as water and sewer. A federal judge has given state lawmakers until June to come up with a feasible solution for handling the heavy volume or risk a court takeover of the entire system. Two other courts are also entertaining motions to put a cap on the prison population. And, in response to yet another case, a federal court has already taken control of the prison health care system, ordering changes that could cost the state as much as $1 billion. The California prison system was undeniably facing a crisis anyway, but pressure from the courts has made prison management and reform one of the most pressing issues in Sacramento this year.

"We are at the point where if we don't clean up the mess, the federal court is going to do the job for us," said Governor Arnold Schwarzenegger. He has asked lawmakers to approve an $11 billion package in response. Most of the money would go toward building more prison and jail capacity. But Schwarzenegger also aims to make good on the promise of rehabilitation suggested by the corrections agency's name change. He wants nearly double the present funding for vocational, educational and drug treatment programs.

In looking to change its approach on corrections, California is just starting to play catch-up with the rest of the country. While no one wants to be accused of being "soft" on crime, fiscal concerns in many states have helped to revive liberal notions that had been abandoned for decades. In the aggregate, state governments are now spending more than $40 billion per year on prisons—five times as much as during the mid-1980s. Corrections departments have become the largest public employers in many states. A few are even spending more on corrections than on higher education. As a result, the ground underlying the corrections debate has clearly shifted. Nearly every state has stepped up its efforts to prepare prisoners for release, hoping that at least some of them will gain the skills and attitude necessary to avoid coming back.

Granted, the word "rehabilitation" is still too charged to return to broad use. The new buzzword is "reentry," a term that tacitly acknowledges that the vast majority of inmates will return to their communities at some point. The problem is that most of them will end up behind bars again, if not for new crimes then for parole violations. In California, seven out of 10 released prisoners are re-incarcerated within three years. That's one of the worst rates in the nation. But most states recognize that if they can cut their recidivism rates by just a small fraction, they will save enormous amounts of money.

Since 2004, for example, Connecticut has been putting more money into reentry programs such as parole, housing and drug treatment. Apparently as a result, the state has seen its prison population decline after a worrisome spike upwards. Connecticut was able to avoid building more prison space, and less crowding meant the cancellation of its multimillion-dollar contract with Virginia to house 500 prisoners it previously had no room for. "Around the country, it's becoming politically safe to do this stuff," says Michael Lawlor, chair of the Connecticut House Judiciary Committee, "because there's something in it for everybody, social progressives and fiscal conservatives."

More policy makers are becoming convinced of the need for offering prisoners some choices other than staring at the wall, but rehabilitation still doesn't sit well with the public.

Of course, not everyone has come around to this way of thinking. The idea that has dominated state corrections policy for more than a decade—that it is better to lock up offenders than waste energy worrying about how they're treated while they're in prison—still has enormous political resonance. And although more policy makers are becoming convinced of the need for offering prisoners some choices other than staring at a wall, the notion of investing in felons for the purposes of rehabilitation still doesn't sit well with the public at large.

In California, voters have strongly indicated their continued desire for a get-tough approach. Last November, they approved one of the harshest sex-offender laws in the country—which, among other things, will put thousands more behind bars. That came on the heels of voter rejection of an attempt to soften the state's "Three Strikes" law, which puts habitual offenders away for decades or for life. "Republicans generally feel we should build more prisons," says Dick Ackerman, the party's leader in the state Senate. "The California taxpayer wants to put these people away."

The Roots of Overcrowding

Like most of the rest of the country, California has spent the past quarter-century on a prison-building spree. The state's prison population has increased eightfold during those years, so that despite nearly tripling the number of its prisons since 1980, the corrections department has just about run out of room. It predicts the system will reach its absolute capacity in June or July, which is just about the time a federal judge might take over the system.

The roots of overcrowding are clear. Beginning in 1976, California's legislature and voters began approving a slew of tougher sentencing laws—some 1,000 altogether, culminating with the 1994 passage of Three Strikes. Although virtually all the laws lengthened sentences, the penal code as a whole has become a hodgepodge. It's easy to sketch out scenarios under which a criminal may face any one of four or five different mandatory sentences—each carrying a different penalty—for the exact same crime.

"The accusations that we became just a warehouse are true."

—James Tilton
California Corrections Secretary

The one thing that has become certain for virtually all prisoners, however, is the date of release. Determinant sentencing has stripped the corrections department of its former authority to make judgments about when and whether a prisoner is ready to be released. Rather than getting time off for good behavior, or shortening their sentences by completing drug treatment programs, prisoners know they will be released on a fixed day, even if they have been dangerous enough to be kept in solitary until the day of their release. "We have more stringent requirements for young people graduating high schools than we do for people being released from prison," says state Senator Mike Machado.

If prisoners have no incentive for participating in rehab programs, there aren't adequate programs available to them anyway. For instance, more than half the state's prisoners are in "high need" of drug treatment, but only about 9 percent of them are likely to be enrolled at any given time, according to the UC Irvine study. Such programs are traditionally understaffed and poorly financed, but overcrowding has meant there's literally no place for them. The state prisons have classrooms and gymnasiums, but many are filled with some of the 19,000 inmates who are sleeping not in cells but in double or triple bunks lined up in every available space. "The accusations that we became just a warehouse are true," says James Tilton, Schwarzenegger's corrections secretary.

Release and Return

Under Schwarzenegger's plan, counties would house more short-term prisoners and help them get access to community-based programs. His proposal includes $5.5 billion for local jails, but counties remain nervous that the state will pass too many costs and responsibilities onto them. According to the sheriff's association in the state, more than 200,000 prisoners at the county level failed in 2005 to serve any or all of their sentences because 20 county jails are under court-ordered population caps, with 12 more maintaining voluntary caps under court pressure. Tilton, undaunted, has been working to convince counties and local law enforcement officials that local programs provide an alternative to the unworkable revolving-door recidivism system currently in place. "My presentation is that, if you want the status quo, if you want an inmate who is not prepared to be in your community, then to be honest you can have that if you like."

With so many of the state's prisoners either functionally illiterate or addicted to drugs (or having a combination of both problems), it's hardly surprising that so many of them return to prison after a brief stint on the outside. In Kansas, says state Representative Pat Colloton, two-thirds of prison admissions are related to parole and probation violations, and 80 percent of these are due to substance abuse or mental illness. In many cases, people are going to prison for violating probation, even though they weren't sentenced to jail time for their original crime.

If their crimes weren't severe enough to warrant a prison sentence in the first place, the state doesn't want them occupying expensive beds or distracting parole officers from more dangerous offenders. Toward that end, Kansas ran a pilot program in Shawnee County that sought to coordinate housing, substance abuse, job training and other programs for parolees. It cut the usual parole-revocation rate from 80 percent to 30 percent. Colloton has introduced twin bills that aim to build on this success by offering grants to more counties. "By giving this support, we can substantially reduce the number of people coming back to jail," she says. "We think that reforming people is the way to go, rather than building more prison beds."

Colloton, a Republican, is not some '60s liberal. Her proposal, like so many among the new generation of rehab programs, would be funded with strings attached. Accountability, after all, has become another universal buzzword. In order to continue to receive funding under Colloton's legislation, a county in Kansas will have to show that it has cut its revocation rate by at least 20 percent. In Oregon, the legislature has imposed a statutory requirement on the corrections department to monitor the success rate of reentry programs. In Washington State, a legislative study found that spending $1,000 per inmate for academic and vocational training programs was a good deal, crediting such programs with savings of more than $10,000 per prisoner in the form of lower crime rates and drops in recidivism of up to 9 percent.

Because the early results look good—and there's suddenly grant money and research available from sources such as the U.S. Department of Justice and the Council of State Governments' new Justice Center—more states are willing to look hard at funding reentry programs as an alternative to spending far more on prison beds. Even in tough-on-crime Texas, which leads the nation not only in executions but also its per capita rate of incarceration, lawmakers are talking seriously about the need to increase programming in prisons and in communities to address illiteracy, drug addiction and other stumbling blocks common to prisoners and parolees. "We're trying to do the smart thing," says Jerry Madden, chairman of the House Committee on Corrections. "The answer is not just building more prisons."

Lack of Political Will

Governor Schwarzenegger has talked seriously about making major changes to California's corrections system throughout the course of his administration. But, according to his critics, whenever push has come to shove, he's stopped pushing. Not long after taking office, Schwarzenegger appointed a prison study commission, headed by former Governor George Deukmejian, and called for an overhaul of the state's overtaxed parole system. So confident was his administration of success with its parole changes—it promised savings of $75 million per year—that it suspended operations at the correctional officer training academy, anticipating the need for fewer officers. But neither the implementation of parole changes nor the savings ever came off.

The lack of new trained officers is just one reason why the corrections department is understaffed by about 4,000 employees. California had one of the nation's lowest guard-to-inmate ratios anyway, but the closure of the training academy has meant hefty overtime payments to those on duty; 6,000 department employees, mostly rank-and-file guards, earned six figures during the past fiscal year. Indeed, the average base salary for prison guards there is 50 percent above the national average.

The guards' main union, the California Correctional Peace Officers Association, has become one of the most powerful forces in Sacramento. It was the leading donor to Schwarzenegger's two immediate predecessors. Schwarzenegger has openly derided the union as a "special interest," sought to cut its power by changing its means of collecting political dues from members, and attempted to shut the union out from prison policy discussions for the first time in years.

The CCPOA also didn't like the fact that he suspended its members' promised pay raises during a tough budget year, or that he tried to revoke some of the managerial control over its members that the union had won from his predecessor, which allows CCPOA to determine which officers will get which jobs 70 percent of the time. After Schwarzenegger unveiled his parole plan, the union helped a victims' rights group air TV ads claiming that the plan would let murderers, rapists and child molesters roam the streets.

Last year, two corrections secretaries quit in the space of a couple of months, later testifying in court that the governor's top political aides had decided to cave in to union demands. The courts grew publicly concerned about the administration's "retreat" from prison reform, with a special master complaining about CCPOA's "disturbing" amount of clout.

But if the union is sometimes cast in the role of villain in California's ongoing prison policy drama, there is plenty of blame left for others. Schwarzenegger called a special session last summer to address the overcrowding issue, asking the legislature to approve $6 billion for prison construction. The Senate passed a heavily revised version of the governor's plan, but the Assembly balked. Legislators claimed they needed more time to address such a complex issue, but the fact that the special session was a failure—coupled with the fact that the Democrats who control the legislature have shown more interest in Schwarzenegger's proposed sentencing commission than his latest construction money request—has led Republicans to level the familiar charge that they are soft on crime and criminals.

Schwarzenegger was seeking changes to the state's sentencing structure even before the U.S. Supreme Court ruled in January that major portions of it are unconstitutional. His fellow Republicans in the legislature claim that a sentencing commission, which would aim to straighten out some of the many inconsistencies in California's penal code, is "code for early release." Sentencing commissions, which have been tried in about 20 states, have not all been successful, but neither have they universally called for shorter sentences.

In North Carolina and Virginia, commonly cited as models in California, sentences for violent crimes were significantly lengthened, although both commissions diverted funds to community-based rehab and reentry programs. But Republican legislators in California are convinced that Democrats mean to use any new sentencing commission as cover for cutting jail time. "My biggest fear is that the liberals are going to drive an agenda where they will give the governor sentencing reform," says Assembly Republican Todd Spitzer, "and will not give any additional resources for prison beds, claiming that sentencing reform is enough to solve the problem."

Chance of a Lifetime

The stop-and-start nature of California's prison debate over the past couple of years has bred plenty of cynicism. But most observers think that the threat of a court takeover will succeed in prodding the political players into finally addressing the problem. Schwarzenegger has gotten nowhere with his earlier prison reform efforts because the political stakes were too high. Now, the dynamic has changed and the penalty for inaction may have become greater than for agreement. No one wants to be blamed when a court orders the release of thousands of convicts or watch the same court freely spend billions of additional dollars from state coffers. The Department of Corrections and Rehabilitation's budget has soared 52 percent over the past five years and is set to exceed $10 billion this year. Those numbers are scary enough without risking the prospect of a court receiver backing up a truck to the state treasury. "We don't need the federal government coming in here and writing blank checks out of our general fund," says Mike Villines, leader of the Assembly Republicans.

Villines, Spitzer and other Republicans clearly mean to keep banging the "tough on crime" gong in order to pressure Schwarzenegger and Democratic legislative leaders. They may or may not succeed in their goals of keeping a sentencing commission's authority limited and prison construction spending high. But even they talk about the need for the state to do a better job with rehabilitation programs in order to cut costly recidivism. The guards' union, for its part, also has embraced the need for rehabilitation programs and publicly stated that sentencing reform is going to happen in California, whether through the legislative process or via court edict.

The debate in California is just beginning, but it's clear that reconciling all the complex and politically touchy issues surrounding sentencing, parole, rehabilitation and, in all likelihood, new prison construction will be tremendously difficult. (To make things even more complicated, the guards' contract is up for renegotiation.) Yet it's quite possible that the state, having let its prison problems grow literally out of its control, will finally take a comprehensive look at solving them.

"Sometimes a crisis will drive decisions, and we are certainly in a crisis situation," says Tilton, the corrections secretary. "This really presents an opportunity that hasn't been around for the 30 years I've been in state government to work through the issues about who should be in prison versus who should be somewhere else."

ALAN GREENBLATT can be reached at agreenblatt@governing.com.

From *Governing,* March 2007, pp. 37–38, 40, 42, 44. Copyright © 2007 by Congressional Quarterly, Inc. Reprinted by permission.

Asking about Family Can Enhance Reentry

MARGARET DIZEREGA AND CAROL SHAPIRO

One simple idea could lead to considerable change as corrections professionals search for innovative, effective and cost-efficient ways to help prepare people who are making the transition from prison to the community: Always ask about the family. Drawing on more than a decade's experience of engaging families that have a member involved with the criminal justice system, the national nonprofit organization Family Justice set its sights on developing a case management tool that would effectively collect information about people's social networks while initiating a dialogue about reentry.

Bolstered by research showing that the organization's strength-based, family-focused approach reduced recidivism and illegal drug use from 80 percent to 42 percent and improved overall family well-being,[1] Family Justice joined with five partners across the country in a dynamic, interactive process to design such a tool. The basic premise was to ask about individuals' family and other social supports in the context of reentry, using a format that is easy to administer and put into practice. The developed instrument is the Relational Inquiry Tool, a series of questions that can change the conversations case managers and other correctional staff have with people who are preparing to leave prison. The first three questions of the eight-question Relational Inquiry Tool are: 1) In thinking about your family support when you get out of prison, what are you most excited about?; 2) In thinking about your family support when you get out of prison, what do you think the greatest challenges will be?; 3) How did you help your family and friends before you came to prison? The questions are always asked in the order listed and they are accompanied with recommended probes that are also open-ended questions that are consistent with the family-focused, strength-based nature of the tool.

The Family Justice project has two main goals:

- The tool can serve as an easy-to-use method of recognizing and reinforcing the positive connections of family and social networks during and after incarcerations; and
- The questions can build rapport between the professional using the tool and the individual transitioning home.

With significant support from the National Institute of Corrections, Family Justice has collaborated on this innovative project with five government and community-based partners: the Massachusetts Executive Office of Public Safety, the Michigan Department of Corrections, the Ohio Department of Rehabilitation and Correction, the Oklahoma Department of Corrections and the Safer Foundation in Chicago.

Why Ask about the Family?

In an Urban Institute study in Chicago, people interviewed four to eight months after their release cited families as "the most important factor" in helping them stay out of prison.[2] A study by the Vera Institute of Justice found that for individuals recently released from prison or jail, "supportive families were an indicator of success across the board, correlating with lower drug use, greater likelihood of finding jobs and less criminal activity."[3]

The corrections field has grown increasingly interested in devising a tool that identifies the strengths of people involved in the criminal justice system and of families and social networks—and one that complements risk and needs assessment instruments. Despite the broad application of data collected by those instruments, they rarely identify how people receive assistance from or provide support to family and other members of their social network. Given the increasing emphasis on reentry as more than 650,000 individuals are expected to leave prison this year,[4] the corrections field must help identify the resources available to people as they return to the community. A simple, effective tool could serve as a catalyst for families and corrections professionals to help create successful reentry plans.

Professionals in the criminal justice field are increasingly recognizing the value of engaging families and their communities, as well as the impact of incarceration on people's children and other loved ones. Although the idea of partnering with families may seem intuitive, the methodology for doing so is not. Current risk and needs assessment instruments focus primarily on indicators of institutional violence or propensity to re-offend, and some of those indicators rely on family histories of substance abuse, criminal justice involvement and other challenges. Though those aspects of a person's past are important, they often lead correctional staff to focus on what an inmate should not do or whom they should avoid. Family Justice's experience suggests that instead of focusing only on deficits, asking about positive social connections and personal strengths and resiliencies can provide case managers with a different entry point to talk about behavior change.

Testing the Relational Inquiry Tool

The government and community-based partners were involved in all aspects of the study, from participating on the National Advisory Board for the Relational Inquiry Tool to scheduling pretest interviews. On the board, the five partners' perspectives were complemented by academics and experts in tool development and inmate reentry. Each of Family Justice's partners selected one pilot location for the tool. Oklahoma and Massachusetts each chose a women's prison; Ohio and Michigan each chose a men's prison; and the Safer Foundation focused on a church-based case management program for adults who have recently been released from prison.

Pretesting

Family Justice staff members conducted pretest interviews with 99 incarcerated and formerly incarcerated individuals at the five pilot sites. Among other questions, respondents were asked about their perceptions or expectations of having such a tool administered by correctional or community supervision staff. They were also asked about previous conversations with correctional staff regarding family strengths and support and were asked whether they thought the tool could accomplish the intended goals.

The design of the Relational Inquiry Tool, especially the order of the questions, is intentional and was validated through focus groups and pretests. The experience of answering one question sets up the others that follow. The questions are consistent with strength-based principles and focus on an individual's social network and family support. The key findings from pretesting are as follows:

- Less than half of the 99 respondents had ever been asked by agency or institution staff about their family. Of those, only 11 people described such questions or conversations as constructive.
- Among 79 respondents, 65 (82 percent) said the tool would help them plan for reentry. Female respondents were more likely to agree (95 percent) than male respondents (78 percent), and former inmates were more likely to agree than current inmates (89 percent vs. 80 percent, respectively).
- A majority of respondents (62 out of 77) thought the tool would help improve the way staff viewed them. Among women, 85 percent agreed; among men,

78 percent agreed. (The questions that correspond to the last two bullet points were added after pretesting was completed in Massachusetts.)

Pilot Testing

The following data are based on assessments of the five pilot sites, four of which were prisons. An eight-item staff feedback assessment was attached to each tool to obtain data on staff's experiences administering it; follow-up phone calls were completed with some pilot testers. Of the 156 tools administered in prisons, 145 were returned with completed assessments. Three key findings emerged:

- Openness between correctional staff and inmates increased by using the tool;
- Using the tool gave correctional staff an increased understanding of the inmate; and
- Both correctional staff and inmates believe the tool will be beneficial in reentry planning.

A Step toward Broader Change

Institutionwide implementation of the Relational Inquiry Tool will create a significant shift in culture. Organizations that integrate the tool into their case management practices must consider how to make other aspects of their work family-focused. Justin Jones, director of the Oklahoma DOC, offered powerful examples of things that must be consistent such as fair phone rates on collect calls from prisons, child-friendly areas for family visitation and parole offices that are welcoming to family members.

By creating a mechanism for different interactions between case managers and inmates, the Relational Inquiry Tool is shifting the way staff view the people with whom they work. According to Jay Glauner, a reentry coordinator with the Ohio Department of Rehabilitation and Correction: "One way the tool really impacted me was the humanization of the offender beyond what a stale file will do. We have a family history section in [a presentencing report], but it's more of a 'Who are your relatives?' question than a 'Who are you close to?' question. This tool could very well create a good framework for productive dialogue when trying to find resources and support for the offender."

By shaping a new conversation with inmates, case managers report that the Relational Inquiry Tool is increasing the level of openness between them and the incarcerated individuals. The 13 minutes on average that case managers spent administering the tool was clearly time well spent. In Massachusetts, for example, the tool increased the correctional program officer's understanding of the inmate every time (n=15). In 14.5 instances, it "really improved" their understanding and the other two times it "somewhat improved" their understanding. For inmates with whom the officers already had a relationship (e.g., the inmate was on their caseload or they had met with the inmate at least once before), Massachusetts correctional program officers reported the degree of openness increased nine out of 10 times as a result of using the tool.

> **Questions about family had typically been part of a routine inventory for intake or risk assessment and were rarely phrased in a strength-based manner or for the purpose of supportive inquiry.**

To understand inmates' perspectives on how the tool could improve their interactions with case managers, Family Justice collected feedback on the tool itself from current and former prisoners. Of the 99 people who participated in the pretest, 54 reported having never been asked questions about family support. Only 11 reported being asked similar questions to those in this tool. When questions had been asked about family in the past, they were not phrased in a similar manner. Questions about family had typically been part of a routine inventory for intake or risk assessment and were rarely phrased in a strength-based manner or for the purpose of supportive inquiry. Several respondents described being asked questions in the past by individuals with whom they did not wish to discuss their families or in a tone that was unsupportive or condescending.

The majority of respondents (80 percent) thought that if case managers used the tool, it would improve how inmates are seen. In focus groups of former inmates, it was clear that sharing certain types of information could enhance their standing with correctional staff. Pretest respondents overwhelmingly thought the tool would help them plan for reentry (82 percent). In the pilot test, eight out of 10 case managers reported that the tool would help them work with people to plan for reentry, suggesting that it is useful in serving this function for staff and inmates alike.

One significant benefit of the tool for respondents is that it can improve their self-perception. Respectively, questions 3 and 4 ask, "How did you help your family and friends before you came to prison?" and "How did your family and friends help you before you came to prison?" Some respondents had difficulty identifying ways they had provided help. Upon further probing, they listed a multitude of things they did to help, including taking care of children, assisting with yard work, tending to a sick relative and being a shoulder to cry on for a friend. Many of those respondents later mentioned that they had not seen themselves as helpful people, but after talking about the positive roles they played for their families, they had a new perspective. Because the tool is designed to be strength-based, it encourages respondents and case managers to talk about strengths in ways they may be unaccustomed to doing.

"Every one of [the Relational Inquiry Tool questions] can be good, and it's based on the time and the place and the intention of the person that's asking," one male focus group participant said. As several current and former inmates expressed during the development of the Relational Inquiry Tool, it will be significantly more effective when case managers follow through on the discussion rather than use it only to prompt the thinking of the inmate. For example, when someone reveals that he or she does not plan to rely on family support for future housing, the expectation is that the case manager will be able to follow up with housing referrals.

Staff at the pilot sites also see the utility of the tool for improving release planning. In states, like Oklahoma, which are considering the role of family and friends in supporting a parolee, the tool could inform the discussion between the parole office and individual under supervision to help identify those support people. To stimulate the long-term integration of the Relational Inquiry Tool into case management practices, Family Justice is interested in exploring how the tool could be incorporated into information technology systems used to manage inmates' files.

A Vehicle for Change

The Relational Inquiry Tool is a promising way to gather information about families and social networks, identifying the resources available to people as they prepare for reentry into their communities. As organizations develop other reentry-related instruments, it is recommended that they use supportive inquiry in an effort to really listen, ask questions about family (broadly defined), and design questions in a way that builds rapport among staff and inmates. Family Justice learned that the introduction of a new tool or program in a correctional setting is more likely to be successful when other changes are taking place to support that innovation. For correctional departments and other criminal justice agencies, incorporating a strength-based, family-focused approach into their work requires dedicated leadership among executives and at the line-staff level.

During the planning process for the Relational Inquiry Tool, Family Justice recommended that partner agencies form diagonal work groups—involving staff at every level of the work force, current and former inmates, and affected family members—throughout the pretesting and piloting phases of the project. By drawing on the resources, experience, and knowledge of the entire work force and of clients and families, the organization stands to gain—as do the individuals, families and communities ultimately served.

Family Justice continues to explore ways to help organizations throughout the country adopt a strength-based, family-focused approach. Recommended changes may include altering the way line staff and managers are recruited, trained and supervised; assessing and changing the way information is collected and used; and conducting an inventory of current practices for visitation, phone calls, education and other family-related opportunities in correctional settings. By working collaboratively and imaginatively—drawing on the strengths of the work force, always asking about families and using the information gathered to identify people's resources as they prepare to re-integrate into the community—the corrections field can make a farther-reaching, longer-lasting impact. Initial evaluation of the Relational Inquiry Tool demonstrates that it can be one vehicle for such change, collecting important information and improving rapport between correctional staff and inmates. Dramatic change can start with just a few questions.

Notes

1. Sullivan, E., M. Mino, K. Nelson and J. Pope. 2002. *Families as a resource in recovery from drug abuse: An evaluation of La Bodega de la Familia.* New York: Vera Institute of Justice.

2. La Vigne, N.G., C. Visher and J. Castro. 2004. *Chicago prisoners' experiences returning home.* Washington, D.C.: Urban Institute.

3. Nelson, M., P. Dees and C. Allen. 1999. *The first month out: Post-incarceration experiences in New York City.* New York: Vera Institute of Justice.

4. In 2004, 672,000 people were released from state and federal prisons, according to the Bureau of Justice Statistics.

Margaret diZerega is senior project associate for Family Justice. **Carol Shapiro** is founder and president of Family Justice.

The Ex-Con Next Door

How communities are preparing for the largest exodus of prisoners in American history.

ALEX KINGSBURY

Building the skin of an airplane is a craft with little tolerance for failure. The rivets that bind the sheets of aluminum must be set cleanly, without burrs or scratches, because just one faulty patch of skin can rip apart an airplane in flight.

The instructors who teach these skills at the minimum-security Winfield Correctional Facility outside Wichita, Kan., have little tolerance for failure, as well. It takes years of good behavior for a prisoner to land a coveted spot in this class, which certifies participants as aircraft sheet metal workers. Yet, as good as they are, the inmates' skills don't guarantee them a job when they get out. Indeed, although subcontractors might accept them, none of the five airplane manufacturing plants that ring Wichita hire ex-felons.

Getting cons to stay ex-cons has long been one of the most vexing challenges of the criminal justice system. One out of every 31 American adults is in jail, on parole, or on probation, and the central reality is this: Nearly everyone who enters the prison system eventually gets out. The problem is, most of those ex-offenders quickly find themselves back inside. Today, ending the cycle of recidivism has become an increasingly urgent problem as communities nationwide are forced to absorb record numbers of prisoners who also often struggle with addiction and other illness.

There are more than 1.5 million people in state or federal prison for serious offenses and 750,000 others in jail for more minor crimes. Prison populations have swelled since the early 1970s, and now offenders are returning to their neighborhoods at a rate of more than 1,400 per day. In 1994, nearly 457,000 prisoners were released from state and federal custody, and in 2005, almost 699,000 prisoners were released. That is the largest single exodus of ex-convicts in American history.

Revolving door. But it's hardly the end of the story. According to the most recent nationwide study on recidivism, in 1994, more than two thirds of prisoners—68 percent—ended up back behind bars within three years of release. It is that figure, little changed for decades, that has community leaders and criminal justice experts focusing on a fresh approach.

The process of coordinated prisoner reintegration is now known as "re-entry," rather than rehabilitation or release. Whereas rehabilitation assumed that individuals could change on their own, re-entry focuses on educating employers and communities about how they can help the offender on the outside. It aims to break though the red tape that has historically delayed social services for felons and to prevent the snags—like drug treatment programs that reject offenders who have been clean only a short time—that keep them from making a healthy return to society.

In practice, that means synchronizing many different social and correctional services while offenders are still inmates and continuing that assistance after their release. Re-entry programs don't necessarily require more funding, just better coordination of existing resources like job training and stable housing. "Rehab is focused on the individual offender; re-entry is about communities, families, children, coworkers, and neighbors," says Amy Solomon, a criminal justice researcher at the Urban Institute.

The state of Kansas has launched several re-entry programs being held up as models. Since the programs were started in 2003, the number of parole absconders has fallen by a third and recidivism has been cut in half. Jesse Howes, a case manager for the Kansas Department of Corrections, meets with selected prisoners during the critical time about eight months before their release and continues to see them on the outside. One of Howes's charges is Michael B. [corrections officials did not allow last names to be used], 44, fresh out of the El Dorado Correctional Facility and working at a Wichita hotel. In 2004, Michael set fire to an empty van after a fight over a girl. It wasn't his first time in prison; he had done a stint for burglary back in 1998 and was charged with escape from custody a year later. Now, after serving nearly three years for the arson conviction, he says he's taking "one baby step at a time." He visits with Howes once a week, to defuse an escalating spat with his boss or to collect coupons for the bus. It's attention to these little things, experts say, that can make the difference between going straight and returning to prison.

Long shot. Lonnie K., 50, is so anxious to leave Winfield that he keeps his release papers and a citation for good behavior

(In thousands)

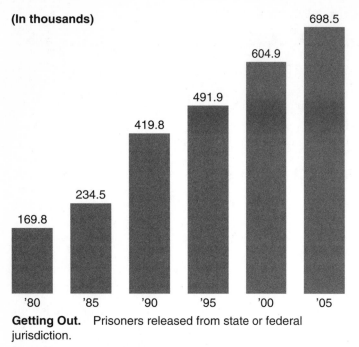

Getting Out. Prisoners released from state or federal jurisdiction.

Source: Bureau of Justice Statistics.

folded in his prison-issue jacket. He hopes to get into a truck-driving school, but he knows it may be a long shot. He's been out a few times before, only to land back in prison after arrests for theft. "I won't even have clothes when I get out," Lonnie says. Howes makes a note to find some threads from the Salvation Army and to set up job interviews for Lonnie. He tries to steer his charges away from low-paying food service or retail jobs. "Unless you can earn a living wage [more than $12 an hour]," Howes says, "you're not going to make it."

Providing free services to murderers and thieves might seem like coddling, but statistics show it's the cheapest and most effective way to keep the public safe. If they can keep just one of the prisoners enrolled in the aircraft sheet metal class out of prison for six months, Wichita officials say, they will save the state money. That's why re-entry programs have made for some unlikely political alliances, including, in Kansas, between conservative GOP Sen. Sam Brownback and Democratic Gov. Kathleen Sebelius. Brownback has sponsored the federal Second Chance Act, which would provide ex-cons with millions of dollars in job training, housing vouchers, and other services. And Sebelius has made helping ex-prisoners a top priority.

In Virginia, meanwhile, YMCAs are working with female offenders and their children. Families are critical to re-entry because they can be both the cause of or the solution to recidivism. Programs in Georgia, supported by a $2 million federal grant, provide job training and mental health services for juvenile offenders. And similarly funded programs in Pennsylvania target offenders 14 to 35 years old.

Holding a job remains the best predictor of success for ex-cons, and employer surveys have found about 80 percent of ex-cons to be diligent, trustworthy, and dependable. Yet employers are still reluctant to hire them. They risk having employees who can be at worst violent and at best antisocial and reap few

An EZ-Pass System for Offenders

New York Uses an ATM-like Kiosk to Track Probationers

Here's how probation once worked in New York City. The offender would report to an overworked officer who may have handled 250 other cases. The officer filled out a paper form that would find its way into a file cabinet in an office never again to see the light of day. "It was a joke," says one former probation officer. "It served neither probationers nor public safety."

In the mid-1990s, faced with shrinking budgets and cuts in staffing, the city began installing a series of kiosks to manage the lowest-risk offenders on probation, expanded to include all low-risk probationers in 2003. (High-risk probationers and sex offenders are still required to deal with officers directly.) Offenders from publicist Lizzie Grubman to rapper Jay-Z, along with thousands of other petty criminals, have reported to the automated kiosks, says Jane Imbasciani, assistant commissioner in the department of probation. Meanwhile, cities in Georgia, Florida, Minnesota, and Illinois have installed similar systems.

The kiosks, which resemble ATMs, ask offenders to scan their hands and respond to some basic questions about their residence, job, and contact with police. The process takes about three minutes. A computer randomly selects users for drug testing, conducted in a small anteroom. "It frees up officers to focus on the more dangerous people, it frees up money, and, frankly, the machines are far better at record keeping," says Department of Corrections Commissioner Martin Horn. The computers also allow officers to track probationers' movements through the computerized self-reporting system, matching crime rates to probationer residency patterns and helping police focus resources. Moreover, in a blow to those who champion stricter sentences for petty crimes, statistics show that some probationers are less likely to commit another crime if their contact with probation officers is minimal.

—A.K.

benefits in return. Employers are eligible for tax credits, and the federal government does bond former inmates up to a few thousand dollars, but small businesses often find the paperwork more trouble than it's worth.

"This is not a question of one kind employer giving a second chance to an ex-con; this is a nationwide problem," says Devah Pager, a professor at Princeton University and author of *Marked: Race, Crime, and Finding Work in an Era of Mass Incarceration.* In studies in New York and Milwaukee, Pager found that employers were half as likely to call applicants with criminal records and even less likely to call them if they were also black.

Marc Lascano, the Austin operations director for a Texas car repair chain, is an exception to that attitude. His Brake Check has hired more than 75 ex-cons in the past five years. More than 80 percent of them have stayed for at least a year, and several have gone into management. "They are disciplined because they are used to following instructions within the corrections system," Lascano says.

The ex-offenders are trained with funds from a state program that has paired thousands of ex-cons with employers. Since 2000, Project RIO (for Reintegration of Offenders) has kept about 40 percent of those who enter the program employed, compared with 24 percent for those who don't enroll. And the recidivism rate for RIO participants was one fifth of that among those who did not participate.

Studies show most ex-cons are reliable, but employers balk at hiring them.

Some states, including New York, have laws restricting employers from considering of criminal records in hiring, but many others do not. Ex-cons are further handicapped because employers can now easily gain access to criminal offender databases when they are performing background checks. The Army, for example, found that more than 8,000 of its new recruits last year had criminal histories. It granted them waivers, but other professions are off limits to ex-cons—teaching and child-care work, of course, but also embalming, limousine driving, fire-fighting, and haircutting.

Back in Wichita, city officials are trying to think beyond individual offenders and toward the community to which they will return. One downtown neighborhood that is flush with ex-cons is a blighted grid of boarded-up houses, empty lots, and scattered trash. Howes, who grew up nearby, imagines prisoners returning to these streets and the hurdles they'll face. But the city, using state and local re-entry funds, is working with developers to change the scene, pairing the unemployed with businesses, targeting healthcare services, even trying to improve math and reading scores for children. "Transforming the physical aspects of the neighborhood is often just as important as helping the individuals," says Sandra Moore, president of Urban Strategies, a St. Louis-based company that is consulting with Wichita.

Orville S., 39, who was sentenced in January 2004 for aggravated sex battery and intentional touching, is now in a Wichita work-release program that keeps him confined at night but allows him to work during the day. He is skilled in plastics manufacturing, but there are no jobs at a local factory. He had a lead on a position at an automotive parts store, but that too came up empty. "Jobs are hard to find because of my crime," he says, after being denied a janitor's job at a local church. But he's hopeful. "I'll find something," Orville says. "I can't afford to get in trouble again."

Prison Inmates Meet Socrates

Lawrence T. Jablecki

Since 1986, as an adjunct professor on the faculty of a college and a university in the state of Texas, I have had direct contact with hundreds of prison inmates enrolled in academic programs for the purpose of completing the associate's, bachelor's, and master's degrees. I am persuaded that this experience permits the following assertions: the overwhelming majority of prison inmates in this country, both state and federal, are not incorrigibly mean or evil, and a correct understanding of the "public interest" dictates that they should be given the opportunity to participate in state and federally funded higher-education programs designed to change their thinking and conduct.

If any reader is tempted to brand me with the pejorative label of a liberal weenie who doesn't believe in the hard coinage of punishment, the following brief comments should suffice to assuage that suspicion. Criminal offenders are in conflict with the norms of society; they are not suffering from psychological disorders that both explain and excuse their conduct. They have consciously and deliberately chosen to commit a crime or, in numerous cases, they consciously and deliberately set themselves up for committing a crime by altering their normal mental and physical capacities. They were free to do otherwise and should be held responsible. Violent predators and many career criminals deserve to be incarcerated for many years, and some should be sentenced to life without the possibility of parole. I have no philosophical objection to capital punishment, but I am opposed to it because innocent persons are convicted and executed.

Now that I have exposed most of the philosophical guts of my position on crime and punishment, the specific purpose of this essay is to elucidate the reasons why I believe that an introduction to the gadfly of Athens is a highly potent crime-prevention initiative that should be made available to a multitude of prisoners.

I graduated from high school in 1958 and the thought of pursuing higher education was almost totally foreign to my mind. Primarily to maintain my association with buddies in my graduating class, I enrolled in a local junior college and unceremoniously flunked out after less than a full semester due to a total lack of interest. I went to work full time and made some very foolish choices that brought me dangerously close to becoming a felonious hoodlum. When not working, I was in the neighborhood bowling alley, where I achieved some local notoriety as the kid with a 200-plus average. In the fall of 1959, motivated mainly by the desire for an adventure away from parental oversight, I enrolled in the four-year college in Oklahoma where my mother had been a student.

Although I was not failing any of my classes during my first semester, I refused to allow any serious reflection and study to engage my mind or interfere with fun, so by January 1960 I was determined to drop out and pursue the career of a professional bowler. The passage of very close to forty years has not significantly dimmed the memory of an event during the same month that marks the beginning of a radical transformation in my thinking and conduct.

Walking to class one afternoon I encountered one of the recognized campus intellectuals. In response to my greeting of "Hello, what do you know?" he made an abrupt stop in front of me and said, "Mr. Jablecki, I do not know anything. I am simply attempting to understand." He then marched past me. Not having a clue as to the meaning of his curt remark, I articulated a response in very unscholarly language. Several days later I asked a senior who was majoring in something called philosophy to explain to me the distinction between knowing and understanding. After his learned discourse, most of which I failed to comprehend, he urged me to remain in school and suggested that in the spring semester I sign up for "Introduction to Philosophy."

Inspired by his apparent wisdom I remained in college and enrolled in "Introduction to Philosophy." In that class the instructor explained the perennial problems of philosophy: I was able to grasp the difference between knowledge and understanding, and I was introduced to the life and teachings of Socrates. During the semester my ambitions, my thinking, and even my behavior changed. I sold my prized black-beauty bowling ball and purchased some philosophical works, which are still in my library. In a very brief period of time a Socratic "conversion" changed the entire course of my life. To the teacher, Dr. Mel-Thomas Rothwell (deceased), I owe an immeasurable debt of gratitude for his patient mentoring until my graduation in 1964.

The relevance of this autobiographical snapshot is that it evidences the view that it is impossible to exaggerate the power of ideas and concepts—for example, justice, truth, goodness, virtue, and beauty—to grab a human mind and redirect a person's life in the manner advocated by Socrates. And, at the risk of making a generalization to which I acknowledge numerous exceptions, a Socratic conversion usually requires the inspired communication of a teacher or mentor who has experienced the transformative power of ideas and concepts.

In the 1986–1987 academic year I was given my first opportunity to introduce Socrates to prison inmates under the auspices of what was at the time Brazosport Junior College in Lake Jackson, Texas. This institution, now known as Brazosport College, continues to provide a two-year course of instruction leading to an associate of arts degree. I taught two courses of "Introduction to Philosophy" to approximately thirty male inmates at the Clemens Unit of the Texas Department of Corrections. I possess no knowledge of the success or failure of any of these men, but I do have some vivid recollections of some of the classes, including our lively discussions of Socrates.

The first session of the first class has left a permanent mark in my bank of memories. Standing in front of a group of men convicted of a range of serious felonies and incarcerated for a substantial number of years can be terrifying, to say the least. I told them that I had agreed to teach this class because of my firm commitment to the views of the German philosopher Immanuel Kant concerning "respect" for all persons as moral agents capable of choices and my equally firm belief that they can change the direction of the remainder of their lives if they choose to do so. This is essentially how I introduce myself to all new classes of prison inmates. And if they perceive that I really mean what I say, the path is clear for some existentially meaningful discussions and insights.

Perhaps the most important fact I can report about these men—inclusive of the inmates I have taught to date—is that, except for a mere few, they do not blame society or others for their criminal behavior. This acceptance of guilt and responsibility is probably at odds with the belief of most people about the supposed rationalizations of criminals. Not unexpectedly, many of the inmates vented their resentment about how they believe they were unfairly treated at one or more steps in our system of criminal justice, and any seasoned practitioner in the system is obliged to acknowledge the truth of some of their claims. The pertinent and critical point, however, is their acceptance of the facts that they made real choices to commit crimes and that society has a right to protect itself by incarcerating malefactors.

These intuitive or pre-philosophical beliefs are fertile ground for introducing the free-will-versus-determinism debate and the arguments employed to justify the institution of punishment. And these issues lead straight to what is usually a hotly contested debate of the Socratic view that persons do not voluntarily or knowingly commit evil or unlawful acts because knowledge and wisdom are the most powerful elements in human life.

When the above issues are examined in philosophy classes in what the inmates refer to as the "free world," they do not convey the same sense of urgency and importance as they do for students confined behind steel bars. One version of determinism is that all so-called free choices are illusory because no human actions or decisions are exempt from an unbroken chain of "causes." Realizing that, if true, this theory could exonerate him from blame and punishment, a convicted murderer eagerly stated, "I would like to think that it was determinism" rather than a choice, and the room was filled with soft laughter. Another student, convicted of aggravated robbery, attempted to articulate the centuries-old view that all persons are born with an innate knowledge of right and wrong—that is, a moral compass called the conscience. Confessing much confusion about how it works, he said, "Now, I done something and I know it was wrong." Following a Socratic unpacking of the words cause and compel, the unanimous decision was that none of them were compelled or forced to commit their crime and they were free to do otherwise.

It should come as no surprise that a discussion of the purpose and justification of punishment with prison inmates, many of whom have been incarcerated for a major portion of their lives, reaches a high level of emotional intensity. No student, in either class, claimed or even implied that he did not deserve to be punished. A chorus of voices, however, condemned the enormous disparity in sentences characteristic of an indeterminate sentencing system and the wide range in which judicial discretion is free to roam.

With no hesitation, one of the men expressed the belief that if he stole a car and Dr. Jablecki stole a car the latter would undoubtedly be gently treated with probation and the former would be sentenced to prison. This, he exclaimed, is not justice or equality, as both committed the same crime and deserved the same punishment.

Heads nodded in agreement and several voiced the caustic remark that the lovely lady of justice wearing the blindfold of impartiality and equality is never blind to the influences of money and status in the community. Anyone, therefore, who plays the role of a Socratic midwife in a similar situation needs to be prepared to maneuver through an emotional minefield in which they will be made aware of all the ugly warts and blemishes in our system of criminal justice.

Now, as implied earlier, I can still almost hear the initial outbursts of disbelief expressed in response to Socrates' belief that no person voluntarily or knowingly commits an evil or wrong act. Socrates, according to the first consensus, had been drinking too much wine or he was an insane old man. The inmates said they knew exactly what they were doing when they committed a murder, robbed a store at gunpoint, sexually assaulted a woman, or cut a drug deal. Assuming the role of Socrates, I called them a collection of ignorant fools incapable of recognizing their best and permanent interests as human beings.

Needless to say, this enlivened the tone of the discussion and set the stage to unpack the meaning of a cluster of relevant words: knowledge, wisdom, ignorance, self-interest mistake, voluntary, involuntary, happiness, and virtue. After several hours of defining and analyzing them, the new consensus was a defense of Socrates' sobriety and the belief that he was a very smart old man. Although I don't have current information on any of the inmates, I believe that most of them made some progress in the ascent from the cave of ignorance and have not forgotten their meeting with Socrates.

In 1988 a fortuitous meeting with George Trabing, the director of the prison program for the University of Houston at Clear Lake, resulted in an invitation for me to join the adjunct faculty of the university. My assignment was to teach a variety of undergraduate and graduate courses in philosophy to prison inmates housed in the Ramsey I prison unit in Rosharon, Texas. During the past ten years, missing only one or two semesters, I have taught a number of classes—including "Metaphysics," "Epistemology," "Philosophy and the Law," "Philosophy and Religion," "Political Philosophy," "Ethics," and "Human Rights and the Justification of Punishment"—in which I inject the life and teachings of Socrates.

The university's bachelor's program was established in 1974; the master's program began in 1988. Four degrees are currently offered to inmates: a B.A. in behavioral sciences, a B.A. in the humanities, an M.A. in literature, and an M.A. in the humanities. As Trabing, Jerry Fryre, and Craig White describe in their 1995 report *Five Year Review: Texas Department of Criminal Justice Outreach Component Human Sciences and Humanities,* the degree in behavioral science contributes to the development of the

> undergraduate student's skills in analytical thinking, written communication, and research; to provide understanding of the customs, languages, values and behaviors of culturally diverse populations, and to educate students to participate as informed, critical citizens of society. . . . The primary mission of the undergraduate and graduate plans in Humanities and literature is to promote cultural literacy and interdisciplinary skills through the study of the liberal arts.

The most important dimension of the mission of all of these educational programs, however, is to promote positive changes in the thinking and conduct of inmates and to reduce the recidivism rate of those who are released on parole. The profound relevance of Socrates' teaching that the "unexamined life is not worth living" and his identification of knowledge and virtue are captured in the five-year review's comments regarding the men who earned their degree in the humanities:

> These students find that courses in history, literature, and philosophy profoundly deepen their sensitivities and expand their horizons. TDCJ students may come from pockets of economic and intellectual poverty from which they have never escaped—they have literally no knowledge of other ways of living. Humanities courses open new realities to them, wholly changing their perspectives about who they are and what the world is about. . . . Such courses are truly revelations, showing ways of living and thinking that they have not encountered before.

Now, as every practitioner in the field of criminal justice should know, the verification of an indisputable causal connection between offenders' completion of any crime-prevention strategy and their subsequent conduct is a tricky enterprise. At the outset, the creators of these academic programs for prison inmates were cognizant of the paramount importance of documenting a bank of data from which they could quantify the apparent successes and failures. The university's most current report was released in January 1995 as a twenty-year history of the program. The report found that more than 200 inmates earned a bachelor's degree, while forty-five earned a master's degree. From 1990 to 1995, of the thirty-nine inmates who earned a bachelor's degree, seventeen were released on parole and two were returned to prison—a recidivism rate of 11 percent. During the same period, of the forty-five who earned a master's degree, nineteen were released on parole and one was returned to prison—a recidivism rate of 5 percent.

To argue that their academic accomplishment is the only factor capable of explaining their successful reintegration into society would be a mistake. The only near definitive answer to this issue is to track a control group of parolees in the same age range and duration of incarceration who have not completed a similar academic program. Although the U.S. Department of Justice did not fund a recent grant proposal from the university to conduct such research, studies conducted in Indiana, Maryland, Massachusetts, New York, and other states have all reported significantly low recidivism rates for inmates in correctional higher-education programs, ranging from 1 percent to 15.5 percent. In addition, my contact with the students in the Texas program—some of whom are now on parole confirms a determination to change and make contributions to society totally unmatched by the majority of inmates who spend their idle time playing dominos, watching television, and reflecting on their perceptions that they are the oppressed victims of society.

Fortunately, I experienced my Socratic "conversion" when I was twenty years old and would not entertain benevolent thoughts toward any person casting doubts on the reality and meaning of that experience. Similarly, five of the former inmates who achieved academic success deserve to be heard. Their comments include:

"My new degrees, new self-image, and newfound confidence in society led me to try something I'd never tried before: a straight lifestyle. . . . Without the formal education which was available through the college program I would still be trying to perfect my technique for a life of crime. Instead, I am giving something back."

"I cannot begin to tell you how much my life has changed as a result of the 'awakening' I received from each . . . of my instructors. The accomplishments I have made since my release would not have been possible without an education."

"Because of my educational pursuits started while incarcerated, I find myself with a master's degree, an L.C.D.C. (licensed chemical dependency counselor), and a position as the manager of client services with a large nonprofit organization. I am forever thankful . . . for the opportunity to change my life."

"For me, the college experience . . . has changed my life. It has allowed me to believe in myself. It has forced me to reevaluate my life without the self-pity or excuse making."

"I firmly believe that education is the key to staying out of prison. . . . My parents are proud of me;

I am respected and consulted by my colleagues; I pay taxes. . . . I hope that I do make a difference in other peoples' lives as a result of my experiences and achievements."

The latter reference to the payment of taxes by a former inmate exposes the shortsighted and factually incorrect arguments of the politicians in Washington, D.C., who have seen to it that prison inmates are ineligible for federal Pell Grant tuition assistance for higher education. In his July 10, 1995, New Yorker article "Teaching Prisoners a Lesson," James S. Kunen draws attention to the critical factual misrepresentations involved in the demise of inmates' eligibility for Pell Grants:

When Bart Gordon, a Democratic representative from Tennessee, sponsored the 1994 crime-bill amendment that barred prisoners from receiving Pell Grants, his aim was to trim the fat in federal education spending. He was under the impression that prisoners were using up something like seventy million dollars a year in Pell Grants that could have gone to more deserving students—those on the outside. Senator Kay Bailey Hutchison of Texas, a Republican who led the fight in the Senate against Pell Grants for prisoners, argued that inmates siphoned off two hundred million dollars and displaced a hundred thousand law–abiding students. In fact, all applicants who meet the grants' need-based eligibility requirements receive Pell Grants, regardless of how many qualifying recipients there are. As a General Accounting Office report explains, "If incarcerated students received no Pell Grants, no student currently denied a Pell award would have received one and no award amount would have been increased." And the amount of money saved by cutting off grants to prisoners is tiny: according to the General Accounting Office, of approximately four million Pell Grant recipients in the 1993–94 academic year, twenty-three thousand were in prison, and they received thirty-five million dollars of the six billion dollars awarded, or about six cents of every ten program dollars.

It would probably be incorrect to suggest that Hutchison and the other members of Congress who helped her destroy hope for thousands of inmates in this country are in the philosophical camp of the ancient Cynics, who were contemptuous of bodily pleasures, sneering fault-finders, and incredulous of human goodness and the capacity to change from vice to virtue. I am persuaded, however, that the policy these politicians approved places them in the category of unmerciful retributivists who sincerely believe in the moral imperative of severe punishment for all criminal offenders—that is, they have no mercy for the wicked.

They are not hypocrites, because they really believe that the construction of new prisons is not a necessary evil but a necessary good. Some of the extremists in this camp probably believe that it would be good policy to literally brand the scarlet letter C (for convict) on the forehead of every prison inmate.

Contrary to the philosophy of unmerciful retributivism, Pell Grants for inmates had the long-range potential of saving billions of tax dollars that will now be spent on the construction and maintenance of prisons and the annual costs of warehousing multitudes of federal and state inmates in what can best be described as toxic waste dumps inhabited by persons with little or no hope for a future that can make life worth living. And equally, if not more important, the advocates of unmerciful retributivism have crafted a policy that unintentionally results in a multitude of new victims of crime perpetrated by parolees who have changed from bad to worse.

Recognizing the existence of an unknown number of contingencies—all of which can influence the success or failure of a parolee armed with a university degree the university's statistics stand in sharp contrast to the fact that, in Texas, between 45 percent and 50 percent of parolees are reincarcerated within three years of the date of their release. Most of them are convicted of new felony offenses, many of which involve victims who suffer (among numerous things) the loss of property, physical injuries, and death. Although it is an expansion of the normal usage of the word, this is an obscenity that in addition to all of the accompanying human suffering is costing taxpayers many millions of dollars every year. In Texas, the annual cost for one prison inmate is close to $20,000—very close to the amount my wife and I pay for our son to attend the prestigious Rice University in Houston—and this cost does not include the maintenance of existing prisons and the construction of new ones. After ten years of almost weekly contact with students in the University of Houston prison program, it has become abundantly clear that if I did not believe in the inmates' capacity to change their totally selfish habits of thought and conduct I would not waste my time on an academic exercise destined to fail. Inmates do not have a "right" to a free university education, nor do they "deserve" it. However, there is an urgent and compelling public interest at stake, justifying the use of tax dollars to create and sustain academic programs for them. Once they grasp the Socratic definition of knowledge and its vast distance from opinions and beliefs, most of my current students articulate the hindsight observation that, had they met Socrates at the age of twenty or earlier, it is not unrealistic to suggest they might not be meeting him now clothed in prison garb. While not willing to fully embrace the contention that during their life of crime they were totally ignorant

and really did not "know" what they were doing, most of my students "see," for the first time, the profound truth of Socrates' doctrine that the possession of knowledge and wisdom can lead to a radical and positive change in both thinking and behavior.

Despite the occasional bitterness aimed at the alleged disparities in the system of criminal justice, during these discussions many of the inmates feel at ease to lay bare their souls and express genuine remorse about the impact of their conduct on parents, spouses, children, and victims. It would be foolhardy to claim or even imply that an encounter with Socrates is a necessary prerequisite to bring the majority of them to a profound existential consciousness of the negative consequences of their crimes. In fact, many of them have previously read several books of Plato's *Republic,* and some have read his *Apology* and *Crito.* But none of them have participated in a methodical unpacking of the content, the profound truth, and the errors in Socratic doctrine and instead have had their emotions shaped by traumatic events in their lives—the death of one or both parents, a divorce decree from a former spouse, children who commit crimes, and a denial of parole. The important claim can be made, however, that the Socratic method of philosophical reflection provides a coherent conceptual framework in which many of these men, for the first time, are "awakened" to a totally new perspective on life.

Prior to my career in criminal justice, when I discovered Great Visions of Philosophy by W. P. Montague, a notation of "good" was made by the following passage:

> There is a great deal of wrong conduct by individuals and by groups that owes its wrongness to want of wisdom rather than to want of will. . . . We all know that boys brought up in a slum district may get the notion that gang loyalty is really better than loyalty to society; the stealing, kidnapping, and even murder are justifiable and thrilling adventures; and that pity for the weak is stupid or unmanly. In these groups the only vices recognized as such will be the vices of cowardice and of treachery or "squealing" on one's "pals." To be a "tough guy" and perhaps the leader of a gang is an activating and in a sense a genuinely moral ideal of many a high-spirited lad, whose courage and energy if directed into other channels might make him not merely a useful citizen but even a hero. It is obvious enough that here the kind of moral reform that is called for is educational in the broadest sense, involving destruction of hideous economic conditions and of the cultural squalor and ignorance that go with them. Not all criminals indeed but probably the majority could be reformed or cured by being given a Socratic wisdom or knowledge of the things

in life that are really worthwhile and an environment that would make it possible to achieve them. Moreover the whole philosophy of punishment would be revolutionized. Prevention rather than cure would be emphasized, and when preventive measures had failed the necessary restraint of the criminal would be accompanied by education rather than by social revenge.

My Socratic conversion justified the use of the word good in response to the above claims. Today, however, I can confidently proclaim the truth of Montague's call for a Socratic revolution in the philosophy of punishment.

According to the most recent estimates released by the U.S. Department of Justice, at the close of 1998 there were 1,232,900 federal and state prison inmates. To advocate the belief that the majority of them could be reformed by a strong dose of Socrates appears to be an incredulous form of idealism completely out of touch with reality. Given the facts that the opinion of the public is that prison inmates should be "better" people when released on parole and that high-school equivalency classes and vocational training programs provided to the majority of them are not designed to foster moral reform, the suggestion that a multitude of inmates should be introduced to Socrates is not a fantasy of an unearthly idealism.

More specifically, I am absolutely convinced that the recidivism rate of former prison inmates can be reduced significantly if, while incarcerated, they are skillfully guided through a systematic discussion of the life and teachings of Socrates as presented by Plate in the *Apology, Crito, Phaedo, Protagaras,* and the analysis of the concept of justice in the *Republic*. This is the largely uncultivated and fertile soil in which federal and state authorities should plant the seeds of carefully designed and well-funded programs capable of tracking the lives of the participants (male and female) and those in control groups for three to five years in order to establish some incontrovertible data regarding the power of education to change the thinking and conduct of former criminal offenders.

So I tell all of my students that the only way to silence the voices of the cynics committed to the view that providing a university or college education to prison inmates is flushing clean dollars down a dirty toilet is to remain crime-free following release on parole. I tell them that the continuation of the program is contingent upon years of cumulative success stories and that their moral obligation to succeed is grounded in the lives of the students who remain behind bars. They are encouraged to contact me after their release, as I may be able to assist them in their search for employment. However, if they call me for help after committing another felony offense, I will volunteer to testify against them. As I said on May 13, 1998, in the conclusion of the commencement address I gave to a group of inmates who had earned either an associate's degree from Alvin Community College in Alvin, Texas, or a bachelor's or master's degree from the University of Houston at Clear Lake:

> The profound sense in which Socrates was correct is precisely why we are here this evening. Collectively, your teachers have guided you on the ascent from the cave of ignorance as articulated by Plate in his *Republic*. You have been led out of the abyss of intellectual and moral darkness and our hope is that you have experienced a genuine Socratic "conversion"— that is, that you have accepted total responsibility for the rottenness of your past conduct and are morally prepared to fulfill your obligations as a member of the human community. . . . [However] I am obliged to tell you that, if you have not or do not experience a Socratic conversion prior to your release, you will be nothing more than a hypocritical, educated crook.

Socrates does not hold all the answers. For example, I readily admit to my students that, although he was committed to the view that humankind is essentially good, Socrates failed to recognize what philosopher David Hume called the incurable weakness in human nature. In his essay *Of the Origin of Government*, Hume comments on the nature of humanity and why it was necessary to invent a system of rules to protect lives and property:

> It is impossible to keep men faithfully and unerringly in the paths of justice. Some extraordinary circumstances may happen, in which a man finds his interests to be more promoted by fraud or rapine than hurt by the breach which his injustice makes in the social union. But much more frequently he is seduced from this great and important but distant interest by the allurement of present, though often very frivolous, temptations. This great weakness is incurable in human nature.

> Men must, therefore, endeavor to palliate what they cannot cure. They must institute some persons under the appellation of magistrates, whose peculiar office it is to point out the decrees of equity, to punish transgressors, to correct fraud and violence, and to oblige men, however reluctant, to consult their own real and permanent interests. In a word, obedience is a new duty which must be invented to support that of justice, and the ties of equity must be corroborated by those of allegiance.

Hume's view of humanity is consistent with Montague's claim that whether we call it "sin" or "selfishness," wrong conduct is due "not to lack of wisdom, but to lack of will. . . . Insight into the nature of the good . . . may be termed a 'necessary,' but not a 'sufficient,' cause of virtue. Wisdom by itself is not enough and great Socrates was wrong in thinking that it was."

Also, almost invariably during our discussions one or more students realize that Socrates' doctrines of humankind and knowledge and virtue are diametrically opposed to the orthodox Christian belief that humans are sinners whose salvation from evil inclinations requires a supernatural infusion of divine grace. The majority of my students, in widely diverse environments, were nurtured in the tradition of Christian theism, and, not surprisingly, a significant number of them are unwilling to concede that Socratic doctrines inflict any serious damage on their religious commitments.

As was the case when I was introduced to Socrates, he can shake unexamined beliefs and faiths. However, unlike any of their other academic classes, it is important that most of my courses contain opportunities for prison inmates to reflect on the most important and enduring questions of human existence. And I can confidently claim that many of them are surprised by the joy of facing the unfathomed depth of Socrates' message to live an examined life.

LAWRENCE T. JABLECKI is the director of the Brazoria County Community Supervision and Corrections Department in Angleton Texas, and has a PhD in political philosophy from Manchester University in Manchester, England.

One Clique

Why Rivals on the Streets Become Allies behind Bars

SHARROD CAMPBELL

Like many custodial agencies, the Georgia Department of Corrections recognizes the existence of security threat groups (STGs). Awareness of the activities of these groups helps to improve the overall security of a facility because, by definition, these various types of associations and groups have the potential to cause disruption. There are four commonly accepted major categories of STGs:

- Street Gangs—Organizations that have their strongest memberships in the communit;
- Prison Gangs—Organizations formed within a penal setting;
- Extremist/Separatist Groups—Organizations with views that promote seperation or superiority of one group over another based on race, religious beliefs or political ideologies; and
- Motorcycle Clubs—Criminal biker organizations that identify with the 1 percent theory (99 percent of bikers are law abiding; therefore, the other 1 percent are outlaws).

Although there are four accepted categories of STGs, the analysis of threats is not limited to inmates who may fall under one of these headings. It is essential that monitoring is not limited to these groups because the culture of a custodial setting often fosters impromptu-situational groups that gravitate together around a particular commonality. These situational groupings and associations must also be monitored because they have the potential to compromise security in correctional settings.

Banding Together

Race is one of the strongest commonality factors among inmates within the correctional system. This primary division is often broken down into other groups or associations within the larger group, and it is where many STG affiliations are found. Within an STG, race or culture is no exception, as evidenced by such groups as the Aryan Brotherhood, Black Guerrilla Family and Mexican Mafia. Although the groups are prison gangs that were founded based on race, there are conflicts that occur between them and other groups organized by race.

For example, there are well-documented conflicts between the Mexican Mafia and La Nuestra Familia, both of which are Hispanic culture/race groups that have a history of violence against each other. Incidents of intra-racial conflicts are not limited to prison gangs formed around race; street gangs also have a history of conflicts between rival groups of the same race. These conflicts often can continue when members of the groups enter the prison system. Conflicts in prisons and in the community between Surenos and Nortenos, Crips and Bloods, and People and Folk gangs have been well-documented by the media. However, in the Georgia correctional system there is a possible factor that appears to cause rival associations within the Hispanic culture to band together. This association has resulted in what appears to be a prison truce within the Hispanic population that includes rival Hispanic STGs.

In Georgia, there has been a steady growth in the general Hispanic population that has affected the overall Hispanic prison population. The Hispanic population currently represents about 5 percent of the incarcerated population. Although 5 percent is a relatively low figure, it is important to note that this percentage also reflects the fact that the population has doubled in number from 2001 to 2006. If that doubling trend continues every six years, it is likely that Hispanics will represent 10 percent of the population by 2013.

This article is not intended to imply that the Hispanic population as a whole inside or outside the Georgia correctional system should be validated as an STG. But, as stated earlier, prison groups associate based on common identifiers and the DOC has noted an alliance among Hispanic inmates that transcends the fiercest street and prison gang alliances for group strength.

The rationale that there is a need for strength among any inmate population is not surprising because it directly relates to a need for security. Although there may be some varied points of view between custodial agencies and inmates as to what constitutes security, both have this need as a primary issue. For the agency, security means equality of safety for all staff, the public and inmates. In inmate circles, security often relates to their ability to control the population because control prevents victimization. Control also gives authority to one group over other weaker inmate populations.

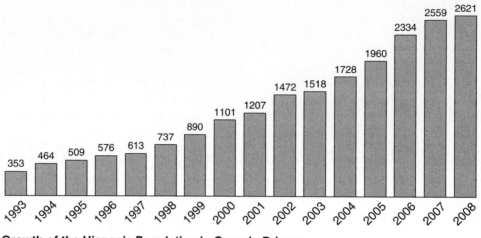

Growth of the Hispanic Population in Georgia Prisons

Within the Georgia penal system, the Hispanic population appears to have the highest overall percentage of STG members. In the general prison population, the security threat population has remained below 4 percent during the past four years, while the percentage of Hispanics in STGs has averaged between 7 percent and 9 percent during the same period.

The higher percentage of STG inmates within the Hispanic population is significant because it supports the possibility that Hispanic STGs have a stronger voice within the larger group. This is critical because validated STGs tend to have a strong organizational structure, which can give the STG a cohesive bond and offer a sense of security to weaker members. Thus, a relationship is developed that creates an atmosphere that forces the individual to remain close to the group. The STG provides security, recreation and a voice to communicate to other groups and prison staff. In return, the member becomes an agent of the STG and must remain loyal. That loyalty may be required in any situation regardless of the type of activity. If the STG has a problem, then the member must be an active part of the solution.

For example, inmates of a race that is outnumbered often believe that they are targeted by the more dominant race. If a minor incident occurs between Hispanic inmates and black inmates, the event may be viewed by the Hispanic inmates as predatory. Events such as thefts are not viewed as isolated events in this perceived power-struggle environment and can trigger group retaliation, which will escalate the conflict. These types of events often reveal that the problem is more complex than the event that triggered the retaliation. There appears to be a collective sense among Hispanic inmates in the Georgia system that this David and Goliath conflict exists because of their small population, which make them appear to be an easy target for black inmates. Their assertion is that banding together will reduce their risk because they will operate as a larger collective—all for one and one for all.

Prison Truce

More than likely, the indoctrination of banding together by race rather than splintering along STG or other variances is instilled early in the incarceration process. In this dynamic, Hispanic inmates will be advised by other Hispanic inmates already in the system that their associations prior to prison are nonessential. A truce between the rival groups must be maintained during their periods of incarceration. For example, it is not uncommon to find an inmate affiliated with a Surenos gang sharing a cell with a Nortenos-affiliated inmate without any open conflict.

Just like other street gangs, Hispanic-affiliated gangs have a history of interpreting the presence of a rival gang member in their area as a violation. The penalty for those violations can lead to the death of the rival gang member. There are no extensive formal associations between rival gang members, and street truces are not often lasting. But because prison presents a special set of circumstances and the probability of victimization and isolation are high, it is better to be with someone of the same culture even if that person is viewed on the streets as a mortal gang enemy.

This association is apparently recognized only during their incarceration, and upon release their street affiliations are reinstated and a rival prior to incarceration is a rival once again. There has been no indication that this truce happens in county and municipal jails; it appears that this alliance only applies to state facilities.

Concerns

There are some concerns about how long this truce will remain a viable factor among this population. Because it is a volatile situational alliance, there is always the possibility of one STG with more membership overriding the other, creating tension in the group. That tension could be expanded as the group becomes larger and more Hispanics enter the system. If the rate of Hispanic inmates continues trending upward, in the next five years their presence may be significant enough that they will begin to splinter into smaller subsets and their alliance may become severed.

It is also possible that other STGs will begin to view the Hispanic population as a threat. This could present a dangerous situation for Hispanic inmates because although they constitute a higher overall percentage of STG members, they still make up a small percentage of the prison population. Therefore, their ability to defend themselves from a collective assault is limited.

Another concern is that the STG's influence over the actions of Hispanic inmates can potentially undermine the penal system's authority to resolve conflicts and address issues. This can have a huge impact on the climate of a facility and the ability of staff to provide a safe and secure environment.

Language is a primary barrier between staff and Hispanic inmates. When a Spanish-speaking inmate is interviewed about a specific incident, there is usually another inmate serving as an interpreter. The inmate interpreter is also a member of the Hispanic inmate population, which means that he can report the information back to the Hispanic gang leaders if the inmate makes an allegation against the group. That interpreter can even change the statement of the inmate interviewee without staff being aware because of the language barrier.

The Georgia DOC has taken steps to reduce this risk by hiring a bilingual investigator and seeking bilingual staff. This provides the department the resources to respond to a crisis involving Hispanic inmates and ensures that the inmates are afforded privacy while giving statements and that the reported statements are accurate accounts of what was said.

Bilingual staff have had a positive effect on communication between correctional staff and inmates. In addition, several staff members have begun to take a strong interest in improving their bilingual skills. How far reaching the effects bilingual staff will have are yet to be determined in mitigating possible conflicts. What is apparent is that it has improved the DOC's ability to accurately assess the Hispanic population's issues and concerns, which allows Hispanic inmates to seek the help of staff in dealing with their issues.

SHARROD CAMPBELL is investigator and STG coordinator for the Georgia Department of Corrections' Office of Investigation and Compliance/Intelligence.

The Professor Was a Prison Guard

JEFFREY J. WILLIAMS

When I was 20, I left college and took a job in a prison. I went from reading the great books as a Columbia University undergraduate to locking doors and counting inmates as a New York State correction officer. Since I'm an English professor now, people never entirely believe me when the issue comes up, probably because of the horn-rimmed glasses and felicitous implementation of Latinate words. I fancied I'd be like George Orwell, who took a job as an Imperial Police officer in Burma and wrote about it in "Shooting an Elephant." I thought I'd go "up the river" to the "big house" and write "Shooting an Inmate" or some such thing. It didn't quite happen that way, although as a professor, I've worked 14 of 16 years in state institutions.

For the most part, I worked at Downstate Correctional Facility, in Fishkill, N.Y. (You can see it in a hollow along the north side of Interstate 84, just east of the Newburgh-Beacon Bridge.) Newly opened and still under construction when I started, in 1979, the place was billed as the prison of the future. It adopted a "campus" style, with clusters of 36 cells arranged in a split-level horseshoe shape, rather than the traditional warehouse style of long rows of 40 or so cells stacked three or four stories high. The new style presumably granted a more pleasant environment, or simply less chaos. Downstate was also threaded with electronic sensors that would supposedly indicate if a cell door was open, or if someone was walking between the rows of razor wire encircling the facility. The electronics were bruited as a wonder solution to security, as well as being more economical, since the old design of a maximum-security prison required a small island of cement, with walls 30 feet high and 20 feet into the ground. The sensors, however, were moody, a sticky door registering locked and unlocked like a temperamental Christmas-tree light, and a raccoon, a bit of rain, or a poltergeist setting off the ones between the fences. Though annoying, they kept you awake if you drew a shift on the berm overlooking the grounds.

Downstate was designed to replace Sing Sing Correctional Facility, in Ossining, as the "classification and reception center" for New York's state prison system. If you were convicted of a felony and sentenced to a sizable term, you were shipped from a county jail to Downstate. County jails are essentially holding tanks, mixing innocent and guilty awaiting trial, 18-year-old shoplifters and 40-year-old murderers awaiting the next stop. State correction officers looked down on the jails as poorly run

zoos, the nursery schools of the prison taxonomy; state officers had substantial training, and state prisons were the higher rehabilitation. Every male inmate in the state system spent his first six weeks at Downstate (women, who at the time numbered less than 5 percent of the prison population, went to Bedford Hills Correctional Facility), taking tests and getting interviewed so counselors could decide where he'd do his time. If he was young, maybe Elmira or Coxsackie; if on a short stretch, a minimum like Taconic; if on a long sentence, behind the high walls of maximums like Great Meadow, Green Haven, Attica, and Clinton. Since most of those convicted came from New York City and environs, Sing Sing had earned the sobriquet "up the river" because it was a 30-mile barge ride up the Hudson. Downstate continued the tradition another 30 miles up, although the present-day conduit is I-84 and the mode of transport a bus.

When you work in prison, just as when you work in academe, you experience a world that has its own language, its own training, its own hierarchy, its own forms of recognition.

Before getting a badge, correction officers did 12 weeks in the training academy in Albany. It was a cross between a military and a technical college, with calisthenics in the morning and classes all day. Wake-up was 6 A.M., with a couple of miles around the track; like in the military, your bed had to be made with crisp corners, belongings neatly stowed in your locker, hair short and face cleanshaven. There were periodic spot inspections, and you got demerits if you missed a step. The academy held hourly classes, punctuated by a bell (lateness was one demerit). One class gave background on the taxonomy and geography of New York's correctional system, from minimum to maximum, prisons dotting the state like community colleges. Another was on relevant law, defining necessary as opposed to excessive use of physical force (one should restrain an inmate from doing harm to himself or others, but not beat him once restrained), and enumerating rights (if an inmate complained of a physical ailment, you had to notify the hospital, even if you thought he was lying). One course covered procedures, detailing how to do a count, how to keep a notebook (in part for legal protection but mostly to pass on information to the next shift), and how to do searches (never ignore an inconvenient corner, even if you don't want to reach, but be careful of hidden pieces of glass or razor blades). One course taught rudimentary psychology, or "interpersonal communication," in which the instructors taught you how to deal with, say, an enraged inmate by responding with something to the effect of, "So you are telling me you're pissed off because. . . . " Although it seemed mindlessly redundant, it was not a bad lesson in how to stop and listen. Prisons, like any social institution, run best when they respond appropriately to needs as well as misdeeds. Contrary to the popular image of sadistic prison guards, the motto the academy drummed into you was "firm, fair, and consistent."

Everyone asks if I carried a gun, but inside the walls you were always outnumbered, and a gun would more likely be used for a takeover or escape. Instead, the most severe weapon was a nightstick. The only place you were issued a gun was on a perimeter post, at one of the gates or on the berm. At the academy, there were classes in weapons—at the time, in the trusty Smith & Wesson .38 revolver, which everyone had to qualify to use; the Remington pump-action shotgun, which you just had to shoot without falling over; and a long-distance .30-30, basically a deer rifle, which granted a special qualification to work in a tower at one of the walled prisons. After you were on the job, you had to qualify with the .38 every year, and, like a field trip, we looked forward to the day we went out to the shooting range. The one part we didn't look forward to was getting tear-gassed, deemed necessary so you knew what it felt like to have the rabid sting of CS or CN gas on your skin and wouldn't panic.

The lessons were usually reinforced with black humor, anecdotes, and morality tales. For example, you can use lethal physical force to prevent an imminent escape but not if an inmate is still on prison grounds. One quip was that if you shot an inmate scaling the fence, you had better make sure he landed on the outside—otherwise you'd end up inside. One story to remind us not to slack off on searches was about an escape from the Fishkill Correctional Facility (actually in Beacon, across the highway from Downstate). The inmate, so the story went, had gotten a gun smuggled in the bottom of a bucket of Kentucky Fried Chicken because the correction officer searching packages had supposedly eaten a piece off the top and passed the bucket through. Another story, to reinforce the rule that you should not eat state food or accept favors, however slight, from inmates, went something like this: An inmate, who worked in the mess hall and prepared the trays that got sent to the blocks for ill or keep-locked inmates, regularly brought BLT's to the correction officer on his block. One day the kitchen officer happened upon the inmate using a bodily fluid as a condiment on the bread. I never knew whether the story was true, but I always brought my lunch.

The first thing you learn when you get behind the walls or concertina wire is that prison has its own language. We received a glossary of terms at the training academy, but, just as with learning a foreign language, the words didn't mean much until you got inside. A prison guard is not a "screw," as in a James Cagney movie, but a "correction officer," or usually just a "CO." A prisoner is not a "convict" but an "inmate." A sentence is a "bid." A cell is a "crib." To calm down is to "chill." A homemade knife is a "shiv."

The university represents the hope, prison the failing, of the meritocracy.

Life in prison is punctuated by counts, three or four for every eight-hour shift. When I was in training at Elmira, which was an old prison with what seemed like mile-long rows of cells three stories high, I remember walking down the narrow runway to take the evening count. There were whispered goads—"CO, you look gooood," "Who you eyeballing?," "Hey motherfucker"—or simply hissing, which was the worst. I didn't turn around to look, since you rarely knew where the voices came from, amidst the echoes of reinforced concrete. Besides, turning would show that they were getting under your skin, which would just fuel the hiss.

What makes time go by in prison is the talk. Talk among the guards was a constant buzz—about life, yesterday's mail, what happened in the visiting room, the food in the mess hall this morning, the lieutenant who was a hard-ass and snuck around at night to catch you sleeping, if you were going fishing on your days off, if you were getting any. With the inmates, though, as in a game of poker, you never let too much show. The one time you worried was when the buzz stopped. You didn't have to know the literary definition of foreshadowing to know that something was aching to happen.

I got good at finding things, as much to stave off boredom as from a sense of duty. Once I found a 10-inch shiv hung in a crevice of cement behind a fuse-box door. It was fashioned from a soup-ladle handle purloined from the kitchen, filed laboriously on cement to a knife edge, its handle wrapped with white athletic tape. I would periodically find jugs of homemade booze, made from fruit and fermented in floor-wax containers, wedged behind a clothes dryer to cook or stowed beneath the bag in a utility vacuum. Once I found a few joints taped under a toilet tank. The joints bothered me more than the rest, not because they were harmful—in fact, one way to still a prison population would be to hand out joints, whereas booze, especially homebrews, tends to prime people for a fight—but because they came from outside. They could have come in through visits, swallowed in a condom, or they could mean a CO or other worker had a business they weren't declaring on their 1040. It violated the boundaries of the place, boundaries that you did not want to get fuzzy.

Prison carries its own set of lessons. One was about how life works, albeit life in a crockpot: mostly by repetition and habit, punctuated by sudden, sometimes scary, but strangely exhilarating moments that shattered the routine. Once when I was at Elmira, whiling away a shift after the inmates were locked in, except for the porters, who did the cleaning, I heard a clomping on the stairs. I looked over to see a porter, head dripping blood, running down the stairs, with another following a few steps back, carrying a piece of jagged glass in his hand. I followed to find two officers on the first tier pinning both inmates to the floor. Danger raises your blood pressure, which isn't good for you over the long term, but acts as a drug in the short.

Another lesson was "Do your job," which was a kind of mantra, repeated by CO's and inmates alike. It meant take your responsibility, don't slough off, don't dump your job on someone else, or you'd be not very tactfully reminded on the cellblock, in the parking lot, or at the next union meeting. The ecological balance of prisons is probably not much more fragile than those of other institutions, or there wouldn't be many prisons still standing, but its imbalances take on a particular intensity. If an inmate had a visitor, you made sure that inmate was escorted to the visiting room right away; otherwise he would have a legitimate beef, which would make life harder for everyone. Especially in the summer, when cement holds heat like barbecue bricks and you didn't want any sparks.

Another lesson was "Don't back down." If an inmate didn't go into his cell at count, you had to confront him and write it up or be ready to hit the beeper you wore on your belt; otherwise, the next day, three people would be lingering at the TV. It was a different kind of lesson than I had learned at Columbia. One might find it in the Iliad but not, in my experience, in most academic venues, where aggression is usually served with the sugary coating of passive circumlocution. I miss the clarity of it and, as with single malt, prefer my aggression straight.

Something else to remember was to the effect of "There but for the grace of God go I." There wasn't much room for moral superiority inside the razor wire, and you quickly lost it if you had it. I worked for a time in draft processing, which is where inmates first arrive after coming through the gates. They got a speech, a shower and delousing, a crew cut, and a khaki uniform cut like hospital scrubs, and then were assigned to a block. To avoid bias, officers generally didn't have access to rap sheets, except in draft and transport, when the sheets were like passports that traveled with the inmates. There was a young kid, maybe 18 or 19, who had been returned from Florida after escaping from a minimum. He had gotten three to five for stealing—taking a joy ride in—a dump truck in upstate New York, and the escape would probably double his sentence. On his sheet, there was an entry that read "act attributed to: drinking a case of beer." I'm not exaggerating.

Prison gave me a kind of adult education that, as a scholarship boy, I had not gotten in the humanities sequence at Columbia. It gave me an education about people, how they get by and how they don't. One of the ways they get by is loyalty. The people I worked with, even some of the inmates, "had my back": If a lieutenant gave you a hard time, the union rep would be in his face. If you were out too late and took a nap in the bathroom, another CO would cover for you. If an inmate saw the superintendent coming while you were watching TV and he thought you did your job, he would warn you. The better species of loyalty is, in fact, not blind: If you screw up, someone you work with should tell you. The corruption of loyalty is when no one says anything.

It's always curious to see how colleagues react when they find out about my time—as I like to put it—in prison. Some are fascinated and quote Cool Hand Luke, but clearly it's just a fantasy to them. Some take on a more serious cast and ask what I think of Foucault's Discipline and Punish, but then prison has become a disembodied abstraction, something they know as much about as dairy farms (as with most prisons, set a long way from any roads they've been on). Some look away, as if I had a swastika tattooed on my forearm. What they don't seem to realize is that correction officers are of the unionized working classes, like cops, whom my colleagues wouldn't hesitate to call if they had an accident or their house was broken into. It is often said that literature expands your world, but it can also close it off.

It is also often said that the university is not the real world, but in my experience each institutional parcel of life has its own world. When you work in prison, just as when you work in academe, you experience a world that has its own language, its own training, its own hierarchy, its own forms of recognition, its own forms of disrepute, and its own wall from the outside. In some ways, prison is the flip side of meritocracy. Both prisons and universities originated in religious institutions and are based on the model of the cloister; both are transitional institutions; both house and grade people; and both marshal primarily the young. The difference, of course, is that the university represents the hope, prison the failing, of the meritocracy. It's an unseemly sign that we invest more in the underside than in the hope.

JEFFREY J. WILLIAMS is a professor of English and literary and cultural studies at Carnegie Mellon University, and editor of the Minnesota Review. His most recent book is the collection *Critics at Work: Interviews, 1993–2003* (New York University Press, 2004).

Supermax Prisons

Jeffrey Ian Ross, PhD

Each time a crime occurs, an arrest is made, the trial ends, and a person is sentenced to prison, the public has a recurring curiosity about where the convict is sent. Over the past two decades, a phenomenal number of individuals have been sentenced to jails and to state or federal prisons.

But this is just the beginning of the journey. Prisoners are classified into a whole host of various kinds of facilities. They typically vary based on the level of security, from minimum to high. But since the mid-1980s, a dramatic change has underscored corrections in the United States and elsewhere. Correctional systems at all levels have introduced or expanded the use of Supermax prisons.

Supermax prisons, also known as Administrative Control Units, Special (or Security) Handling Units (SHU), or Control Handling Units (CHU) (Here, "CHUs" is pronounced "shoes."), are stand-alone correctional facilities, wings or annexes inside an already existing prison. They are a result of the recent growth in incarceration that has occurred throughout many of the world's advanced industrialized countries.

There is, however, a well-documented turning point in the history of Supermax prisons. In October 1983, after the brutal and fatal stabbings of two correctional officers by inmates at the federal maximum-security prison in Marion, Illinois, the facility implemented a 23-hour-a-day lockdown of all convicts. The institution slowly changed its policies and practices and was retrofitted to become what is now considered a Supermax prison. Then, in 1994, the federal government opened its first Supermax prison in Florence, Colorado, specifically designed to house Supermax prisoners. The facility was dubbed the "Alcatraz of the Rockies."

Research on Supermax Prisons

Although much has been written on jails, prisons, and corrections, the mass media and academic community have been relatively silent with respect to Supermax prisons—and with good reason. It is difficult for journalists and scholars to gain access to prisoners, correctional officers, and administrators inside this type of facility. Reporting on correctional institutions has never been easy, and many editors and reporters shy away from this subject matter. Correctional professionals are also reluctant to talk with outsiders for fear that they may be unnecessarily subjected to public scrutiny.

Numerous books on corrections, jails, and prisons have been published for trade, classroom, and professional audiences; only a few monographs offer an in-depth look at Supermax prisons. In December 2002, the American Correctional Association (the largest professional association for correctional practitioners in the United States) published *Supermax Prisons: Beyond the Rock.* This edited monograph, consisting of seven chapters written by prison officials, is more of a technical guide for prison administrators who run one of these types of facilities. Unfortunately, it suffers from the biases of its sponsor and limited targeted audience. *The Big House: Life Inside a Supermax Security Prison* (June 2004) is a memoir written by Jim Bruton, former warden of the Minnesota Correctional Facility-Oak Park Heights facility. Although pitched as a memoir of a Supermax administrator, Oak Park is without question primarily a maximum-security facility with only one of the nine complexes used as an Administrative Control Unit (or Supermax). Largely because of the numerous entertaining anecdotes, in many respects the book's treatment is superficial. Moreover, Bruton is overly self-congratulatory about his ability to solve problems on his watch and thus serious scholars have easily dismissed the book.

There has also been a handful of publicly available government reports published on the topic of Supermax prisons. These have consisted primarily of statistical compilations outlining the numerous Supermax facilities throughout the United States and the composition of the inmates housed within.

The academic treatments (journal articles or chapters in scholarly books) fall into three groups: general overviews, those that focus on the individuals that are sent to solitary confinement or Supermax prisons, and those that focus on the effects of Supermax prisons. The research centers disproportionately on American Supermax prisons and, while this is a start, this literature treats Supermax prisons in isolation of other countries' experiences. Rigorous comparative examinations of foreign-based Supermax prisons have yet to be performed.

There are many unanswered questions about Supermax prisons. Why are Supermax prisons necessary? What particular circumstances led to the creation of Supermax prisons in different states and countries? Is the construction and increased reliance on Supermax institutions due to the fact that today's prisoners are more incorrigible and dangerous, and thus more difficult to handle? Or is it a reflection of the correctional system's failure or mismanagement, or pressures by the general public for a get-tough stance against dangerous criminals? Who are the typical persons sent to Supermax prisons? Why have the Supermax prisons and similar institutions in other countries engendered intense public outcry? What are the similarities and differences among American supermaxes and comparable facilities elsewhere?

The academic treatments (journal articles or chapters in scholarly books) fall into three groups: general overviews, those that focus on the individuals that are sent to solitary confinement or Supermax prisons, and those that focus on the effects of Supermax prisons.

Why Supermaxes Have Proliferated

Since the mid-1980s, many state departments of corrections have built their own Supermax prisons. Several reasons can account for their proliferation. First, many states had similar experiences to the blood that spilled at Marion. In Minnesota, for example, the escape of a prisoner, kidnapping of correctional officers, fatal stabbing of a warden, and a series of prison disturbances in the early 1970s created an environment that was ripe for the construction of a new facility that would house the "worst of the worst." Another explanation for the growth of Supermax prisons lies in the development of a conservative political ideology that began during the Reagan administration (1981–1989). As a response to an increased public fear of crime and to the demise of the "rehabilitative ideal," a punitive agenda took hold of criminal justice and led to a much larger number of people being incarcerated.

Reagan's Republican successor, George H.W. Bush, continued this approach from 1989 to1993. Since then several factors prompted a dramatic increase in the number of people entering jails and prisons: the construction of new correctional facilities; new and harsher sentencing guidelines (particularly "truth in sentencing" legislation, mandatory minimums, and determinant sentencing); the passage of "three strikes you're out" laws and the war on drugs.

In short, many of the gains that were part of the so-called "community corrections era" of the 1960s were scaled back. Congress and state legislatures passed draconian laws that reversed such time-honored practices as indeterminate sentencing and invoked a host of laws that lengthened prison sentences for convicted criminals.

Another factor that contributed to the growth of Supermaxes is the careerism of correctional administrators. Some have argued that without the leadership of particular wardens, government rainmakers, and commissioners and/or secretaries of respective state Departments of Corrections, Supermax facilities would not ever have been built in the first place. Finally, it should be understood that, in many respects, Supermaxes symbolize the failure of rehabilitation and the inability of policymakers and legislators to think and act creatively regarding incarceration. Supermax prisons are excellent examples of the way that America, compared to other countries, has dealt with lawbreakers.

Originally designed to house the most violent, hardened, and escape-prone criminals, Supermaxes are increasingly used for persistent rule-breakers, convicted leaders of criminal organizations (e.g., the mafia) and gangs, serial killers, and political criminals (e.g., spies and terrorists). In some states, the criteria for admission into a Supermax facility and the review of prisoners' time inside (i.e., classification) are very loose or even nonexistent. These facilities are known for their strict lockdown policies, lack of amenities, and prisoner isolation techniques. Escapes from Supermaxes are so rare that they are statistically inconsequential.

In the United States alone, 6.47 million people are under the control of the criminal justice system. Approximately 2.3 million are behind bars in jails or prisons, while 3.8 million are on probation and 725,527 are on parole. The Supermaxes, maintained by the Federal Bureau of Prisons (FBOP) in Marion and Florence, for example, incarcerate 1,710 people—including such notable political criminals as "Unabomber" Ted Kaczynski and Oklahoma City bombing co-conspirator Terry Nichols.

Nevertheless, only a fraction of those incarcerated in state and federal prisons are sent to a Supermax facility. In 1998, approximately 20,000 inmates were locked up in this type of prison, representing less than 2 percent of all the men and women currently incarcerated across the country. Most of the U.S. Supermaxes, such as the federal facility in Florence, are either brand new or nearly so; others, however, are simply free-standing prisons that have been retrofitted. Meanwhile, the number of convicts being sent to Supermax prisons is steadily growing.

Many prisons have earned their individual reputations largely through well-known events that have taken place within their walls and have subsequently been covered by the media. Places like Attica, Folsom, San Quentin, Sing Sing, and Stateville are etched in the consciousness of many Americans. The Supermaxes, on the other hand, are known for their conditions and effects on prisoners within their walls.

Conditions of Confinement

Although cells vary in size and construction, they are generally built to the dimensions of 12 by 7 feet. A cell light usually remains on all night long, and furnishings consist of a bed, a desk, and a stool made out of poured concrete, as well as a stainless steel sink and toilet.

One of the more notable features of all Supermax prisons is the fact that prisoners are usually locked down 23 out of 24 hours a day. The hour outside of the prison is typically used for recreation or bathing/showering. Other than their interaction with the supervising correctional officers (COs), prisoners have virtually no contact with other people (either fellow convicts or visitors). Access to phones and mail is strictly and closely supervised, or even restricted. Reading materials are often prohibited. Supermax prisoners have very limited access to privileges such as watching television or listening to the radio.

Supermax prisons also generally do not allow inmates either to work or congregate during the day. In addition, there is absolutely no personal privacy; everything the convicts do is monitored, usually through a video camera that is on all day and night. Any communication with the correctional officers most often takes place through a narrow window on the steel door of the cell, and/or via an intercom system.

In Supermaxes, inmates rarely have access to educational or religious materials and services. Almost all toiletries (e.g., toothpaste, shaving cream, and razors) are strictly controlled. When an inmate is removed from his cell, he typically has to kneel down with his back to the door. Then he is required to place his hands through the food slot in the door to be handcuffed.

In spite of these simple facilities and the fact that prisoners' rehabilitation is not encouraged (and is next to impossible under these conditions), Supermax prisons are more expensive to build and to run than traditional prisons.

Prisoners are sentenced or transferred to Supermaxes for a variety of reasons that often boil down to a judge's sentence, classification processes, and inmates' behavior while they are incarcerated.

Officially, prison systems design classification categories as a means to designate prisoners to different security levels. Typically, the hard-core, violent convicts serving long sentences are assigned to maximum-security facilities; the incorrigible prisoners serving medium-length sentences are sentenced to medium-security prisons; and the relatively lightweight men serving short sentences are sentenced to minimum-security camps, farms, or community facilities.

For some convicts, the decision of where they will be sent is made long before they hop on their very first prison van. In the sentencing phase of a trial, the judge may specify where the convict will spend his or her time. For example, Ramzi Yousef, the convicted bomber in the 1993 attack on the World Trade Center, was sent directly to the federal Supermax in Florence, Colorado. Depending on sentencing guidelines and an individual's criminal history, officials must determine which security level is most appropriate for each convict. Alternatively, prisoners who are new to the system will be transferred to a receiving and departure setting, where they are classified into the appropriate receiving facility.

The classification of inmates serves many functions for the Department of Corrections (DOC) and the individual correctional institutions. In general, this process determines which facility and security level is best suited to each prisoner. This decision may ultimately facilitate a prisoner's rehabilitation and/or protect correctional officers from being hurt (as officials clearly do not want, for example, a violence-prone convict in a minimum-security prison). Classification also saves taxpayers money (since sending too many prisoners to higher-security prisons, which are more costly to operate, results in a greater expense) and saves the Department of Corrections resources.

Where a convict is sent depends on a number of factors. The division of probation and parole usually prepares a Pre-Sentence Investigation, which is another attempt by the criminal justice system to collect a prisoner's personal information. The probation or parole officer reviews a number of factors relevant to the convict's circumstances, including criminal history. They prepare a report, which makes a recommendation as to which facility would best suit the particular criminal. This report is then shared with the judge, defense attorney, and prosecutor—and the judge retains the ability to accept or dismiss the recommendation. By the same token, some well-heeled and high-profile defendants (e.g., Martha Stewart) or their loved ones may employ the services of sentencing consultants like Herb Hoelter of the National Center for Institutions and Alternatives. For a hefty fee, these hired individuals can prepare a report that recommends where a client should be sentenced. The defendant's attorney then passes the report on to the prosecutor (and judge) in hopes that it may ultimately influence the presiding judge.

In most lock-ups and prisons, the majority of the inmates do not get into trouble because they follow the rules. The problem population comprises approximately 1 percent of the prisoners in an institution. When there is an incident, such as a stabbing on a tier, correctional officers cannot place all of the suspects on administrative segregation (i.e., "in the hole"). But when this type of extreme punishment becomes the norm for a particular prisoner, the administration is usually prompted to transfer the inmate to a higher-security prison. Over time, a prisoner who repeatedly finds himself in this type of situation becomes more and more likely to end up at a Supermax facility.

Typically, the hard-core, violent convicts serving long sentences are assigned to maximum-security facilities; the incorrigible prisoners serving medium-length sentences are sentenced to medium-security prisons; and the relatively lightweight men serving short sentences are sentenced to minimum-security camps, farms, or community facilities.

Effects of Incarceration

All told, the isolation, lack of meaningful activity, and shortage of human contact take their toll on prisoners. Supermax residents often develop severe psychological disorders, though, unfortunately, we do not have specific psychological data, per se, on individuals kept in these facilities. However, numerous reports based on anecdotal information have documented the detrimental effects of these facilities.

The conditions inside Supermax prisons have led several corrections and human rights experts and organizations (like Amnesty International and the American Civil Liberties Union) to question whether these prisons are a violation of (1) the Eighth Amendment of the U.S. Constitution, which prohibits the state from engaging in cruel and unusual punishment, and/or (2) the European Convention on Human Rights and the United Nations'

Universal Declaration of Human Rights, which were established to protect the rights of all individuals, whether living free or incarcerated. According to Roy D. King, in an article published in the 1999 volume of *Punishment and Society,* "Although the effective reach of international human rights standards governing the treatment of prisoners remains uncertain, there seems little doubt that what goes on in a number of Supermax facilities would breach the protections enshrined in these instruments. . . . The International Covenant on Civil and Political Rights, which the United States has ratified, for example, has a more extensive ban on 'torture, cruel, inhuman or degrading treatment or punishment' than the Eighth Amendment prohibition of 'cruel and unusual' punishment, and requires no demonstration of intent or indifference to the risk of harm, on the part of officials" (164).

Supermax prisons have plenty of downsides, and not just as far as the inmates are concerned. Some individuals have suggested that Supermax prisons are all part of the correctional industrial complex (i.e., an informal network of correctional workers, professional organizations, and corporations that keep the jails and prisons system growing). Most of the Supermaxes in the United States are brand new or nearly so. Others are simply freestanding prisons that were retrofitted. According to a study by the Urban Institute, the annual per-cell cost of a Supermax is about $75,000, compared to $25,000 for each cell in an ordinary state prison.

Future Prospects

The United States has plenty of super-expensive Supermax facilities—two-thirds of the states now have them. But these facilities were designed when crime was considered a growing problem; the current lower violent-crime rate shows no real sign of a turn for the worse. However, as good as these prisons are at keeping our worst offenders in check, the purpose of the Supermax is in flux.

No self-respecting state director of corrections or correctional planner will admit that the Supermax concept was a mistake. And you would be wrong to think that these prisons can be replaced by something drastically less costly. But prison experts are beginning to realize that, just like a shrinking city that finds itself with too many schools or fire departments, the Supermax model must be made more flexible in order to justify its size and budget.

One solution is for these facilities to house different types of prisoners. In May 2006, Wisconsin Department of Corrections officials announced that, over the past sixteen years, the state's Supermax facility in Boscobel—which cost $47.5 million (in 1990) and holds 500 inmates—has always stood at 100 cells below its capacity. It is now scheduled to house maximum-security prisoners—serious offenders, but a step down from the worst of the worst.

The Maryland Correctional Adjustment Center, a.k.a. the Baltimore Supermax prison, opened in 1989 at a cost of $21 million with room for 288 inmates. Like its cousin in Wisconsin, the structure has never been at capacity. Not only does it hold the state's most dangerous prisoners, it also houses 100 or so inmates who are working their way through the federal courts and serves as the home for Maryland's ten death row convicts.

Converting cells is one approach, but not the only one. Other ideas include building more regional Supermaxes and filling them by shifting populations from other states. This would allow administrators to completely empty out a given Supermax, and then close it down or convert it to another use.

There is also the possibility that some elements of the Supermax model could be combined with the approaches of more traditional prisons, creating a hybrid that serves a wider population. But different types of prisoners would have to be kept well away from each other—a logistical problem of no small concern.

The invention and adoption of Supermax prisons is perhaps the most significant indictment of the way we run correctional facilities and/or what we accomplish in correctional facilities. Most relatively intelligent people know that the United States incarcerates more people per capita than any other advanced industrialized country. And the average American rarely questions this fact. Then again, many people believe that individuals doing time are probably guilty anyway. Thus reforming or changing prisons is and will remain a constant struggle.

JEFFREY IAN ROSS, PhD is an Associate Professor in the Division of Criminology, Criminal Justice and Social Policy, and a Fellow of the Center for International and Comparative Law at the University of Baltimore. He has researched, written, and lectured on national security, political violence, political crime, violent crime, corrections, and policing for over two decades. Ross' work has appeared in many academic journals and books, as well as popular outlets. He is the author, co-author, editor and co-editor of twelve books including most recently *Special Problems in Corrections* (Prentice Hall, 2008). He has also appeared as an expert commentator on crime and policing issues in many media outlets such as newspapers, magazines, and nationally televised shows. His website is www.jeffreyianross.com.

From *Society,* Vol. 44, No. 3, March/April 2007, pp. 60–64. Copyright © 2007 by Jeffrey Ian Ross. Reprinted by permission of the author.

The Results of American Incarceration

**Any answer to the question "What do we get from imprisonment?"
has to recognize that U.S. imprisonment operates differently
than it does in any other democratic state in the world.**

TODD R. CLEAR

Let's begin with a little thought experiment. Today, there are 1.3 million federal prisoners; over 2 million citizens are incarcerated in state prisons and local jails. Imagine that those numbers grow methodically for the next generation. By the time people born today reach their thirtieth birthday, there will be over 7 million prisoners and, if local jails are counted, more than 10 million locked up on any given day. How are we to react to such daunting numbers?

First, let's agree that the experiment seems unrealistic. This kind of growth would result in about 2 percent of the population incarcerated on any given day. Taken as a percentage of males aged 20–40 (most of those behind bars are from this group), the proportion locked up would be stupefying.

A rational person might say, "State and local governments have trouble affording today's prisons and jails, so how could they pay for such a mind-boggling expansion? What kind of society could justify locking up so many of our young men?"

After a bit more thought, that person might also say, "Well, if we are going to do it, then at least we will eliminate a lot of crime."

This is perhaps a disturbing thought experiment, but it is not a far-fetched one.

The 'War' on Crime

To illustrate, go back a full generation, to the beginning of the 1970s. Richard Nixon is president, and we are having a bit of a "war" on crime (puny, by today's standards). Crime rates seem disturbingly high, and the nightly news seems dominated by stories about disorder in the streets.

Imagine, for a moment, attending a futurist seminar, and the speaker has turned his attention to the topic of social control. He has said a few words about the coming days of electronic surveillance through bracelets on people's ankles and wrists, pictures and home addresses of convicted criminals displayed for all to see at the touch of a keyboard, detention in an offender's home enforced by threat of prison, chemical testing of a person's cells—detectable from saliva left at the scene of a crime—instead of fingerprints to prove guilt at trial, and so on. The audience would rightfully have been a bit awed by the prospect.

Then he makes the most stunning prediction of all. He says, "In the next 30 years, the prison population is going to grow by 600 percent. Instead of today's 200,000 prisoners, we will have more than 1.3 million."

Anyone who heard such predictions in the early 1970s would have been more than a bit skeptical. But they have all come true.

Any answer to the question, "What do we get from imprisonment?" has to begin with a frank recognition that incarceration in the United States today operates differently than in any other modernized or democratic state in the world, and that this phenomenon has resulted from very recent changes in U.S. penal policy. Today, we lock up our fellow citizens at a rate (700 per 100,000) that is between 5 and 10 times higher than in comparable industrial democracies.

A Washington, D.C., prison reform group, the Sentencing Project, has offered these comparisons: European states such as Germany, Sweden, France, the Netherlands, and Switzerland have incarceration rates of less than 100 per 100,000, one-seventh of ours. The big lock-up states—England, Spain, Canada, and Australia—have prison/jail rates of between 100 and 200, or one-fourth of ours. Our only competitors are Russia and South Africa, with prison-use levels that are 90 and 60 percent of ours, respectively.

That is not the whole story. Our world leadership in the use of prison is a fairly recent accomplishment. U.S. prison population statistics go back to 1925, when there were about 100,000 prisoners. Between 1925 and 1940, a period of fairly substantial immigration and U.S. population growth, the number of prisoners doubled. During the years of World War II, the prison population dropped by about a third. (Most observers think this drop was due to the large number of young men in the armed forces and unavailable for imprisonment). Between 1945 and 1961, the number of prisoners grew by 68 percent, to a high of about 210,000 in the early 1960s, staying more or less stable into the 1970s.

U.S. Leads World in Incarceration

- Today, the United States locks up its citizens at a rate (700 per 100,000) that is between 5 and 10 times higher than in comparable industrial democracies.
- In European states such as Germany, Sweden, France, the Netherlands, and Switzerland, incarceration rates are under 100 per 100,000.
- The big lockup states—England, Spain, Canada, and Australia—have prison/jail rates of between 100 and 200, or one-quarter of ours.
- The only competitors for prison and jail use are Russia and South Africa, with levels that are 90 and 60 percent of ours, respectively.
- Since the 1990s, almost all the growth in the prison population has been due to longer sentences, not more crime or prisoners.
- In effect, the U.S. anomaly in prison use results mostly from the policies we enact to deal with crime, much less than from crime itself.

Social scientists looked at these numbers and saw a pattern of profound stability. In 1975, two researchers from Carnegie-Mellon University, Alfred Blumstein and Jacqueline Cohen, argued that after accounting for such factors as war, immigration, and changes in youth population, there had been a "homoeostatic" level of stability in punishment for the first three-quarters of the twentieth century. That theory no longer applies. Between 1971 and 2002, the number of prisoners grew by an astounding 600 percent. Why did everything change?

Why the Growth in Crime?

It is easy to say that prison populations grew because crime—or at least violent crime—grew. But this view turns out to be simplistic. In their recent book, *Crime Is Not the Problem*, UCLA criminologists Franklin Zimring and Gordon Hawkins point out that several countries have violent crime rates that rival ours, yet use prison less readily than we do. Moreover, those European countries with low rates of incarceration seem to have property crime rates that are not so different from ours.

Besides, the growth of the U.S. prison population has been so consistent for a generation that nothing seems to affect it much. Since 1980, for example, prison populations grew during economic boom times and recessions alike; while the baby boomers were entering their crime-prone years and as they exited those years; and as crime dropped and while it soared.

Today's nationally dropping crime rates—a trend in some big cities that is almost a decade long—suggest that prison growth has helped make the streets safer. But when we take the long view, aside from burglary (which has dropped systematically for 20 years), today's crime rates are not very different than at the start of the big prison boom in the 1970s. Since then, crime rates went up for a while, down for a while, back up again, and are now (thankfully) trending downward. Prison populations, by contrast, went only one way during this entire period: up.

Blumstein and Department of Justice statistician Allen Beck have studied trends in criminal justice since the 1980s to better understand what accounts for the recent growth in the prison population. They argue that you can divide the growth into three distinct periods. In the late 1970s and early 1980s, prisons grew because crime was growing and more criminals were being sentenced to prison. In the 1980s into the beginning of the 1990s, prison growth was partly due to crime rates, but it was much more a product of greater numbers of criminals being sentenced to prison and of longer terms for those sentenced there.

By the 1990s and into the early 2000s, the story has changed, and almost all of the growth in the prison population is due to longer sentences, not more crime or more prisoners. In effect, the U.S. anomaly in the use of prison is a result mostly of the policies we enact to deal with crime, and much less of crime itself.

A Street's-Eye View

But all of this exploration looks for broad patterns. What about the view from the streets? John DiIulio of the University of Pennsylvania, former codirector of the White House Office on Faith-Based Initiatives, once observed, "A thug in jail can't shoot my sister?" Isn't it apparent on its face that a person behind bars is someone from whom the rest of us are pretty safe?

Yes, but that may not be the most effective way to deter crime. The irony is that while people who are behind bars are less likely to commit crimes, that may not mean those crimes are prevented from occurring.

Drug crime is the obvious example. Almost one-third of those sent to prison are punished for drug-related crimes, and one prisoner in four is serving time for a drug crime. In most of these cases, the criminal activity continued without noticeable interruption, carried out by a replacement. One of the recurrent frustrations of police work is to carry out a drug sweep one day, only to see the drug market return in a matter of hours. Locking up drug offenders is not an efficient strategy for preventing drug crime.

This line of analysis can be misleading, though, because most drug offenders are not specialists in drug crime. Analyses of criminal records show that people in prison who are serving time for drug-related activity typically have arrests and/or convictions for other types of offenses. Doesn't locking them up for drugs prevent the other crimes from happening? At least some other crime is prevented, but not as much as might be thought.

A few years ago, Yale sociologist Albert Reiss reported that about half of all criminal acts are perpetrated by young offenders acting in groups of two or more. Rarely are all of the members of the group prosecuted for the crime. This discovery led to a string of studies of what has been referred to as "co-offending," the commission of crimes by multiple offenders acting in concert. When one person out of a group is arrested and imprisoned, what impact does the arrest have on the crimes the group had been committing? A lot rides on the nature and behavior of criminal groups.

Much research is now under way to better understand how crimes are committed by offenders acting alone and in a group. It would be convenient if criminal groups had stable leaders and were systematic in the way they planned criminal activity. If so, arresting the leaders might break up the groups, and strategies of deterrence might reduce the likelihood of criminal actions. Neither characteristic applies.

Criminologist Mark Warr of the University of Texas has studied the way young males form co-offending groups and engage in criminal acts. He reports that leadership is sporadic and often interchangeable, that criminal actions are spontaneous, and that co-offending groups are loosely formed and vary over time. His findings suggest that well-respected strategies of targeted prosecution and focus on leaders of criminal activity are likely to have diminishing returns in crime prevention. As Rutgers University's Marcus Felson has argued, this analysis of dynamic, spontaneous, loosely organized criminal activity applies not simply to some youth but to most gang behavior. Arresting one person in the network and sending him to prison is far from a guarantee that the crime that person was involved in will stop.

Are Crime and Punishment Connected?

None of this is to argue that imprisonment prevents no crime. Professor David W. Garland of New York University School of Law, one of the most widely respected social critics of imprisonment, puts it well when he says that only the naive would claim that prisons and crime are unrelated. But even if it is recognized that crime and prisons are connected, under close scrutiny, we can find various reasons why wildly growing rates of imprisonment might not lead willy-nilly to wildly reducing rates of crime. Said another way, we can find explanations for the fact that the period in which incarceration has grown so much has not been matched by a corresponding drop in crime.

A new literature is emerging about the unintended consequences of incarceration. Prison populations, for example, are drawn predominantly from the ranks of poor people from minority groups. Today, one in eight black males aged 25–29 is locked up; this rate is almost eight times higher than for white males. Estimates reported by the Department of Justice indicate that of black males born today, 29 percent will go to prison for a felony offense, while currently 17 percent of all African-American

males have spent time in prison. These rates are about six times higher than for white males.

Patterns of racial segregation mean that imprisonment also concentrates residentially. James Lynch and William Sabol, researchers from the Urban Institute, have estimated that in some very poor neighborhoods in Washington, D.C., and Cleveland, Ohio, upwards of 18–20 percent of adult males are locked up on any given day. New York City's Center for Alternative Sentencing and Employment Services reported that in 1998, in two of Brooklyn's poorest Council Districts, one person went to prison or jail for every eight resident males aged 20–40.

These high rates of incarceration, concentrated among poor minority males living in disadvantaged locations, are a new phenomenon that results from a generation of prison population growth in the United States. Social scientists are beginning to investigate whether this socially concentrated use of prison sentences has long-term effects on such factors as neighborhood order, family structure, and child development.

One can imagine, for example, that a neighborhood where a large proportion of parent-age men are missing is a neighborhood that would grapple with a number of problems, from family stability to child supervision. My own research with my colleagues Dina Rose and Elin Waring seems to suggest that high incarceration rates produce socially destabilizing results that may be a factor in sustaining high rates of crime.

The prison is a blunt social instrument, while crime is a much more nuanced social problem. Given what we know about crime, it should not surprise us that so much prison has provided so little in the way of broad public safety.

When trying to weigh the benefits of prison, perhaps we are used to asking the wrong question. We tend to ask about whether prison is a good idea compared to alternative sentencing. In today's America, this may be a fascinating question but it is not a very meaningful one. The more appropriate question would be, "Given our experience with incarceration over the last century, what might we expect from further increases in its use; what might happen if we began to cut back in its use?" This question, which we might perhaps save for another day, would recognize the political reality that U.S. prison rates are going to be internationally out-of-scale for a long time. The only question we face is, how much?

TODD R. CLEAR is Distinguished Professor in Community Justice and Corrections at John Jay College of Criminal Justice in New York City.

From *WorldandIJournal.com*, December 2003, pp. 18–21. Copyright © 2003 by World and I Online. Reprinted by permission.

Article 44

Partnering with Law Enforcement

Ashbel T. Wall II and Tracey Z. Poole

The primary mission of law enforcement is to maintain peace and order and provide a safe environment. In these respects, it is fundamentally aligned with the mission of the corrections field. Although each domain has its own role and perspective, the goal of public safety requires integration and activities that interlock and interconnect. The message must be sent, from the top, that this approach is a priority at the highest level.

There are several underlying assumptions that must be in play if prisoner reentry is to be effective. All of them support the argument that corrections and law enforcement must come together to further these important ideas:

- Prisoner reentry is a statewide issue;
- The current approach to corrections is costly and the outcomes are not great;
- Solutions do not lie solely within correctional departments;
- Both human services and law enforcement must join together with corrections;
- Communities and community-based agencies must be part of the process;
- It is possible to create models that cut across existing bureaucratic structures;
- The work must involve changes in organizational culture and attitudes;
- Communication and data-sharing are essential; and
- Success can (and should) be measured.

Perhaps the most important outcome of the partnerships formed between probation and parole officers and police officers is the sense of mutual respect and connection that develops from working in tandem on a regular basis. It is unusual to hear of probation and parole officers described as "the two new rock stars of the city," but that is how Col. Dean Esserman, the Providence police chief, described Rhode Island DOC probation officers Yolanda Harley and Geneva Brown at a recent gathering that included members of his staff, DOC officials and a reporter from *The Providence Journal*. Esserman added, "And I intend to buy tickets to their concert someday."

The chief said he is enthusiastic about this "remarkable partnership" between his department and the DOC and its role in enhancing public safety in the state's largest city. The Providence police officers are now wired into the DOC's inmate database, INFACTS, and can access it from laptops in their cruisers or from police headquarters and substations. Within moments of arrest, police officers can determine whether individuals are on probation or parole, download offenders' photos, and review other important details about their incarceration history.

Meeting probationers where they live is one of the cornerstones of probation. As a result of the partnership between the DOC and the police department, Brown and Harley have moved out of their comfort zone—working previously in the Superior Court and the District Court—and now have offices right alongside the police substation in District 7, a neighborhood with a startlingly high number of probationers. Historically, probation officers had been frustrated because they were desk-bound in the courthouse. Today, these two officers' entire caseloads live within a 10-minute drive. Brown and Harley conduct weekly home visits, participate in ride-alongs with the police and attend weekly staff meetings in Esserman's office to share information about probationers on their caseloads. They say they cannot imagine returning to "the old way" of doing business.

The willingness of District 7's Lt. Michael Correia and his staff to welcome probation officers into their substation and to work hand in glove with them has sent a message across the city that the DOC and the Providence Police Department will partner in every way possible to ensure the safety of the city's residents. Harley and Brown have been pioneers in this effort. Their supervisor and all of the administrators in probation and parole have been instrumental in making this relationship successful.

Once a month, new probationers from the district are invited to the District 7 substation for a "meet 'n greet" attended by critical staff from the police department and probation and parole. Their photos are taken and included in a personalized meet 'n greet flier, which is a handy way for police and probation officers to quickly identify and keep tabs on probationers. "Right away when they come in the room," Correia said, "they know something's different." Micheline Lombardi, who supervises Harley and Brown, sees these gatherings as an opportunity to show probationers that "we're not the enemy. [We want] to help them change the way they look at life and make better choices." Lombardi added: "This is a long-term partnership. We're taking it to the next level. Other districts now want what District 7 has."

Rhode Island's probation officers have among the highest caseloads in the country. While the state needs more officers, its fiscal crisis has made it imperative that new and creative options be considered. Since this partnership has only existed for about seven months, it is too early to generate hard data on the impact the partnership is having on recidivism. However, the sentiment shared by the police department and the DOC is that people behave better when they are being watched, and this collaboration greatly increases the level of supervision.

Of the approximately 20,000 Rhode Islanders on probation or parole in the state's communities, 6,600 lived in the city of Providence as of year-end 2007, according to the Rhode Island DOC's Planning and Research Unit. This partnership is bringing the focus of supervision down to the neighborhood level, and it shows that working together every day really makes the system work. It is a smart investment because it increases the state's ability to prevent re-offending, which involves

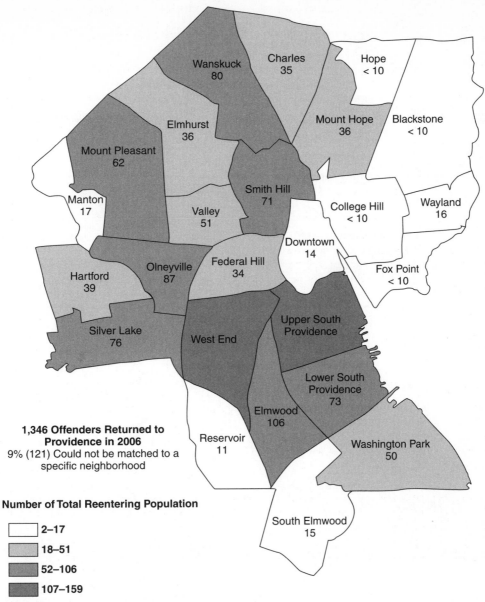

1,346 Offenders Returned to Providence in 2006
9% (121) Could not be matched to a specific neighborhood

Number of Total Reentering Population

☐	2–17
▨	18–51
▨	52–106
▨	107–159

Distribution of Providence's Reentering Population by Neighborhood, 2006

Data Source: R.I. Department of Corrections, 2006 Sentenced Releases.

additional victimization; leads to a churning of offenders through the correctional system; and drives up crowding and costs.

The DOC is interested in developing similar relationships in cities across the state and recently launched an initiative in Warwick, Rhode Island's second largest community. About 75 probationers residing in that city were invited to the police department for a meet 'n greet involving the Warwick Police Department and the DOC's probation and parole staff. They were addressed by A.T. Wall II, the corrections director; Lt. Thomas Hannon, Warwick Police Department; Robert Corrente, U.S. attorney for the state of Rhode Island; Col. Stephen McCartney, Warwick Chief of Police; and Christine Imbriglio, supervisor of Kent County Probation. Several community service providers also attended, including the Kent Center, Kent House, Vantage Point, Assisted Recovery, Addiction Recovery Institute, the Department of Human Services and West Bay Community Action. These providers were available at the conclusion of the presentation to offer assistance and information to attendees. Warwick Mayor Scott Avedesian dropped in on the gathering and also met with local politicians, probation and parole staff, the chief, and others in the neighborhood of

Oakland Beach to discuss expanding the partnership to include more communities. "I'm enthusiastically supporting this and look forward to further expanding the partnership," McCartney said.

Regional Reentry Councils

The battle for successful reentry is ultimately won or lost on the ground in individual communities. The DOC has begun the process of creating local reentry councils in communities with the highest concentration of returning offenders—thus far in Newport, Providence, Pawtucket and Woonsocket. The reentry councils comprise local elected officials, upper managers from local service providers, senior probation and parole staff, law enforcement personnel, and representatives from faith-based organizations and the business sector. These councils are beginning to make an impact on the lives of the men and women in the affected communities who leave prison with the often daunting goal of never coming back.

The purpose of these regional councils is to create a seamless transition for offenders from prison back into their home communities by

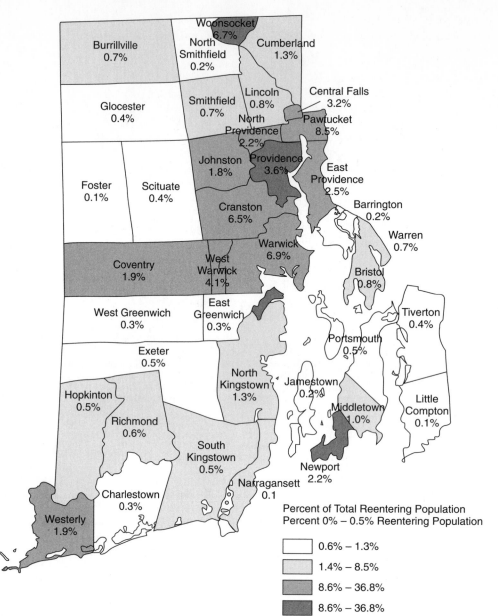

Distribution of Rhode Island's Reentering Population by Municipality, 2006, 3,654 Offenders Returned to Rhode Islands in 2006

Data Source: R.I. Department of Corrections, 2006 Sentenced Releases

resolving the specific barriers—finding employment, health care and affordable housing—that often lead to a downward spiral. The councils also serve as advocates for effective inmate reentry. They have the local credibility to point out that reentry is an issue of community safety, and it affects every member of a community, whether directly or indirectly.

Newport's Council

Spearheaded by the faith community in Newport, the regional reentry council there was the first to get off the ground in Rhode Island and has transformed the way the DOC and other social service agencies are able to assist inmates returning to this city.

At a recent meeting of the council, DOC probation and parole and transitional services staff; representatives of local agencies such as a faith-based nonprofit for ex-offenders and a local homeless shelter; the area hospital's social worker; mental health providers; the community police officer; and the city's part-time reentry coordinator

gathered around the table to discuss the list of specific individuals to be released from prison in the next six months.

Newport's Key Players

"All of you are able to tell us things about these people we never would have known otherwise," noted Sister Teresa Foley, professional/transitional services coordinator for the DOC. "The interchange of information has been wonderful and has allowed us to do better planning by knowing all of these interconnections."

Roberta Richman, assistant director for rehabilitative services for the DOC, has been a driving force in getting these regional councils off the ground. She is pleased to see each council taking on a unique shape specific to the character and size of the community. "These people [returning offenders] are not an island unto themselves," Richman said during a council meeting in Newport. "The police know them. Many of you around the table know them. This is where they have grown up and we at the DOC couldn't possibly serve them as well without the helpful information you're all able to provide us with. We share information and the responsibility for being there for people who are trying hard and can't do it alone."

The Rev. Cheryl Robinson runs Turning Around Ministries, a Newport nonprofit that mentors returning offenders for 18 months and helps them with needs such as food, clothing, shelter, and GED preparation or accessing college courses—all of the things that can become stumbling blocks and force someone back into old, harmful patterns. Robinson has been a leader on the Newport Reentry Council since it began.

Cheryl Newsome plays an equally pivotal role as Newport's part-time reentry coordinator. She works with landlords to find housing for clients and accompanies them to court, homeless shelters or mental health appointments. Both Newsome and Robinson travel to the DOC in Cranston once a month to attend discharge-planning meetings.

Tom Reiser is a clinician with CODAC Behavioral Healthcare, and his presence at the council meetings enables his staff to expedite the process of getting offenders enrolled in treatment within days of their release. His agency offers counseling and assessment and acts in coordination with East Bay Community Action. The two agencies work closely with DOC probation and parole staff and provide reports to the courts.

Nancy Hallman, probation and parole supervisor for Newport County, has found the regional council immensely helpful to her and her staff. "Even if someone is on straight probation [never incarcerated]," she noted, "we know we can contact someone from the council for assistance. With our heavy caseloads, having these community networking connections has taken some of the burden off of probation."

Sue Windsor is a social worker with Newport Hospital. She encourages reentering offenders to get a primary care physician if they do not have one and works with discharge planning to ensure that services offenders receive in prison will continue. Windsor also works with probation and parole to ensure that released offenders have the medications they need.

Fernando Comas, probation officer in the sex offender unit who attends council meetings when a sex offender is on the release list, visits these offenders while they are still incarcerated to set them up with the services they will need upon release. "They function much better when people are involved and respond well to a helping hand," he said. "We work to help them reenter society and allow people to observe that they can function normally."

Also in attendance when possible are Christine Green, DOC discharge planner (contracted through the Urban League), who sets up court-ordered treatment and provides follow-up with clients for about a year; and Anna Harrison-Auld, administrator for adult outpatient and emergency services with Newport Country Community Mental Health Center. "We prioritize inmates when they're released," Harrison-Auld explained. "They can walk in on the day of discharge and have an application."

Newport as a Model

Thanks to this partnership, offenders returning to Newport are set up with coordinated services and are better able to function, unlike in past years when they would leave prison and get on a bus with nothing but a trash bag full of their belongings. The hope is to secure additional funding so a reentry center can be set up in downtown Newport and the results of these efforts can be tracked more formally. At one meeting, a discharge planner mentioned that only one of her clients has returned to prison out of all those released to Newport in the previous six or seven months. Robinson is only aware of two of her clients who have returned to prison. They were the ones who refused help.

Perhaps this model is so successful in Newport because of its small size and the close proximity of service providers. Maybe it is the fact that Jimmy Winters, community police officer and another important member of the council, has known most of the returning offenders and their extended families for much of their lives. Whatever the reason, it seems to be working.

Expanding the Effort

Providence Mayor David Cicilline has appointed his police chief to co-chair the reentry council there and has obtained grant money to hire a full-time reentry coordinator. In Pawtucket and Warwick, similar initiatives are just getting off the ground. In order for these efforts to be successful, three legs of the stool need to be in place to provide ex-offenders with the stability they need to reenter society.

Richman, who has been at this work for much of her 30-year DOC career, said: "First, prison officials need to begin preparing [offenders] for life outside the prison walls before they leave us. Then, the community has to put aside the stigma of dealing with people who have been incarcerated. But, most important, the offenders themselves have to want to make the necessary changes."

Perhaps Cicilline said it best in his keynote address to the DOC's offender reentry strategic-planning retreat back in September. The biggest challenge, as he sees it, is on an emotional level. Most Rhode Islanders' gut reaction to the thought of devoting resources to ex-offenders is negative. It does not make sense to them. Those professionals engaged in this work see the benefits, but how do they persuade the public? Clearly not with logic and evidence alone, according to Cicilline. It is really a matter of using different language to talk about this work so that it is not focused on individual offenders. It has to be about communities protecting themselves—people who do not want to be victims or to have their own neighbors victimized again. Any community that neglects this work is risking the safety of its citizens. "We are not building an ex-offender community support system but a community protection strategy," Cicilline argued. "Changing our language in this discussion really isn't political spin. It really is about communities."

The two successful emerging partnerships with law enforcement and the four regional reentry councils in Rhode Island all play a critical role in the state's commitment to effective prisoner reentry. It is through deliberate connections at the ground level that Rhode Island will begin to see a drop in recidivism rates and save taxpayer money by ensuring that the thousands of people released from prison each year will stay out. It is about a whole new way of doing business in corrections, and like any change, there are bound to be growing pains. In the long run, though, the gain will far exceed the pain.

ASHBEL T. WALL II is director of the Rhode Island Department of Corrections. **TRACEY Z. POOLE** is chief of information and public relations for the Rhode Island Department of Corrections.

Test-Your-Knowledge Form

We encourage you to photocopy and use this page as a tool to assess how the articles in *Annual Editions* expand on the information in your textbook. By reflecting on the articles you will gain enhanced text information. You can also access this useful form on a product's book support website at *http://www.mhhe.com/cls*.

NAME:

DATE:

_____

TITLE AND NUMBER OF ARTICLE:

_____

BRIEFLY STATE THE MAIN IDEA OF THIS ARTICLE:

_____

LIST THREE IMPORTANT FACTS THAT THE AUTHOR USES TO SUPPORT THE MAIN IDEA:

_____

WHAT INFORMATION OR IDEAS DISCUSSED IN THIS ARTICLE ARE ALSO DISCUSSED IN YOUR TEXTBOOK OR OTHER READINGS THAT YOU HAVE DONE? LIST THE TEXTBOOK CHAPTERS AND PAGE NUMBERS:

_____

LIST ANY EXAMPLES OF BIAS OR FAULTY REASONING THAT YOU FOUND IN THE ARTICLE:

_____

LIST ANY NEW TERMS/CONCEPTS THAT WERE DISCUSSED IN THE ARTICLE, AND WRITE A SHORT DEFINITION:

We Want Your Advice

ANNUAL EDITIONS revisions depend on two major opinion sources: one is our Advisory Board, listed in the front of this volume, which works with us in scanning the thousands of articles published in the public press each year; the other is you—the person actually using the book. Please help us and the users of the next edition by completing the prepaid article rating form on this page and returning it to us. Thank you for your help!

ANNUAL EDITIONS: Criminal Justice 10/11

ARTICLE RATING FORM

Here is an opportunity for you to have direct input into the next revision of this volume.
We would like you to rate each of the articles listed below, using the following scale:

1. **Excellent: should definitely be retained**
2. **Above average: should probably be retained**
3. **Below average: should probably be deleted**
4. **Poor: should definitely be deleted**

Your ratings will play a vital part in the next revision.
Please mail this prepaid form to us as soon as possible.
Thanks for your help!

RATING	ARTICLE	RATING	ARTICLE
	1. What Is the Sequence of Events in the Criminal Justice System?		21. Illegal Globally, Bail for Profit Remains in U.S.
	2. Plugging Holes in the Science of Forensics		22. Avoiding Sixth Amendment Suppression: An Overview and Update
	3. Does Proximity to Schools Tempt Former Sex Offenders?		23. When Our Eyes Deceive Us
	4. Stereotype, Then and Now		24. Abandoning Places
	5. The Death of the War on Drugs		25. When Evidence Is Ignored: Residential Restrictions for Sex Offenders
	6. Of Crime and Punishment: Experts Explore Issues in the Legal Limelight		26. When the Poor Go to Court
	7. Serving Life for Providing Car to Killers		27. Justice & Antonin Scalia: The Supreme Court's Most Strident Catholic
	8. Do Batterer Intervention Programs Work?: Two Studies		28. America's Imprisoned Kids
	9. Telling the Truth about Damned Lies and Statistics		29. The 21st Century Juvenile Justice Work Force
	10. Identity Theft Trends: Abuse of Social Security Numbers		30. Teens Caught in the Middle: Juvenile Justice System and Treatment
	11. Violence and the Remaking of a Self		31. Jail Time Is Learning Time
	12. Understanding Stockholm Syndrome		32. Lifers as Teenagers, Now Seeking Second Chance
	13. Judge Steven Leifman Advocates for the Mentally Ill		33. Violence in Adolescent Dating Relationships
	14. Victim Satisfaction with the Criminal Justice System		34. Mentally Ill Offenders Strain Juvenile System
	15. Policing in Arab-American Communities after September 11		35. Inmate Count in U.S. Dwarfs Other Nations'
	16. Racial Profiling and Its Apologists		36. Felon Fallout
	17. Our Oath of Office: A Solemn Promise		37. Asking about Family Can Enhance Reentry
	18. Stress Management . . . and the Stress-Proof Vest		38. The Ex-Con Next Door
	19. Judging Honesty by Words, Not Fidgets		39. Prison Inmates Meet Socrates
	20. Law Enforcement Perspective on the Use of Force: Hands-On, Experiential Training for Prosecuting Attorneys		40. One Clique: Why Rivals on the Streets Become Allies behind Bars
			41. The Professor Was a Prison Guard
			42. Supermax Prisons
			43. The Results of American Incarceration
			44. Partnering with Law Enforcement

BUSINESS REPLY MAIL
FIRST CLASS MAIL PERMIT NO. 551 DUBUQUE IA

POSTAGE WILL BE PAID BY ADDRESSEE

McGraw-Hill Contemporary Learning Series
501 BELL STREET
DUBUQUE, IA 52001

ABOUT YOU

Name

Date

Are you a teacher? ❑ A student? ❑
Your school's name

Department

Address   City   State   Zip

School telephone #

YOUR COMMENTS ARE IMPORTANT TO US!

Please fill in the following information:
For which course did you use this book?

Did you use a text with this ANNUAL EDITION? ❑ yes ❑ no
What was the title of the text?

What are your general reactions to the Annual Editions concept?

Have you read any pertinent articles recently that you think should be included in the next edition? Explain.

Are there any articles that you feel should be replaced in the next edition? Why?

Are there any World Wide Websites that you feel should be included in the next edition? Please annotate.

May we contact you for editorial input? ❑ yes ❑ no
May we quote your comments? ❑ yes ❑ no

NOTES

NOTES

NOTES

NOTES